Foreword

Jesse James responded to the question, "Why rob banks?" with the obvious answer, "That's where the money is." The obvious answer to "Why a casebook for pharmacy practice in the community setting?" would have to be "That's where the patients are." The imperative for patient-centered care delivered in the "everywhere" location of community pharmacy practice has never been greater. One needs only to look at the extremely diverse set of diseases and conditions contained in this casebook to appreciate the impact pharmacists can have on patients who seek patient care services in the community pharmacy.

Since 1999 and thanks to the many publications on the safety of health care published by the Institute of Medicine, the world has come to appreciate what pharmacists have realized for decades, if not centuries: Without oversight and interventions provided by the medication use specialist, drug therapy often fails to achieve the objectives for care that prescribers intended and patients need. Accumulated evidence indicates that pharmacists possess the essential knowledge, skills, abilities, and attitudes to help make medications work and to decrease the risk of avoidable drug-related problems.

It is not easy though. Managing systems of drug distribution for safety and accurate preparation of medications for patients has always been pharmacists' highest priority. With dispensing volumes at all time highs and dispensing revenues per prescription near record lows, pharmacy practices struggle to find the resources to fully engage in pharmaceutical care, medication therapy management, or service development.

This casebook is a unique new resource to help make the transition to a patient-centered approach a more reasonable goal. Cases are stories and stories are a powerful tool for learning. Whether you are a seasoned pharmacist looking to sharpen your insights in patient management with common or not so common conditions or a new practitioner fortifying the amazing education you just received from your alma mater, these cases can help you see new aspects of patients and their diseases. Furthermore, the casebook could be used even earlier for a student pharmacist to learn how to apply knowledge to care for patients in the community pharmacy setting. In turn, this knowledge can be used to make you a better practitioner of patient-centered care.

The collective goal of the profession of pharmacy is that patient care will be the standard of care provided in all settings, especially the community pharmacy. After all, that is where the patients are and where they want to remain. The alternative to well-managed drug therapy and controlled diseases is institutional care, or worse.

This is our future and the future is now! Your patients deserve nothing less than your full investment in achieving safe and effective medication therapy. The cases and practice pearls contained in this casebook should help you and your patients achieve those goals.

LUCINDA L. MAINE, PhD, RPh
Executive Vice President and CEO
American Association of Colleges of Pharmacy

Preface

Community pharmacy practice has evolved to allow many pharmacists to take a more active role in patient care and medication management. Schools and colleges of pharmacy may employ faculty members specializing in community pharmacy to train students in innovative community pharmacy practice. In addition, there has been a surge in the number of pharmacy graduates pursing residency training in community pharmacy practice. However, there are few, if any, teaching and learning resources focused solely on the management of patients in the community pharmacy practice setting. Although patients often present with chronic conditions similar to those in other practice environments, there are many opportunities and barriers unique to community practice. The community pharmacist must often efficiently and effectively serve as a disease state manager, medication manager, clinician, educator, counselor, coach, personnel supervisor, and small business owner, all while providing outstanding patient care and upholding unerring standards of safety in dispensing medications. Pharmacy educators need teaching tools and resources to train current and future community pharmacists to succeed in implementing innovative patient care services in this dynamic and sometimes challenging environment.

Many pharmacy schools use cased-based or active learning methods to teach student pharmacists in the classroom and during advanced practice experiences. No published casebooks currently exist that focus on community pharmacy practice. To fill this void, pharmacy faculty and preceptors must write their own cases or use general therapeutic texts that present patient care problems in a health-system or ambulatory care environment. Often, cases in these traditional texts do not provide an adequate model of patient care in community pharmacy practice. For example, most traditional therapeutic cases set in a health-system practice provide learners with a patient's entire medical profile, including diagnoses and a complete medication list, along with assumed access to the prescribing clinician. In the community setting, though, pharmacists rarely have this type of medical information and are required to discern the right course of action without this information or easy prescriber access. The community pharmacist needs to be able to choose the correct recommendation or course of action, but also to consider practice-specific issues that affect their ability to provide patient care such as available inventory, formulary considerations, limited after-hours access to prescribers, legal concerns, potential medication errors, and others. Finally, there are teaching opportunities unique to community practice in the areas of documentation of patient care services, establishment of a new service, preventive medicine, self-care, or personal health that are often not emphasized in traditional texts.

For this reason, the editors developed this casebook based solely in the community setting to give learners (student pharmacists, residents, and pharmacists) a chance to discuss and learn from cases that closely resemble the patients they will see in the community pharmacy setting. This casebook covers common disease states that are seen in community pharmacy practice. It also includes cases about preventive medicine and personal health care such as immunizations and age-based health screenings. Other cases focus on development and implementation of patient care services in the community pharmacy practice setting.

Patient presentation in the community pharmacy varies greatly from day to day, and from patient to patient. For this reason, each case in this text is presented differently and includes unique teaching points about medication management, drug therapy selection, and/or opportunities and challenges unique to the community pharmacy setting. Generally, cases in this book are written with presentation to the community pharmacy counter or within an innovative patient care service provided in the pharmacy with or without a chief complaint. Case authors provide limited information about the patient, such as age, gender, race, allergies, and medication profile, similar to what a community pharmacist may be able to access. Each case includes learning objectives and questions for the learner to answer about how the pharmacist should manage the patient. These questions cover topics that include inquiries about appropriate medication therapy and management, collaborative practice, preventive medicine measures, self-care and nonprescription medicines, patient education, and follow-up. Each case lists additional activities to allow learners to delve deeper into the topic when desired and a list of references.

The cases use examples of "real-world" pharmacy records and patient care forms, such as those many community pharmacists would use in day-to-day practice. The casebook also contains an appendix that lists abbreviations used in the pharmacy records and forms. Many of the cases have incorporated the Medication Therapy Management (MTM) Core Elements developed by the American Pharmacists Association and National Association of Chain Drug Stores. However, instructors could use any case in the book to teach the concepts of MTM. For example, for each case, instructors could ask the learner to develop a Personal Medication Record (PMR) and Medication Action Plan (MAP) for the patient. The core elements and forms for developing a PMR and a MAP are available at http://www.pharmacist.com/AM/Template.cfm?Section= Search1&section=Jan_March6&template=/CM/Content Display.cfm&ContentFileID=3839.

The editors intend for this casebook to be used by faculty to bring community pharmacy patient care topics into the classroom, by preceptors to reinforce topics during advanced practice experiences, by residency preceptors to enhance discussions with community pharmacy residents, and by pharmacists to enhance their skills in management of patients in the community setting. This casebook has a companion answer key for instructors to use as a teaching and resource guide. As with any published textbook,

instructors should verify that guidelines and/or standard of care has not changed before relying solely on the answer key. Answer keys often contain additional teaching or clinical pearls for instructors to emphasize when teaching from the case. It is the editors' hope that these cases will enhance pharmacotherapy teaching and learning in the community practice setting by providing an educational resource that is geared toward community pharmacy.

JEAN-VENABLE "KELLY" R. GOODE

LYNNE M. ROMAN

KRISTIN W. WEITZEL

December 2008

Contents

COMMUNITY PHARMACY PRACTICE CASE STUDIES

NOTICE

Drug therapy and other treatment information are evolving constantly, because of ongoing research and clinical experience, and are often subject to interpretation. The publisher, editors, authors, and other contributors have made every effort to ensure the accuracy and completeness of the information presented in this publication. However, these parties cannot be held responsible for the continued accuracy of the information, any inadvertent errors or omissions, or the application of this information, and shall have no liability to any person or entity with regard to claims, loss, or damage caused or alleged to be caused, directly or indirectly, by the use of the information contained herein. Readers are advised that decisions regarding any treatment, including drug therapy, must be based on the independent judgment of the clinician, changing information about a treatment or drug (e.g., as reflected in the literature and manufacturer's most current product information), and changing medical practices.

The authors and other contributors have written this book in their private capacities. No official support or endorsement by any federal or state agency or pharmaceutical company is intended or inferred.

COMMUNITY PHARMACY PRACTICE CASE STUDIES

Jean-Venable "Kelly" R. Goode, PHARMD, BCPS, FAPHA, FCCP
Professor and Director
Community Pharmacy Practice and Residency Programs
Virginia Commonwealth University School of Pharmacy
Richmond, Virginia

Lynne M. Roman, PHARMD
Pharmacist Manager
Target Pharmacy
Ellicott City, Maryland

Kristin W. Weitzel, PHARMD, CDE
Assistant Editor
Pharmacist's Letter and *Prescriber's Letter*
Director of Editorial Projects
Therapeutic Research Center
Stockton, California
Clinical Associate Professor (Adjunct)
University of Florida College of Pharmacy
Gainesville, Florida

American Pharmacists Association®
Improving medication use. Advancing patient care.
APhA

Washington, D.C.

Managing Editor: Linda L. Young
Editorial Services: DataMasters Professional Editing Services, Eileen Kramer,
Acquiring Editor: Sandra J. Cannon
Publications Professionals, LLC, Robert Reynolds, Linda Young
Compositor: Maryland Comp
Cover Designer: Richard Muringer, APhA Creative Services

Published by the American Pharmacists Association
1100 15th Street, NW, Suite 400
Washington, DC 20005-1707
www.pharmacist.com

To comment on this book via e-mail, send your message to the publisher at
aphabooks@aphanet.org

Library of Congress Cataloging-in-Publication Data

Community pharmacy practice case studies / [edited by] Jean-Venable
"Kelly" R. Goode, Lynne M. Roman, Kristin W. Weitzel.
     p. ; cm.
  Includes bibliographical references.
  ISBN 978-1-58212-105-5
  1. Pharmacy—Case studies. 2. Community health services—Case studies. I. Goode,
Jean-Venable "Kelly" R. II. Roman, Lynne M. (Lynne Marie) III. Weitzel, Kristin W. IV.
American Pharmacists Association.
  [DNLM: 1. Community Pharmacy Services—organization & administration—
Problems and Exercises. 2. Drug Therapy—methods—Problems and Exercises. 3. Patient
Care Planning—Problems and Exercises. 4. Pharmacies—organization &
administration—Problems and Exercises. QV 18.2 C734 2009]

RS122.3.C66 2009
615'.1—dc22
                        2008050816

Dedication

This casebook is dedicated to the memory of Mario M. Zeolla, PharmD, BCPS, an emerging leader in community pharmacy practice. Mario's death cut short a bright future and the pharmacy profession lost an extraordinary teacher and role model. His devotion to teaching will always be remembered. We will continue to be inspired by his example.

It is in Mario's spirit and enthusiasm for teaching and community practice that we launch this book; hoping many more student pharmacists, residents and pharmacists will learn to enhance their community pharmacy practice and the care of their patients.

A teacher affects eternity; he can never tell where his influence stops.
—Henry Brooks Adams

Acknowledgments

The editors would like to thank Terry L. Schwinghammer for his guidance and advice about editing and publishing a casebook. We would also like to thank the many community pharmacy practitioners and pharmacy faculty members who contributed their knowledge and expertise to this casebook as authors, reviewers, and consultants.

We would also like to thank Sandy Cannon and Julian Graubart, American Pharmacists Association. Their wisdom and encouragement were invaluable as we worked through, and learned about, compiling and editing a casebook.

Finally, we are indebted to our families for their unwavering understanding, support, and encouragement during the completion of this book.

Contributors

Nicole Paolini Albanese, PharmD
Clinical Assistant Professor, Department of Pharmacy Practice, University at Buffalo School of Pharmacy and Pharmaceutical Sciences, Buffalo, New York

Marialice S. Bennett, RPh, FAPhA
Professor of Clinical Pharmacy, The Ohio State University College of Pharmacy, Columbus, Ohio

Nancy Brahm, PharmD, MS, BCPP, CGP
Clinical Associate Professor, The University of Oklahoma College of Pharmacy–Tulsa, Tulsa, Oklahoma

Ericka L. Breden, PharmD, BCPP, CGP
Clinical Pharmacy Specialist, Psychiatry, and Associate Clinical Professor, Pharmacy and Psychiatry, Virginia Commonwealth University Health System, Richmond, Virginia

Amber Briggs, PharmD, BC-ADM
Clinical Pharmacist and Pharmacy Consultant, Central Peninsula Hospital, Soldotna, Alaska

Kelly Brock, PharmD
Independent Consultant, Irvine, California
*At the time of writing:
Western University of Health Sciences College of Pharmacy, Pomona, California

Kimberley C. Brown, PharmD
Science and Research Liaison, Tibotec Therapeutics Clinical Affairs, Division of Ortho Biotech Clinical Affairs, LLC, Jacksonville, Florida
*At the time of writing:
HIV Clinical Specialist, Rainbow Center–Shands Jacksonville, Jacksonville, Florida

Lakesha M. Butler, PharmD
Clinical Assistant Professor, Southern Illinois University Edwardsville School of Pharmacy, Edwardsville, Illinois

Bruce R. Canaday, PharmD, BCPS, FASHP, FAPhA
Clinical Professor and Vice-Chair, Division of Pharmacy Practice and Experiential Education, University of North Carolina Eshelman School of Pharmacy, Chapel Hill, North Carolina
*At the time of writing:
Director, Department of Pharmacotherapy, South East Area Health Education Center (SEAHEC), Wilmington, North Carolina

Kimberly A. Cappuzzo, PharmD, MS, CGP
Assistant Professor, Department of Pharmacy, Virginia Commonwealth University School of Pharmacy, Richmond, Virginia

Kara M. Carruthers, BS, PharmD
Director of Clinical Services, Main at Locust Pharmacy Clinic and Medical Supply, Davenport, Iowa

Jennifer Cerulli, PharmD, BCPS, AE-C
Associate Professor of Pharmacy Practice, Union University Albany College of Pharmacy, Albany, New York

Sweta Chawla, BS, PharmD, MS
Assistant Professor of Pharmacy Practice, Arnold & Marie Schwartz College of Pharmacy, Long Island University, Brooklyn, New York

Antoinette B. Coe, BA
Doctor of Pharmacy 2009 Candidate, Virginia Commonwealth University

School of Pharmacy, Richmond, Virginia

Heather Brennan Congdon, PharmD, CACP, CDE
Assistant Professor and Assistant Dean for Shady Grove, University of Maryland School of Pharmacy, Shady Grove Campus, Rockville, Maryland

Kimberly M. Crosby, PharmD, BCPS
Clinical Assistant Professor, Department of Clinical and Administrative Sciences, The University of Oklahoma College of Pharmacy–Tulsa, Tulsa, Oklahoma

Andrea DiFalco, PharmD
Lake Norman Regional Medical Center, Cornelius, North Carolina
*At the time of writing:
Community Pharmacy Practice Resident, Clinical Instructor, Department of Pharmacy, Virginia Commonwealth University School of Pharmacy, Richmond, Virginia

Holly Divine, PharmD, CGP, CDE
Clinical Associate Professor, Department of Pharmacy Practice and Science, University of Kentucky College of Pharmacy, Lexington, Kentucky; Clinical Pharmacist and Co-Founder, PharmacistCARE Program, Lexington, Kentucky

Dee Dugan, PharmD
Assistant Professor, Department of Pharmacy Practice, Samford University McWhorter School of Pharmacy, Birmingham, Alabama
*At the time of writing:
Assistant Professor of Pharmacy Practice, Palm Beach Atlantic University Lloyd L. Gregory School of Pharmacy, West Palm Beach, Florida

Angela M. Dyer, PharmD
Anticoagulation Clinic Manager,
Williamson Medical Center,
Franklin, Tennessee
*At the time of writing:
Clinical Pharmacist, Health
Management Corporation,
Richmond, Virginia

Darla Klug Eastman, PharmD
Assistant Professor of Pharmacy
Practice, Drake University College
of Pharmacy and Health Sciences,
Des Moines, Iowa
*At the time of writing:
Pharmacy Practice Resident,
Iowa Methodist Medical Center,
Des Moines, Iowa

Michael E. Ernst, PharmD, BCPS
Associate Professor (Clinical),
Division of Clinical and
Administrative Pharmacy,
College of Pharmacy and Department
of Family Medicine, Roy J. and
Lucille A. Carver College of
Medicine, The University of Iowa,
Iowa City

Emily Evans, PharmD, AE-C, CDM
Assistant Professor, Department of
Clinical and Administrative
Sciences, The University of
Louisiana at Monroe College of
Pharmacy, Shreveport, Louisiana

**Jeffery D. Evans, BS Chem,
PharmD**
Assistant Professor, Department of
Clinical and Administrative
Sciences, University of Louisiana at
Monroe College of Pharmacy,
Shreveport, Louisiana

**Jonathan D. Ference, PharmD,
BCPS**
Clinical Assistant Professor, The
University of Oklahoma College of
Pharmacy–Tulsa and Adjunct
Assistant Professor, The University of
Oklahoma College of
Medicine–Tulsa, Tulsa, Oklahoma

Stefanie Ferreri, PharmD, CDE
Clinical Assistant Professor and
Director, Community Pharmacy
Residency Program, University of
North Carolina Eshelman School of

Pharmacy, Chapel Hill, North
Carolina

Eric Frontera-Zayas, PharmD
Staff Pharmacist, WalMart Pharmacy,
Sunrise, Florida
*At the time of writing:
Community Pharmacy Resident,
Nova Southeastern University
College of Pharmacy, Fort
Lauderdale, Florida

Sharon B. S. Gatewood, PharmD
Assistant Professor, Virginia
Commonwealth University School of
Pharmacy, Richmond, Virginia

Nicole M. Gattas, PharmD, BCPS
Assistant Professor of Pharmacy
Practice, St. Louis College of
Pharmacy, St. Louis, Missouri

Denise Glasser, PharmD
Pharmacy Manager, Target
Pharmacy, Gainesville, Virginia

**Jeffery A. Goad, PharmD, MPH,
FCPhA, FCSHP**
Associate Professor of Clinical
Pharmacy, Coordinator, Community
Pharmacy Program, and Director,
Community Pharmacy Practice
Residence, University of Southern
California School of Pharmacy, Los
Angeles, California

**Jean-Venable "Kelly" R. Goode,
PharmD, BCPS, FAPhA, FCCP**
Professor and Director, Community
Pharmacy Practice and Residency
Programs, Virginia Commonwealth
University School of Pharmacy,
Richmond, Virginia

Molly E. Graham, PharmD
Assistant Professor of Pharmacy
Practice, Texas Tech University
Health Sciences Center School of
Pharmacy, Abilene, Texas
*At the time of writing:
PGY2 Ambulatory Care Resident in
Primary Care, Coastal Area Health
Education Center and New Hanover
Regional Medical Center,
Wilmington, North Carolina

Heather Allison Greene, PharmD
CVS Pharmacy, Richmond, Virginia

*At the time of writing:
Assistant Professor of Pharmacy,
Department of Pharmacy, Virginia
Commonwealth University School of
Pharmacy, Richmond, Virginia

Ron Gregory, PharmD
*At the time of writing:
Community Pharmacy Practice
Resident and Clinical Instructor,
Virginia Commonwealth University
School of Pharmacy and Kroger
Pharmacy, Richmond, Virginia

Stuart T. Haines, PharmD, BCPS
Professor, University of Maryland
School of Pharmacy and Clinical
Specialist, University of Maryland
Medical Center, Baltimore, Maryland

Deanne L. Hall, PharmD, CDE
Assistant Professor and Director,
Ambulatory Care Pharmacy
Residency, Department of Pharmacy
and Therapeutics, University of
Pittsburgh School of Pharmacy,
Pittsburgh, Pennsylvania

Hind I. Hamid, PharmD
Clinical Pharmacist, St. Vincent's
Health System, Birmingham,
Alabama; Assistant Professor of
Pharmacy Practice, McWhorter
School of Pharmacy, Samford
University, Birmingham, Alabama
*At the time writing:
Resident, Jefferson County
Department of Health and McWhorter
School of Pharmacy, Samford
University, Birmingham, Alabama

Dana P. Hammer, RPh, MS, PhD
Director, Bracken Pharmaceutical
Care Learning Center and Teaching
Certificate Program in Pharmacy
Education, Department of Pharmacy,
University of Washington School of
Pharmacy, Seattle, Washington

**Judy Sommers Hanson, PharmD,
CDM**
Manager, Shared Faculty and
Clinical Education, Walgreens
Health Initiatives, Deerfield, Illinois

Pamela C. Heaton PharmD
Assistant Professor of Pharmacy Practice, Division of Pharmacy Practice, University of Cincinnati College of Pharmacy, Cincinnati, Ohio

Katherine Heller, PharmD
Walgreen's Health Initiative, Orlando, Florida
*At the time of writing:
Assistant Professor of Pharmacy Practice and Coordinator, CityFit – Wellness Programs, Palm Beach Atlantic University Lloyd L. Gregory School of Pharmacy, West Palm Beach, Florida

Richard N. Herrier PharmD
Clinical Associate Professor, Departments of Pharmacy Practice and Science, University of Arizona College of Pharmacy, Tucson, Arizona

Michael Hogue, PharmD
Assistant Professor, Department of Pharmacy Practice, Samford University McWhorter School of Pharmacy, Birmingham, Alabama

Carson Huntoon, PharmD
Hoagland Pharmacy, Bellingham, Washington
*At the time of writing:
Doctor of Pharmacy Student, University of Washington School of Pharmacy, Seattle, Washington

Holly Hurley, PharmD
Assistant Professor, Department of Pharmacy, University of Appalachia College of Pharmacy Grundy, Virginia

Lisa D. Inge, PharmD
Jacksonville Assistant Campus Director and Clinical Assistant Professor, Department of Pharmacy Practice, University of Florida College of Pharmacy, Jacksonville, Florida

Brandon T. Jennings, PharmD
Assistant Professor (Clinical), Department of Pharmacotherapy, University of Utah College of Pharmacy, Salt Lake City, Utah
*At the time of writing:

Community Pharmacy Practice Resident and Clinical Instructor, Department of Pharmacy, Virginia Commonwealth University School of Pharmacy, Richmond, Virginia

Carrie Foust Koenigsfeld, PharmD
Associate Professor of Pharmacy Practice, Drake University College of Pharmacy and Health Sciences, Des Moines, Iowa

Kristin Kouski, PharmD
Ukrop's Super Market Pharmacy, Inc., Richmond, Virginia
*At the time of writing:
Community Pharmacy Practice Resident and Clinical Instructor, Virginia Commonwealth University School of Pharmacy and Richmond Apothecaries, Richmond, Virginia

Brice A. Labruzzo, PharmD
Assistant Professor, University of Louisiana at Monroe College of Pharmacy, Baton Rouge, Louisiana

Annie Lam, PharmD, CGP, FASCP
Senior Lecturer, Department of Pharmacy and Director, University of Washington School of Pharmacy Residency Programs, University of Washington School of Pharmacy, Seattle, Washington

Roger D. Lander, PharmD, FASHP, FCCP
Professor of Pharmacy Practice, McWhorter School of Pharmacy, Samford University, Birmingham, Alabama; Pharmacist, Jefferson County Department of Health, Birmingham, Alabama

Stacy Lauderdale, PharmD, BCPS
Assistant Professor and Drug Information Specialist, Department of Pharmacy Practice, Samford University McWhorter School of Pharmacy, Birmingham, Alabama

Christine Lee, PharmD
Clinical Assistant Professor and Assistant Director for Clinical Services for the Maryland P3 Program, University of Maryland School of Pharmacy, Baltimore, Maryland

Maria Maniscalco-Feichtl, PharmD
Assistant Professor, Department of Pharmacy Practice, Pharmacist, Clinic Pharmacy, and Director, Community Pharmacy Practice Residency, Nova Southeastern University College of Pharmacy, Fort Lauderdale, Florida

Macary Weck Marciniak, PharmD, BCPS
Clinical Associate Professor, University of North Carolina Eshelman School of Pharmacy, Chapel Hill, North Carolina
*At the time of writing:
Associate Professor, Department of Pharmacy Practice, Union University Albany College of Pharmacy, Albany, New York

Jennifer McFee, PharmD, CDM
Staff Pharmacist, Walgreens, Chicago, Illinois
*At the time of writing:
Department of Pharmacy Practice, University of Illinois at Chicago College of Pharmacy, Chicago, Illinois

Bella H. Mehta, PharmD, BS
Assistant Professor of Clinical Pharmacy and Director, Clinical Partners Program, Division of Pharmacy Practice and Administration, The Ohio State University College of Pharmacy, Columbus, Ohio

Allana Mehlhorn, PharmD, BCPS
Associate Professor of Pharmacy Practice, Palm Beach Atlantic University, West Palm Beach, Florida

Kimberly D. Mitchell, PharmD
Assistant Professor, Department of Pharmacy Practice, Southwestern Oklahoma State University College of Pharmacy, Tulsa, Oklahoma

David A. Mott, PhD
Associate Professor, Sonderegger Research Center, University of Wisconsin–Madison School of Pharmacy, Madison, Wisconsin

Warren A. Narducci, PharmD, RPh, FAPhA
Hy-Vee Pharmacy, Shenandoah, Iowa
*At the time of writing:
Nishna Valley Pharmacy, Shenandoah, Iowa

Amy Nicholas, PharmD, CDE
Assistant Professor, Department of Pharmacy Practice and Science, University of Kentucky College of Pharmacy, Lexington, Kentucky

Sarah Parnapy, PharmD
Assistant Professor, Pharmacy Practice, Bernard J. Dunn School of Pharmacy, Shenandoah University, Winchester, Virginia

Elizabeth Peterson, PharmD
Primary Care Resident, Ralph H. Johnson VA Medical Center, Charleston, South Carolina
*At the time of writing:
Doctor of Pharmacy 2008, University of Wisconsin–Madison School of Pharmacy, Madison, Wisconsin

Erin C. Raney, PharmD, BCPS
Associate Professor of Pharmacy Practice, Midwestern University College of Pharmacy–Glendale, Glendale, Arizona

Jennifer L. Rodis, PharmD
Assistant Professor of Clinical Pharmacy, The Ohio State University College of Pharmacy, Columbus, Ohio

Magaly Rodriguez de Bittner, PharmD, BCPS, CDE
Chair and Professor, Department of Pharmacy Practice and Science, University of Maryland School of Pharmacy, Baltimore, Maryland

Lynne M. Roman, PharmD
Pharmacist Manager, Target Pharmacy, Ellicott City, Maryland

Janelle Ruisinger, PharmD
Clinical Assistant Professor, Community Pharmacy Residency Coordinator, Department of Pharmacy Practice, The University of Kansas Medical Center, Kansas City, Kansas

Melody Ryan, PharmD, BCPS, CGP
Associate Professor, Pharmacy Practice and Science Department, University of Kentucky College of Pharmacy and Associate Professor (Joint Appointment), Department of Neurology, University of Kentucky College of Medicine, Lexington, Kentucky; Neurology Clinical Pharmacy Specialist, Lexington Veteran Affairs Medical Center, Lexington, Kentucky

Catrina Schwartz, PharmD
Clinical Assistant Professor, Department of Pharmacotherapy, Washington State University College of Pharmacy, Spokane, Washington

Jeri J. Sias, PharmD
Clinical Associate Professor, The University of Texas at El Paso/The University of Texas at Austin Cooperative Pharmacy Program, El Paso, Texas

Patricia W. Slattum, PharmD, PhD, CGP
Associate Professor of Pharmacy and Vice-Chair for Graduate Studies, Geriatric Specialist, Department of Pharmacy, Virginia Commonwealth University School of Pharmacy, Richmond, Virginia

Audrey Smith, PharmD, MBA
Clinical Pharmacist, Emergency Department, University of Kansas Hospital, Kansas City, Kansas
*At the time of writing:
Community Pharmacy Resident, University of Kansas School of Pharmacy and Hen House Pharmacy, Overland Park, Kansas

Margie E. Snyder, PharmD
Community Practice Research Fellow, University of Pittsburgh School of Pharmacy, Pittsburgh, Pennsylvania
*At the time of writing:
Pharmacy Practice Resident, University of Pittsburgh School of Pharmacy, Pittsburgh, Pennsylvania

Melissa A. Somma, PharmD, CDE
Assistant Professor of Pharmacy & Therapeutics, University of Pittsburgh School of Pharmacy, Pittsburgh, Pennsylvania

Dennis D. Stanley, BS
Manager, Wellness Center, Ukrop's Pharmacy; Clinical Assistant Professor, Virginia Commonwealth University School of Pharmacy, Richmond, Virginia

Gilbert A. Steiner, PharmD, CPP
Clinical Associate Professor of Pharmacy Practice, Campbell University School of Pharmacy, Buies Creek, North Carolina

J. Tyler Stevens PharmD
Assistant Professor, Virginia Commonwealth University School of Pharmacy, Richmond, Virginia
*At the time of writing:
Community Pharmacy Practice Resident, Virginia Commonwealth University School of Pharmacy and Buford Road Pharmacy, Richmond, VA

Erin L. St. Onge, PharmD
Assistant Dean and Director, University of Florida College of Pharmacy–Orlando Campus, Apopka, Florida

Rebecca L. Stovall, PharmD
Clinical Pharmacist, Okmulgee Indian Health Center, Okmulgee, Oklahoma
*At the time of writing:
Community Pharmacy Resident, May's/Drug Warehouse Pharmacy, Tulsa, Oklahoma

Jennifer M. Strickland, PharmD, BCPS
Director of Pharmacy, Lakeland Regional Medical Center, Lakeland, Florida

Kelly Swensgard PharmD
Adjunct Assistant Professor of Pharmacy Practice, University of Cincinnati College of Pharmacy, Cincinnati, Ohio; Clinical Pharmacist, CVS Pharmacy, Cincinnati, Ohio

James R. Taylor, PharmD, CDE
Clinical Assistant Professor,
Department of Pharmacy Practice,
University of Florida College of
Pharmacy, Gainesville, Florida.

Nimita Thekkepat, PharmD, MBA
Assistant Professor of Pharmacy
Practice and Community Clinical
Pharmacist, St. Louis College of
Pharmacy, St. Louis, Missouri

Michelle Herbert Thomas, PharmD, CDE
Clinical Director, Richmond
Apothecaries, Inc., Richmond,
Virginia

Renee Ahrens Thomas, PharmD, MBA
President, RBT Consulting, Reston,
Virginia
*At the time of writing:
Associate Professor, Pharmacy
Practice, Bernard J. Dunn School of
Pharmacy, Shenandoah University,
Winchester, Virginia

Bradley P. Tice, PharmD, PMP
Chief Clinical Officer, PharmMD
Solutions, LLC, Brentwood,
Tennessee

Margaret Tomecki, PharmD, FAPhA
Senior Manager, Practice
Development and Research,
American Pharmacists Association,
Washington, DC
*At the time of writing:
Coordinator, Academic Programs,
Clinical Assistant Professor,
Department of Pharmacy Practice,
University of Illinois at Chicago
College of Pharmacy, Chicago, Illinois

Andrew P. Traynor, PharmD, BCPS
Assistant Professor and Assistant
Director, Pharmaceutical Care
Residency Program, University of
Minnesota–Duluth College of
Pharmacy, Duluth, Minnesota

Vicki L. Wade, PharmD
Staff Pharmacist, Carolinas
Rehabilitation, Charlotte, North
Carolina
*At the time of writing:
Staff Pharmacist, Carolinas
Medical Center, Charlotte, North
Carolina

Kristin W. Weitzel, PharmD, CDE
Assistant Editor, *Pharmacist's Letter*
and *Prescriber's Letter*, and Director of

Editorial Projects, Therapeutic
Research Center, Stockton,
California; Clinical Associate
Professor (Adjunct), University of
Florida College of Pharmacy,
Gainesville, Florida

Adam C. Welch, PharmD
Assistant Professor, Pharmacy
Practice, Wilkes University Nesbitt
School of Pharmacy, Wilkes-Barre,
Pennsylvania

Katherine E. Werner, PharmD
Clinical Pharmacist-Provider,
Department of Defense–MEDDAC,
Evans U.S. Army Community
Hospital, Department of Pharmacy,
Ft. Carson, Colorado

Amy L. Whitaker, PharmD
Assistant Professor,
Virginia Commonwealth University
School of Pharmacy, Richmond,
Virginia

Mario M. Zeolla, PharmD, BCPS (deceased)
Associate Professor of Pharmacy
Practice, Union University Albany
College of Pharmacy, Albany,
New York

Principles of Incorporating Patient Care into a Community Practice

Section

1

1 Entrepreneurship in Pharmacy

Bradley P. Tice

Objectives

1. Discuss the basic characteristics of an entrepreneur.

2. Develop a feasibility analysis and pro forma cash flow statement.

3. Describe the value of extracurricular activities and experiential aspects of developing entrepreneurial capabilities.

Traditionally, entrepreneurship in pharmacy is thought of as starting and running an independently owned pharmacy store. The focus of this case is to extend the discussion of entrepreneurship in pharmacy to the identification and pursuit of opportunities that are related to pharmacy practice, and that might arise from the pharmacist's specialized body of knowledge, skills, and professional practice.

Scenario

Ben Jacobs grew up in a mid-sized family and has two brothers and a sister. His parents owned and operated three sandwich shops in the small city where they lived. The town had a population of about 40,000. Pharmacist Jacobs worked in the sandwich shops from the time he was 12 years old. At first he did general cleaning and stocking and, as he gained experience, rotated through all areas of the business including delivery to customers, in-store service delivery, inventory management, and catering. He also had some exposure to running the business. His father stressed the importance of relationships and being involved in the community. For this reason, while growing up, pharmacist Jacobs was highly involved in community and church activities. This involvement extended to his professional organizations during pharmacy school and now to state and national pharmacy associations. During college he was also involved with many campus-wide organizations outside of pharmacy, and he has begun to get involved in the local civic organizations in the city where he now lives.

Pharmacist Jacobs graduated from an accredited college of pharmacy in May of 1998 with his Doctor of Pharmacy degree. Upon graduation he began work as an employee staff pharmacist in June 1998 for a large pharmacy company. Initially, as was typical, he worked at multiple stores, filling in for other pharmacists on vacation, sick days, and other time off (i.e., floater pharmacist). After about 8 months, he was placed full-time in one of the slower stores in the market. The pharmacy staff consisted of two other full-time pharmacists and six technicians. The pharmacists dispensed about 1400 prescriptions per week. The clientele was primarily a poorer population, resulting in a prescription mix that was about 60% Medicaid.

Pharmacist Jacobs was excited about the start of his career and really enjoyed helping people. He found the people who came to his store to be very friendly and willing to listen to his help. They did not have a lot of money to pay for expensive health care services, and many of them did not have a regular medical doctor. As a result, many of them turned to him for medical assistance. Frequently, people would come to him for help in the area of wound care. He constantly found himself assisting patients in the first-aid section, so he made sure to keep himself up to date in first aid and wound care management by attending numerous continuing education sessions and even consulting with a physician specialist in the area.

One day, pharmacist Jacobs decided to put together a special kit that included items for basic first aid and some special instructions that had proved very helpful to his patients. The kit became known as "Ben's Kit" (Case Table 1–1) and was a popular item in the pharmacy. The kit was based on techniques that he had learned from an Australian pharmacist who specialized in wound care. The kit contained materials that did not require compounding but, at the same time, were not typically found in nonprescription sections of the pharmacy. The necessary items, along with the special instructions, were simply put in a clear plastic bag and labeled "Ben's Kit." The price included a

CASE Table 1–1   Ben's Kit
Red Desert Dust[a] (20 g)
Colloidal silver (3 mL)
Sterile gauze
Wound tape
Instructions

[a] Contains Australian seasonings.
Note: Ben's Kit is for case study use only and does not represent any legitimate wound care treatment.

modest markup. The pharmacy staff appreciated pharmacist Jacobs' effort because it significantly reduced the time required for patient consultations and seemed to help the patients. He continued using the kit and assisting patients with wound care. Physicians even began making referrals for Ben's Kit. Within 24 months, however, he was transferred to another store.

The new store had a much different clientele and was much busier. This store was open 24 hours and dispensed about 3200 prescriptions a week. Five full-time pharmacists and one part-time pharmacist staffed the store, with 17 technicians in various full- and part-time roles. Pharmacist Jacobs was surprised to find that he was not able to spend as much time with patients and found that the clientele, which was much more affluent, wanted quick answers and overall was more demanding.

He had brought over a supply of Ben's Kits but found that the new staff did not really buy into the concept and were not focused on patients because they were so busy. Still, he kept a supply of kits on hand and found them to be useful for quick solutions to first-aid questions. Patients sometimes balked at the packaging, but word quickly spread about the effectiveness of Ben's Kits. Furthermore, one of the pharmacists in the store was trying to start a diabetes care service. She asked pharmacist Jacobs to teach her about wound care and began using the kits with her diabetes patients. The physicians she worked with also really liked the kits and began sending her referrals. The one good aspect of the new store was that pharmacist Jacobs could charge four times the price that he had charged at his old store. Originally, he was ordering the products through the store for a cost of about $3.29 and selling them for $4.49. At the new store he could charge $17.99 for the same kit.

By this time, pharmacist Jacobs had been at the new store about 18 months. The lack of time with patients and overall busyness was really draining him. The "newness" of his career had started to wear off, and he felt he was ready for a new challenge. He wondered if he could do something bigger with Ben's Kits, but he did not have any background in business or a lot of extra money to start a company on his own.

Pharmacist Jacobs decided to contact the local university's business school to see if any classes that might help him were available. He was directed to the school's entrepreneurship program and connected with a professor who specialized in new opportunities. The professor spent a good amount of time with him and introduced him to some basic frameworks of entrepreneurship (Case Figures 1–1 and 1–2).

Questions and Activities

Pharmacist Jacobs' first concern is that he does not "feel" that he is an "entrepreneur." The professor asks him to describe what he thinks an entrepreneur "is."

1. a. Describe your concept of an entrepreneur and what you view as the characteristics of a successful entrepreneur.

   b. What type of training does one need to be an entrepreneur?

Pharmacist Jacobs describes his idea and experience to the professor and asks the professor for his opinion of the idea. The professor replies that one of the key components of pursuing a new idea is researching the idea and performing a feasibility analysis. The professor refers pharmacist Jacobs to Case Figure 1–1 and suggests that he perform a feasibility analysis on the four areas in the second column.

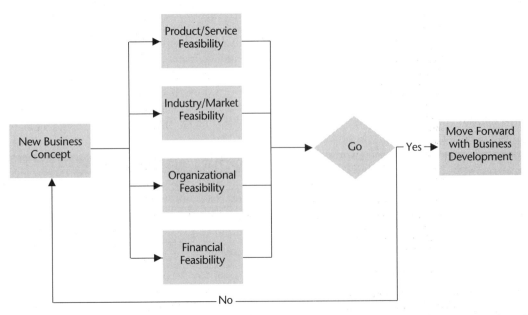

CASE Figure 1–1 Determination of feasibility of a new business concept. (*Source:* Reproduced with permission from Barringer BR, Ireland RD. *Entrepreneurship: Successfully Launching New Ventures.* Upper Saddle River, NJ: Pearson Prentice Hall; 2006.)

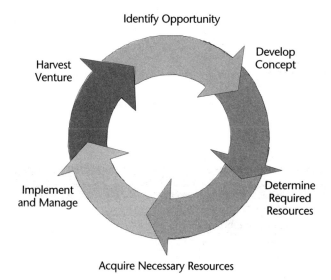

Identify Opportunity

Develop Concept

Determine Required Resources

Acquire Necessary Resources

Implement and Manage

Harvest Venture

Step in Entrepreneurship Process	Elements of Research
Identify the opportunity	Changing demographics Emergence of new market segments Process needs New technologies Incongruities Regulatory change Social change
Develop the concept	New products New services New markets New organizational structure/forms New technologies New sales or distribution channels
Determine the required resources	Skilled employees General management expertise Marketing and sales expertise Technical expertise Financing Distribution channels Sources of supply Production facilities Licenses, patents, and legal protection
Acquire the necessary resources	Debt Equity Leveraging Outsourcing Leasing Contract labor Temporary staff Supplier financing Joint ventures Partnerships Barter Gifts
Implement and manage	Implementation of concept Monitoring of performance Payback for resource providers Reinvestment Expansion Achievement of performance goals
Harvest the venture	Absorption of new concept into mainstream operations Family business succession Sell venture Go public Shut down venture

CASE Figure 1–2 The entrepreneurship process. (*Source:* Adapted with permission from reference 6.)

2. Develop a feasibility analysis for Ben's Kit. (*Note:* This activity may require the learner to make feasibility assumptions from a scenario provided by the instructor or to develop a scenario using appropriate variables [e.g., amount of capital available to invest, size of market, salaries and other expenses, volume discounts of costs of goods, etc.] and then make feasibility assumptions.) Provide a rationale/description for the assumptions. For instance, describe how the marketing costs will drive the revenue assumptions, and explain the basis for the estimate of sales volume (number of kits sold).

After performing the feasibility analysis, pharmacist Jacobs decides to pursue the opportunity. To realize his goal, he needs to get others to invest in his concept/business.

3. Develop a short statement that could be used to quickly get buy-in from potential investors.

After performing the feasibility analysis, pharmacist Jacobs is much more knowledgeable about this opportunity. He has identified the size of the market and his target customers, and understands the overall business landscape. Armed with this knowledge, he is now ready to develop some financial projections.

4. Develop a simplified pro forma cash flow statement that describes the financial potential for the opportunity. Include a top section that lists the projected income and a bottom section that describes expenses. The bottom section should be broken down into "variable costs" and "fixed costs."

5. Pharmacist Jacobs' current employment by a pharmacy company is a key aspect of this case. What are some potential advantages and disadvantages of this situation?

6. Using the case information and Case Figure 1–1, describe how pharmacist Jacobs' extracurricular and professional activities can benefit him in the pursuit of this opportunity.

7. One of the most important statements for a new opportunity is the pro forma cash flow statement. This statement identifies sources of income and expenses. Why is this statement so important?

Information Sources

1. Miner JB. *The Four Routes to Entrepreneurial Success.* San Francisco: Berrett-Koehler; 1996.

2. Porter ME. *Competitive Advantage.* New York: The Free Press; 1985.

3. Zaltman G. *How Customers Think: Essential Insights Into the Mind of the Market.* Boston: Harvard Business School Press; 2002.

4. Frank MO. *How to Get Your Point Across in 30 Seconds or Less.* New York: Pocket Books; 1986.

5. Barringer BR, Ireland RD. *Entrepreneurship: Successfully Launching New Ventures.* Upper Saddle River, NJ: Pearson Prentice Hall; 2006.

6. Morris MH, Kuratko DF. *Corporate Entrepreneurship.* Fort Worth, Tex: Harcourt College Press; 2003.

2 Developing a Business Plan

Jennifer L. Rodis

Objectives

1. Identify the rationale and key components of a business plan for development of a patient care service in a community pharmacy.

2. Describe a pharmacist-run patient care service in a concise and clear manner that is understandable and appealing to various stakeholders.

3. Conduct a needs assessment to determine the logistics of implementing, marketing, and billing for a pharmacist-run patient care service.

4. Analyze costs and create a financial plan.

5. Determine strategies to measure outcomes.

This case will help learners to identify the elements of a business plan, provide the resources to guide the learner through the process of developing a business plan, and describe a community pharmacy scenario with which the learner can create a business plan. Developing a business plan is a complex, multistep process that has been broken down into the essentials for this case.

Development Process

The process for developing a business plan for a patient care service in a community pharmacy involves multiple steps. These steps ultimately lead to the creation of a dynamic document that guides development of the service, communicates the goals of the service to multiple stakeholders, and identifies a means to measure the success of the service. The specific elements of a business plan have been described by various authors and organizations, whose descriptions vary slightly in terminology and organization.[1-5] Case Table 2–1 lists the components of a business plan as described by Philips and Larson.[1] This case will address the needs assessment, financial analysis, and outcomes assessment components of a business plan.

An effective business plan involves a sound needs assessment, often referred to as a "SWOT" analysis, which identifies and categorizes internal strengths and weaknesses (SW) and external opportunities and threats (OT) that are related to service implementation. An effective SWOT analysis helps the business planner fully evaluate the phar-

CASE Table 2–1 Ten Basic Elements of a Business Plan
Executive summary
Description of the business
Description of the product or service
Sales and marketing
Requirements
Costs
Pricing and reimbursement
Financing
Financial data analysis
Concluding narrative

Source: Reference 1.

macy environment and identify potential target groups for marketing, collaboration, and/or competition—as well as establish a niche for the pharmacy service. The SWOT analysis helps the business planner determine that the service being proposed is not only feasible but also meets the needs and desires of the environment.

The financial analysis, another key element of the business plan, includes pricing the service as one of the main goals. It is also important for community pharmacists to evaluate the options available for billing and receiving compensation for the provision of patient care services.[6-12]

The business plan also serves as a guide to measure the success of the service. A good business plan identifies the key outcomes that will be evaluated to determine the success of the service. The developer considers clinical, humanistic, and economic outcomes, and then selects outcomes to measure according to the interests of key stakeholders; it is often helpful to ask stakeholders what outcome data they would like to see.

Scenario

Pamela Jacobs is a pharmacist in a small chain pharmacy in a rural town with a population of approximately 18,000. The population demographics for the town are described in Case Table 2–2. The pharmacy chain involves a total of five stores, two located in the town where the pharmacy originated and three in neighboring smaller towns; pharmacist Jacobs works in one of the two stores in the original

CASE Table 2–2	Population Demographics for Zip Code of Pharmacy
Gender	
Male	53%
Female	47%
Age (years)	
<19	27.7%
20–34	18.5%
35–54	28.3%
55–64	9.5%
65–74	8.2%
75	7.8%
Race and ethnicity	
White	86%
Black or African American	8%
Asian or Pacific Islander	5%
Other	1%

town. Her pharmacy serves a diverse population of patients with regard to age, disease states, and socioeconomic status. The pharmacy is located about half a mile from the county hospital and about one and a half miles from a building that houses a private physician practice. One physician, in particular, from this practice calls the pharmacy one to two times per week with a medication question or to discuss a specific patient case. Approximately 15% of the prescriptions filled at the pharmacy are hospital discharge prescriptions for nonlocal patients who live more than 15 miles away; the majority of prescriptions are filled for local residents.

Store hours vary from store to store within the chain. The two original stores are open Monday through Friday, 9 am to 7 pm, and Saturday, 9 am to 5 pm, and closed on Sundays and holidays.

Pharmacist Jacob's store is staffed by three pharmacists, four technicians, and three cashiers. Pharmacist shifts are 9 am to 5 pm, 10 am to 6 pm, and 11 am to 7 pm; technician shifts are 9 am to 5:30 pm, 10:00 am to 6:30 pm, and 10:30 am to 7 pm. Pharmacist and technician staffing overlaps between 11 am to 5 pm, Monday through Friday, and from 10 am to 2 pm on Saturdays. Pharmacist Jacobs and one other pharmacist work full-time (40 hours per week), whereas the third pharmacist works part-time (32 hours per week). The three pharmacists have worked together for approximately 4 years; the first two pharmacists had worked together for 3 years before pharmacist Jacobs joined the team 4 years ago. All but one of the four technicians have been with the small chain for more than 5 years. The new technician joined the team a year ago. The other technicians have worked together at this pharmacy for 3 years. All technicians are certified. The pharmacy staff work very

well together and maintain an excellent rapport with patients and local physician offices.

The pharmacy chain already offers some select expanded patient care services for their patients, including:

- Free delivery to patients within city limits.
- Glucometer training.
- Cholesterol screening using Cholestech LDX.
- Blood glucose testing.

The services are offered by appointment and to walk-ins during regular store hours. Pharmacists and technicians are involved in the delivery of these services: Technicians complete the point-of-care paperwork for the appropriate tests; pharmacists complete the testing and provide the patient counseling and education. The services are fee-for-service. For the past 3 months, this store has been the most successful store in the small chain with regard to the number of screenings and profits. The staff at this store are motivated and interested in advanced patient care services.

There are four other pharmacies within a 5-mile radius of this pharmacy: a grocery store chain pharmacy, two national chain pharmacies, and an independent pharmacy. Of these pharmacies, only the independent pharmacy offers any advanced patient care services, which include diabetes education and wellness screenings (blood pressure, blood glucose, and weight monitoring). Also located within this 5-mile radius are a self-insured automobile factory, a YMCA, and a senior residential facility that offers assisted and independent living opportunities.

Pharmacist Jacobs recently attended a meeting of her state professional association and listened to a presentation by a community pharmacist who offers comprehensive medication therapy reviews in her pharmacy. Pharmacist Jacobs would like to integrate this service into her pharmacy environment. Her vision for the comprehensive medication therapy review includes the following:

- At the initial face-to-face appointment or phone call interview, the pharmacist will compile a complete medical history, including medications.
- Between the first and second visit, the pharmacist will:

   —Evaluate the medication profile.

   —Gather relevant education materials.

   —Put together a medication record, a medication action plan, and a letter detailing the pharmacist's recommendations for the patient.

- During the second face-to-face appointment, the pharmacist will review the medication profile with the patient, and offer any needed education, counseling, or recommendations for optimizing the patient's drug therapy.

The pharmacist will communicate with the patient's physician about recommendations related to any medication-related problems identified during the first and/or second patient visit. The pharmacist will also follow up with the patient as needed to provide further education and counseling, and will periodically review the medication profile to identify any new medication-related problems.

Pharmacist Jacobs sees this new service as an opportunity to take the patient care at her pharmacy to the next level. She creates the documentation forms, protocols for patient care, and researches training programs for pharmacists on conducting comprehensive medication therapy reviews. The next step is to develop a business plan to share her idea with the pharmacy chain owner and receive approval to move forward with implementation of the new patient care service.

Questions and Activities

1. Analyze the pharmacy's environment, and use a SWOT analysis to determine whether the proposed comprehensive medication therapy review service is feasible.

2. What specific characteristics of this pharmacy may pose barriers or contribute to the success of implementing this service?

3. Write a mission statement, and list short- and long-term goals for the service.

4. Identify the key stakeholders for this patient care service, and discuss marketing strategies specific to each stakeholder.

5. Determine how the benefits differ when marketing to each stakeholder (i.e., physician vs. patient).

6. Conduct a financial analysis to determine a price range for the comprehensive medication therapy review service.

Available resources to assist with this financial analysis include purchasing the Cost of Service Calculator from PharmAccount (https://www.pharmaccount.com/Default.asp) or working through the cost-calculator worksheet put together by the National Institute for Pharmacy Care Outcomes.[11,12]

7. Identify available billing options and decide on the most appropriate billing process for this pharmacy.

8. Generate a list of the costs, direct and indirect, that may be involved in the start-up of the service.

9. List outcome measures that determine the success of this service, including the mechanisms for gathering the data for the outcome assessment.

10. Compose for the pharmacy chain owner an executive summary of the business plan for implementation of the comprehensive medication therapy review service.

Additional Activities

1. Create a business plan to implement comprehensive medication therapy reviews to be provided by community pharmacists in a local physician's office. Consider the differences in marketing, billing techniques, and personnel costs in this setting.

2. Develop a presentation to formally present the business plan to the small chain pharmacy's owner.

3. Create a survey that could be given to patients visiting a community pharmacy to assess their satisfaction with the pharmacy and their interest in participating in pharmacist-run patient care services provided by the pharmacy.

4. Choose a local community pharmacy, and identify potential collaborating and/or competing organizations within a 5-mile radius of the pharmacy. (Try using Google maps [pharmacies, physician offices, community organizations] and the pharmacy's list of physicians, and calling the local small business association.)

5. Use data at www.census.gov to assess the population demographics in a local pharmacy's zip code.

6. Create a survey for patients to evaluate their outcomes from a patient care service.

Information Sources

1. Hagel HP, Rovers JP. *Managing the Patient-Centered Pharmacy.* Washington, DC: American Pharmaceutical Association; 2002:146–65.

2. Rovers JP, Currie JD, Hagel HP, et al. *A Practical Guide to Pharmaceutical Care.* 2nd ed. Washington, DC: American Pharmacists Association; 2003:287–93.

3. Cipolle RJ, Strand LM, Morley PC. *Pharmaceutical Care Practice.* 2nd ed. New York: McGraw-Hill; 2004:343–6.

4. Cohn KH, Schwartz RW. Business plan writing for physicians. *Am J Surg.* 2002;184:114–20.

5. Schneider JE. The way to a powerful business plan. *Drug Discov Today.* 2002;7:342–5.

6. Hogue MD. *The Pharmacist's Guide to Compensation for Patient Care Services.* Washington, DC: American Pharmacists Association; 2002.

7. Snella KA, Trewyn RR, Hansen LB, et al. Pharmacist compensation for cognitive services: focus on the physician office and community pharmacy. *Pharmacotherapy.* 2004;24:372–88.

8. Beatty SJ, Rodis JL, Bellebaum KL, et al. Community and ambulatory pharmacy evaluation of patient care services and billing

patterns before implementation of Medicare Part D. *J Am Pharm Assoc.* 2006;46:707–14.

9. Norton JL, Gibson DL. Establishing an outpatient anticoagulation clinic in a community hospital. *Am J Health Syst Pharm.* 1996;53:1151–7.

10. American Medical Association Bookstore. Current Procedural Terminology References. Available at: https://catalog.ama-assn.org/Catalog/home.jsp. Last accessed October 26, 2008.

11. Rupp MT. *Pricing Pharmacist Care Services.* 2nd ed. Washington, DC: American Pharmacists Association; 2007. Available for purchase at: http://www.ncpanet.org.

12. PharmAccount. Cost of Service Calculator. Available for purchase at: https://www.pharmaccount.com/Default.asp. Last accessed October 26, 2008.

13. Holdford DA. *Marketing for Pharmacists.* 2nd ed. Washington, DC: American Pharmacists Association; 2007.

3 Pharmacy Workflow

Sharon B. S. Gatewood

Objectives

1. Develop the most efficient workflow for processing prescriptions.

2. Identify the roles of both the pharmacist and the technician within the workflow.

3. Explore the benefits of an automated workflow system for the pharmacy.

4. Identify possible pharmacy technologies that could improve the workflow.

Scenario

Audra Matthews is a newly licensed pharmacist who has been hired as a staff pharmacist in a brand-new pharmacy. The pharmacy is located in an up-and-coming urban setting with a middle- to upper-level income population. She is one of three full-time pharmacists who work in the pharmacy on a regular basis. The schedule allows for some overlap between the pharmacists. One full-time and two part-time technicians work in the pharmacy as well. The hours of operation are Monday through Saturday, 9 am to 9 pm, and Sunday, 11 am to 6 pm. The prescription volume ranges from 300 to 400 per day, with an average of about 1900 prescriptions per week. The pharmacy has automation that includes interactive voice response, voicemail, and a small, portable counting device. Patient care services provided at the pharmacy include blood pressure monitoring, diabetes screening, cholesterol screening, and medication therapy management services.

Although Audra Matthews is a new pharmacist, she has been asked to evaluate the workflow for addition of a diabetes education program for the pharmacy. Case Figure 3–1 shows the existing layout of the pharmacy.

Questions and Activities

1. What is pharmacy workflow?

2. With the existing layout, what would be the most efficient workflow in this pharmacy for processing a prescription?

3. What tasks must generally be completed by a pharmacist?

4. What tasks may generally be completed by a technician?

5. Generate a schedule for the day. What are the job responsibilities for each person?

6. Identify some physical changes to the pharmacy layout that may improve the workflow and reduce the time it takes to fill a prescription.

7. Identify some staffing changes to the pharmacy schedule that may improve the pharmacy workflow.

8. What technology is available to enhance pharmacy workflow?

9. What types of clinical activities can be incorporated into the pharmacy workflow?

10. Would an automated workflow system be beneficial in this pharmacy? Why or why not?

11. What are the advantages and disadvantages for this pharmacy to have a drive-thru window?

Additional Activities

1. Research the laws in your state regarding the duties and capabilities of pharmacy technicians. In addition, define the ratio of pharmacist to technicians in the pharmacy.

2. Design your own pharmacy layout with efficient workflow for processing prescriptions. (The number of prescriptions filled daily is 300 to 400.)

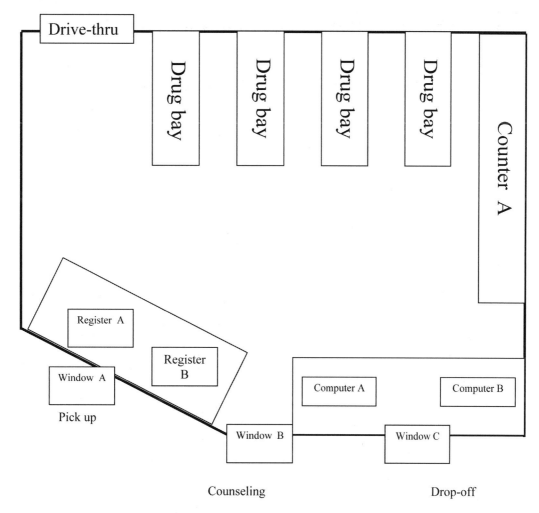

CASE Figure 3–1 Original pharmacy layout.

Information Sources

1. Rovers JP, Currie JD, Hagel HP, et al. *A Practical Guide to Pharmaceutical Care*. 2nd ed. Washington, DC: American Pharmacists Association; 2003:253–66.

2. Pai AK. Integration of a clinical community pharmacist position: emphasis on workflow design. *J Am Pharm Assoc*. 2005; 45:400–3.

3. Angelo LB, Ferreri SP. Assessment of workflow redesign in community pharmacy. *J Am Pharm Assoc*. 2005;45:145–50.

4. Angelo LB, Christensen DB, Ferreri SP. Impact of community pharmacy automation on workflow, workload, and patient interaction. *J Am Pharm Assoc*. 2005;45:138–44.

5. Helling DK, Nelson KM, Ramirez JE, et al. Kaiser Permanente Colorado Region Pharmacy Department: innovative leader in pharmacy practice. *J Am Pharm Assoc*. 2006;46:67–76.

4 Marketing Pharmacy Services

Bradley P. Tice

Objectives

1. Analyze a situation with regard to developing a patient care service in a pharmacy practice, and be able to identify and bring together components of the practice to establish an effective marketing plan for a new pharmacy service.

2. Apply principles for marketing products and services to be able to discuss and develop a marketing plan for a pharmacy service.

3. Justify the need for resources to market pharmacy services.

4. Establish the value of a pharmacy service and determine a price at which to offer the service.

This case discusses the opportunity to implement new pharmacy services in diabetes in a busy community pharmacy setting. The focus of the case is to provide enough background to provide the foundation for developing a marketing plan, discussing the various aspects of marketing— internally and externally—and establishing pricing, as well as to discuss the differences in marketing services versus products.

Scenario

Pharmacist Rebecca Smith is an employee at a pharmacy in a metropolitan area with a population of more than 400,000. She works for a pharmacy company that has 14 stores in the metropolitan area and a total of 147 stores in a four-state area. After being employed with the company for 3 years and working at this store location for 1 year, pharmacist Smith, along with four other pharmacists in her metropolitan area, was sent to a 2-day certificate training program in diabetes. The district pharmacy supervisor for the 23 stores in the metropolitan area has charged these five pharmacists with developing a program to serve the needs of the pharmacies' patients with diabetes. The pharmacies have never offered any services like these before, but the supervisor read a recent demographic report of the city that identified 14% of the population as having diabetes (the national average is 7%). A high percentage of this population is younger than 20 years (5% compared with the national average of 0.22%), 14% of the population is aged 20 to 60 years (national average 9.6%), and 24% is older than 60 years (national average

20.9%). The pharmacists who attended the program are excited about the opportunity; however, they realize now that they are back in their pharmacies, everything is business as usual. They feel they have a lot to offer all the patients with diabetes who come to their stores, but they also realize that their patients do not see them any differently yet. In addition, the other staff pharmacists are not sure how adding this service will impact them.

The program described at the meeting focused primarily on advanced aspects of the disease including sick day management, blood glucose monitoring, pattern management and insulin therapy, preventive care (e.g., foot and eye examinations, immunizations), and nutrition. It also included a module on marketing and pricing services. To help the pharmacist attendees in their effort to start a diabetes service, the program materials included a "menu" of services that could be delivered (Case Table 4–1). The marketing module of the program also included a handout "Marketing 101" (Case Figure 4–1) to help with the start-up of the service.

CASE Table 4–1 "Menu" of Services	
Service	**Fee**
Comprehensive program (includes medication review, four educational classes, training for blood glucose monitoring, and monitoring for adherence and guideline assessment)	
Training	
Use of blood glucose monitors	
Blood glucose monitoring	
Insulin injection technique	
Education	
Sick day management	
General diabetes education	
Preventive services education (immunizations, foot care, eye care, etc.)	
Other Services	
Insulin pattern management	
Medication review	
Adherence monitoring	
Guideline assessment and monitoring	
Grocery store tour on healthy eating and reading food labels	

Marketing 101

Marketing is an area that often is not well understood, especially by pharmacists because it is not a part of their traditional training. At the same time, it may be the biggest determining factor to business success. Having a product (or service) that nobody knows about will not generate much success. In addition, the perceptions that patients gain on the basis of marketing can shape their expectations and even the amount they are willing to pay for the product (or service). For this diabetes certificate program, we have included a basic module on marketing. This summary sheet can be used as a quick reference tool. It is not exhaustive, but it can help you get started and remember some key points. It is important to remember that marketing is as much, or more of, an art than it is a science. One key is to simply get started. Do your best to see what does and does not work, but realize that one of the biggest frustrations with marketing, as well as spending money on marketing, is that it can be difficult to quantify results for a specific marketing initiative.

The Four P's[1]

- *Product.* The actual physical goods or service(s) that you are offering a patient to satisfy a need.
- *Price.* The dollar amount you are charging for your product(s). Price is a marketing tool because it affects the number and type of patients who purchase the product. Price also affects their perceptions of the value and quality of your product.
- *Promotion.* The tools, methods, and skills to communicate the product(s). Examples include advertising, publicity, direct sales, and personal selling.
- *Place.* The place and time that the product is offered.
- *Positioning* (*often called the fifth P*). How you want your product to be viewed by others.

Aspects of Marketing Services

Aspects of marketing *services* rather than products include:

- *Intangible.* Unlike products, services do not sit on shelves. They are non-inventoried. For someone to purchase a service, they must understand it and be able to "visualize" it. To reduce uncertainty, buyers look for signs of service quality by looking at the people, place, equipment, material, and prices where the service is offered.
- *Inseparable.* Services are typically produced and consumed at the same time. For this reason, both the patient and server affect the service outcome. This relationship also causes the patient to be highly interested in who the provider is.
- *Variable.* Services are highly variable, depending on who provides them and even when they are provided.
- *Perishable.* Services cannot be "stored." Fluctuations in demand can make it difficult to staff efficiently.

Rogers' Five Factors of Product Diffusion[2]

- *Relative advantage.* The degree to which a product is better than the product it replaces.
- *Compatibility.* The degree to which a product is consistent with existing values and experiences.
- *Complexity.* The degree to which a product is difficult to understand and use.
- *Trialability.* The degree to which a product may be experimented with on a limited basis.
- *Observability.* The degree to which product usage and impact are visible to others.

Examples of Marketing Methods

- *Word of mouth.* Word of mouth is often the most powerful method of marketing, but it can also be the most difficult to achieve. Generating positive statements from people's experiences with your products and getting them to talk about it is the ultimate goal.

- *Advertising.* Advertising is easy to do but is the most expensive. In this method, the store likely has weekly flyers or other advertisements that might provide space for pharmacy advertising. It is often difficult to get this space; at least 8 to 13 weeks of lead time is required.
- *Public relations.* Public relations is accomplished through public service announcements on the radio and free notices in newspapers, and so forth. These efforts are less costly than advertising and can be perceived as more credible because they are not paid advertisements. However, public relation efforts can be more difficult to achieve and control.
- *Direct mail.* Current direct mail efforts are less effective than in the past, but there is a reason for all the junk mail. *Note:* It generally takes 7 to 11 "hits" on a person before they make the purchase decision.
- *In-store.* In-store marketing is generally easy to do but does sometimes requires permission and coordination with the store director. Examples include signs, brochures, prescription bag stuffers, badges, giveaways, banners, in-store radio announcements, and so forth.
- *Personal selling.* Personal selling requires some training, but the key is for staff to be well prepared for when the other marketing methods bring in "buyers." Personal selling is also necessary and effective when identifying potential patients and then helping them identify and understand how the product(s) will benefit them.

Pricing Strategies

One of the most common and costly mistakes is basing pricing too much on what the cost is to make and deliver the product(s). An ancient Chinese proverb states "The way the table gets treated depends upon the price for which it is sold." Pricing is a tool that can be used to control and affect the perception and uptake of the product. Some pricing strategies are[3]:

- *Skim pricing.* Skim pricing is designed to capture the highest margins at the expense of high sales volumes. It involves setting prices that are high relative to most purchasers' willingness to pay. This strategy is viable only when sales revenue from a price-insensitive segment exceeds that received from selling to a larger market at a lower price. Skim pricing can also be used to control and manage the volume of product purchased. "Sequential skimming" is when the price is dropped once the top segment of the market has been "skimmed off." The price is then lowered to capture sales from the next lower market tier. This strategy is often used in technology sales.
- *Penetration pricing.* Penetration pricing involves setting a low price to attract and hold a large base of purchasers. Prices are not necessarily cheap, but they are low compared with the perceived economic value. This strategy can be used to keep competition from entering the market. Its disadvantage is that it can undermine the perceived quality of the product when it enters the market and will not work when product quality is difficult to evaluate.
- *Value-based pricing.* Value-based pricing involves determining the dollar value benefit for the purchaser and pricing toward that dollar amount. This strategy can result in higher profit margins, but the value must be based on a short "mean time to payback" (MTB). The MTB should generally be less than 1 year for purchasers to regain their investment. As the MTB increases, the decision to buy will be more difficult for the purchaser.
- *Cost-plus pricing.* Cost-plus pricing involves determining the costs involved in making and delivering the product, including operational costs, and adding a "fair" amount above that. Difficulties with this strategy are that costs are most often underestimated and what is "fair" to the seller might not seem fair to the purchaser.

CASE Figure 4–1 Basic marketing principles.

The district pharmacy supervisor feels that he has done a lot by simply sending the pharmacists to the training, paying their way, and giving them the opportunity. He has not been able to give the five pharmacists any specific time during their workweek to develop the program but does expect them to deliver one. He has promised that, if they are able to deliver results, he will be able to work in extra staff to cover the hours required to deliver this service. There is no budget for the pharmacists to work from, but they are able to make requests to their store supervisors and the district pharmacy supervisor.

Overview of the General Health Care Landscape

Pharmacists in the state where pharmacist Smith works are active and well organized. They are generally recognized as leaders in the country with regard to pushing pharmacy services forward. The pharmacy association has many programs on patient care practice and advancing pharmacy services. There have also been several demonstration projects in the state that have helped establish the value of pharmacist services. Still, pharmacist services are mostly thought of in the traditional sense of filling and dispensing prescription orders.

Other health care professionals are similarly progressive within their areas, and some turf issues do exist. Physicians are open to working with pharmacists on a one-on-one basis. The board of pharmacy and board of medicine have come together to establish collaborative practice guidelines in the state, which enable pharmacists to set up protocols with physicians that allow pharmacists to deliver a higher level of direct patient care. Still, the physician associations often raise objections to advanced pharmacy practices extending "too far" into patient care. Occasionally legislation is also introduced to limit the extent to which pharmacists are able to extend their practices. Nurse practitioners are also active within the state.

The city has three main hospitals. Two of them have nurse-led diabetes programs that are offered free to anyone with diabetes. The hospital closest to the store does not have a diabetes program.

Pharmacy and Store

Pharmacist Smith's pharmacy is a busy store with a weekly prescription volume of approximately 2400 prescriptions. She is a staff pharmacist and works 40 hours a week. The pharmacy also has a pharmacy manager and two other pharmacists, for a total of four pharmacists, who staff the hours of operation of 8 am to 10 pm, Monday through Friday, Saturday, 8 am to 6 pm, and Sunday, 9 am to 5 pm. A total of seven technicians also work at the store. Two of these technicians have worked in the pharmacy for more than 10 years each and are well established in dispensing roles. One technician is a very quick learner and is able to function independently in many roles. Two of the technicians are less experienced and require a fair amount of oversight. The remaining two technicians work 10 to 15 hours each week, primarily evenings and weekends. The pharmacy manager's focus is on prescription volume. His salary is just above that of the staff pharmacists, but they all receive performance bonuses based on prescription volume. The pharmacy manager's incentive is significantly larger than the staff pharmacists' because of his managerial responsibilities.

The pharmacy is part of a grocery store that is the second-ranked store in the market. The pharmacy manager reports to the grocery store director, but the pharmacy is also directly supervised by the district pharmacy manager who has received upper management's approval to test the implementation of a diabetes program in this market. However, the grocery store director was not included.

The pharmacy has a typical counter area for patient counseling but does not have a private area for sit-down counseling. Options for a sit-down area include partitioning off some of the waiting area or using the break room in the store. The store also has a training room that can be used for education classes.

Relationships with physicians' offices, which are considered good, typically consist of requesting refills for patients and taking new prescriptions. The staff has paid a lot of attention to answering their calls quickly and establishing good rapport. Still, when the pharmacists make therapeutic recommendations, they generally catch the physicians' offices off guard, thus indicating that deep relationships have not been established with the physicians' offices. One office, that of Dr. Steve Barry, does seem more open and appreciative of their efforts. Pharmacist Smith has interacted with him at church and continuing education events.

The pharmacy staff has generally good relationships with its patients. However, with such a large prescription volume, it can be difficult to recognize every person when they come in. The company recently performed a patient satisfaction survey. The results can be seen in Case Table 4–2.

Competition

The store has competition from two major chain pharmacy companies in the market. One chain company currently has 8 stores in the market; another has 17 stores. Each chain has a pharmacy within a one-block radius of pharmacist Smith's store, with one located at the same intersection. Neither of the chain pharmacies has programs similar to the diabetes program being developed; however, one does offer adult immunizations through their pharmacists. The other offers influenza immunizations in the fall through nurses and has started to put in acute care clinics. So far three clinics have been established, but none is within 5 miles of pharmacist Smith's store yet. The Visiting Nurses Association is also active and well organized in the city and provides numerous services. Several independently owned pharmacies also exist in the area, one of which is

CASE Table 4–2   Patient Satisfaction Survey Results

Category	Results[a]
Satisfaction with Current Services	
Overall satisfaction with pharmacy services[b]	4.1
Satisfaction with speed of pharmacy service	3.9
Overall convenience of pharmacy service	4.1
Location of pharmacy store	4.3
Price of medications	3.6
Friendliness of pharmacy staff	4.4
Importance of Service Areas	
Speed of service	4.3
Convenience	4.6
Location	4.6
Price	4.5
Friendliness of staff	4.2
Accuracy in dispensing medications	5.0
Counseling on medications	4.1
Pharmacist management of medications	3.4
Additional service offerings	3.9
Types of Additional Services of Interest	
Educational classes on medical conditions	3.4
Health care library with videos	4.1
Weight loss classes	3.8
Health care brochures (free)	4.2
Individualized sessions on medical conditions	3.3
Individualized sessions on medications	3.7
Automated refill services	4.0
Prescription delivery	4.2

[a] Survey used a scale of 1–5, with 5 as the highest score.
[b] Result is for a separate question, not an average of rankings for individual questions.

CASE Table 4–3   Demographics within 5 Miles of Store

Gender for Households	
Male	45%
Female	55%
Age for Households	
17 or younger	35%
18–24	14%
25–44	17%
45–64	13%
65+	21%
Average age (years)	38.4
Race and Ethnicity for Households	
White	47%
Black or African American	22%
American Indian and Alaska Native	3%
Hispanic or Latino	23%
Bosnian	5%

CASE Table 4–4   Demographics for Metropolitan Area

Gender for Households	
Male	42%
Female	58%
Age for Households	
17 or younger	29%
18–24	16%
25–44	15%
45–64	17%
65+	23%
Average age (years)	39.6
Race and Ethnicity for Households	
White	38%
Black or African American	24%
American Indian and Alaska Native	4%
Hispanic or Latino	27%
Bosnian	7%

approximately 2 miles away. This pharmacy is well-known for patient care and has developed extensive services. Another independent pharmacy, approximately 5 miles away, has a focus on compounding.

Demographics

The store is located in a part of the city that is considered middle class. The population has an even mix of white- and blue-collar workers, with many "office-type" workers and also many workers who are employed nearby at a tire manufacturing plant. Demographics within 5 miles of the store are described in Case Table 4–3. The demographics for the entire metropolitan area are included in Case Table 4–4.

Questions and Activities

1. On the basis of their training in the certificate program, the five pharmacists decide that they can offer all the services listed in Case Table 4–1. The pharmacists understand the need to clearly define the products they will be offering. Using the patient satisfaction survey results (Case Table 4–2), demographic information, and other information provided in the case, develop and define each product.

2. Discuss the various pricing strategies (Case Figure 4–1) and their pros and cons for this situation. Establish a pricing strategy for the overall mix of products/services. For each product/service defined, establish a price that fits within that strategy.

3. Use the Marketing 101 tool (Case Figure 4–1) to devise a marketing strategy to effectively market the diabetes services. Include an analysis of how Rogers'

five factors of product diffusion impact the development and marketing of the service.

4. Describe how the services will provide value to patients, and how they will see and experience that value.

5. What factors could cause concern for pharmacy staff/management and the district manager, but could also help identify the need for "internal marketing," that is, marketing to people within the organization to obtain buy-in and support? What would be an effective internal marketing strategy?

6. How will the current environment and level of competition affect the types of services that the pharmacists choose to deliver? What "threats" and "opportunities" can be identified?

7. What types of promotions can be delivered within the budget constraints of the case? Discuss the advantages and disadvantages of the examples in the Marketing 101 tool (Case Figure 4–1), and identify additional marketing opportunities that fit within the case.

8. Describe and discuss the current employment setup and how it affects the likelihood for success in marketing the program. What are some of the strengths and weaknesses of this model? What would be a more ideal employment arrangement?

Information Sources

1. Zaltman G. *How Customers Think: Essential Insights Into the Mind of the Market*. Boston: Harvard Business School Press; 2003.

2. Edersheim EH. *The Definitive Drucker*. New York: McGraw-Hill; 2007.

3. Gourville JT. *Note on Innovation Diffusion: Rogers' Five Factors*. Boston: Harvard Business School Publishing; 2005.

4. Kotler P. *Marketing Management*. Upper Saddle River, NJ: Prentice Hall Press; 1998.

5. Nagle TT. Holden RK. *The Strategy and Tactics of Pricing*. Vol 3. Upper Saddle River, NJ: Prentice Hall Press; 2002.

5 Documentation of Patient Care in the Community Pharmacy Setting

Jennifer Cerulli

Objectives

1. Identify the reasons to document patient care encounters.

2. Describe the desired characteristics of a pharmacy documentation system.

3. List the essential elements to be documented by a community pharmacist from the perspective of the pharmacy, the physician/health care team, and the third-party payer.

4. Develop the documentation tools needed for community pharmacy practice (SOAP notes, physician letters).

Scenario

Paul Potter is a pharmacist and pharmacy owner of an independent pharmacy in a suburban town. The pharmacy services currently offered include free weekly blood pressure assessment for patients, as well as an asthma education and a medication therapy management program. During the dispensing and counseling process for an albuterol nebulizing solution prescription, the mother of a 4-year-old female child named Annie expressed that she was unsure when to use this new medication. She had obtained some medications from this pharmacy and another medication as a physician sample. She did not know the name of the other medication. After pharmacist Potter described the pharmacy's asthma program, the mother scheduled an appointment for a session.

The mother brought all of Annie's medications to the appointment; they included Proventil metered-dose inhaler (MDI) with AeroChamber (given as a physician sample; mother is not clear on the directions for use); albuterol nebulizing solution (use 1 vial every 4 hours as needed for shortness of breath); loratadine oral syrup (5 mg/5 mL) 1 teaspoonful by mouth every day; and a cough and cold nonprescription medication (decongestant/antihistamine combination). The mother alternates use of Proventil and albuterol about 4 to 5 times per week when Annie has shortness of breath and coughing. Annie takes loratadine

each day, but her mother noticed a constant runny nose, so she gives her the cough and cold medication a few times a week. Until pharmacist Potter reviewed the medications with the mother, she was unaware that Proventil MDI and albuterol nebulizer solution were the same medication with the same indication.

Pharmacist Potter provided Annie's mother with an overview of asthma and described how the medications work to improve breathing. He described the expected results, adverse effects, and administration technique for each medication or device. The cleaning procedure for the holding chamber and inhaler was also reviewed. Pharmacist Potter described how to determine when the MDI was empty (i.e., the floating technique does not work). He suggested that the mother talk with the physician and request an asthma action plan, which would define how often to use the rescue medications and how much to use. Pharmacist Potter also discussed methods to control possible asthma triggers. He provided the mother with a symptom and medication diary to track the frequency of albuterol use, triggers, and symptoms. Because the child is only 4 years old, the use of a peak flow meter was not discussed.

Annie's mother seemed pleased with her visit and walked away with a list of items to discuss with the physician at the next visit. As she left, pharmacist Potter contemplated how to document this visit and how to communicate to the physician that he felt Annie might now need controller therapy for her asthma. He recalled an old saying: "If you didn't document it, you didn't do it."

Questions and Activities

1. Identify the challenges that the pharmacist may encounter when attempting to document patient care.

2. Describe the ideal characteristics of a pharmacy documentation system that the pharmacist should consider when choosing a system.

3. What are the advantages and disadvantages of pen-and-paper documentation versus an electronic documentation system?

4. Identify the critical elements needed to document a patient care encounter and intervention.

5. Write a SOAP note based on the encounter.

6. Create a document that the pharmacist can use to forward his interventions and recommendation to the child's physician.

Additional Activities

1. Compare and contrast electronic and Internet-based documentation systems that are available for use in the community pharmacy setting.

2. Design a documentation form template that can capture the encounter information for a pen-and-paper patient chart system, and that would enable the pharmacist to assess the overall quality of the asthma program in the future.

Information Sources

1. Currie JD. Documentation. In: Rovers JP, Currie JD, eds. *A Practical Guide to Pharmaceutical Care*. 3rd ed. Washington DC: American Pharmacists Association; 2007:139–60.

2. American Pharmacists Association, National Association of Chain Drug Store Foundation. *Medication Therapy Management in Community Pharmacy Practice: Core Elements of an MTM Service*. Version 1.0. J Am Pharm Assoc. 2005;45:573–9. Also available at: http://www.pharmacist.com/MTM.

3. Currie JD, Doucette WR, Kuhle J, et al. Identification of essential elements in the documentation of pharmacist-provided care. *J Am Pharm Assoc*. 2003;43:41–9.

4. Brock KA, Casper KA, Green TR, et al. Documentation of patient care services in a community pharmacy setting. *J Am Pharm Assoc*. 2006;46:378–84.

5. Bennett M, Wedret JEJ, eds. *Collaborative Pharmacy Practice: Guidelines and Tools*. Washington DC: American Pharmacists Association; 2004.

6. Yee CM, Kohli J. Computerized documentation by pharmacists of medication therapy management services in a community pharmacy [letter]. *J Am Pharm Assoc*. 2008;48:4–6.

6 Compensation for Patient Care in the Community Pharmacy Setting

Andrew P. Traynor

Objectives

1. Describe the difference between compensation and reimbursement.

2. List the different possible payers of patient care services in a community pharmacy.

3. Design a fee structure for patient care services delivered in a community pharmacy.

4. Explain the credentialing process for becoming a provider with insurance carriers.

5. Apply current medication therapy management CPT codes to a fee structure for a medication therapy management service.

Lack of compensation and uncertainty regarding billing processes have been identified as key obstacles to implementation of patient care services in the community pharmacy setting.[1] For those providing patient care in community and ambulatory settings, Beatty and colleagues[2] identified reasons why pharmacists may not bill or charge for their services.

It is vital to understand terminology related to compensation for cognitive services. Nutescu and Klotz[3] outlined this terminology, as well as additional resources related to compensation, for a wide variety of patient settings. Hogue[4] explained that two of the most important terms to consider initially are "reimbursement" and "compensation" because these terms are often used interchangeably. Incorporating patient care in the community practice provides stand-alone value and/or adds value to drugs or devices; thus, compensation is the goal and the preferred term to use.

Snella and colleagues[5] have summarized approaches for pharmacists in clinics and community pharmacies to secure compensation for cognitive services. These services include laboratory services, immunizations, and various education and management services. The first step in establishing compensation is to complete a review of the potential payer mix that represents one's patients. This mix may consist of various insurances including Medicare, Medicaid, and private insurance. Outside of the Medicare Part D provision, which requires plan sponsors to offer medication therapy management (MTM) services in conjunction with a prescription drug benefit,[6] compensation strategies with insurance companies should focus on billing the patient's medical benefits as opposed to prescription benefits. Third-party payers usually require that health care professionals become credentialed before they can become a provider and receive compensation for patient care services. The credentialing processes and requirements may vary depending on the payer.

Models of Medicaid-sponsored cognitive services exist and represent different payment mechanisms. Examples of pharmacists' relationships with managed care organizations have been described; these organizations may provide a source of compensation for cognitive services.[3] Another source of income is contracts between pharmacists and self-insured employer groups for disease management and medication therapy management.[7] Although third-party payers are a dominant market segment, rising health care costs and increased patient responsibility for those costs present an opportunity to bill patients directly as sources of compensation. Finding ways to work with these payers has been suggested as a strategy to improve compensation.[8]

Scenario

Joe Johnson is a pharmacist in an independent pharmacy, ABC Pharmacy, in a rural town with a population of approximately 11,000. Pharmacist Johnson took this position after his residency because of the potential to further develop patient care services. The pharmacy owner is quite interested in providing this service to his patients and wants to ensure that the practice is sustainable. The pharmacy serves a variety of patients with regard to age, disease states, and socioeconomic status. The pharmacy is located across the street from a private practice medical building. A small critical access hospital is also located in the community.

The pharmacy is open Monday through Friday, 8 am to 8 pm, Saturday, 9 am to 5 pm, and closed on Sundays and holidays. It is staffed by three pharmacists (including pharmacist Johnson and the owner), four technicians, and three cashiers. Pharmacist and technician shifts are 8 am to

4:30 pm, 10 am to 6:30 pm, and 12 pm to 8:30 pm. The pharmacy staff is a good team and works very well together; the staff also has excellent relationships with patients and the local physician office.

The pharmacists counsel on each prescription (new and refill) as well as all devices that patients use. Pharmacist Johnson has recently reviewed an abundance of information related to the Asheville Project; he also just attended a meeting of his state professional association and listened to a presentation regarding delivery of MTM services. He would like to integrate this service in the pharmacy. His vision for the MTM service includes the following:

- Face-to-face appointments with patients and communication with local physician offices will be undertaken to gather complete medical history, including medications.

- According to the findings at the visit, the pharmacist will educate the patient, develop a patient-specific care plan with the patient, and communicate this care plan to the patient's physician as written documentation.

- All patient encounters will be documented in an electronic documentation system.

- Follow-up with the patient will occur as needed to provide further counseling and to periodically review medication use and health to identify any drug-related problems.

On the basis of the results of the Asheville Project, pharmacist Johnson has approached local self-insured employers to propose MTM as a benefit for their employees. The largest employers in the community that offer a health insurance benefit include the local health system (300 employees), the city (150 employees), the paper mill (250 employees), and a locally based trucking company (100 employees). Diabetes, hypertension, hyperlipidemia, arthritis, obesity, asthma, and chronic obstructive pulmonary disorder are common conditions requiring medical visits and use of prescription drugs. The employers are receptive to the idea but want to see more evidence of how it will work.

Pharmacist Johnson offers to provide MTM services to 10 volunteers as an example of the service that he will provide, and the recommendations that he will make to improve patient care and reduce the amount of money the employers spend on health care. The first of the 10 patients currently has diabetes, hypertension, and hyperlipidemia. The patient is currently taking eight medications for these chronic conditions. Pharmacist Johnson identifies two drug therapy problems in this patient.

Pharmacist Johnson will meet with the rest of the patients in this pilot and report back to the employer group with a summary of the results and further specifics related to the

CASE Table 6–1	2007 Estimated Delivery Costs for MTM Services at ABC Pharmacy
Categories of Cost	**Cost**
Pharmacist salary	$95,000
Pharmacist benefits	$23,750
Working space	$12,000
Marketing	$6,000
Computer and documentation software	$10,000
Utilities	$2,400
Support personnel	$45,000
Clinical equipment (stethoscopes, blood pressure cuff, scale, etc.)	$1,000
Office supplies	$5,000
Practice liability insurance	$150

service's cost. Case Table 6–1 represents resources that will be required for provision of the MTM service.

Questions and Activities

1. Identify reasons why pharmacists may not bill or charge for their services.

2. Explain the difference between the terms "reimbursement" and "compensation."

3. Explain the billing terminology for patient care services:

   a. CPT code
   b. ICD-9 code
   c. RBRVS
   d. X-12 platform
   e. NCPDP platform

4. According to the Lewin[9] report, what is an appropriate amount to charge for MTM services?

5. Using Case Tables 6–1 and 6–2, determine a rate of compensation for each level of payment for an MTM service.

6. Using the MTM services CPT codes in Case Table 6–3, assign CPT codes to each level of payment outlined in question 5.

7. In addition to using the RBRVS, what additional strategies may be used to account for and bill for services provided?

8. Compile an informational document that contains a summary of the literature outlining the benefits of pharmacists providing patient care.

CASE Table 6–2 MTM Compensation Scale

Level	Assessment of Drug-Related Needs	Identification of Drug Therapy Problems	Complexity-of-Care Planning and Follow-Up Evaluation
1	Problem-focused: at least 1 medication	Problem-focused: 0 problems	Straightforward: 1 medical condition
2	Expanded problem: at least 2 medications	Expanded problem: at least 1 problem	Straightforward: 1 medical condition
3	Detailed: at least 3–5 medications	Detailed: at least 2 problems	Low complexity: at least 2 medical conditions
4	Expanded detailed: at least 6–8 medications	Expanded detailed: at least 3problems	Moderate complexity: at least 3 medical conditions
5	Comprehensive: ≥9 medications	Comprehensive: at least >4 problems	High complexity: at least ≥4 medical conditions

Source: Minnesota Department of Human Services. Provider Update PRX-06-02: Medication Therapy Management Services. Available at: http://www.dhs.state.mn.us/main/idcplg?IdcService=GET_DYNAMIC_CONVERSION&RevisionSelectionMethod=LatestReleased&dDocName=id_055325. Last accessed October 25, 2008.

CASE Table 6–3 CPT Codes for MTM Services

Code	Description
99605	Billing code for a first-encounter service performed face-to-face with a patient in a time increment of up to 15 minutes
99606	Code for use with the same patient in a time increment of up to 15 minutes for a subsequent or follow-up encounter
99607	Add-on code that may be used to bill for additional increments of 15 minutes of time to either of the preceding codes

Source: American Pharmacists Association Newsroom. MTM CPT Codes Made Permanent. Available at: http://www.pharmacist.com. Last accessed October 25, 2008.

9. Using the fee structure and CPT code utilization developed in questions 5 and 6, complete the Centers for Medicare and Medicaid Services (CMS) 1500 form for the first pilot MTM patient encounter.

Additional Activities

1. Create a referral form that may be used by physicians to refer patients to your patient care service. On this form, consider various elements that may be required for billing (ICD-9-CM codes) and for providing proof of medical necessity to third-party payers.

2. Upon approval of the MTM benefit for the employer groups' employees, what should the pharmacist evaluate to demonstrate the employer's return on investment?

3. Research existing MTM services covered by third parties; include available Medicaid and Medicare Part D programs; and compare compensation rates for these programs.

4. Choose a local community pharmacy; identify services that may be implemented; and create fee structures for these services in light of the pharmacy payer mix, patients' needs, and costs for providing patient care.

5. After reviewing the paper by Snella and colleagues,[5] describe the difference in billing strategies and opportunities for pharmacist services in the community pharmacy and physician office settings.

Information Sources

1. McDonough RP, Rovers JP, Currie JD, et al. Obstacles to the implementation of pharmaceutical care in the community setting. J Am Pharm Assoc. 1998;28:87–95.

2. Beatty SJ, Rodis JL, Bellebaum KL, et al. Community and ambulatory pharmacy evaluation of patient care services and billing patterns before implementation of Medicare Part D. J Am Pharm Assoc. 2006;46:707–14.

3. Nutescu EA, Klotz RS. Basic terminology in obtaining reimbursement for pharmacists' cognitive services. Am J Health Syst Pharm. 2007;64:186–92.

4. Hogue MD. The Pharmacist's Guide to Compensation for Patient Care Services. Washington DC: American Pharmacists Association; 2002.

5. Snella KA, Trewyn RR, Hansen LB, et al. Pharmacist compensation for cognitive services: focus on the physician office and community pharmacy. Pharmacotherapy. 2004;24:372–88.

6. Centers for Medicare and Medicaid Services. Medicare Part D Manual, Chapter 7, pages 6–14. Available at: http://www.cms.hhs.gov/PrescriptionDrugCovContra/Downloads/PDBManual_Chapter7.pdf. Last accessed October 25, 2008.

7. Garrett DG, Bluml BB. Patient self-management program for diabetes: first-year clinical, humanistic, and economic outcomes. J Am Pharm Assoc. 2005;45:130–7.

8. Bennett MS, Blank D, Bopp J, et al. Strategies to improve compensation for pharmaceutical care services. J Am Pharm Assoc. 2000; 40:747–55, 870–2.

9. Davanzo J, Dobson A, Koenig L, et al. Medication Therapy Management Services: A Critical Review. Falls Church, Va: The Lewin Group; 2005.

7 Documentation and Compensation for Medication Therapy Management Services under Medicare Part D

Dee Dugan and Katherine Heller

Objectives

1. Identify the patients who are eligible for receiving Medicare Part D benefits with regard to pharmacist-provided medication therapy management services.

2. Describe the pharmacy services that may be billed through Medicare Part D.

3. Outline the core documentation elements that ensure continuity of quality patient care, provide documentation for compensation, and limit liability.

4. Complete a sample Centers for Medicaid and Medicare Services 1500 form for a basic medication therapy management service visit by using a National Provider Identification number as well as appropriate CPT and ICD-9 codes.

Scenario

You are a pharmacist at a local community pharmacy in rural South Florida called Sands Pharmacy. Today's date is January 16. You have been recently hired to assist with the expansion of the owner's patient care clinic. The clinic currently has 30 patients enrolled for diabetes care. Your specialty interest is cardiovascular disease and prevention and wellness. You honed your skills in these areas through your community practice residency. Although you have previously billed for providing patient care, you are still learning this critical skill.

Early on a Saturday morning, Mr. and Mrs. Lo-Kay shuffle into the store and toward the pharmacy. You note that Mr. Lo-Kay is being particularly attentive to his diminutive wife and that she is somewhat pale and drawn in appearance. Upon reaching the pharmacy counter, Mrs. Lo-Kay is clutching a container of Prilosec OTC. Becoming concerned, you leave your computer terminal and ask, "Are you doing OK, Mrs. Lo-Kay?" Mr. Lo-Kay responds with a frown, "My wife is feeling very poorly. She was very sick to her stomach all last night and started throwing up this morning. We saw on the television that Prilosec OTC is

doctor recommended for stomach upset. Do you think this will help her?"

Upon further questioning, Mr. and Mrs. Lo-Kay reveal the following about her condition: Her stomach has been feeling progressively worse over the last week. Her first symptom was nausea, which was intermittent and "not very bothersome." She was able to alleviate the nausea with ginger and saltine crackers. Last night, Mrs. Lo-Kay was unable to relieve the symptoms, which progressively worsened until she began vomiting. She remains nauseated but has been able to taker her medications as well as eat and drink "a little." She denies any change in bowel or bladder habits. She reports that she has felt shaky over approximately the last 12 hours and that she has experienced a change in vision marked by yellowed discoloration of objects since early this morning. Mr. Lo-Kay noted that her hands had developed a slight tremor since this morning.

When asked if she is taking any other medications—nonprescription medications, nutritional supplements, or herbal products—Mrs. Lo-Kay answers that she takes a low-dose aspirin tablet every day. She then proceeds to tell you of her health troubles, which started during her trip to Beijing, China. Mrs. Lo-Kay refilled her prescription medications 2 days before leaving the United States. (Case Table 7–1 is a printout of Mrs. Lo-Kay's prescription medication profile.) She reports having some trouble with her heart while in China, which she described as feeling "jumpy" and leaving her feeling somewhat breathless. Her mother recommended the family herbalist who gave Ms. Lo-Kay a mixture of Ren Shen (dried ginseng root) and Shu Di (Chinese foxglove, the herbal from which digitalis is derived). She has been taking this mixture for 7 days; use of the mixture is concurrent with the onset of her nausea. The Lo-Kays have been back in the States for 2 days. She denies any missed doses and keeps a medication box.

Suspecting digoxin toxicity, you perform the following physical assessment: BP L arm 145/82 mm Hg; pulse 40 bpm and irregular; HEENT–PERRLA with photophobia.

CASE Table 7–1 Prescription Medication Profile

Anna Lo-Kay
1234 Beach Shore Dr.
Riviera Beach, FL 33333

Phone: 561-222-1212 **DOB:** 1/29/1935 **Insurer:** Medicare/BCBS

Allergies/Intolerances: PCN (rash)

Rx No.	Drug Name	Directions	Date	R/F	Prescriber	Qty	RPh
660111	Lisinopril 40 mg	1 tablet by mouth every morning	12/1	8	Shatner	31	LSN
660112	Coreg 25 mg	1 tablet by mouth twice daily	12/1	6	Shatner	62	LSN
660113	Furosemide 40 mg	1 tablet by mouth every morning	12/1	9	Shatner	31	LSN
660114	Digoxin 0.125 mg	1 tablet by mouth every morning	12/1	6	Shatner	31	LSN
660115	Pravastatin 40 mg	2 tablets by mouth every evening	12/1	4	Kirk	62	LSN
660116	Nitrostat 0.4 mg	1 tablet as directed	12/1	3	Shatner	25	LSN
660117	Warfarin 3 mg	1 tablet as directed	12/1	6	Shatner	62	LSN
660111	Lisinopril 40 mg	1 tablet by mouth every morning	10/31	9	Shatner	31	NUN
660112	Coreg 25 mg	1 tablet by mouth twice daily	10/31	7	Shatner	62	NUN
660113	Furosemide 40 mg	1 tablet by mouth every morning	10/31	10	Shatner	31	NUN
660114	Digoxin 0.125 mg	1 tablet by mouth every morning	10/31	7	Shatner	31	NUN
660115	Pravastatin 40 mg	2 tablets by mouth every evening	10/31	5	Kirk	62	NUN
660116	Nitrostat 0.4 mg	1 tablet as directed	10/31	4	Shatner	25	NUN
660117	Warfarin 3 mg	1 tablet as directed	12/1	7	Shatner	62	NUN
660111	Lisinopril 40 mg	1 tablet by mouth every morning	9/30	10	Shatner	31	JSD
660112	Coreg 25 mg	1 tablet by mouth twice daily	9/30	8	Shatner	62	JSD
660113	Furosemide 40 mg	1 tablet by mouth every morning	9/30	11	Shatner	31	JSD
660114	Digoxin 0.125 mg	1 tablet by mouth every morning	9/30	8	Shatner	31	JSD
660115	Pravastatin 40 mg	2 tablets by mouth every evening	9/30	6	Kirk	62	JSD
660116	Nitrostat 0.4 mg	1 tablet as directed	9/30	5	Shatner	25	JSD
660117	Warfarin 3 mg	1 tablet as directed	9/30	8	Shatner	62	JSD

Questions and Activities

1. What is the definition of pharmacist-provided medication therapy management (MTM) services?

2. What are the core elements of pharmacist-provided basic MTM services?

3. Which of these MTM services are covered by Medicare Part D? How are these services paid?

4. List the different payment sources for MTM services besides Medicare Part D.

5. Is the patient, Mrs. Lo-Kay, eligible for MTM services through Medicare Part D? What are the eligibility criteria?

6. On the basis of the information in this case, what would be the most appropriate MTM service(s) for which Mrs. Lo-Kay is eligible?

Medication Therapy Review for _____   DOB: _____

Site of Visit:	Consent: □ Given (*patient initials*)
Date of Visit: Length of Visit:	Allergies:

Service(s) Rendered: □ Medication Therapy Review (MTR) *Comprehensive*   □ Medication Therapy Review (MTR) *Targeted*

□ Medication Action Plan (MAP)   □ Personal Medication Record (PMR)

Purpose of Visit/CC:

Relevant History: (HPI, ROS, MedHx, PMH, FHx, SHx)

Pertinent Physical Examination:

Clinical Impression(s):

Plan for Care:

Plan for Follow-Up:	RPh-Provider Name: License Number: Signature:

CASE Figure 7–1 Sample medication therapy review form. (For more complex patient cases, this form may need to be expanded to allow appropriate documentation.)

7. What documentation should be created for a medication therapy review (MTR)?

8. Create a targeted MTR for Mrs. Lo-Kay. (See Case Figure 7–1 for a sample form.)

Mrs. Lo-Kay returns on February 14 for a comprehensive MTR. The pharmacist acquires the following information from Mrs. Lo-Kay:

- *Aspirin not taken with food in patient concurrently taking warfarin.*

- *Nonadherence to Coreg at evening dose: "I just can't remember to take it."*

- *Nonproductive, chronic cough linked with lisinopril.*

9. Create a personal medication record (PMR) and a medication action plan (MAP) for Mrs. Lo-Kay. (See Case Figures 7–2 and 7–3, respectively, for sample forms.) Use the information above in addition to the previous case description to create Mrs. Lo-Kay's PMR and MAP.

10. What are the necessary steps to complete before submitting a pharmacist billing for MTM services through Medicare Part D?

11. What factors should a pharmacist consider when setting a fee for MTM services?

12. How do pharmacists submit claims for MTM services through Medicare Part D?

13. What components should be included in documentation of patient care services to justify billing for those services?

14. What other MTM services could be offered to Mrs. Lo-Kay in the future?

15. The pharmacist has already obtained her National Provider Identification (NPI) number: 0123456789. The pharmacy address is 555 Wellness Way, Riviera Beach, FL 33333. During the first targeted MTR for Mrs. Lo-Kay, the pharmacist received permission from Mrs. Lo-Kay to put her signature on file (SOF) for completion of future CMS 1500 forms. In a phone call to Mrs. Lo-Kay's physician, the pharmacist received the following diagnosis code for Mrs. Lo-Kay: E855.8 for digoxin toxicity and 427.3 for atrial fibrillation. Complete a CMS 1500 form for the targeted MTR MTM service and the comprehensive MTR MTM service. Use Case Figure 7–4 to assist you with this process and the following ICD-9 codes:

- Digoxin toxicity: E855.8 Other specified drugs acting on central and autonomic nervous systems

- Nonadherence to congestive heart failure regimen: 428.0

Personal Medication Record for _____   Prepared by: _____

Date Created: _____   **Reported Medication Allergies with Reaction:** _____

Please list all medications including prescription, nonprescription, herbal, vitamins, and other supplements.

	Medicine #1	Medicine #2	Medicine #3	Medicine #4	Medicine #5	Medicine #6	Medicine #7
Drug Name							
Dosage							
Intended Use							
Directions							
How long taken?							
Precautions							
Discontinued?	Yes/No	Yes/No	Yes/No	Yes/No	Yes/No	Yes/No	Yes/No
Why discontinued?							
MD Name							
MD Contact Information							

CASE Figure 7–2 Sample personal medication record. (*Source:* This form is based on forms developed by the American Pharmacists Association and the National Association of Chain Drug Stores Foundation. Reproduced with permission from APhA and NACDS Foundation.)

Sands Pharmacy

Medication Action Plan for _____ DOB: _____

Date Created: _____   **Reported Medication Allergies with Reaction:** _____

Prepared by: _____   **Pharmacy Contact Information:** _____

	Drug Name:	Drug Name:	Drug Name:	Drug Name:
Description of Drug-Related Issue				
Date Drug-Related Issue Identified				
Suggested Action				
Person Responsible				
Date Action Taken				
Result of Action				

CASE Figure 7–3 Sample medication action plan. (*Source:* This form is based on forms developed by the American Pharmacists Association and the National Association of Chain Drug Stores Foundation. Reproduced with permission from APhA and NACDS Foundation.)

1500

HEALTH INSURANCE CLAIM FORM

APPROVED BY NATIONAL UNIFORM CLAIM COMMITTEE 08/05

PICA | PICA

1. MEDICARE (Medicare #) MEDICAID (Medicaid #) TRICARE CHAMPUS (Sponsor's SSN) CHAMPVA (Member ID#) GROUP HEALTH PLAN (SSN or ID) FECA BLK LUNG (SSN) OTHER (ID) | 1a. INSURED'S I.D. NUMBER (For Program in Item 1)

2. PATIENT'S NAME (Last Name, First Name, Middle Initial) | 3. PATIENT'S BIRTH DATE MM DD YY SEX M F | 4. INSURED'S NAME (Last Name, First Name, Middle Initial)

5. PATIENT'S ADDRESS (No., Street) | 6. PATIENT RELATIONSHIP TO INSURED Self Spouse Child Other | 7. INSURED'S ADDRESS (No., Street)

CITY STATE | 8. PATIENT STATUS Single Married Other Employed Full-Time Student Part-Time Student | CITY STATE

ZIP CODE TELEPHONE (Include Area Code) ( ) | | ZIP CODE TELEPHONE (Include Area Code) ( )

9. OTHER INSURED'S NAME (Last Name, First Name, Middle Initial) | 10. IS PATIENT'S CONDITION RELATED TO: | 11. INSURED'S POLICY GROUP OR FECA NUMBER

a. OTHER INSURED'S POLICY OR GROUP NUMBER | a. EMPLOYMENT? (Current or Previous) YES NO | a. INSURED'S DATE OF BIRTH MM DD YY SEX M F

b. OTHER INSURED'S DATE OF BIRTH MM DD YY SEX M F | b. AUTO ACCIDENT? YES NO PLACE (State) | b. EMPLOYER'S NAME OR SCHOOL NAME

c. EMPLOYER'S NAME OR SCHOOL NAME | c. OTHER ACCIDENT? YES NO | c. INSURANCE PLAN NAME OR PROGRAM NAME

d. INSURANCE PLAN NAME OR PROGRAM NAME | 10d. RESERVED FOR LOCAL USE | d. IS THERE ANOTHER HEALTH BENEFIT PLAN? YES NO If yes, return to and complete item 9 a-d.

READ BACK OF FORM BEFORE COMPLETING & SIGNING THIS FORM.
12. PATIENT'S OR AUTHORIZED PERSON'S SIGNATURE I authorize the release of any medical or other information necessary to process this claim. I also request payment of government benefits either to myself or to the party who accepts assignment below.

SIGNED DATE | 13. INSURED'S OR AUTHORIZED PERSON'S SIGNATURE I authorize payment of medical benefits to the undersigned physician or supplier for services described below.

SIGNED

14. DATE OF CURRENT: MM DD YY ILLNESS (First symptom) OR INJURY (Accident) OR PREGNANCY(LMP) | 15. IF PATIENT HAS HAD SAME OR SIMILAR ILLNESS. GIVE FIRST DATE MM DD YY | 16. DATES PATIENT UNABLE TO WORK IN CURRENT OCCUPATION MM DD YY MM DD YY FROM TO

17. NAME OF REFERRING PROVIDER OR OTHER SOURCE | 17a. 17b. NPI | 18. HOSPITALIZATION DATES RELATED TO CURRENT SERVICES MM DD YY MM DD YY FROM TO

19. RESERVED FOR LOCAL USE | 20. OUTSIDE LAB? YES NO $ CHARGES

21. DIAGNOSIS OR NATURE OF ILLNESS OR INJURY (Relate Items 1, 2, 3 or 4 to Item 24E by Line)
1. 3. | 22. MEDICAID RESUBMISSION CODE ORIGINAL REF. NO.
2. 4. | 23. PRIOR AUTHORIZATION NUMBER

24. A. DATE(S) OF SERVICE From MM DD YY To MM DD YY	B. PLACE OF SERVICE	C. EMG	D. PROCEDURES, SERVICES, OR SUPPLIES (Explain Unusual Circumstances) CPT/HCPCS MODIFIER	E. DIAGNOSIS POINTER	F. $ CHARGES	G. DAYS OR UNITS	H. EPSDT Family Plan	I. ID. QUAL.	J. RENDERING PROVIDER ID. #
1								NPI	
2								NPI	
3								NPI	
4								NPI	
5								NPI	
6								NPI	

25. FEDERAL TAX I.D. NUMBER SSN EIN | 26. PATIENT'S ACCOUNT NO. | 27. ACCEPT ASSIGNMENT? (For govt. claims, see back) YES NO | 28. TOTAL CHARGE $ | 29. AMOUNT PAID $ | 30. BALANCE DUE $

31. SIGNATURE OF PHYSICIAN OR SUPPLIER INCLUDING DEGREES OR CREDENTIALS (I certify that the statements on the reverse apply to this bill and are made a part thereof.) SIGNED DATE | 32. SERVICE FACILITY LOCATION INFORMATION a. NPI b. | 33. BILLING PROVIDER INFO & PH # ( ) a. NPI b.

NUCC Instruction Manual available at: www.nucc.org | PLEASE PRINT OR TYPE | APPROVED OMB-0938-0999 FORM CMS-1500 (08-05)

CARRIER — PATIENT AND INSURED INFORMATION — PHYSICIAN OR SUPPLIER INFORMATION

CASE Figure 7–4 Sample CMS 1500 form.

- Adverse event secondary to lisinopril therapy: 995.2

- ASA with warfarin taken without food: V65.43, V58.83, V58.66, V58.61

16. What are the barriers to pharmacists providing MTM services in the community pharmacy setting? What are some solutions to removing these barriers?

Additional Activities

1. Compare and contrast the different MTM programs available through Medicare Part D, including the process for documentation and billing for the services.

2. Develop a business plan for implementing MTM services for Medicare patients in a community pharmacy.

3. Develop a marketing message about MTM services to "sell" the value to patients.

Information Sources

1. Bluml BM. Definition of medication therapy management: development of professionwide consensus. *J Am Pharm Assoc* 2005;45:566–72.

2. American Pharmacists Association, National Association of Chain Drug Stores Foundation. *Medication Therapy Management in Pharmacy Practice. Core Elements of an MTM Service. Version 2.0.* Washington, DC: American Pharmacists Association; March 2008. Available at: http://www.pharmacist.com. Last accessed November 7, 2008.

3. Centers for Medicare & Medicaid Services. Medicare Program–General Information Overview. Available at: http://www.cms.hhs.gov/MedicareGenInfo. Last accessed November 7, 2008.

4. Centers for Medicare & Medicaid Services. Outreach and Education, Medicare Learning Network Educational Web Guides–Documentation Guidelines for E&M Services. Available at: http://www.cms.hhs.gov/MLNEdWebGuide/25_EMDOC.asp#TopOfPage. Last accessed November 7, 2008.

5. Snella KA, Trewyn RR, Hansen LB, et al. Pharmacist compensation for cognitive services: focus on the physician office and community pharmacy. *Pharmacotherapy* 2004;24:372–88.

6. Thomson CA. National billing codes announced for pharmacists' clinical services. *Am J Health Syst Pharm* 2005;62:1640–2.

8 Practice-Based Research in the Community Pharmacy Setting

David A. Mott and Elizabeth Peterson

Objectives

1. Define pharmacy practice-based research.

2. Discuss the importance of practice-based research for community pharmacy practice, including its benefits and challenges.

3. Apply practice-based research concepts to develop research questions and projects for community pharmacy practice.

4. Describe the key steps for implementing a practice-based research project in a community pharmacy.

5. Identify and analyze published community pharmacy research projects.

Scenario

Market Stop is a regional grocery store chain with 25 stores and pharmacies. The chain serves mostly a suburban population. On average the pharmacies fill 160 prescriptions per day. The pharmacy hours are 9 am to 9 pm, Monday through Saturday. Six of the pharmacies have three full-time pharmacists and four full-time technicians. All other pharmacies have two full-time pharmacists and three full-time technicians. The pharmacists serve as preceptors for advanced community pharmacy practice advanced experiential experiences (APPEs). Usually, each pharmacy has three to five student pharmacists per year, with each student present for 5 weeks.

The pharmacy in each store offers the following patient care services: comprehensive adult immunizations, smoking cessation, medication therapy management, screenings for blood glucose, cholesterol, blood pressure, body composition, and bone mineral density. An American Diabetes Association–recognized diabetes education program is also offered. Four pharmacies have a comprehensive pretravel health program. In addition, the grocery store chain has collaborative practice agreements with a physician for asthma, hyperlipidemia, and diabetes programs. The chain is also actively promoting an associate wellness program.

You are the pharmacist who oversees the patient care programs for the chain. As part of your position, you want to conduct some research projects to help improve the process of providing patient care, and to help document the quality of patient care that the pharmacists are providing in the community.

Questions and Activities

1. Define pharmacy practice-based research.

2. Why is practice-based research important for community pharmacy practice?

3. Who are the stakeholders for practice-based research in community pharmacy practice?

4. Identify the benefits to community pharmacists of getting involved with practice-based research.

5. Identify some barriers to community pharmacists participating in practice-based research.

6. How do community pharmacists get involved in practice-based research?

7. Identify some potential collaborators for community pharmacists interested in conducting practice-based research.

8. Name four published research projects conducted in community pharmacy settings.

9. Identify some of the issues and/or problems with the current literature that describes research in community pharmacy practice. How could these issues and/or problems be addressed in future practice-based research?

10. What types of research can be conducted in community pharmacy practice?

11. What is the process for conducting a practice-based research project in a community pharmacy?

12. What must the community pharmacist consider in terms of protection of human subjects when conducting practice-based research?

13. Develop a research question for the pharmacy case.

14. Describe how you will conduct the project to answer this research question. Include the research design to use, the variables to measure, and the tools to be used in collecting data.

15. Identify types and sources of funding that might be available for community pharmacy practice-based research projects.

Additional Activities

1. Research and discuss how practice-based research networks could be incorporated in community pharmacies.

2. Complete a grant application for your research idea for the case.

3. Complete an investigational review board application at your university for your research idea for the pharmacy case.

4. Investigate journal requirements for publishing practice-based research.

Information Sources

1. US Department of Health and Human Services, Agency for Healthcare Research and Quality. AHRQ Support for Primary Care Practice-Based Research Networks (PBRNs): Fact Sheet. Available at: http://www.ahrq.gov/research/pbrn/pbrnfact.htm. Last accessed November 1, 2008.

2. Cranor CW, Bunting BA, Christensen DB. The Asheville Project: Long-term clinical and economic outcomes of a community pharmacy diabetes care program. *J Am Pharm Assoc.* 2003;43:173–48.

3. Goode JV, Swiger K, Bluml BM. Regional osteoporosis screening, referral, and monitoring program in community pharmacies: findings from Project ImPACT: Osteoporosis. *J Am Pharm Assoc.* 2004; 44:152–60.

4. Krass I, Armour CL, Mitchell B, et al. The Pharmacy Diabetes Care Program: assessment of a community pharmacy diabetes service model in Australia. *Diabet Med.* 2007;24:677–83.

5. Laufenberg-Horstmann E, DeVore E, Bassuener K. The Coulee Region Community Pharmacy Asthma Intervention study. *J Am Pharm Assoc.* 2006;46:738–46.

6. Rossi P, Freeman H, Lipsey M. *Evaluation.* 6th ed. Thousand Oaks, Calif: Sage Publications; 1999.

7. Campbell D, Stanley J. *Experimental and Quasi-experimental Designs for Research.* Boston: Houghton Mifflin; 1963.

8. *Conducting a Practice-Based Project: A Guide for Community Pharmacy Residents and Preceptors.* Washington, DC: American Pharmacists Association; 2006.

9. Lipowski EE. Practice-based research networks: why, what, who, and how. *J Am Pharm Assoc.* 2008;48:142–52.

10. Goode JR, Mott DA, Chater R. Collaborations to facilitate success of community pharmacy practice-based research networks. *J Am Pharm Assoc.* 2008;48:153–62.

Principles of
Managing Patients in
the Community
Pharmacy Setting

9 Patient Care Process

Kelly Brock

Objectives

1. Outline the patient care process involved in a community pharmacy setting.

2. Analyze the core elements of a medication therapy management service in a community pharmacy setting.

3. Describe the components of a comprehensive medication therapy review.

4. Develop a personal medication record for a patient.

5. Design a patient-specific medication action plan.

Scenario

Today's date is September 29. Mary Smith presents to the pharmacy with the prescriptions shown in Case Figures 9–1, 9–2, and 9–3. The technician gathers information from Mrs. Smith and processes the three prescriptions. The prescriptions are now ready for your initial review.

Questions and Activities

1. What should be the first step in the patient care process?

2. What information must be included on a prescription for it to be considered a valid prescription?

3. Three new prescriptions (Plavix, lisinopril, and metoprolol tartrate) were processed for Mr. Smith. Case Table 9–1 is a printout of Mr. Smith's prescription

---

Noah James, MD
10 Main Street
Iowa City, IA 52240

FOR Michael Smith   DOB 6/21/55

ADDRESS 15 Hawkeye Drive   DATE 9/29

        Lisinopril 10 mg
        1 po qd
        #30

REFILL____ TIMES   DR. _____

DEA NO_____

CASE Figure 9–2 Prescription #2 for patient Michael Smith.

Noah James, MD
10 Main Street
Iowa City, IA

FOR Michael Smith   DOB 6/21/55

ADDRESS 15 Hawkeye Drive   DATE 9/29

        Metoprolol tartrate 100mg
        1 po bid
        #60

REFILL____ TIMES   DR. _____

DEA NO_____

CASE Figure 9–1 Prescription #1 for patient Michael Smith.

Noah James, MD
10 Main Street
Iowa City, IA

FOR Michael Smith   DOB 6/21/55

ADDRESS 15 Hawkeye Drive   DATE 9/29

        Metoprolol tartrate 100mg
        1 po bid
        #60

REFILL____ TIMES   DR. _____

DEA NO_____

CASE Figure 9–3 Prescription #3 for patient Michael Smith.

CASE Table 9–1 Prescription Medication Profile

Michael Smith
15 Hawkeye Drive
Iowa City, IA 52246

Phone: 319-537-5808   **DOB:** 06/21/85   **Insurer:** Prescription drug plan: 3 co-payment levels: $10/$25/$50

Allergies/Intolerances: NKDA   **Medical Conditions:** Asthma

Rx No.	Drug Name	Directions	Date	R/F	Prescriber	Qty	Cost	RPh
612507	Lisinopril 10 mg	1 tablet by mouth every day	9/29	1	James	30	10.00	KB
612508	Metoprolol tartrate 100 mg	1 tablet by mouth twice daily	9/29	5	James	60	8.99	KB
612509	Plavix 75 mg	1 tablet by mouth every day	9/29	5	James	30	50.00	KB
611001	Albuterol inhaler	2 puffs every 4–6 hours as needed	9/1	As needed	Block	1	10.00	JJ
611002	Advair	1 inhalation twice daily	9/1	3	Block	1	25.00	JJ
611001	Albuterol inhaler	2 puffs every 4–6 hours as needed	8/15	As needed	Block	1	10.00	JJ
611001	Albuterol inhaler	2 puffs every 4–6 hours as needed	8/2	As needed	Block	1	10.00	JJ
611002	Advair	1 inhalation twice daily	8/2	4	Block	1	25.00	JJ
611001	Albuterol inhaler	2 puffs every 4–6 hours as needed	7/18	As needed	Block	1	10.00	JJ
611001	Albuterol inhaler	2 puffs every 4–6 hours as needed	7/4	As needed	Block	1	10.00	JJ
611002	Advair	1 inhalation twice daily	7/4	4	Block	1	25.00	JJ

medication profile. Review the new prescriptions against Mr. Smith's profile. What problem(s) do you identify during this review?

The prescriptions are reprocessed for Mr. Smith. Case Table 9–2 is a printout of Mr. Smith's prescription medication profile.

4. As part of the patient care process, what should you review during a prospective DUR?

5. Perform a prospective DUR for Mr. Smith. What do you conclude from the DUR?

6. On the basis of the DUR, what intervention(s), if any, would be necessary before filling the prescriptions for Mr. Smith?

7. The prescriptions are filled and you perform a final check before dispensing the prescriptions. Mr. Smith has joined his wife at the pharmacy counter after running errands. What are the pertinent topics to address during patient education?

8. While providing patient education, you notice that Mr. Smith is holding packages of nonprescription aspirin and ibuprofen. What would be the most appropriate approach to this situation?

After evaluating Mr. Smith's prescription profile, you determine that he would be a good candidate for your medication therapy management (MTM) service. You explain the new program to Mr. Smith and he agrees to enroll. He would like to set up his first appointment for next week.

CASE Table 9–2 Prescription Medication Profile (Reprocessed Prescriptions)

Michael Smith
15 Hawkeye Drive
Iowa City, IA 52246

Phone: 319-537-5808 **DOB:** 06/21/55 **Insurer:** Prescription drug plan: 3 co-payment levels: $10/$25/$50

Allergies/Intolerances: NKDA **Medical Conditions:** Hypothyroidism, depression, dyslipidemia

Rx No.	Drug Name	Directions	Date	Refills	Prescriber	Qty	Cost	RPh
011507	Lisinopril 10 mg	1 tablet by mouth every day	9/29	1	James	30	10.00	KB
011508	Metoprolol tartrate 100 mg	1 tablet by mouth twice daily	9/29	5	James	60	8.99	KB
011509	Plavix 75 mg	1 tablet by mouth every day	9/29	5	James	30	50.00	KB
011404	Tricor 145 mg	1 tablet by mouth every day	9/10	3	Hall	30	25.00	JJ
011403	Niaspan 1000 mg	1 tablet by mouth at bedtime	9/10	3	Hall	30	25.00	JJ
011402	Avandia 4 mg	1 tablet by mouth every day	9/10	3	Hall	30	25.00	JJ
011401	Synthroid 100 mcg	1 tablet by mouth every day	9/10	3	Tucker	30	10.00	JJ
011404	Tricor 145 mg	1 tablet by mouth every day	8/14	4	Hall	30	25.00	JJ
011403	Niaspan 1000 mg	1 tablet by mouth at bedtime	8/14	4	Hall	30	25.00	JJ
011402	Avandia 4 mg	1 tablet by mouth every day	8/14	4	Hall	30	25.00	JJ
011401	Synthroid 100 mcg	1 tablet by mouth every day	8/14	4	Tucker	30	10.00	JJ
011301	Zoloft 100 mg	1 tablet by mouth every day	8/14	4	Tucker	30	50.00	JJ
011404	Tricor 145 mg	1 tablet by mouth every day	7/16	4	Hall	30	25.00	JJ
011403	Niaspan 1000 mg	1 tablet by mouth at bedtime	7/16	4	Hall	30	25.00	JJ
011402	Avandia 4 mg	1 tablet by mouth every day	7/16	4	Hall	30	25.00	JJ
011401	Synthroid 100 mcg	1 tablet by mouth every day	7/16	4	Tucker	30	10.00	JJ
011301	Zoloft 100 mg	1 tablet by mouth every day	7/16	4	Tucker	30	25.00	JJ

9. Describe the five core elements of an MTM service as identified by the model framework for implementing effective MTM services in pharmacy practice, which was developed by the American Pharmacists Association (APhA) and the National Association of Chain Drug Stores (NACDS) Foundation.

During the initial MTM visit, you gather the following information. Mr. Smith recently had a myocardial infarction and is now starting new medications. He has had high cholesterol for many years. After his heart attack, the physician told him that he would need to make a lot of changes in his life so that he would not end up back in the hospital. Mr. Smith realizes that he could probably lead a healthier life, and he knows he should quit smoking. However, no one has ever explained to him what lifestyle changes would be most beneficial for his health conditions

He is concerned about his health, but he is not sure if he can afford all of his medications. The new medication, Plavix, is really expensive, and someone told him that he would have to take the medication for a year after his heart attack because of the stent in his heart. Mr. Smith has been taking Zoloft for several years; 2 months ago, the co-pay for his Zoloft changed from $25.00 to $50.00 a month. He stopped taking the Zoloft last month because it was so expensive, but he feels that his depression is getting worse. He does not understand why the co-pay changed, but he is not sure he can afford the medication, especially with his new medications. He heard that a generic product is available for Zoloft. Upon further questioning, the patient says that before his heart attack, he had been diagnosed with a thyroid problem, depression, and high cholesterol. He has not been to his primary care physician for almost 2 years.

Using the information provided by Mr. Smith and the information in his prescription medication profile, you complete a comprehensive medication therapy review (MTR).

10. What elements should you assess during a comprehensive MTR?

11. What drug-related or disease-related problems were identified during the MTR? Prioritize the identified problems.

12. What are the components of a personal medication record (PMR) as identified by the model developed by APhA and the NACDS Foundation?

13. Using the available information, develop a PMR for Mr. Smith.

14. What are the components of a medication action plan (MAP) as identified by the model developed by APhA and the NACDS Foundation?

15. Design a MAP for Mr. Smith.

16. Would you need to gather any additional information about this patient before conducting an intervention? If so, how would you gather this information?

17. What intervention(s) would be necessary to resolve Mr. Smith's drug-related or disease-related problems?

18. How would you communicate your intervention/recommendation to the patient?

19. How would you communicate your intervention/recommendation to the patient's other health care provider(s)?

20. What factors would impact the time to follow up with Mr. Smith?

21. What information should be included in the documentation of MTM services?

22. What are the potential barriers to the patient care process?

Additional Activities

1. Describe how the patient care process might differ for a follow-up visit.

2. Describe how the patient care process might differ if the patient refused an appointment with the pharmacist.

3. Identify limitations of relying on electronic prospective DUR systems.

4. Compare and contrast pharmaceutical care and MTM.

5. Identify potential solutions for the identified barriers to the patient care process.

6. Research collaborative practice laws in your state and how these laws affect the patient care process.

Information Sources

1. American Pharmaceutical Association. *Principles of Practice for Pharmaceutical Care*. Washington, DC: American Pharmaceutical Association; 1996.

2. Hepler CD, Strand LM. Opportunities and responsibilities in pharmaceutical care. *Am J Hosp Pharm*. 1990:47:533–43.

3. Rovers JP. Patient data collection. In: Rovers JP, Currie JD, eds. *A Practical Guide to Pharmaceutical Care*. 3rd ed. Washington, DC: American Pharmacists Association; 2007:47–88.

4. Tomechko MA, Strand LM, Morley PC, et al. Q and A from the pharmaceutical care project in Minnesota. *Am Pharm*. 1995; NS35(4):30–9.

5. Fulda TR, Lyles A, Pugh MC, et. al. Current status of drug utilization review. *J Manag Care Pharm*. 2004;10:433–41.

6. Rovers JP. Identifying drug therapy problems. In: Rovers JP, Currie JD, eds. *A Practical Guide to Pharmaceutical Care*. 3rd ed. Washington, DC: American Pharmacists Association; 2007:23–47.

7. Rovers JP. Patient data evaluation. In: Rovers JP, Currie JD, eds. *A Practical Guide to Pharmaceutical Care*. 3rd ed. Washington, DC: American Pharmacists Association; 2007:89–106.

8. Rovers JP. Patient care plan development. In: Rovers JP, Currie JD, eds. *A Practical Guide to Pharmaceutical Care*. 3rd ed. Washington, DC: American Pharmacists Association; 2007:107–38.

9. American Pharmacists Association, National Association of Chain Drug Stores Foundation. *Medication Therapy Management in Pharmacy Practice. Core Elements of an MTM Service Model. Version 2.0*. Washington, DC: American Pharmacists Association; March 2008.

10. McGivney MS, Meyer SM, Duncan-Hewitt W, et al. Medication therapy management: its relationship to patient counseling, disease management, and pharmaceutical care. *J Am Pharm Association*. 2007;47:620–8.

11. Currie JD, Doucette WR, Kuhle J, et. al. Identification of essential elements in the documentation of pharmacist-provided care. *J Am Pharm Assoc*. 2002;43:41–9.

12. Currie JD. Documentation. In: Rovers JP, Currie JD, eds. *A Practical Guide to Pharmaceutical Care*. 3rd ed. Washington, DC: American Pharmacists Association; 2007:139–60.

13. McDonough RP. Obstacles to pharmaceutical care. In: Rovers JP, Currie JD, eds. *A Practical Guide to Pharmaceutical Care*. 2nd ed. Washington, DC: American Pharmaceutical Association; 2003: 267–78.

10 Professionalism in the Community Pharmacy Setting

Dana P. Hammer and Carson Huntoon

Objectives

1. Define professionalism.

2. Describe factors that influence professionalism in pharmacy practice.

3. Discuss challenges that community pharmacy practitioners face with regard to professionalism.

4. For specific scenarios (1) identify professionalism issues and (2) strategize methods for improving professionalism.

Pharmacists have traditionally been held in high esteem by the public, ranking prominently in polls for trust, ethics, and honesty. As health care providers, pharmacists certainly should be held to high standards of practice in the care of patients. This level of professionalism is increasingly important as the health care system and needs of society continue to evolve. The clinical pharmacy movement, which gained momentum in the 1970s, continues to grow and expand. Many pharmacists and practices have embraced and implemented pharmaceutical care and medication therapy management to make a significant difference in patients' lives. True professionals serve their patients with the patient's best interests in mind: They maintain their intellectual competence to make the best clinical, evidence-based decisions for their patients, and they accept responsibility for these decisions. State and national pharmacy associations frequently report about their individual member pharmacists who are improving health in their communities and making their profession proud.

Maintaining and enhancing this professionalism can seem rather daunting, as reflected in daily news reports of professionals, celebrities, high-ranking officials, and other role models engaging in some sort of unprofessional, unethical, or even criminal behavior. Apparently no profession is immune—these behaviors have been cited in physicians, lawyers, clergy, accountants, nurses, professors, and others. Some see these same trends occurring in pharmacy: There are accounts of greedy, unethical, or uncaring pharmacists in the press. These situations may be compounded by the standards of practice in some pharmacies, where it seems the emphasis is not on improving patient health but on the quick dispensing of prescription medications to store customers. Related to this situation, the structure of the U.S. health care system in general does not necessarily support a more professional role for pharmacists.

This case presents specific scenarios and asks questions that will help pharmacists to (1) discuss the concept of professionalism and its role in pharmacy practice, (2) identify situations in practice in which professionalism can be improved, and (3) create and implement strategies to improve these situations. If the pharmacist's role in patient care is to be preserved and expanded in our current health care system, pharmacists and the sites in which they practice need to embrace the ideals of professionalism. These ideals also affect staff members, patients, and other health care providers whom pharmacists serve. Although creating a culture of professionalism is not easy, implementing small, incremental changes in one's practice will go a long way in establishing this foundation.

Before reviewing the specific scenarios below, the pharmacist should consider general questions about professionalism in pharmacy practice.

General Questions

1. What is professionalism?

2. What factors influence professionalism in pharmacy practice?

3. What are some of the challenges that community pharmacy practitioners face with regard to professionalism?

Scenario 1

You have just arrived at Joe's Pharmacy, a small independent pharmacy, for a job interview. You have heard good things about this pharmacy with regard to its customer service and helpful staff. As you enter the pharmacy, you observe that the aisles are closely spaced and arranged in such a way that it is difficult to navigate through the store.

The items on the shelves are not arranged in a logical manner; many products are dusty and have tipped over or are located at the back of the shelf. The shelf items include several products that you have seen on television commercials and deem their benefits as questionable. A local hip-hop radio station is playing on the overhead speaker system.

As you navigate your way to the prescription filling area in the back of pharmacy, you realize that it is very hard to determine the locations of the pick-up and drop-off stations. The visible filling area is extremely cluttered and you notice that the staff seem to be very busy. The pharmacist is rapidly checking prescriptions as a staff member clad in a T-shirt and jeans quickly walks from one end of the pharmacy to the other while filling prescriptions. The phone rings constantly. As you observe patients pick up their prescriptions, you notice the absence of a private or even semi-private counseling area. There is also no formal waiting area or any sign of patient care services other than dispensing. When pharmacist Reynolds finally comes over to greet you, you comment that the pharmacy is not quite what you expected. He says, "Customers have been filling their medications here for years and they keep coming back."

Scenario 1 Questions

1. What impression might a new patient have of this pharmacy?

2. What potential areas could be improved to enhance the professional image of this pharmacy?

3. If you were employed at this pharmacy, what strategies would you devise to improve these areas?

4. How would you discuss these strategies with the pharmacy owner?

Scenario 2

You are a staff pharmacist and preceptor who has worked at the same community pharmacy for several years. Over the last year or so, you have observed a steady increase of prescription volume to the point that you are beginning to feel frustrated. Lately, you often arrive early or stay late to "stay on top" of the workload, and you are not able to spend sufficient time with the student pharmacists rotating through the site. Staffing has not increased in several years; during certain times of the day you are the only pharmacist. The technician and clerk work extremely hard and many times seem overburdened by their workloads. You believe that the addition of another technician, as well as some additional part-time pharmacist coverage to assist during the busiest times, would greatly help. You approach the pharmacy manager with your ideas, but she is not receptive to the changes and states that she wants you and the staff to spend less time counseling the patients so that you can concentrate on filling prescriptions. She is even considering cutting staff hours because of financial shortages from slow Medicare Part D reimbursement. You are frustrated by the situation and strongly consider updating your résumé to look for another job.

Scenario 2 Questions

1. What issues in this pharmacy detract from its professionalism?

2. What ideas could improve patient care and professionalism in this pharmacy?

3. How would you justify to the manager that your ideas should be supported by store management?

4. What strategies would you devise to implement your ideas?

Scenario 3

You are a new pharmacy manager in a community pharmacy. It is your first day on the job, and you are currently covering the regular staff pharmacist's lunch hour. A woman arrives at the pharmacy counter with a prescription to be filled. You talk with the woman and learn that the prescription is for her young child who has an ear infection and is waiting in the car. You tell the mother that the prescription will be filled as quickly as possible, and she goes to sit in the waiting area nearby. You put the prescription in cue to be processed by one of the technicians. When you go to check other waiting prescriptions, you notice that the two technicians are openly engrossed in detailed conversation about a raucous party they attended the previous night. The prescription for the child sits on the pharmacy counter. The mother steps up to the prescription counter and impatiently demands the whereabouts of her child's medication, as well as makes some heated and rude comments about the "lazy technicians" and "lousy pharmacy service." One of the technicians retorts to the woman that if she does not like the service she can take her lousy prescription elsewhere. The two get into a shouting match.

Scenario 3 Questions

1. What issues in this situation detract from the pharmacy's professionalism?

2. How would you handle the immediate situation with the mother?

3. How would you handle the immediate situation with the technicians?

4. What strategies would you devise to prevent these situations from happening again?

Information Sources

1. Merriam-Webster. Merriam-Webster's Collegiate Dictionary, 10th ed. Springfield, Mass: Merriam-Webster; 1997:930.

2. APhA-ASP/AACP-COD Task Force on Professionalism. White paper on pharmacy student professionalism. *J Am Pharm Assoc.* 2000;40:96–102.

3. Beardsley RS. Chair report of the APhA-ASP/AACP-COD Task Force on Professionalization: enhancing professionalism in pharmacy education and practice. *Am J Pharm Educ.*1996;60:26S–8S.

4. Medical Professionalism Project. Medical professionalism in the new millennium: a physician charter. *Ann Intern Med.* 2002;136: 243–6.

5. Greenwood E. Attributes of a profession. *Soc Work.* 1957;2:44–55.

6. Wilensky HL. The professionalization of everyone? *Am J Soc.* 1964;70:137–46.

7. Vollmer HM, Mills DL. *Professionalization.* 1st ed. Englewood Cliffs, NJ: Prentice-Hall. 1966:65.

8. Hall RH. Professionalization and bureaucratization. *Am Soc Rev.* 1968;33:92–104.

9. Strauss G. Professionalism and occupational associations. *Indus Rel.* 1963;II(3):8–9.

10. Parsons T. *The Social System.* Glencoe, Ill: The Free Press. 1951:454.

11. American Board of Internal Medicine Committees on Evaluation of Clinical Competence and Clinical Competence and Communication Programs. *Project Professionalism.* Philadelphia: American Board of Internal Medicine; 2001:5–6.

12. Purkerson Hammer D, Mason HL, Chalmers RK, et al. Development and testing of an instrument to assess behavioral professionalism of pharmacy students. *Am J Pharm Educ.* 2000;64:141–51.

13. Hammer, D.P. Improving professionalism in your practice. *Drug Store News.* October-December 2002:19–24.

14. Hammer DP, Berger BA, Beardsley RS, et al. Student professionalism. *Am J Pharm Educ.* 2003;67(3):article 96.

15. Chalmers RK. Contemporary issues: professionalism in pharmacy. *Tomorrow's Pharm.* March 1997:10–2.

11 Health Disparities in the Community Pharmacy Setting

Jeri J. Sias

Objectives

1. Describe unique health disparities that exist among various racial and ethnic populations.

2. Identify barriers to pharmaceutical care that patients from different cultures may experience in a community pharmacy.

3. Analyze U.S. Census data to make broad suggestions about the types of pharmacy services that may be appropriate for diverse communities.

4. Identify legal documents that affect provision of services to persons with limited English proficiency.

5. Identify opportunities in community pharmacy practice to understand diverse cultures and to implement changes in the pharmacy setting.

Methods to Improve Care across Cultures in a Community Pharmacy

You are a pharmacist who has worked several years for a chain pharmacy practice located in a large city in the southern region of the United States. You have just been promoted to district manager. The district office has received several complaints over the past year regarding patient dissatisfaction with the patient care service in different segments of the city. Furthermore, medication errors have been caught at the point of counseling on refills, and the pharmacist has identified inappropriate use of the medication. You understand that some of the concerns may be related to difficulties that the pharmacists and staff are having because they work in a diverse community. You are asked to help resolve these issues. To familiarize yourself with the situation, you decide to evaluate the current pharmacy setting while obtaining background information about the diverse cultures served by the pharmacies.

One pharmacy-based article provides the following broad suggestions for ways to improve care across cultures[1]:

- *Evaluate your own culture.* It is important to self-reflect and take time to understand what makes you and your pharmacy unique. By evaluating your own cultural identity and personal values, you can better understand other cultures and the differences that may exist between you and another culture. Furthermore, each pharmacy has its own "culture," and by understanding what the pharmacy culture is, pharmacists can better understand if they provide services that are open and inviting to other cultures.

- *Learn about your community.* Learning basic information about the community served by the pharmacy helps put patient care in context. Online census data, map search engines, and local/state health department Web sites are tools that can help you get started.

- *Develop communication skills.* What communications skills do pharmacists and pharmacy personnel need to serve different communities? Understanding communications styles can be critical to good patient care. For example, do patients in your community use direct eye contact or do they need personal space when communicating with the pharmacist? Furthermore, are unique language concerns present in your community? What education level do your patients have? If a large portion of your patients speak a different language, an interpreter and bilingual written materials may be needed. If patients have low literacy, the pharmacy may need to have written information adapted to a lower grade level or rely more heavily on oral communication.

- *Use community resources.* Become familiar with community resources. What markets and restaurants do your patients go to? Where do the children go to school? What civic or religious organizations are in the community? These resources can be key to an expansion of patient care services in the pharmacy and also to a better understanding of the culture.

After reviewing these four guidelines, you complete a brief inventory (Case Figure 11-1) to start your evaluation of the culture and values of the pharmacists and staff in your district.

To learn about the communities served by your pharmacies, you turn to the U.S. Census data for your city and find the information (Case Table 11-1). In your background

Understanding the Culture and Values within the Pharmacy Setting

Time:
- ☐ Time is money
- ☐ People should be punctual
- ☐ Live for the future
- ☐ The future holds the answers
- ☐ Work to live

- ☐ Time is relative
- ☐ Time with the patient is most important
- ☐ Live in the moment
- ☐ The past holds the answers
- ☐ Work to earn money

- ☐ Remember the past

- ☐ Work to save money

Medication use:
- ☐ Herbal products generate revenue
- ☐ Treatment is more important than prevention
- ☐ A higher being has ultimate control of health

- ☐ Herbs have valuable healing properties
- ☐ Prevention is more important than treatment
- ☐ Medications will improve health

Community values:
- ☐ Treat the individual one at a time

- ☐ Medicine can control nature
- ☐ The elderly are respected and wise
- ☐ Value youth over age
- ☐ Fate (or high being) has control over my life

- ☐ Treat the family and you treat the individual
- ☐ Nature is more powerful than medicine
- ☐ The elderly are often ill and frail
- ☐ Value age over youth

- ☐ Value all ages equally

For good communication with the patient, the following should occur:
- ☐ Direct eye contact
- ☐ Talk more than listen
- ☐ Close personal space helps convey interest in the patient
- ☐ The pharmacist should be able to give the patient a hug
- ☐ Use written information in appropriate languages
- ☐ Patients should learn to speak English

- ☐ Indirect eye contact
- ☐ Listen more than talk
- ☐ Distance maintains a more professional environment
- ☐ The pharmacist should not touch the patient
- ☐ Use verbal counseling

- ☐ Use an interpreter

CASE Figure 11–1 Sample inventory for evaluating the culture of pharmacists and pharmacy staff.
Source: Reference 2.

CASE Table 11–1   U.S. Census Data for a Metropolitan Area

	United States	State	City	Zip Code #1	Zip Code #2	Zip Code #3	Zip Code #4
Population	281,421,906	20,851,820	656,562	22,534	30,110	26,825	26,023
Median age (years)	35.3	32.3	29.6	29.8	28.3	21.2↓	38.3↑
65 years and older	12.4%	9.9%	6.7%	12.4%↑	8%	1.3%	7.2%
White	75.1%	71%	65.4%	30%↓	40.8%	74.6%	92.1%↑
African American	12.3%	11.5%	10%	23.7%	31.8%↑	3%	0.6%↓
AmericanIndian/ Alaska Native	0.9%	0.6%	0.6%	1%↑	0.6%	0.3%	0.2%
Asian	3.6%	2.7%	4.7%	0.4%	1.2%	14.9%↑	4.4%↓
Pacific Islander	0.1%	0.1%	0.1%	0%	0.1%	0.1%	0%
Hispanic/Latino	12.5%	32%	30.5%	67.7%↑	42.3%	10.1%	5.1%↓
<High school education	19.6%	24.4%	16.6%	53.7%↑	30.2%	3.1%	1.9%↓
Born outside of United States	11.1%	13.9%	16.6%	21%	25.1%↑	14%	8.3%↓
English not spoken at home	17.9%	31.2%	31.1%	57%↑	39.2%	25.2%	11.8%↓
Per-capita income	$21,857	$19,617	$24,163	$10,719↓	$15,441	$11,350	$58,310↑

Arrows (↑↓) indicate highs or lows in comparison with city, state, and/or U.S. data.
Source: Reference 3.

reading, you come across a definition for "health disparities" and find information that helps you understand the health care needs that may be affecting your diverse communities. According to Healthy People 2010, a U.S. government initiative for disease prevention and health promotion objectives for the Nation, one of the two main goals is to "eliminate health disparities."[2] You identify six national focus areas for health disparities among racial and ethnic minorities.[3]

- Infant mortality
- Cancer screening and management
- Cardiovascular disease
- Diabetes
- HIV infection/AIDS
- Immunizations

Furthermore, other existing disparities that seem to disproportionately affect racial and ethnic minorities are mental health, hepatitis, syphilis, and tuberculosis.

Using national vital statistics, you identify mortality data that are based on the five predominant racial and ethnic groups in the United States (Case Table 11–2). Although you understand that the statistics may differ for your city, the data provide some broad epidemiologic information that helps you understand what diseases and problems are the leading causes of mortality in diverse racial/ethnic populations.

As you work on a process to develop communication skills among the staff in your pharmacies, you learn about one model or continuum for cultural competency (Case Figure 11–2). In this continuum, you identify different levels of cultural competency that you may be able to apply to your

CASE Table 11–2 Ten Leading Causes of Death, by Race/Ethnicity: United States, 2002

	American Indian		Asian/Pacific Islanders		Black		Hispanic		White	
	Rank	% Total Deaths	Rank	% Total Deaths	Rank	% Total Deaths	Rank	% Total Deaths	Rank	% Total Deaths
Diseases of heart	1	19.9	2	26.0	1	26.8	1	23.8	1	28.9
Malignant neoplasms	2	17.5	1	26.1	2	21.6	2	19.8	2	22.9
Accidents (unintentional injuries)	3	12.0	4	4.9	5	4.3	3	8.6	5	4.3
Diabetes mellitus	4	6.0	5	3.5	4	4.4	5	5.0	6	2.8
Cerebrovascular diseases	5	4.6	3	9.2	3	6.5	4	5.5	3	6.6
Chronic liver disease and cirrhosis	6	4.4	15	0.8	15	0.9	6	2.9	12	1.1
Chronic lower respiratory diseases	7	3.6	7	3.0	8	2.7	8	2.6	4	5.5
Intentional self-harm (suicide)	8	2.6	8	1.7	16	0.7	11	1.7	10	1.4
Influenza and pneumonia	9	2.4	6	3.1	11	2.0	9	2.4	7	2.8
Assault (homicide)	10	2.2	13	1.0	6	2.9	7	2.7	20	0.4
Nephritis, nephrotic syndrome, and nephrosis	11	1.8	9	1.7	9	2.6	12	1.6	9	1.6
Septicemia	12	1.6	10	1.1	10	2.1	15	1.3	11	1.3
Alzheimer's disease	14	0.9	14	0.9	14	1.2	16	1.3	8	2.6
HIV	18	0.5	23	0.3	7	2.7	13	1.6	22	0.3
Certain conditions originating in the perinatal period	NA	NA	NA	NA	12	1.7	10	2.1	20	0.3

NA, not available.
Source: Reference 4.

Proficiency
Pharmacy personnel hold culture in high esteem and value positive role of culture in health and well-being.

Competency
Pharmacy personnel accept and respect differences. Continuous self-assessment and expansion of cultural knowledge resources occur.

Pre-competency
Pharmacy personnel desire to deliver high-quality services and are committed to civil rights. However, they may feel one change in the system is adequate.

Blindness
Pharmacy provides services with a philosophy of no bias—believes that if the system works, all people will be served with equal effectiveness.

Incapacity
Pharmacy culture makes biased decisions with clients from other cultures and perpetuates stereotypes.

Destructiveness
Pharmacy culture devalues cultures and individuals through attitudes, policies, and practices.

CASE Figure 11–2 Cultural competency continuum. *Source:* Adapted from reference 6.

pharmacy setting. You also learn about the culturally and linguistically appropriate services (CLAS) standards and the requirements for persons with limited English proficiency under Title VI of the Civil Rights Act of 1964.[4,5] The CLAS document contains 14 standards that focus on culturally competent care, language access services, and organizational support.

Scenario

While working in zip code #1, you encounter the following situation. Gloria Elena Diaz is a 63-year-old Latin American female who is filling her first prescription with you. She enters with her grandson who is about 8 years old. When you start to ask her how you can help, she starts to speak in Spanish quickly and looks at her grandson for help. The grandson says that she needs a prescription for her diabetes. You address the patient by her first name and smile frequently at her, but you find it difficult to communicate with her and often catch yourself talking with only her grandson. Although the patient is friendly, she is withdrawn and looks down and away from you frequently. After filling the prescription for insulin, providing the patient written instructions in Spanish, and providing counseling on dosing through her grandson, you feel frustrated about not being

able to talk to the patient and wish that you had someone to at least help you interpret the conversation with the patient.

You discuss the situation with the staff pharmacist in zip code #1. The staff pharmacist says to you, "Don't worry. That always happens here. It's the patient's responsibility to learn English. After all you gave her the written instructions in Spanish. I can't keep up with all of the changes here. I tell them what the medicine is for, and I have done my best. Diabetes is genetic and she doesn't keep her weight down, so it's ultimately her responsibility."

Questions and Activities

1. Using the "understanding culture and values" template (Case Figure 11–1), how would you describe your own values. What are your general perceptions of the values and culture of community pharmacy and/or pharmacists? Compare your perceptions to those of your classmates. What similarities and differences do you find? To what do you attribute the similarities and/or differences?

2. Why is it important to work toward cultural competency in a pharmacy setting? Provide at least five

reasons and justify them. (See www11.georgetown.edu/research/gucchd/nccc/foundations/need.html.)

3. Using the six focus areas for health disparities discussed previously and sources for national health information, further describe the unique health disparities that exist among various racial and ethnic populations in the United States.

4. Identify barriers to patient care that patients from different cultures may experience in a community pharmacy.

5. Analyze the U.S. Census data to make broad suggestions about the types of pharmacy services that may be appropriate for the diverse communities in the scenario (Case Table 11-1).

6. Review the six focus areas (question 2) to decrease health disparities. What services could pharmacies provide to address these disparities?

7. What legal responsibilities do pharmacists have to provide care to persons under the CLAS standards (www.omhrc.gov/assets/pdf/checked/finalreport.pdf) and for persons with limited English proficiency (www.lep.gov)?

8. What other Internet resources are available to learn about health disparities and improve cultural competency?

9. Identify opportunities in pharmacy practice to use community resources in understanding diverse cultures and implementing changes in the pharmacy setting. What community organizations could a pharmacist use? What type of work could you do with these community organizations?

10. On the basis of the scenario, where would you place yourself, as the new district manager, on the cultural competency continuum (Case Figure 11−2)? Why? Where would you place the staff pharmacist and why?

11. Go to the National Vital Statistics Web site and evaluate the report "Deaths: Leading Causes for 2004" [in the United States] (www.cdc.gov/nchs/data/nvsr/nvsr56/nvsr56_05.pdf). On the basis of the scenario, what do the mortality data reveal about Hispanic women who are the same age as the patient? How do these statistics compare with women of other racial and ethnic groups of the same age? Use Figure Case 11−3 as a worksheet to list the top 5 leading causes of death (and percentages). How could you incorporate this knowledge into your pharmacy practice? Why is it important?

12. What communication concerns arise in the scenario? How could you work to resolve these issues?

Additional Activities

1. Conduct a census data search using the address of the community pharmacy where you work or are an intern. Compare and contrast demographic, economic, and social characteristics for your community with those of other neighborhoods/zip codes in your city, and with the city and state characteristics.

2. Describe the current culture of a "typical" community pharmacy in your city. If you were a patient, what information would you need to be comfortable to take your medication correctly or to select a nonprescription medication or device?

3. Look up information online from your city/county health department to identify the prevalence of various diseases and health problems in your area.

4. Go on a 30-minute walking tour around the neighborhood of the community pharmacy where you work or are an intern. Identify potential community partners for conducting pharmacy-related or health-related activities.

5. Participate in an activity in which you are immersed in a situation that requires you to be exposed for at

Top Five Leading Causes of Death among U.S. Females, 55–64 Years

	All Races	African American	American Indian	Asian American	Hispanic	White
1						
2						
3						
4						
5						

CASE Figure 11–3 Sample worksheet for comparison of leading causes of death among older U.S. females.

least 30 minutes to a few hours of a different language. For example, rent or go to a foreign-language film and watch it without reading the subtitles. Visit a religious event that is conducted in a different language. Visit a local market where people speak a different language. Observe and listen. During the experience, keep a mental note (or take notes) about the following:

- What communication did you understand or not understand?

- What mannerisms (e.g., hand gestures, eye contact) did you notice in this different culture?

- What was comfortable about the situation? What was awkward?

- How would you feel if you were a patient from this culture who was walking into the pharmacy where you work or intern? Comfortable? Frustrated? What questions do you think you would have? How would you try to communicate with the pharmacist?

- How do you think you would provide pharmacy services to a patient who comes from this culture?

6. Develop a plan for implementing culturally diverse education for the pharmacy staff in your district.

7. Look for other Web sites that focus on cultural competency and health disparities. Develop a resource list for learning about different populations.

References

1. Brown CM, Nichols-English G. Dealing with patient diversity in pharmacy practice. *Drug Top*. September 6, 1999.

2. U.S. Department of Health and Human Services, Office of Disease Prevention and Health Promotion. Healthy People 2010. Available at: http://www. healthypeople.gov/. Last accessed October 25, 2008.

3. Centers for Disease Control, Office of Minority Health and Health Disparities. Eliminating Racial & Ethnic Health Disparities. Available at: http://www. cdc.gov/omhd/About/disparities.htm. Last accessed October 25, 2008.

4. Cross T, Bazron B, Dennis K, Isaacs M. *Towards a Culturally Competent System of care*. Washington, DC: Georgetown University. 1989.

5. U.S. Department of Health and Human Services, Office of Minority Health. *National Standards for Culturally and Linguistically Appropriate Services in Health Care*. Washington, DC: Department of Health and Human Services; 2001. Available at: http://www. omhrc.gov/assets/pdf/checked/finalreport.pdf. Last accessed October 25, 2008.

Other Information Sources

1. Limited English Proficiency: A Federal Interagency Website. U.S. Department of Justice. Civil Rights Division. Available at: http://www.lep.gov/. Last accessed October 25, 2008.

2. National Center for Cultural Competence. The Compelling Need for Cultural and Linguistic Competence. Available at: http://www11.georgetown.edu/ research/gucchd/nccc/foundations/ need.html. Last accessed October 25, 2008.

3. Heron MP. *Deaths: Leading Causes for 2004*. [Table 1: Deaths, Percentage of Total Deaths, and Death Rates for the 10 Leading Causes of Death in Selected Age Groups, by Race and Sex: United States, 2004.] Hyattsville, Md: National Center or Health Statistics; November 20, 2007. National Vital Statistics Reports, Vol. 56, No. 5. Available at: http://www.cdc. gov/nchs/data/nvsr/nvsr56/ nvsr56_05.pdf. Last accessed October 25, 2008.

4. Spector RE. *Cultural Diversity in Health and Illness*. Upper Saddle River, NJ: Pearson Prentice Hall, 2004.

5. U.S. Census Bureau. American FactFinder. Available at: http://www.factfinder.census.gov. Last accessed October 25, 2008.

12 Patient Safety in Community Pharmacy Practice

Antoinette B. Coe and Kristin W. Weitzel

Objectives

1. Identify areas of community pharmacy practice that are prone to medication errors.

2. Develop procedures and policies for documenting medication errors and implementing a continuous quality improvement process.

3. Identify the strategies and systems that a community pharmacy can use to prevent medication errors and improve patient safety.

Scenario 1

You are the pharmacy manager for a large independent pharmacy. A medication error is brought to your attention by one of your staff pharmacists. Katrina Cox, a long-time patient of the pharmacy, is a 50-year-old female with type 2 diabetes, hypertension, and hyperlipidemia. For the last 3 years, Ms. Cox has refilled a prescription for 100 mg Toprol XL tablets at your pharmacy. She has participated in the pharmacy-based diabetes management classes and blood pressure monitoring program provided by your clinical pharmacist, and she takes an active role in her health care. Ms. Cox brought in a new prescription 3 days ago for her usual Toprol XL dose. She came into the pharmacy this morning to ask if a different product was dispensed because "her pills look different than last time." She brought her prescription vial with her to show the pharmacist. Your staff pharmacist relays to you that the tablets inside the vial do not match the label of 100 mg Toprol XL tablets. The staff pharmacist says that she was the one who checked the prescription and that she does not remember talking to the patient. She has pulled the hard copy of the original prescription and verified that it was written for Toprol XL. Ms. Cox's patient profile confirms that she has been on this medication at the same dose of 100 mg daily for some time and has never received Topamax.

The tablets were identified as 100 mg Topamax tablets by using the tablet's imprint code. Ms. Cox is concerned about any "bad things" that might happen to her because of the mix-up. She would also like to know how this error occurred and what will be done to prevent its recurrence.

Background Pharmacy Information

This independent pharmacy has been owned by the same family for more than 30 years. Its owners, who are pharmacists, are well-known for their service to the community. Patients prefer this pharmacy because of the individualized patient care they receive and their relationship with their pharmacist. The majority of patients have been using this pharmacy for many years. In fact, many of the patients tell stories of their parents bringing them to the pharmacy as children.

As the pharmacy manager, you are responsible for the supervision of the pharmacy staff. The staff includes three full-time staff pharmacists, one part-time staff pharmacist, one part-time clinical pharmacist, two part-time pharmacy interns, three full-time pharmacy technicians, and one part-time pharmacy technician. The pharmacy is open from 8 am to 10 pm, Monday to Friday, and from 10 am to 7 pm, Saturday and Sunday. Typically, two staff pharmacists and two pharmacy technicians work during business hours Monday through Friday. There are fewer personnel on Saturday and Sunday: only one staff pharmacist and one pharmacy technician. The clinical pharmacist, who sees patients by appointment or leads group education classes, has a variable schedule. The pharmacy interns work less than 10 hours per week, with their schedules revolving around their classes and examinations.

The daily pharmacy prescription volume is approximately 200 to 300 prescriptions, with an average weekly volume of 1700. The majority of the pharmacy's patients are referred from large family physician and pediatric practices located nearby. The pharmacy is designed with specific areas for prescription drop-off, pick up, and private patient counseling. A pharmacy technician receives the prescription from the patient, asks the patient questions regarding any drug allergies or new information, and enters the information into the computer system. The prescription hard copy and pharmacy label are placed into a color-coded basket. Another pharmacy technician will take this basket and prepare the medication for the pharmacist to review. The pharmacy uses a bar code scanner to match the bar codes on the pharmacy label to the drug manufacturer's bottle. It is pharmacy policy that the pharmacy technicians obtain the pharmacist's approval or input for any drug allergies, drug interactions, or questions. The pharmacist performs the final check before the prescription is ready for pick up, and then counsels the patient on both new and refill prescriptions. The pharmacists take an active role in helping patients select nonprescription medications, herbal products, and other dietary supplements.

In addition to dispensing medications, the pharmacy offers several health promotion, education, and screening opportunities. A large classroom is located behind the pharmacy. This classroom is used by the clinical pharmacist for diabetes, hyperlipidemia, hypertension, and asthma education or management classes. The clinical pharmacist has recently designed and implemented a medication therapy management service for patients who take more than one chronic medication or have a specified disease state.

Questions and Activities

1. What physical assessment should be performed or questions asked of the patient today to determine the clinical impact of this medication error?

2. After assessing the patient for any harm, what additional follow-up (if any) with the patient or prescriber would you recommend?

3. Identify at least three opportunities by the pharmacy staff to prevent this error. How would you correct these deficiencies?

4. What strategies could have been used to prevent this problem?

5. What internal pharmacy documentation is necessary? Explain why documentation requirements may vary from state to state or in different pharmacy settings.

6. When an error or misfill is detected in the community pharmacy, it is often necessary to identify a tablet or capsule that a patient received to determine what medication was dispensed. What reference sources can the community pharmacist use to identify tablet imprint codes?

Ms. Cox returns to the pharmacy a month later with a new prescription for Biaxin XL 500 mg, #14, take 2 tablets by mouth daily for 7 days. The pharmacy technician typing the prescription into the computer asks the pharmacist to override the drug interaction warning screen. Upon review, the pharmacist notices a drug interaction between clarithromycin and the patient's simvastatin, which she takes at a dose of 20 mg nightly at bedtime. The pharmacy computer system lists the interaction as moderate.

7. What is the interaction between simvastatin and clarithromycin? What are the possible clinical outcomes of concurrent use of the two medications?

8. What actions would you take as the pharmacist today in light of this interaction?

Additional Activities

1. What is a prospective DUR process? Explain its importance in improving patient safety.

2. List specific strategies that can be used to reduce medication errors in high-risk patient populations such as pediatric and elderly patients.

3. What is medication reconciliation? List steps the community pharmacist can take to improve patient safety and minimize medication errors for patients recently discharged from a health system or hospital.

4. Using the following Web sites as a reference, list three examples of look-alike, sound-alike medication errors. Describe methods or systems that a pharmacist can use to prevent this type of error.

   - Centers for Drug Evaluation and Research (www.fda.gov/cder/drug/MedErrors/nameDiff.htm)
   - Institute for Safe Medication Practices (www.ismp.org/Tools/confuseddrugnames.pdf)

5. The National Coordinating Council for Medication Error and Reporting Prevention (NCC MERP) recognizes a medication error index that classifies errors on the basis of outcomes (www.nccmerp.org/medError CatIndex.html). Describe the nine categories.

6. Using the NCC MERP algorithm, categorize the patient case error (www.nccmerp.org/medErrorCat Index.html).

7. The USP Medication Errors Reporting Program is offered in conjunction with the Institute for Safe Medication Practices (ISMP) and as a partner of the FDA MedWatch program. The USP program recommends that health care professionals voluntarily report actual or potential medication errors. These medication errors include problems with the interpretation, calculation, administration, or understanding of verbal and written orders. The information gathered is used for educational programs to prevent future medication errors. Using the details from the patient case, complete an error reporting form found at one of the following links:

   - USP Medication Errors Reporting Program—provides background information (www.usp.org/hqi/patientSafety/mer)
   - USP Medication Errors Reporting Program form (www.usp.org/pdf/EN/patientSafety/medform.pdf)
   - FDA MedWatch (www.fda.gov/medwatch/index.html)

- Institute for Safe Medication Practices (www.ismp.org/orderforms/reporterrortoismp.asp)

8. Use the ISMP publication *Medication Safety Self Assessment for Community/Ambulatory Pharmacy* to evaluate a pharmacy that you currently work in or have worked in the past. This document is available at www.ismp.org/survey/NewMssacap/Index.asp. Discuss results with the pharmacist at that practice, a case leader, and/or other students.

9. Interview two community pharmacists from different practice sites about their experience with a medication error. Compare and contrast their experiences and company policies for handling medication errors. List steps that could have been taken in each case to prevent the error.

10. The ISMP has developed a list of high-alert medications (www.ismp.org/Tools/highalertmedications.pdf). The following mini-cases are based on high-alert medications. Choose one or more of the mini-cases, and list the potential negative outcomes of an error, common causes of errors with this drug or drug class, and strategies to prevent errors and improve patient safety.

Mini-Case A: Warfarin

Andrea Hall is a 65-year-old female with a history of hypothyroidism. She has been taking 100 mcg of levothyroxine (Synthroid, others) daily for more than 10 years. She comes into the pharmacy with a new prescription for warfarin 3 mg daily. The patient tells you that she was recently in the hospital and diagnosed with atrial fibrillation. She mentions that she has been having some pain in her joints lately and has to take 1 to 2 naproxen tablets daily for pain relief.

a. List potential drug interactions in this patient's regimen.

b. List three potential medication errors commonly seen with warfarin. Identify strategies to prevent these medication errors.

c. Warfarin has a required medication guide that is included with dispensed prescriptions. Is it considered a medication error to "forget" to include the medication guide? Why or why not?

Mini-Case B: Insulin

Joel Zimmerman is a 30-year-old male with type 1 diabetes. He currently takes Lantus once daily and NovoLog with his meals. He had a new prescription for NovoLog Flexpen filled 2 days ago at your pharmacy. The patient has brought his box of Flexpens into the pharmacy and says that he received the wrong medication. You look at the box and see that the pharmacist filled the prescription with the NovoLog Mix 70/30 Flexpen instead of the correct NovoLog. Mr. Zimmerman says that he used the insulin for 2 days before he noticed the mistake. You look at the hard copy of the prescription to verify the correct medication and at the boxes of the NovoLog Flexpens in the pharmacy refrigerator. You notice that the two boxes appear very similar.

a. Why are dispensing and administration errors more common with insulin products?

b. What strategies can the pharmacy use to prevent this type of error?

Mini-Case C: Methotrexate

Maria Lopez is a 38-year-old female recently diagnosed with rheumatoid arthritis. She said that she wakes up with stiffness and pain in her ankles and wrists, and feels like her joints are hot. She has also been feeling weak and tired lately. She recently started going for short daily walks and eating a healthy diet to lose weight. Her doctor has prescribed 7.5 mg methotrexate 1 tablet by mouth weekly, and a 1 mg folic acid tablet daily. She said that her doctor told her to take an NSAID for the next couple of months for pain until the methotrexate starts working. She would like to get your recommendation for an appropriate NSAID.

a. List potential dosing, dispensing, and administration errors with once-weekly oral methotrexate.

b. What strategies can be used to minimize medication errors with once-weekly methotrexate?

c. While looking in your computer system for more information to answer the patient's question, you notice a drug interaction alert for methotrexate and NSAIDs. How would you counsel Mrs. Lopez about this interaction and choosing an NSAID?

Information Sources

1. Topamax [package insert]. Titusville, NJ: Ortho-McNeil Neurologics; March 2007.

2. Toprol XL [package insert]. Wilmington, Del: AstraZeneca LP; July 2007.

3. Medication errors and patient safety resources. *Pharm Lett Prescrib Lett* 2007;23(5):230501.

4. Meadows M. Strategies to reduce medication errors: how the FDA is working to improve medication safety and what you can do to help [serial online]. *FDA Consum Mag.* 2003;37(3). Available at: http://www.fda.gov/fdac/features/2003/303_meds.html. Last accessed August 17, 2008.

5. Zocor [package insert]. Whitehouse Station, NJ: Merck and Co; May 2007.

6. Biaxin XL [package insert]. North Chicago, Ill: Abbott Laboratories; March 2007.

7. Molden E, Andersson KS. Simvastatin-associated rhabdomyolysis after coadministration of macrolide antibiotics in two patients. *Pharmacotherapy.* 2007;27:603.

Personal Health Care and Preventive Medicine

Section

3

Age-Based and Gender-Based Screenings

Objectives

1. Apply preventive guidelines from different sources to make recommendations for a patient.

2. Identify barriers to patients receiving appropriate preventive services.

3. Determine screening tests that may be offered in the community pharmacy setting.

4. Describe factors that must be considered before providing a screening in the community pharmacy.

Scenario 1: Determining Recommendations for Preventive Services

Mrs. Smith comes into your independent community pharmacy for a refill on her glipizide. She is a 64-year-old white female and a well-known cynic when it comes to the health care system. You had to convince her to fill her glipizide medication 6 years ago when she was diagnosed with a "touch of the diabetes," and you are surprised that she still takes it today. Although Mrs. Smith has health insurance through her union job at a local supermarket, she does not believe much in seeing physicians, taking medications, or any other preventive services. She does not even check her blood glucose. She feels that she is healthy for the most part (and her physician agrees, refilling her glipizide sometimes

without seeing her). She is overweight at 5 feet 1 inch and 150 pounds.

Mrs. Smith is married to a truck driver from the same company; they both smoke. They have two healthy children; at the age of 42 she had a hysterectomy. You are aware that Mrs. Smith's mother filled Fosamax 70 mg weekly from you twice, but she said it was too expensive and now buys just calcium. Mrs. Smith's father passed away at a young age from a heart attack.

Today when Mrs. Smith comes in to pick up her glipizide, she says that her employer is offering a health fair screening day, and she wants to know if it is worth the cost to have the blood tests and mammogram. She mentions that she wants to know all the necessary information about the screenings so that she can do it all in one visit and "get it over with if I have to."

General guidelines for preventive care are available from different governmental and private associations. Case Table 13–1 contains a non-comprehensive list of sources for guidelines on preventive services.

Scenario 1 Questions and Activities

1. Using the guidelines in Case Table 13–1, determine which preventive health screenings or tests you should recommend for Mrs. Smith. How often should she receive these preventive tests (according to the

CASE Table 13–1 Sources for Guidelines for Preventive Services (General and Disease-Specific Examples)	
Organization and/or Publication	**Web Site[a]**
United States Preventive Services Task Force (USPSTF): Pocket Guide to Clinical Preventive Services, 2007; Electronic Preventive Service Selector (ePSS; downloadable to PDA)	www.ahrq.gov/clinic/uspstfix.htm
Agency for Healthcare Research and Quality (AHRQ) Preventive Services	www.ahrq.gov/clinic/prevenix.htm
American Academy of Family Physicians (AAFP)	www.aafp.org
American College of Physicians	www.acponline.org
American College of Obstetricians and Gynecologists (ACOG)	www.acog.com
American Diabetes Association (ADA)	www.diabetes.org
American Heart Association (AHA)	www.americanheart.org
American Cancer Society (ACS)	www.cancer.org

[a] Last accessed October 25, 2008.

guideline you list)? Compile a list for this patient that includes the test, frequency, and the guideline (source) for the information.

2. Mrs. Smith's work is offering a thyroid stimulating hormone (TSH) test, a full cholesterol panel, and a fasting glucose test for $25. The mammography van will also be there. Are these screenings appropriate for Mrs. Smith? After answering this question for each test, justify your answer.

3. Do you recommend that Mrs. Smith receive the preventive screenings from the health fair at work? Why or why not?

4. Because Mrs. Smith seems so interested in health today, you also decide to reiterate the care that she should receive to prevent complications specifically from diabetes. List the diabetes-specific preventive care measures you should discuss with her, even if her diabetes is under control.

5. Mrs. Smith will qualify for Medicare in a few months. What preventive screenings does Medicare pay for?

6. Discuss whether or not the frequency of the screenings listed in question 5 are clearly stated in the guidelines?

7. What are the potential barriers to delivering preventive services?

Scenario 2: Providing Preventive Services in Your Community Pharmacy

After Mrs. Smith's visit, you start thinking about providing some health screenings as an added service for your patients. The owner does not care which screenings are offered as long as they are beneficial to your patient population, are in line with current guidelines, and generate a profit.

Scenario 2 Questions and Activities

1. Your first step is to determine all the possible tests that you can perform in the pharmacy. Of course, there are many kinds of "screenings" to consider.

   a. List examples of screening tests that you have to draw blood to complete.

   b. List examples of screening tests that you complete by asking the patient questions from a validated survey.

   c. List other screening tests that you could complete in your pharmacy but are not included in a or b.

2. Now that you have the list of possible screening tests, you have to determine profitability, feasibility, and a need in your population. Listed below are factors to consider in determining the feasibility of providing a particular screening. What do you need to consider for each factor to develop a screening service?

   - Patient population
   - Other providers
   - Payment
   - Training and regulations
   - Practice site needs

3. You are considering a "Heart Healthy Program" that offers screening for cholesterol, blood pressure, and awareness of cardiovascular risk factors. First, you need to determine whether your pharmacy has the potential to be successful with this type of program. What is the target population of this program?

4. The other staff pharmacist is not sure that he is sufficiently up-to-date on the clinical skills required to perform this program. What recommendations do you make?

You have to determine which cholesterol-measuring device to purchase. Of the several options available, one device measures only total cholesterol (TC) and high-density lipoproteins (HDLs), whereas another offers different cartridges to measure TC, a total lipid panel, glucose level, and even liver function tests (LFTs). The more comprehensive machine is much more expensive.

5. The pharmacy manager says you have to purchase a machine that can measure the full cholesterol panel. Why is he insisting on the more expensive machine?

6. How much does it cost to provide a test, excluding the cost of the machine? Use the costs in Case Table 13–2. Assume that the process takes 15 minutes and pharmacist time is $50 per hour.

7. How much would you charge the patient considering the cost for this screening? How many tests do you need to provide at this cost to pay for the machine?

8. Are there other costs that you did not consider in determining the cost for question 7? If yes, what are they?

9. The Occupational Safety and Health Administration (OSHA) is an agency that protects workers from harm on the job (www.osha.gov). It regulates the work environment to keep workers safe. Why would you have to consider OSHA regulations when performing a cholesterol test?

10. The Clinical Laboratory Improvement Act (CLIA) Amendments were established in 1988 to ensure quality standards for laboratory testing. When does a pharmacy need a CLIA certificate?

CASE Table 13–2 Start-Up Costs for Cholesterol Screenings	
Service/Supply	**Cost**
Cholestech LDX System (includes printer with 100 labels, Optics check cassette, 200 capillary tubes, plunger and lancets, pipette, 50 pipette tips, accessory tray, user manual, training video, and procedure manual CD)	$2115.00
Lipid profile + glucose cartridges, box of 10 (includes TC, HDL, triglycerides, TC/HDL ratio, estimated LDL, VLDL, and glucose)	$110.00
Results brochures (#50)	$15.00
Gloves, adhesive bandages, cotton gauze pads	$10.00
Total cost for start-up supplies	$3226.00

You would also like to consider screening patients for strep throat using the QuickVue In-Line One-Strep A Test. You know a physician who will collaborate with you on a standing order to treat patients who test positive and recommend nonprescription treatment or referral for those who test negative. Your pharmacy has a CLIA certificate of waiver.

11. Does the QuickVue In-Line One-Strep A Test fall under the "CLIA-waived" status? Where did you find this information?

After developing a business plan, policies and procedures, documentation system, and liability clause for the Heart Healthy Program, you finally want to start offering the service. You put up a poster that reads "CHOLESTEROL AND HYPERTENSION SCREENINGS" next to your register. After a month, this marketing is obviously not working; patients rarely inquire about the service just from the poster. You want to develop a more comprehensive marketing strategy to include your current patients and others who do not normally come to your pharmacy.

12. Describe two strategies to market to current patients. Describe why you think these marketing strategies will be more successful, and what challenges need to be considered before choosing that form of marketing. Consider these three elements in your answer: strategy, advantages, and challenges.

13. Describe two strategies to market to people who are not currently patients of the pharmacy. These strategies should differ from those used for current patients. Describe why you think these marketing strategies will be successful and what challenges need to be considered before choosing that form of marketing.

14. Successful marketing tells the patient the benefits that they will receive from the product, not just the product's features. Case Figure 13–1 lists some "features" of the cholesterol program. Describe these features in terms of a "benefit" that the patient will receive from the service; an example of a benefit is given.

15. You realize that your staff also needs to start talking to patients about the service. Write a 15-second informational piece that your staff can use to learn about the cholesterol service and then to promote the service to your patients. Include the product definition, an explanation of its benefits, and the price.

Alex Kasper responds to your marketing campaign and comes in for a screening. This 40-year-old white male is obese, but he currently has no medical conditions. He says that cholesterol problems run in his family; his father had a heart attack when he was 44. His fasting results are as follows:

- Total cholesterol: 282
- LDL: 195
- HDL: 36
- Triglycerides: 255
- Fasting glucose: 142 mg/dL

16. Communicate the results of the lipid and glucose screening tests to Alex Kasper, and counsel him on the next steps that he should take.

17. After several months of conducting cholesterol screenings using the Cholestech LDX, a local physician's office calls. One of the patients who had their cholesterol tested at your pharmacy followed up on their high cholesterol readings. The physician wants to know why the pharmacy's results differ from the office's readings. Justify the machine you are using and account for the difference in results.

Feature	Benefit
Cholesterol medication assessment	Helps people understand how their medication works
Test levels of TC, HDL, LDL, and TG	
Cardiovascular risk factor assessment	
Patient education of the results	

CASE Figure 13–1 Sample marketing worksheet to determine talking points for cholesterol screening tests.

Additional Activities

1. List the preventive services that apply to both males and females. Research the available screening devices for osteoporosis screening or A1c screenings. How do they compare with the gold standard for diagnosis?

2. Develop a patient education leaflet for reporting and interpreting the results of a cholesterol screening.

3. List the topics that should be addressed in a policy and procedure manual for screening services in a community pharmacy.

4. Develop a business plan for provision of screening services in a community pharmacy.

5. Investigate three survey-type screening tools for disease. Find at least one of the three on the Internet by searching in the manner that patients would if they thought they had a disease (e.g., migraines, asthma, or Alzheimer's disease). Determine the validity of each screening tool. Who developed the screening tool? Is it validated. If so, how? If it is not validated, is it still useful and in what capacity? Justify your answer with primary literature when appropriate.

Information Sources

1. American Academy of Family Physicians. Summary of Recommendations for Clinical Preventive Services. Revision 6.3, March 2007. Available at: http://www.aafp.org/online/etc/medialib/aafp_org/documents/clinical/clin_recs/cps.Par.0001.File.tmp/August2006CPS.pdf. Last accessed October 25, 2008.

2. US Preventive Services Task Force. *The Guide to Clinical Preventive Services, 2006: Recommendations of the U.S. Preventive Services Task Force.* Rockville, Md: US Department of Health and Human Services, Agency for Healthcare Research and Quality; 2006. AHRQ Publication No. 06-0588. Available at: http://www.ahrq.gov/clinic/pocketgd.pdf. Last accessed October 25, 2008.

3. American Diabetes Association. Standards of medical care in diabetes—2007. *Diabetes Care.* 2007; 30(suppl 1):S4–S41.

4. American Association of Clinical Endocrinologists and the American College of Endocrinology. AACE medical guidelines for the management of diabetes mellitus: the AACE system of intensive diabetes self-management—2002 update. *Endocr Pract.* 2002;8 (suppl 1):40–82.

5. Centers for Disease Control and Prevention. Recommended Adult Immunization Schedule. Available at: http://www.cdc.gov/vaccines/recs/schedules/adult-schedule.htm. Also available from the Immunization Action Coalition in laminated paper copy at: http://www.immunize.org/immschedules. Last accessed October 25, 2008.

6. Centers for Disease Control and Prevention. Prevention of herpes zoster. Recommendations of the Advisory Committee on Immunization Practices (ACIP) *MMWR Morb Mortal Wkly Rep* 2008;57(RR-5):1–30.

7. Centers for Medicare & Medicaid Services. Your Guide to Medicare's Preventive Services. Baltimore, Md: US Department of Health and Human Services; 2004. CMS Publication No. 10110. Available at: http://www.medicare.gov/Publications/Pubs/pdf/10110.pdf. Last accessed October 25, 2008.

8. US Department of Health and Human Services. Preventive Services: A Healthier US Starts Here. Available at: http://www.medicare.gov/Health/Overview.asp. Last accessed October 25, 2008.

9. National Heart, Lung, and Blood Institute. Complete Report: *Seventh Report of the Joint National Committee on Prevention, Detection, Evaluation, and Treatment of High Blood Pressure.* Baltimore, Md: US Department of Health and Human Services, National Institutes of Health, National High Blood Pressure Education Program; August 2004. NIH Publication No. 04-5230. Available at: http://www.nhlbi.nih.gov/guidelines/hypertension/jnc7full.pdf. Last accessed October 25, 2008.

10. National Cholesterol Education Program. *Third Report of the Expert Panel on Detection, Evaluation, and Treatment Of High Blood Cholesterol in Adults (Adult Treatment Panel III): Full Report.* Bethesda, Md: National Institutes of Health, National Institutes of Health, National Heart Lung Blood Institute; September 2002. NIH Publication No. 02-5215. Available at: http://www.nhlbi.nih.gov/guidelines/cholesterol/atp3full.pdf. Last accessed October 25, 2008.

11. Grundy SM, Cleeman JI, Merz NB, et al. Implications of recent clinical trials for the National Cholesterol Education Program Adult Treatment Panel III Guidelines. *Circulation.* 2004;110:227–39.

12. US Department of Labor, Occupational Safety and Health Administration. Bloodborne Pathogens Standards 1910.1013. Available at: http:// http://www.osha.gov/pls/oshaweb/owadisp.show_document?p_table=STANDARDS&p_id=10051. Last accessed October 25, 2008.

13. US Department of Health and Human Services, Centers for Medicare and Medicaid Services. Clinical Laboratory Improvement Amendments (CLIA) Overview. Available at: http://www.cms.hhs.gov/CLIA/01_Overview.asp#TopOfPage. Last accessed October 25, 2008.

14. US Department of Health and Human Services, Centers for Disease Control and Prevention. CLIA. Available at: http://www.phppo.cdc.gov/clia/default.aspx. Last accessed October 25, 2008.

15. US Food and Drug Administration, Center for Devices and Radiological Health. CLIA – Clinical Laboratory Improvement Amendments. Available at: http://www.fda.gov/cdrh/clia. Last accessed October 25, 2008.

16. Rosenthal WM, Briggs GC, Rosenthal T. *Ambulatory Care Clinical Skills Program: Practice Management Module.* Bethesda, Md: American Society of Health-Systems Pharmacists; 1999.

17. Rovers JP, Currie JD, Hagel HP, et al. *A Practical Guide to Pharmaceutical Care.* 2nd ed. Washington, DC: American Pharmacists Association; 2003.

18. Cholestech Corporation. Cholestech LDX. Available at: http://www.cholestech.com. Last accessed October 25, 2008.

19. Carter BL, Dent LA, Ernst ME, et al. *Resource Kit: Community Pharmacy.* Kansas City, Mo: American College of Clinical Pharmacy; 2002.

20. Hagel HP, Rovers JP. *Managing the Patient-Centered Pharmacy.* Washington, DC: American Pharmacists Association; 2002.

21. Holdford D. *Marketing for Pharmacists.* Washington, DC: American Pharmacists Association; 2003.

22. Goode JV, Nau D, Layson-Wolf C, et al. *Diabetes Management Services: A Pharmacist's Resource Guide.* Washington, DC: American Pharmacists Association; 2004.

23. Anderson AS, Goode JV. Engaging students in wellness and disease prevention services. *Am J Pharm Educ.* 2006;70(2):1–8.

24. Ciardulli LM, Goode JV. Using health observances to promote wellness in community pharmacies. *J Am Pharm Assoc.* 2003;43:61–8.

25. Rosenthal WM. Establishing a pharmacy-based laboratory service. *J Am Pharm Assoc.* 2000;40:146–56.

14 Adult Immunization

Jean-Venable "Kelly" R. Goode and Dennis D. Stanley

Objectives

1. Define the role of pharmacists in pharmacy-based immunization programs.

2. Describe the principles and procedures for developing a pharmacy-based immunization program, including legal and regulatory issues as well as practical issues.

3. Develop an appropriate vaccination plan including dosage, timing, and spacing of vaccines that is based on a patient's age, risk factors for disease, and immunization and medication history.

4. Evaluate a medical and medication history to identify precautions and contraindications for immunization.

5. Describe appropriate administration of vaccines including timing and spacing of both inactive and live attenuated vaccines.

Scenario

Main Street Community Pharmacy is located in a state where pharmacists are allowed to administer any type of adult immunizations. The pharmacy offers influenza immunizations any time during the day or during clinics. Other adult immunizations are offered any time during the day or by appointment. All the pharmacists have completed the American Pharmacists Association's Pharmacy-Based Immunization Delivery Certificate Training Program. The pharmacy has been providing immunizations in the community for 10 years.

Harold Walters, a 62-year-old African American male, presents to the community pharmacy in mid-October to ask questions about "diabetes meters" and to have his new prescriptions filled (Case Figures 14–1 and 14–2). His prescription profile is presented in Case Table 14–1. Mr. Walters was recently diagnosed with diabetes. In addition, Mr. Walters presents with a number of items for purchase, including a box of condoms and a bottle of enteric-coated aspirin. He is very excited because his first granddaughter was born 4 weeks ago. He notices your sign "Protect the ones you love—get your influenza shot." He requests information about the influenza shot. He heard that it can give you the "flu."

Questions and Activities

1. What are the roles of pharmacists in pharmacy-based immunization delivery? Identify potential activities at each level for a community pharmacist to include in his or her practice.

2. List the factors that a pharmacist should consider when implementing an immunization service in a community pharmacy.

3. What laws and regulations must pharmacists follow when they are involved in administering immunizations to patients?

4. What do you tell Mr. Walters about the influenza vaccine?

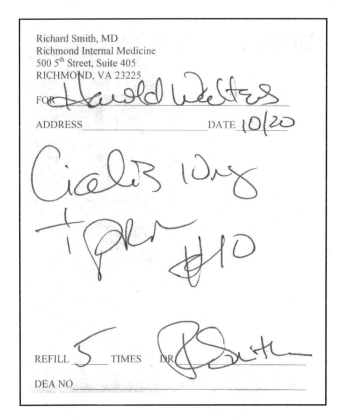

Richard Smith, MD
Richmond Internal Medicine
500 5th Street, Suite 405
RICHMOND, VA 23225

FOR Harold Walters

ADDRESS _____ DATE 10/20

Cialis 10mg
↑ prn #10

REFILL 5 TIMES DR _____

DEA NO _____

CASE Figure 14–1 Prescription #1 for patient Harold Walters.

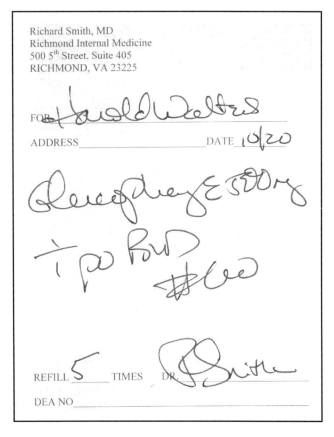

Richard Smith, MD
Richmond Internal Medicine
500 5th Street, Suite 405
RICHMOND, VA 23225

FOR _Harold Walters_

ADDRESS_____ DATE _10/20_

REFILL _5_ TIMES DR. _Smith_

DEA NO_____

CASE Figure 14–2 Prescription #2 for patient Harold Walters.

5. Is Mr. Walters a candidate for the influenza vaccine? Why or why not?

6. When is the most appropriate time to administer the influenza vaccine? Why?

Mr. Walters agrees to receive the influenza vaccine. He completes an immunization waiver form (Case Figure 14–3).

7. What pertinent screening questions need to be asked before administering the patient's influenza vaccination?

8. How do inactivated and live vaccines differ? Name the inactivated and live-attenuated vaccines available in the United States.

The pharmacist notes that the patient has brought his immunization record card with him and asks to look at it (Case Figure 14–4).

9. Where would you find information about which vaccines Mr. Walters needs today?

10. Identify other immunizations that Mr. Walters needs according to his medication and immunization history. Include the rationale for each vaccination.

CASE Table 14–1 Patient Prescription Medication Profile

Harold Walters
1000 Gaskins Road
Richmond, Virginia 23238

Phone: 804-335-9988   **DOB:** 04/06/44   **Insurer:** CIGNA

Allergies/Intolerances: PCN, codeine, and IVP dyes

Notes: Widower

Rx. No.	Drug Name	Directions	Date	R/F	Prescriber	Qty	RPh
621753	Ventolin inhaler	Inhale 2 puffs every 6 hours as needed	9/1	1	Hall	1	PR
620987	Hydrochlorothiazide 25 mg	1 tablet every day for blood pressure	9/1	3	Smith	30	PR
621753	Ventolin inhaler	Inhale 2 puffs every 6 hours as needed	8/15	2	Hall	1	RG
621753	Ventolin inhaler	Inhale 2 puffs every 6 hours as needed	8/1	3	Hall	1	RG
620987	Hydrochlorothiazide 25 mg	1 tablet every day for blood pressure	7/23	4	Smith	30	PR
621753	Ventolin inhaler	Inhale 2 puffs every 6 hours as needed	7/1	4	Hall	1	RG
621634	Naproxen 500 mg	1 tablet twice daily as needed for knee pain	6/5	0	Hall	30	RG
620987	Hydrochlorothiazide 25 mg	1 tablet every day for blood pressure	6/1	5	Smith	30	PR
621075	Ciprofloxacin 500 mg	1 tablet twice daily for 3 days	5/30	0	Hall	12	RG
621074	Malarone	1 tablet every day	5/30	0	Hall	23	RG
620987	Hydrochlorothiazide 25 mg	1 tablet every day for blood pressure	4/28	6	Smith	30	PR
620986	Ventolin inhaler	Inhale 2 puffs every 6 hours as needed	4/28	2	Hall	1	PR

Name _HAROLD WALTERS_

Street _1000 GASKINS ROAD_

City _Richmond_ State _VA_ Zip _23238_

Main Street Community Pharmacy
Immunization Program

Phone (_804_) _885-9988_ (Male) Female

Birth date _4_ / _6_ / _44_ E-mail: _____

SS# ___-___-___ Medicare # _∅_

Allergies _____

Physician _Smith_

The following questions will help us determine which vaccines may be given to you today. Please check the appropriate answer. If any question is not clear, please ask us to explain it.

	DATE:			DATE:			DATE:		
	YES	NO	Don't Know	YES	NO	Don't Know	YES	NO	Don't Know
1. Are you sick today or do you currently have a fever or infection?		✓							
2. Do you have allergies to medications, eggs, thimerosal, any vaccine, or any vaccine component?		✓							
3. Have you ever had a serious reaction after receiving a vaccination?		✓							
4. Do you, any person who lives with you, or any person you take care of have cancer, leukemia, AIDS, hepatitis, or any other immune system problem?		✓							
5. Do you, any person who lives with you, or any person you take care of take cortisone, prednisone, other steroids, anticancer drugs or X-ray treatments?		✓							
6. During the past year have you received a transfusion of blood or plasma, or been given a medicine called immune globulin?		✓							
7. Do you have seizure or brain problems?		✓							
8. For women: Is it possible that you are pregnant or may become pregnant in the next month?									
9. Have you received any vaccinations in the past 4 weeks?		✓							
Did you bring your immunization record with you?	✓								

I certify that I am at least 18 years old and hereby give my consent to the staff of Main Street Community Pharmacy to administer the vaccine(s) listed below. I understand that it is not possible to predict all possible side effects or complications associated with vaccines. I, on behalf of myself, my heirs, executors, personal representatives, agents, successors and assigns hereby agree to release indemnify and hold harmless Main Street Community Pharmacy, Inc., its subsidiaries, divisions, affiliates, agents, officers, directors, contractors and employees from any and all claims arising out of, in connection with, or in any way related to the administration of the vaccines listed below.

I agree that Main Street Community Pharmacy will notify my physician of vaccines received.

I HAVE RECEIVED THE FOLLOWING VACCINE INFORMATION STATEMENTS AND EXPLANATION OF POSSIBLE ADVERSE EFFECTS:

VIS _Influenza_ VERSION(year) _current_ VIS _____ VERSION(year) _____

VIS _____ VERSION(year) _____

❖ **I AGREE TO WAIT NEAR THE VACCINATION LOCATION FOR APPROXIMATELY 20 MINUTES FOR OBSERVATION BY A MAIN STREET COMMUNITY PHARMACY'S PHARMACIST.**

Signature _Harold Walters_ Date _10_ / _20_ / ____

Date	Vaccine Name and Manufacturer	Lot # and Exp. Date	Dose, Route, Site	Administered by (and Title)
			R L	
			R L	
			R L	

CASE Figure 14–3 Immunization waiver form.

Adult Immunization Record Card

Name: Harold Walters   DOB: 4/6/44

Date	Vaccine	Dose/Site	Healthcare Provider
4/6/92	Td	0.5mL IM Deltoid	S Thomas, RN
8/10/02	Td	0.5mL IM Deltoid	J Roberts RN

Notes: Childhood vaccines administered w/o varicella.   S Thomas, RN

CASE Figure 14–4 Immunization record.

11. What are the contraindications and precautions for the newly recommended vaccines? Determine whether Mr. Walters has any precautions or contraindications to these vaccines.

12. Give the dosage, route, and site of administration for each of the recommended vaccines. Can you give all the vaccines today? Why or why not?

13. How could the pharmacist decrease the number of injections that Mr. Walters will need today?

14. Explain the procedure for administering intramuscular and subcutaneous immunizations to adult patients, including recommended needle sizes for adults.

15. What elements of documentation are required after administration of a vaccine?

16. Identify the elements of patient education that Mr. Walters should receive. Provide written and verbal counseling information.

17. What should the pharmacist do if Mr. Walters calls back the next day and reports an adverse effect such as a painful swollen arm that occurred after the vaccination?

18. Complete the Vaccine Adverse Event Reporting System form (vaers.hhs.gov/pdf/vaers_form.pdf).

19. When will Mr. Walters need to return for any needed booster doses or other vaccines?

20. What should you do if Mr. Walters does not return to receive his needed vaccines?

Additional Activities

1. Compare and contrast the differences in state laws concerning pharmacists' and student pharmacists' authority to administer immunizations.

2. Review the most current immunization recommendations for adolescents, and provide a summary of how your recommendations for this case would differ if this person were an 18-year-old female with no immunizations since kindergarten.

3. Evaluate the Institute of Medicine's reports about adverse effects from vaccinations, and determine what information you would provide to patients who are wary of vaccinations.

4. Investigate immunization coalitions in your area, and brainstorm how pharmacists could be involved with immunization coalitions.

5. Develop a business plan for implementing a year-round immunization program in a community pharmacy.

Information Sources

1. American Pharmacists Association. *Pharmacists as Vaccine Advocates. A National Certificate Program for Pharmacists Self-Study Learning Program*. Module 1. Rev 10th ed. Washington, DC: American Pharmacists Association; March 2006.

2. Centers for Disease Control and Prevention. Prevention and control of influenza. Recommendations of the Advisory Committee on Immunization Practices (ACIP). *MMWR Morb Mortal Wkly Rep.* 2008;57(Early Release):1–60.

3. Centers for Disease Control and Prevention. *Epidemiology and Prevention of Vaccine-Preventable Diseases*. Atkinson W, Hamborsky J, McIntyre L, Wolfe S, eds. 10th ed. Washington DC: Public Health Foundation; 2007.

4. Grabenstein John D. *ImmunoFacts. Vaccines and Immunologic Drugs 2007*. St Louis: Facts and Comparisons; 2006.

5. Centers for Disease Control and Prevention. Preventing tetanus, diphtheria, and pertussis among adolescents: use of tetanus toxoid, reduced diphtheria toxoid and acellular pertussis vaccine. Recommendations of the Advisory Committee on Immunization Practices (ACIP). *MMWR Morb Mortal Wkly Rep.* 2006;55(RR-3): 1–34.

6. Halperin S, Sweet L, Baxendale D. How soon after a prior tetanus-diphtheria vaccination can one give adult formulation tetanus-diphtheria-acellular pertussis vaccine? *Pediatr Infect Dis J.* 2006;25:195–200.

7. Centers for Disease Control and Prevention. Prevention of herpes zoster. Recommendations of the Advisory Committee on Immunization Practices (ACIP). *MMWR Morb Mortal Wkly Rep.* 2008;57(RR-5):1–30.

8. Centers for Disease Control and Prevention. Prevention of pneumococcal disease. Recommendations of the Advisory Committee on Immunization Practices (ACIP). *MMWR Morb Mortal Wkly Rep.* 1997;46(RR-8):1–24.

9. Centers for Disease Control and Prevention. A comprehensive immunization strategy to eliminate transmission of hepatitis B virus infection in the United States. Recommendations of the Advisory Committee on Immunization Practices (ACIP). *MMWR Morb Mortal Wkly Rep.* 2006;55(RR-16):1–33.

10. Centers for Disease Control and Prevention. Prevention of hepatitis A through active or passive immunization. Recommendations of the Advisory Committee on Immunization Practices (ACIP). *MMWR Morb Mortal Wkly Rep*. 2006;55(RR-7):1–23.

11. Centers for Disease Control and Prevention. General recommendations on immunization. Recommendations of the Advisory Committee on Immunization Practices (ACIP). *MMWR Morb Mortal Wkly Rep*. 2006;55(RR-15):1–37.

12. American Pharmacists Association. *Clinical Considerations. A National Certificate Program for Pharmacists Self-Study Learning Program. Module 3*. Rev 10th ed. Washington, DC: American Pharmacists Association; March 2006.

15 Global Health Threats and the Role of the Community Pharmacist

Katherine E. Werner

Objectives

1. Identify the top seven biological threats that the United States faces.

2. Identify patient-specific variables that may affect treatment choices, and design an appropriate regimen to treat exposure to a biological threat.

3. Identify/differentiate between a drug–drug, drug–nutraceutical, and drug–disease problems versus disease state progression in a given patient.

4. Design a treatment regimen for individuals exposed to an individual who has been exposed to a biological threat. Include the appropriate government agencies that should be notified.

5. Describe the pathophysiology of the biological agent, its clinical features and diagnostic criteria, progression of the disease, and appropriate medical management plus any caveats that differentiate the biological agent from the naturally occurring disease.

6. Describe tools used in prevention of exposures to biological agents (both pre- and postexposure) and any adverse reactions associated with these tools.

Scenario

You work as a community pharmacist at Drugs R Us and your license is up for renewal. To meet your biannual continuing education (CE) requirements of 32 hours for license renewal, you recently completed an online CE program "The Pharmacist's Response to Bioterrorism" hosted by the Maryland Board of Pharmacy. After completing the program, you feel prepared to handle any challenge you encounter.

Within the shopping center where Drugs R Us Pharmacy is located, there is a 24-hour walk-in clinic called Sick Call. Late one Friday you are staffing the pharmacy when a familiar patient Bob Barker presents at the counter to ask a few questions. You notice that he is sweating and is a bit flushed. Mr. Barker works for FedEx, loading trucks in the evenings. He tells you that for the last 24 to 48 hours he has felt as if he is getting sick. Mr. Barker says that he feels feverish and nauseated, and has had a cough for the last month, which has also worsened. He attributes the cough to seasonal allergies. He also has not had much of an appetite for the last 3 days and has been taking his prescription Motrin around-the-clock to help with his overall malaise. He would like you to recommend a nonprescription product to assist with his "flu-like" symptoms. He also expresses concern about being sick because his 10-year anniversary is in a few days. The patient excuses himself to use the men's room; while he is away, you review his current medication profile (Case Table 15–1).

After evaluating Mr. Barker's medication profile and prescription history, you have some targeted questions that you would like to ask him. You also make a list of possible nonprescription medications to discuss with him. When he returns from the bathroom, you review his medication allergies/drug intolerances with him to ensure that the list is complete. Mr. Barker confirms the information. He has been treated for both hypertension and benign prostatic hyperplasia for the last several years, and he is concerned about the effects of blood pressure medications on his libido. When asked about his cough, he says that he has been coughing for at least 2 to 3 weeks. He had bought some generic Robitussin DM, but it did not help. He tends to cough more at night than in the morning. Until 2 days ago the cough had been nonproductive; then he started coughing up some ugly-looking sputum. After work yesterday, he went to Sick Call and saw Dr. Baxter who gave him a prescription for an antibiotic. Mr. Barker has not yet filled the prescription because he does not like antibiotics. He also complains that lately because of job stress (mainly related to increased workload and longer hours), he has had terrible heartburn and feels that his Zantac is not working as well. The heartburn is relieved only by Tums, which he has been eating like they are "going out of style" at least 6 times a day.

Mr. Barker remarks that he has been exhausted and was so tired several nights ago at work that he dropped a package and the box split open, spewing a white powder all over his uniform. Because he was afraid of being reprimanded at

CASE Table 15–1   Prescription Medication Profile

Bob Barker
812 Hollins Street
Baltimore, MD 21201

Phone: 410-685-4040   **DOB:** 7-24-1965   **Insurer:** United Health

Allergies/Intolerances: Cough with Lotrel (2/22)

Nonprescription: Centrum and saw palmetto supplement

Rx No.	Drug Name	Directions	Date	R/F	Prescriber	Qty	RPh
653421	Ibuprofen 800 mg	1 tablet by mouth with food three times daily as needed	3/28	0	Johnson	90	KW
654987	Ranitidine 150 mg	1 tablet by mouth twice daily for acid reflux	2/22	1	Johnson	180	RL
655678	Vardenafil 10 mg	1 tablet by mouth 1 hour before intercourse	2/22	11	Johnson	36	RL
655677	Zestoretic 10/12.5	1 tablet by mouth every morning for high blood pressure	2/22	3	Johnson	30	RL
654521	Ibuprofen 800 mg	1 tablet by mouth with food three times daily as needed	2/22	1	Johnson	90	RL
654821	Alfuzosin 10 mg	1 tablet by mouth every evening for prostate	2/1	1	Johnson	90	KW
655288	Lotrel 5/10	1 tablet twice daily as needed for HSV outbreaks	12/3	3	Johnson	90	GH
654987	Ranitidine 150 mg	1 tablet by mouth twice daily for acid reflux	11/20	2	Johnson	180	RL
654821	Alfuzosin 10 mg	1 tablet by mouth every evening for prostate	11/3	2	Johnson	90	KW
654521	Ibuprofen 800 mg	1 tablet by mouth with food three times daily as needed	11/3	2	Johnson	90	KW
653287	Ranitidine 150 mg	1 tablet by mouth twice daily for acid reflux	9/30	0	Johnson	180	KW
653563	Tamsulosin	1 capsule by mouth every evening	8/30	0	Johnson	90	RL
653287	Ranitidine 150 mg	1 tablet by mouth twice daily for acid reflux	7/3	1	Johnson	180	RL
653798	Naproxen 500 mg	1 tablet by mouth every 12 hours as needed	6/1	0	Johnson	40	RL
653563	Tamsulosin 0.4 mg	1 capsule by mouth every evening	5/25	1	Johnson	90	KW
653421	Ibuprofen 800 mg	1 tablet by mouth with food three times daily as needed	5/10	3	Johnson	90	KW
653287	Ranitidine 150 mg	1 tablet by mouth twice daily for acid reflux	3/29	2	Johnson	180	RL

work by his new supervisor, he did not report the incident to anyone and re-taped the box before the evening shift supervisor returned from his dinner break. He continued to work in the area for another 4 hours. When asked when his cough began to worsen, he confirms that it worsened today at work. However, the fever and nausea began late the day before. Because he has been feeling worse, he wants to know if he should fill the prescription Dr. Baxter gave him yesterday (Case Figure 15–1).

Questions and Activities

1. Identify all patient-specific medical problems and the drugs used to treat them. Include problems that are not being addressed.

2. On the basis of the patient's current and past drug regimens, create a problem list that identifies all possible drug–drug, drug–nutraceutical, and drug–disease

Dr. Keith Baxter, MD
Sick Call
2003 N. Charles Street
Baltimore, MD 21201
410-685-2717

    For: Bob Barker (DOB 7-24-1965)
    Address: 812 Hollins Street, Baltimore, MD
        410-685-4040

    SIG: Cipro 500 mg
         Take 1 tablet po bid for 10 days
         #QS

Keith Baxter, MD
(electronic signature on file)

CASE Figure 15–1 Prescription for patient Bob Barker.

problems. What counseling tips might you want to reinforce with this patient?

3. Are any potential unidentified drug–disease issues not being addressed?

4. Currently, what are the top seven proposed biological threats to the United States?

5. How many categories of critical biological agents exist? Which category do the top seven threats fall under? What differentiates these agents from other infectious agents?

6. If you suspect that this patient has been exposed to a biological agent, which of the above threats would be the most likely etiology? What are the next steps to take?

7. What are the goals of pharmacotherapy, drug(s) of choice for this biological agent, and counseling pearls that need to be discussed with this individual? What alternative therapies exist?

8. What are the most common side effects of the drugs of choice for this biological agent?

9. What interventions are necessary to implement appropriate treatment in this individual and/or people exposed to this individual? Who is at risk?

10. How does one handle postexposure prophylaxis for individuals suspected to be exposed to this biological threat?

Additional Activities

1. Compare and contrast the differences in epidemiology of naturally occurring anthrax versus weaponized anthrax. What is the proposed staging on inhalation anthrax?

2. List and compare the clinical features of cutaneous anthrax versus inhalation anthrax versus gastrointestinal/oropharyngeal anthrax.

3. Discuss the evolution of the anthrax vaccine. Which vaccine is currently recommended? Who should receive the vaccine?

4. How can inhalation anthrax be differentiated from influenza-like illness and community-acquired pneumonia?

5. What therapeutic considerations must be considered when dealing with special populations such as pediatric patients, pregnant women, and immunocompromised individuals?

Information Sources

1. Kloner RA, Jackson G, Emmick JT, et al. Interaction between the phophodiesterase 5 inhibitors, tadalafil, and two alpha blockers, doxazosin and tamulosin in healthy normotensive men. *J Urol.* 2004;172(5 pt 1):1935–40.

2. Levitra (package insert). West Haven, Conn: Bayer Pharmaceuticals; 2005.

3. Braeckman J. The extract of *Serenoa repens* in the treatment of BPH: a multicenter open study. *Curr Ther Res.* 1994,55:76–84.

4. Gerber GS, Zagaja GP, Bales GT, et al. Saw palmetto (*Seronoa repens*) in men in lower urinary tract symptoms: effects on urodynamic parameters and voiding symptoms. *Urology* 1998;51:1003–7.

5. Brogden RN. *Seronoa repens* (Permixon). A review of its pharmacology and therapeutic efficacy in BPH. *Drugs Aging.* 1996;9:379–95.

6. Salvetti A, Pendrilli R, Magagna A, et al. Differential effects of selective & nonselective prostaglandin synthesis inhibition on the pharmacological responses to captopril in patients with essential hypertension. *Clin Sci.* 1982, 63:2615–35.

7. Swartz SL, Williams GH. Angiotensin-converting enzyme inhibition & prostaglandins. *Am J Cardiol.* 1982; 49:1405–9.

8. Goldstone R, Martin K, Zipster R, et al. Evidence for a dual action of converting enzyme inhibitor on blood pressure in normal man. *Prostaglandins.* 1981;22:587–98.

9. Walden RJ, Owens CW, Graham BR, et al. NSAIDS and the control of hypertension: pilot study. *Br J Clin Pharmacol.* 1991;33:241P.

10. Duffin D, Leahey W, Brennan G, et al. The effects of indomethacin on the anti-hypertensive response to enalapril and lisinopril. *Br J Clin Pharmacol* .1992;34:456P.

11. Brown CH. Effect of rofecoxib on the antihypertensive activity of lisinopril [letter]. *Ann Pharmacother.* 2000;34:1486.

12. Gurwitz, JH, Everitt DE, Monane M, et al. The impact of ibuprofen on the efficancy of the antihypertension treatment with HCTZ in elderly persons. *J Gerontol A Biol Sci Med Sci.* 1996;51:M74–9.

13. Klassen D, Godfriend JL, Schona AA, et al. Assessment of blood pressure during treatment with naproxen or ibuprofen on hypertension patients treated with HCTZ. *J Clin Pharmacol.* 1993;33:971–8.

14. Knauf H, Bailey MA, Hasenfuss G, et al. The influenxe of anti-inflammatory drugs on thiazide-induced hemodynamic and saluretic effects. *Eur J Clin Pharmacol.* 2006;62:885–92.

15. Bhagat K. Effects of NSAIDs on hypertension control using ACE inhibitors and thiazide diuretics. *East Afr Med J.* 2001;78:507–9.

16. Kirchner KA, Brandon S, Mueller RA, et al. Mechanism of attenuated HCTZ response during indomethacin administration. *Kidney INT.*1987;31:1097–103.

17. Mihaly GW, Marino AT, Webster LK, et al. High dose of antacids (Mylanta II) reduces the bioavailability of ranitidine. *Br Med J.* 1982;285:998–99.

18. Desmond PV, Harman PJ, Gannoulis N, et al. The effect of antacids and food on the absorption of cimetidine and ranitidine. *Gastroenterology.* 1986;90:1393.

19. Donn KH, Eshelman FN, Plachetka JR, et al. The effects of antacids and propanotheline on the absorption of oral ranitidine. *Pharmacotherapy.* 1984;4:89–92.

20. Mantyla R, Mannisto PT, Vuorela A, et al. Impairment of captopril bioavailability by concomitant food and antacid intake. *Int J Clin Pharmacol Ther Toxicol.* 1984;22:626–9.

21. Hakim R, Tolis G, Goltzman, et al. Severe hypercalcemia associated with HCTZ and calcium carbonate therapy. *Can Med Assoc J.* 1979;121:591–4.

22. Drinka PJ, Nolten WE. Hazards of treating osteoporosis and hypertension concurrently with calcium, vitamin D, and distal diuretics. *J Am Geriat Soc.* 1984;32:405–7.

23. Meehan PJ, Rosenstein NE, Gillen M, et al. Responding to detection of aerosolized *Bacillus anthracis* by autonomous detection systems in the workplace. *MMWR Morb Mortal Wkly Rep.* 2004;53 (Early Release);1–11.

24. Centers for Disease Control and Prevention. Update: investigation of anthrax associated with intentional exposure and interim public health guidelines. *MMWR Morb Mortal Wkly Rep.* 2001;50:889–93.

25. Centers for Disease Control and Prevention. Update: Investigation of bioterrorism-related anthrax and interim guidelines for exposure management and antimicrobial therapy. *MMWR Morb Mortal Wkly Rep.* 2001;50:909–19.

26. Conoj, Cragan JD, Jamieson DJ, et al. Prophylaxis and treatment of pregnant women for emerging infections and bioterrorism emergencies. *Emerg Infect Dis.* 2006;12:1631–7.

27. Mayer TA, Bersoff-Matcha S, Murphy C, et al. Clinical presentation of inhalational anthrax following bioterrorism exposure: report of 2 surviving patients. *JAMA.* 200128;286:2549–53.

28. Guarner J, Jerrigan JA, Shieh, et al. Pathology and pathogenesis of bioterrorism-related inhalational anthrax. *Am J Pathol.* 2003;163:701–9.

29. LaForce MF. Anthrax. *Clin Infect Dis.* 1994;19:1009–14.

30. Young JAT, Collier RJ. Attacking anthrax, *Sci Am.* 2002;286:48–9.

31. Cieslak TJ, Eitzen EM. Clinical and epidemiological principles of anthrax. *Emerg Inf Dis.* 1999;5:552–5.

32. Inglesby TV, Henderson DA, Bartlett JG, et al. Anthrax as a biological weapon. *JAMA.* 1999;281:1735–45.

33. Inglesby TV, O'Toole T, Henderson DA, et al. Anthrax as a biological weapon, 2002. updated recommendations for management. *JAMA.* 2002;287:2236–52.

34. Jernigan JA, Stephens DS, Ashford DA, et al. Bioterrorism-related inhalational anthrax: the first 10 cases reported in the United States. *Emerg Infect Dis.* 2001;7:933–44.

35. Centers for Disease Control and Prevention. Update: Investigation of bioterrorism-related anthrax – Connecticut, 2001. *MMWR Morb Mortal Wkly Rep.* 2001;50:1077–9.

36. Joellenbeck LM, Zwanziger L, Durch JS, et al. The anthrax vaccine: is it safe? Does it work? Washington DC: National Academies Press; 2002.

37. Demicheli V, Rivetti D, Deeks JJ, et al. The effectiveness and safety of vaccines against human anthrax: a systematic review. *Vaccine.* 1998;16:880–4.

38. Centers for Disease Control and Prevention. Use of anthrax vaccine in the US: recommendations of the Advisory Committee on Immunization Practices. *MMWR Morb Mortal Wkly Rep.* 2000;49 (RR-15):1–20.

39. Khan AS, Sage MJ, Groseclose SL, et al. Biological and chemical terrorism: strategic plan for preparedness and response. *MMWR Morb Mortal Wkly Rep.* 2000;49(RR-4):1–14.

40. Kaufmann AF, Meltzer MI, Schmid GP. The economic impact of a bioterrorist attack: are prevention and postattack intervention programs justifiable? *Emerg Inf Dis.* 1997;3:83–94.

41. Hupert N, Cuomo J, Callahan MA, et al. *Community-Based Mass Prophylaxis: A Planning Guide for Public Health Preparedness.* Rockville, MD: Agency for Healthcare Research and Quality; August 2004. AHRQ Publication No. 04-0044.

42. Centers for Disease Control and Prevention. Emergency Preparedness and Response. Available at: http://www.bt.cdc.gov. Last accessed November 1, 2008.

43. Agency for Healthcare Research and Quality. Bioterrorism and Other Public Health Emergencies: Tools and Models for Planning and Preparedness. Community-Based Mass Prophylaxis. A Planning Guide for Public Health Preparedness. Available at: http://www.ahrq.gov/research/cbmprophyl. Last accessed November 1, 2008.

16 Nutrition

Renee Ahrens Thomas

Objectives

1. Summarize the 2005 Dietary Guidelines for Americans in the areas of calorie, fat, and sodium intake.

2. Review a completed food diary and suggest basic changes that can decrease calories, fat, and salt.

3. Identify guides that can help direct the choice of proper portion sizes.

4. Outline a monitoring plan, including monitoring parameters, for someone who has requested help in modifying his or her diet.

Scenario

You are a community pharmacist at a local retail pharmacy. As one of six pharmacists in a busy store, you rotate duties with the other pharmacists. Some days you dispense prescriptions; other days you work with patients in the clinical office. Today is your day to dispense prescriptions. Beth Smalley, a new patient to your pharmacy, brings in a script for atenolol 25 mg, 1 tablet daily, #30, no refills. After you fill it, you spend some time counseling her on the medication. When you ask her about her diet and physical activity plans, she confesses that she exercises on a fairly regular basis but has "absolutely no idea" where to start with her diet. You talk with her about your pharmacy's clinical services and suggest that she make an appointment to come in and talk about her diet. She asks when you will next be in the clinical office and schedules an appointment for the end of the week. Because you will be talking with her about her diet, you hand her several blank food diaries, and ask her to record everything that she eats over the next few days before she comes in for her appointment.

During Mrs. Smalley's initial visit to your clinical services office, you take a brief medical and medication history. She is a 45-year-old African American female who has an unremarkable past medical history. Currently, she is taking a multivitamin daily. She tells you that over the last 10 years, both her weight and blood pressure have increased. The doctor just diagnosed her with hypertension. This diagnosis concerns her because her father died of a heart attack in his early 50s. In addition, her brother was diagnosed with hypertension last month, prompting her to see her physician for a blood pressure check. Her blood pressure today is 150/80 (adult cuff, left arm, sitting).

Mrs. Smalley says that she tries to exercise four times a week. Currently, she is walking for 20 minutes at a time but plans to increase the duration of exercise as she can. Her diet is variable. She and her husband enjoy eating out; they eat out four times a week. She says that her weakness is chocolate and salty foods; she "can't go more than a few hours without a snack." Because she and her husband are "empty-nesters," they often eat in front of the television. She does not like vegetables very much but does eat a few fruits. Her husband enjoys red meat, so they eat about four servings a week. Her dairy intake is erratic, with most of it coming from yellow cheeses. When you ask her about her food diaries, she pulls out yesterday's diary (Case Table 16–1).

Questions and Activities

1. On the basis of the patient's presentation, identify the problem for which she seeks help today.

2. What are the goals of therapy for this patient?

3. Identify available treatment alternatives for this patient's problem.

4. Identify the interventions needed to solve the problem and the anticipated outcomes of this intervention.

5. According to the 2005 Dietary Guidelines for Americans[1]:

   a. What is the patient's estimated daily caloric requirement?
   b. How many servings of fruits and vegetables, whole grains, and dairy products should she consume a day?
   c. What percentage of her daily calories should come from total fat and saturated fat?
   d. What should be her daily intake limit for sodium?
   e. What should be her daily alcohol consumption?

CASE Table 16–1   Sample Food Diary

Date: 5/26

Description of Food Intake (Including Drinks)	Time	Emotions
Breakfast	7:30 am	Tired and hungry
Egg and Cheese McMuffin		
Orange juice		
Coffee with creamer and sugar		
Lunch	12:00 pm	Hungry
Peanut butter sandwich on white bread		
Apple		
Potato chips		
Coke (12-ounce)		
Two chocolate chip cookies		
Dinner	6:00 pm	A little hungry
T-bone steak (8-ounce)		
Garlic mashed potatoes		
Steamed carrots in butter		
Two glasses of red wine		
Chocolate cheesecake		
Snacks		
Snickers candy bar	10:00 am	Stressed
Bag of Doritos	3:00 pm	Bored
Popcorn	10:00 pm	

6. After reviewing the patient's food diary, identify some initial suggestions that you could give her?

7. The patient says that she would like to work on her snacking habits first. What are initial suggestions to help her change her snacking habits?

8. What are some easy suggestions to help a patient remember practical portion sizes?

9. What intervention (e.g., patient recommendation, call to provider or family member, contact emergency services, etc.) is necessary to implement this treatment?

10. What monitoring parameters available in the community pharmacy setting should be used to evaluate the therapy in this patient, including efficacy and adverse effects?

11. Develop an action plan for the patient; include short-term and long-range goals.

12. What are the pertinent topics to address during patient education?

13. Develop a follow-up plan for this patient; include the time to follow up and method of contact.

Additional Activities

1. Create a sample menu for this patient using the National Heart, Lung, and Blood Institute's online menu planner (hp2010.nhlbihin.net/menuplanner/menu.cgi).

2. Research and give examples of the following behavioral modifications and how they could affect this patient: self-monitoring, cognitive restructuring, stimulus control, problem solving, relapse prevention, and social support.

Information Sources

1. US Department of Health and Human Services, US Department of Agriculture. Dietary Guidelines for Americans 2005. Available at: http://www.health.gov/dietaryguidelines/dga2005/document/pdf/DGA2005.pdf. Last accessed July 24, 2008.

2. Gentry M. Portions in perspective. *Am Inst Cancer Res Newsl.* 2006;92:3.

17 Managing the Use of Dietary Supplements

Mario M. Zeolla

Objectives

1. Describe the federal regulations governing the production and sale of dietary supplements in the United States.

2. State four key issues that should be addressed during patient counseling on the use of any dietary supplement.

3. Discuss potential limitations of the available scientific evidence supporting the safety and efficacy of dietary supplements.

4. Given a patient who requests a recommendation for the use of a dietary supplement, develop a response that considers the available evidence regarding safety and efficacy of these agents, and patient-specific characteristics.

Scenario

Today is September 1. Greg Little, a 70-year-old white male, presents to the pharmacy counter with questions about the use of some "OTC medications" for his knee pain. The patient says that he started using Osteo Bi-Flex about a week ago. He is considering stopping use of the supplement because a friend who is nurse told him that these products do not work and may cause problems with his other medical conditions. He also says that he does not think the product has helped with his knee pain so far. He asks your opinion of the product and whether he should continue to use it or perhaps try some other supplement.

When asked about his medication use, Mr. Little says that he currently takes four prescription medications and three nonprescription products. The nonprescription agents include aspirin 81 mg, Osteo Bi-Flex two caplets three times daily, and Garlique 1 tablet once daily. The patient has no known drug or food allergies. His current prescription medications as listed in the pharmacy's dispensing software are shown in Case Table 17–1.

When questioned about his arthritis symptoms, the patient says he has had pain in his right knee for about a year, and that it recently worsened over the past few months. He denies pain at rest but rates his pain as 7 or 8 on a scale of 1 to 10 when he walks or jogs. He had initially used nonprescription pain relievers such as Advil and Tylenol to treat the pain, but he did not think they helped much. He was prescribed another medication for arthritis by his physician a few months ago; however, he stopped using it after a week because it bothered his stomach. He also says that his physician told him his cholesterol levels are "excellent." Mr. Little thought they could be better though and decided to begin taking garlic supplements a few months ago after hearing a commercial by Larry King on the radio.

Questions and Activities

1. On the basis of the patient's presentation and drug therapy, identify any medication-related problem(s) related to the dietary supplements that he is currently taking. Provide supporting details to explain each problem.

2. What intervention(s) (e.g., patient recommendation, call to provider or family member, contact emergency medical services, etc.) are necessary to resolve the medication-related problems identified? Explain the rationale for each intervention.

3. What monitoring measures available in the community pharmacy setting should be used to evaluate therapy in this patient, including efficacy and adverse effects?

4. Develop a follow-up plan for this patient; include time to follow up and method of contact.

The patient agrees to your recommendations but asks whether he should consider taking one of the other dietary supplements marketed for lowering of cholesterol.

5. a. What other dietary supplements have been studied for hyperlipidemia?

   b. Have any of these agents been shown to significantly reduce lipid levels?

   c. Would you recommend any of these supplements to this patient? Why or why not?

6. What additional information points and rationale should be addressed when counseling this or any patient who uses dietary supplements?

CASE Table 17–1   Prescription Medication Profile

Greg Little
2113 Vista Drive
Sarasota, FL 34236

Phone: 941-244-0105   **DOB:** July 10, 1937   **Insurer:** CIGNA

Rx No.	Drug Name	Directions	Date	R/F	Prescriber	Qty	RPh
631493	Altace 10 mg	1 capsule every day	4/21	5	Jones	30	KT
632192	Glucophage XR 500 mg	4 tablets every day	5/22	5	Jones	120	JN
631493	Altace 10 mg	1 capsule every day	5/22	4	Jones	30	JN
632411	Zocor 40 mg	1 tablet every day	5/23	5	Jones	30	JN
633234	Nabumetone 500 mg	2 tablets every day with food	5/30	4	Jones	30	KT
631493	Altace 10 mg	1 capsule every day	6/21	3	Jones	30	JN
632192	Glucophage XR 500 mg	4 tablets every day	6/21	4	Jones	120	JN
632411	Zocor 40 mg	1 tablet every day	6/21	4	Jones	30	JN
631493	Altace 10 mg	1 capsule every day	7/21	2	Jones	30	KT
632192	Glucophage XR 500 mg	4 tablets every day	7/21	3	Jones	120	KT
632411	Zocor 40 mg	1 tablet every day	7/21	3	Jones	30	KT
637321	Hydrochlorothiazide 25 mg	1 tablet every day	7/21	4	Jones	30	KT
631493	Altace 10 mg	1 capsule every day	8/23	1	Jones	30	JN
637321	Hydrochlorothiazide 25 mg	1 tablet every day	8/23	3	Jones	30	JN
632192	Glucophage XR 500 mg	4 tablets every day	8/26	2	Jones	120	KT
632411	Zocor 40 mg	1 tablet every day	8/26	2	Jones	30	KT

7. How are dietary supplements regulated in the United States? List four important aspects of these regulations that pharmacists should understand and be familiar with.

8. Review Case Figure 17–1. Compare and contrast how the requirements for dietary supplement labels differ from those for other nonprescription medications.

9. How is the manufacturing of dietary supplements regulated by the Dietary Supplement Health and Education Act of 1994?

10. What are the limitations of the current regulatory process in terms of ensuring that dietary supplements are safe?

11. What are the limitations of the current regulatory process in terms of ensuring that dietary supplements are effective?

Additional Activities

1. Identify reliable resources and references on dietary supplements for community pharmacists to use in their practice. Discuss advantages and disadvantages of each source from the standpoint of a community pharmacist.

2. Search the Internet for consumer information about dietary supplements. Evaluate the quality and reliability of information found in terms of authorship, attribution/referencing, currency, and potential bias.

3. Develop a business plan for incorporating a patient care program for dietary supplements in a community pharmacy setting.

Supplement Facts

Serving Size: 1 Tablet   Servings per Container: 30

Amount Per Serving		% DV
Vitamin C (as ascorbic acid)	**500mg**	**833%**
MegaImmuneBoost® Proprietary Blend 462mg		*****
Echinacea (purpurea), Zinc sulfate, Propolis, Andrographis, Panax Ginseng, Astralgus, Garlic (standardized to 1.3% alliin content), Great Plantain.		

* Daily Value (DV) not established.
  Other ingredients: Calcium phosphate, Cellulose, Stearic Acid, Polyethylene Glycol, Aluminum Lake, Titanium Dioxide, FD&C Red No. 10

CASE Figure 17–1 Sample dietary supplement label.

Information Sources

1. Richy F, Bruyere O, Ethgen O, et al. Structural and symptomatic efficacy of glucosamine and chondroitin in knee osteoarthritis: a comprehensive meta-analysis. *Arch Intern Med.* 2003;163:1514–22.

2. Clegg DO, Reda DJ, Harris CL, et al. Glucosamine, chondroitin sulfate, and the two in combination for painful knee osteoarthritis. *N Engl J Med.* 2006;354:795–808.

3. Hoffer LJ, Kaplan LN, Hamadeh MJ, et al. Sulfate could mediate the therapeutic effect of glucosamine sulfate. *Metabolism.* 2001;50: 767–70.

4. Stumpf JL, Lin SW. Effect of glucosamine on glucose control. *Ann Pharmacother.* 2006;40:694–8.

5. Shapiro K. *Natural Products: A Case-Based Approach for Healthcare Professionals.* Washington DC: American Pharmacists Association; 2006:115–33.

6. Stevinson C, Pittler MH, Ernst E. Garlic for treating hypercholesterolemia. A meta-analysis of randomized clinical trials. *Ann Intern Med.* 2000;133:420–9.

7. Steiner M, Li W. Aged garlic extract, a modulator of cardiovascular risk factors: a dose-finding study on the effects of AGE on platelet functions. *J Nutr.* 2001;131(3s):980S–4S.

8. Piscitelli SC, Burstein AH, Welden N, et al. The effect of garlic supplements on the pharmacokinetics of saquinavir. *Clin Infect Dis.* 2002;34:234–8.

9. Markowitz JS, Devane CL, Chavin KD, et al. Effects of garlic (Allium sativum L.) supplementation on cytochrome P450 2D6 and 3A4 activity in healthy volunteers. *Clin Pharmacol Ther.* 2003;74:170–7.

10. Ulbricht CE, Basch EM. *Natural Standard Herb & Supplement Reference.* Glucosamine. St Louis: Elsevier Mosby; 2005:388–403.

11. Caron MF, White CM. Evaluation of the antihyperlipidemic properties of dietary supplements. *Pharmacotherapy.* 2001;21:481–7.

12. Chen JT, Wesley R, Shamburek RD, et al. Meta-analysis of natural therapies for hyperlipidemia: plant sterols and stanols versus policosanol. *Pharmacotherapy.* 2005;25:171–83.

13. Berthold HK, Unverdorben S, Degenhardt R, et al. Effect of policosanol on lipid levels among patients with hypercholesterolemia or combined hyperlipidemia: a randomized controlled trial. *JAMA.* 2006; 295:2262–9.

14. Blendon RJ, DesRoches CM, Benson JM, et al. Americans' views on the use and regulation of dietary supplements. *Arch Intern Med.* 2001;161:805–10.

15. National Institutes of Health, National Center for Complementary and Alternative Medicine. Statistics on CAM Use in the United States,. Available at: http://nccam.nih.gov/news/camstats.htm. Last accessed July 16, 2008.

16. Shapiro K. *Natural Products: A Case-Based Approach for Healthcare Professionals.* Washington DC: American Pharmacists Association; 2006:1–14.

17. Taylor CL. Regulatory frameworks for functional foods and dietary supplements. *Nutr Rev.* 2004;62: 55–9.

18. Harris IM. Regulatory and ethical issues with dietary supplements. *Pharmacotherapy.* 2000;20:1295–302.

18 Dietary Supplements

Bella H. Mehta

Objectives

1. Identify potential drug–herb and disease–herb interactions through a comprehensive medication review.

2. Design a therapeutic plan for a patient interested in natural medicines.

3. Develop a communication plan to provide information about natural medicines to patients and health care providers.

4. List appropriate resources for evidence-based information on natural products.

Scenario

You are a pharmacist at Buckeye Pharmacy, an independent pharmacy situated within a medical office complex. Physicians practicing in adjacent offices include family medicine physicians, obstetrician/gynecologists, and cardiologists. Often, patients who come to your store are coming directly from their physician appointments with new prescriptions or are sent over by the physicians for in-depth counseling services. Your pharmacy offers disease management, wellness and prevention, and patient education for specialty pharmacy services (rheumatoid arthritis, hepatitis C, and multiple sclerosis) in addition to comprehensive medication reviews. You have a strong interest in complementary and alternative medicines, so physicians send many patients to you for medication therapy management services with a focus on natural medicines.

One afternoon, Asha Shah, a 54-year-old Indian woman, one of your regular patients, comes to the counter. She has a scheduled appointment with you today for a natural medicines consultation. She is excited to have an appointment with someone whom she considers to be unbiased and able to provide reliable information.

You have already pulled Ms. Shah's drug profile from your records (Case Table 18–1). Her nonprescription medication history includes:

- Aspirin 81mg 1 tablet every day.
- Vitamin E 200 IU 1 capsule every day.

- Oscal Ultra (600 mg calcium carbonate plus Vitamin D) 2 tablets every day.
- Triphala Extract (Triphala fruit extract [terminalia chebula, terminalia bellerica, emblica officinalis] 120 mg) 1 tablet three times daily.

Before today's visit, you had Ms. Shah complete a Buckeye Pharmacy Patient Profile (Case Figure 18–1), so you know the patient's current and past medical history.

Ms. Shah had indicated to you when she first made her appointment that she had a number of questions about natural products. She would like to know what to take to help her with her hot flashes—they are keeping her up at night. She tells you that she has stopped her prescription hormone replacement therapy (HRT) because of everything that she has heard on the news. In addition, her mother and one of her sisters died of breast cancer, which she believes was a result of their HRT use. She is also interested in stopping as many of her medications as she can and wants to know if a natural product is available for her heart. Her father had his first heart attack at 45 years and died of a heart attack at the age of 55 years. There is a strong family history of heart disease among uncles and cousins as well.

You know that she does not smoke and drinks only occasionally (one to two drinks per month). She is a vegetarian and does not want to consume anything that contains meat products including fish and poultry.

As you begin your appointment, you notice that she has picked up supplements in the herbal product aisle while she was waiting for you. She wants to know your opinion of these specific products: Eskimo-3 (fish oils containing eicosapentaenoic acid [EPA] and docosahexaenoic acid [DHA]), GarliX (6500 mcg of allicin and 14,300 mcg of alliin), Valer-A-Somn (valerian 150 mg), and EchniGold (echinacea angustifolia 200 mg, goldenseal 250 mg, vitamin C 9 mg).

She has also brought some of the laboratory work that you had requested. She participated in a work wellness fair last month and brought the results of her lipid profile.

- Blood pressure: 124/81 mm/Hg
- Fasting blood glucose: 96 mg/dL

CASE Table 18–1   Prescription Medication Profile

Asha Shah
123 Cannon Drive
Columbus, OH 43210

Phone: 614-293-5000   **DOB:** 4/3/52   **Insurer:** Anthem

Allergies/Intolerances: NKDA

Rx No.	Drug Name	Directions	Date	R/F	Prescriber	Qty	RPh
640140	Hydrochlorothiazide 25 mg	1 tablet by mouth every day	9/20	2	Wang	30	GB
640141	Metoprolol tartrate 50 mg	2 tablets by mouth every day	9/20	2	Wang	120	GB
640139	Lipitor 40 mg	1 tablet by mouth at bedtime	9/20	2	Wang	30	GB
641088	Z-Pak	2 tablets by mouth on day 1, 1 tablet daily on days 2–5	8/17	0	Chavez	1	WH
641977	Premphase	1 maroon tablet on days 1–14; 1 light blue tablet on days 15–28	7/6	6	Flanigan	1	GB
641977	Premphase	1 maroon tablet on days 1–14; 1 light blue tablet on days 15–28	5/30	7	Flanigan	1	GB
640140	Hydrochlorothiazide 25 mg	1 tablet by mouth every day	5/30	3	Wang	30	GB
640141	Metoprolol tartrate 50 mg	2 tablets by mouth every day	5/30	3	Wang	120	GB
640139	Lipitor 40 mg	1 tablet by mouth at bedtime	5/30	3	Wang	30	GB

- Total cholesterol (TC): 215 mg/dL
- Low-density lipoprotein(LDL): 137 mg/dL
- High-density lipoprotein (HDL): 47 mg/dL
- Triglycerides (TG): 155 mg/dL
- TC/HDL: 4.6

Questions and Activities

1. On the basis of the patient's presentation and drug therapy, identify the drug- or disease-related problem, and state the current drug therapy for the problem.

2. What are the goals of pharmacotherapy for this patient?

3. Identify the most appropriate resources that a pharmacist can use to find information on herbs and other dietary supplements.

4. Identify the different prescription treatments and natural alternatives available for the patient's drug therapy problems. Assess known safety/efficacy issues with the herbs and other dietary supplements, including potential drug–herb interactions, for the related conditions.

5. Complete a medication action plan for this patient prior to the appointment (Case Figure 18–2).

6. What drug(s), dosage form(s), schedule(s), and duration(s) of therapy are optimal for the treatment of this patient's problem?

7. What information should the pharmacist provide about the additional supplements that the patient picked up at the pharmacy (Eskimo-3 [fish oils containing EPA 210–270 mg and DHA 125–175 mg] 500 mg per capsule; GarliX [6500 mcg of allicin and 14,300 mcg of alliin]; Valer-A-Somn [valerian root 150 mg]; and EchniGold [*Echinacea angustifolia* 200 mg, goldenseal 250 mg, vitamin C 9 mg]) and the product that she is already using (Triphala Extract containing triphala fruit extract [*Terminalia chebula, Terminalia bellerica, Emblica officinalis*] 120 mg 1 tablet three times daily)?

8. What monitoring parameters available in the community pharmacy setting should be used to evaluate therapy in this patient, including efficacy and adverse effects? What monitoring parameters should the pharmacist recommend that the patient discuss with her physician?

9. What nondrug therapies or lifestyle modifications might be useful in managing the patient's problem?

10. What are the pertinent topics to address during patient education?

Buckeye Pharmacy
1 Scarlet Way
Columbus, OH 43210
(614) 293-8000

PATIENT PROFILE SHEET

Patient Information

Shah	Asha	B	Gender: M (F)
Pt Name (Last)	(First)	(MI)	

123 Canon Dr.   Columbus   OH   Phone#: 293-5000
(Street)   (City)   (State)

DOB: 4/3/52   SS#_____   Ht 60   Wt 154

Patient Medical Information

Please indicate which of the following medical conditions you have been told by a physician that you have:

- ☐ Angina (Chest pain)
- ☐ Asthma
- ☐ A.fib/irregular heart rate
- ☐ Blood clots
- ☐ Cancer
- ☐ CHF
- ☐ Depression

- ☐ Diabetes
- ☐ Epilepsy
- ☐ GERD
- ☐ Glaucoma
- ☑ High blood pressure
- ☑ High cholesterol
- ☐ Kidney disease

- ☐ Liver disease
- ☐ Migraines
- ☐ Nervous disorders
- ☐ Obstructive lung disorder
- ☐ Thyroid disorders
- ☐ Ulcers
- ☐ Other:

Please indicate if you are allergic to any of the following and the reaction that you had:

- ☐ Aspirin_____
- ☐ Codeine_____
- ☐ Erythromycin_____
- ☐ Others(please describe):_____ None

- ☐ Penicillin_____
- ☐ Sulfa_____
- ☐ Tetracyline_____

CASE Figure 18–1 Sample pharmacy patient profile. *(Continued)*

11. Develop a follow-up plan for this patient; include time to follow up or method of contact.

12. What should be included in documentation to communicate natural product recommendations to the patient's physicians?

Additional Activities

1. Investigate which of the following herbs or dietary supplements have some evidence for safety and efficacy: green tea, ginger, ginkgo biloba, glucosamine and chondroitin, and peppermint.

Family History

Is there is history of any of the following diseases in your mother, father, brother(s) or sisters (s)?:

Disease	N	Y	Don't know
Heart attack	☐N	☑Y	☐Don't know
Stroke	☑N	☐Y	☐Don't know
Diabetes	☑N	☐Y	☐Don't know
Cancer	☐N	☑Y	☐Don't know
High cholesterol	☐N	☐Y	☑Don't know
Blood clot	☑N	☐Y	☐Don't know

Lifestyle Information

Are you pregnant? ☐Y ☑N ☐Attempting to conceive

Mark one: ☑Married ☐Divorced ☐Single

Occupation: _Convenience Store Assistant Manager_

Which form of tobacco do you use?
☐Cigarettes ☐Tobacco ☐Snuff ☐Pipes ☐Bidis ☑None

For how many years? _____ How much? _____

Do you drink alcohol? ☑Y How many drinks do you have each week? _1-2/month_
☐N

Do you follow any special diets? ☑Y Please specify: _Vegetarian – No meat products_ ☐N

Recent Hospitalizations

Year	Hospital	Reason

CASE Figure 18–1 *(Continued).*

Prescription Medications

Date	Medication name	How much	How often	Doctor	For what
	Hydrochlorothiazide	25mg	Daily	Wang	BP
	Metopral	50mg	Twice Daily	Wang	BP
	Lipitor	40mg	Daily	Wang	Cholesterol
	Prem-Phase	1 tablet	Daily	Flanigan	Hot flashes
	Z-pack	250mg	Daily	Chavez	Infection

Over-the-Counter Medications

Please indicate which of the following conditions you treat with non-prescription products:

- [ ] Allergies
- [x] Cough and cold
- [ ] Constipation
- [ ] Diarrhea
- [ ] Eye problems
- [ ] First aid
- [x] Headache
- [ ] Heartburn/stomach acid
- [ ] Intestinal gas
- [ ] Lice
- [x] Muscle aches/pains
- [x] Pain
- [x] Sinus congestion/sinus pain
- [ ] Skin conditions (e.g. poison ivy)
- [ ] Sunburn
- [ ] Temperature - fever
- [ ] Vaginal yeast infections
- [ ] Vitamins/minerals
- [ ] Other (please specify):
- [ ] Other (please specify):

Please indicate if you use any of the following herbs and dietary supplements:

- [ ] Bee pollen
- [ ] Coenzyme Q10
- [ ] Echinacea
- [ ] Fish oils/Omega-3
- [ ] Garlic
- [ ] Gingko biloba
- [ ] Ginseng
- [ ] Glucosamine
- [ ] Melatonin
- [ ] Peppermint
- [ ] Saw palmetto
- [ ] Soy
- [ ] St. John's Wort
- [ ] Valerian
- [ ] Alternative hormone replacement therapy
- [ ] Athletic enhancement supplements
- [ ] Weight loss supplements
- [ ] Protein powders/shakes
- [x] Other (please specify): Triphala Extract
- [ ] Other (please specify):

I confirm that the information provided above is accurate to the best of my knowledge. Because information changes periodically, I will inform the pharmacy of any changes that occur to the above information. I also authorize release of any medical or other information necessary to process and fill my prescriptions and other claims.

Signature: _Asna Shd_ Date: _10/3_

CASE Figure 18–1 *(Continued).*

Medication Therapy Management Service

Medication Action Plan
Patient: _____
Date: _____
Primary Physician: _____   Phone: _____

Medication-Related Issue	Proposed Action	Notes	Responsible Person	Contacted / Result of Action	Notes
☐ Adverse drug reaction ☐ Administration/technique ☐ Duplicate therapy ☐ Drug–drug interaction ☐ Formulary/lower cost ☐ Goals/monitoring: _____ ☐ Incorrect prescribed dose ☐ Incorrect prescribed med ☐ Patient nonadherence ☐ Untreated disease state ☐ Unnecessary medication ☐ Other:	☐ Contact provider ASAP ☐ Contacted provider via phone ☐ Sent/faxed letter to provider ☐ Disease education ☐ Referral to disease state management: _____ ☐ Follow up with patient ☐ Other: _____			**Contacted** ___ **Date** ___ **Result of Action** ☐ Intervention accepted ☐ Intervention denied ☐ Patient follow-up on ☐ Pending ☐ Lost to follow-up #1 ___ #2 ___ #3 ___	
☐ Adverse drug reaction ☐ Administration/technique ☐ Duplicate therapy ☐ Drug interaction ☐ Formulary/lower cost ☐ Goals/monitoring: _____ ☐ Incorrect prescribed dose ☐ Incorrect prescribed med ☐ Patient non-compliance ☐ Untreated disease state ☐ Unnecessary medication ☐ Other:	☐ Contact provider ASAP ☐ Contacted provider via phone ☐ Sent/faxed letter to provider ☐ Disease education ☐ Referral to disease state management: _____ ☐ Follow up with patient ☐ Other			**Contacted** ___ **Date** ___ **Result of Action** ☐ Intervention accepted ☐ Intervention denied ☐ Patient follow-up on ☐ Pending ☐ Lost to follow-up #1 ___ #2 ___ #3 ___	
☐ Adverse drug reaction ☐ Administration/technique ☐ Duplicate therapy ☐ Drug interaction ☐ Formulary/lower cost ☐ Goals/monitoring: _____ ☐ Incorrect prescribed dose ☐ Incorrect prescribed med ☐ Patient nonadherence ☐ Untreated disease state ☐ Unnecessary medication ☐ Other:	☐ Contact provider ASAP ☐ Contacted provider via phone ☐ Sent/faxed letter to provider ☐ Disease education ☐ Referral to disease state management: _____ ☐ Follow up with patient ☐ Other:			**Contacted** ___ **Date** ___ **Result of Action** ☐ Intervention accepted ☐ Intervention denied ☐ Patient follow-up on ☐ Pending ☐ Lost to follow-up #1 ___ #2 ___ #3 ___	

CASE Figure 18–2 Sample medication action plan. (*Source:* Adapted from The Ohio State University College of Pharmacy Clinical Partners Program.)

2. You are put in charge of ordering herbal medications to stock in the community pharmacy. How do you evaluate which products to stock in the pharmacy?

3. Search the Internet to learn what information consumers might find about herbal medications.

4. Develop a business plan for incorporating a patient care program for the herbal medications.

5. Identify pertinent literature about HRT, and discuss the risk versus benefit.

Information Sources

1. National Institutes of Health, National Heart, Lung, and Blood Institute. Third Report of the National Cholesterol Education Program Expert Panel on Detection, Evaluation, and Treatment of High Blood Cholesterol in Adults (ATP III): Final Report. Bethesda, Md: National Institutes of Health; September 2002. NIH Publication No. 02-5215. Available at: http://www.nhlbi.nih.gov/guidelines/cholesterol/atp3full.pdf. Last accessed November 10, 2008.

2. Grundy SM, Cleeman JI, Merz C, et al. Implications of recent clinical trials for the National Cholesterol Education Program adult treatment panel III guidelines. *Circulation.* 2004;110:227–39.

3. The North American Menopause Society. Treatment of menopause-associated vasomotor symptoms: position statement of The North American Menopause Society. *Menopause.* 2004;11(1):11–33.

4. Nappi RE, Malavasi B, Brundu B, et al. Efficacy of Cimicifuga racemosa on climacteric complaints: a randomized study versus low-dose transdermal estradiol. *Gynecol Endocrinol.* 2005;20:30–5.

5. Setchell KD, Brown NM, Lydeking-Olsen E. The clinical importance of the metabolite equol—a clue to the effectiveness of soy and its isoflavones. *J Nutr.* 2002;132:3577–84.

6. Chenoy R, Hussain S, Tayob Y, et al. Effect of oral gamolenic acid from evening primrose oil on menopausal flushing. *BMJ.* 1994;308:501–3.

7. Shuster J. Black cohosh root? chasteberry tree? seizures! *Hosp Pharm.* 1996;31:1553–4.

8. Hirata JD, Swierz LM, Zell B, et al. Does dong quai have estrogenic effects in postmenopausal women? A double-blind, placebo-controlled trial. *Fertil Steril.* 1997;68:981–6.

9. Baber RJ, Templeman C, Morton T, et al. Randomized placebo-controlled trial of an isoflavone supplement and menopausal symptoms in women. *Climacteric.* 1999;2:85–92.

10. Knight DC, Howes JB, Eden JA. The effect of Promensil, an isoflavone extract, on menopausal symptoms. *Climacteric.* 1999;2:79–84.

11. Komesaroff PA, Black CV, Cable V, et al. Effects of wild yam extract on menopausal symptoms, lipids and sex hormones in healthy menopausal women. *Climacteric.* 2001;4:144–50.

12. Harris WS. n-3 fatty acids and serum lipoproteins: human studies. *Am J Clin Nutr.* 1997;65:1645S–54S.

13. Wang C, Chung M, Balk E, et al. *Effects of Omega-3 Fatty Acids on Cardiovascular Disease Effects of Omega-3 Fatty Acids on Cardiovascular Disease.* Evidence Report/Summaries No. 94. AHRQ Publication Contract No. 290-02-0022. Bethesda, Md: National Library of Medicine; March 2004. AHRQ Publication No. 04-E009-2. Available at: http://www.ncbi.nlm.nih.gov/books/bv.fcgi?rid=hstat1a.chapter.38290. Last accessed November 10, 2008.

14. Yzebe D, Lievre M. Fish oils in the care of coronary heart disease patients: a meta-analysis of randomized controlled trials. *Fundam Clin Pharmacol.* 2004;18:581–92.

15. Kris-Ehterton PM, Harris WS, Appel LJ, American Heart Association Nutrition Committee. Fish consumption, fish oil, omega-3 fatty acids, and cardiovascular disease. *Circulation.* 2002;106:2747–57.

16. Stevinson C, Pittler MH, Ernst E. Garlic for treating hypercholesterolemia: a meta-analysis of randomized clinical trials. *Ann Intern Med.* 2000;133:420–9.

17. Gardner CD, Lawson LD, Block E, et al. Effect of raw garlic vs. commercial garlic supplements on plasma lipid concentrations in adults with moderate hypercholesterolemia: A randomized clinical trial. *Arch Int Med.* 2007;167:346-53.

18. Lucas EA, Wild RD, Hammond LJ, et al. Flaxseed improves lipid profile without altering biomarkers of bone metabolism in postmenopausal women. *J Clin Endocrinol Metab.* 2002;87:1527–32.

19. Jenkins DJ, Kendall CWC, Vidgen E, et al. Health aspects of partially defatted flaxseed, including effects on serum lipids, oxidative measures, and ex vivo androgen and progestin activity: a controlled, crossover trial. *Am J Clin Nutr.* 1999;69:395–402

20. American Heart Association. Cholesterol-lowering drugs. 2006. Available at: http://www.americanheart.org/presenter.jhtml?identifier=163. Last accessed November 10, 2008.

21. National Institutes of Health, National Heart Lung and Blood Institute. Seventh Report of the Joint National Committee on Prevention, Detection, Evaluation, and Treatment of High Blood Pressure (JNC VII). Bethesda, Md: National Institutes of Health; 2004. NIH Publication No. 04-5230. Available at: http://www.nhlbi.nih.gov/guidelines/hypertension/jnc7full.htm. Last accessed November 10, 2008.

19 Smoking Cessation

Denise Glasser

Objectives

1. List motivational factors for smoking cessation given a specific case.

2. Develop a comprehensive smoking cessation plan for a specific case.

3. Compare and contrast the various nicotine replacement products.

4. Compare the mechanism of action of nicotine replacement products with prescription medications.

5. Analyze patients' barriers to smoking cessation and devise an action plan.

6. List nonpharmacologic methods to deter a nicotine craving.

Scenario

Today, a pharmacy customer presents to your community pharmacy with a prescription for Chantix (varenicline). While at the drop-off window, the patient says that the physician assistant thought this medication was the best thing to help him quit smoking. The patient has not filled any prescriptions at your pharmacy before. His information is as follows:

Greg Nelson
13301 Gateway Drive
Gainesville, VA 20155
Phone: 571-262-5061   DOB: 07/10/66   Insurer: MedcoHealth
Allergies: NKDA

After transmitting the prescription to the insurance company, you receive a rejection notice stating that smoking deterrents are not covered under the subscriber's plan.

When the gentleman returns you find out the following:

- He is an information technology specialist and has been smoking for 25 years.

- He smokes on average a pack a day, but on a stressful day he may smoke 1 1/2 packs.

- He recently became engaged to a nonsmoker and would like to quit before his wedding 3 months from now.

- Although he is willing to spend some money on some kind of therapy to "keep the edge off," he does not want it to break the bank.

- He smokes most of his cigarettes on his drive into work and back home. He can sometimes sit in his car for 2 hours if traffic is bad enough.

- At work he takes smoke breaks every 2 hours with his coworkers. It is at this time that he catches up on all his gossip.

- He smokes very little at night and weekends because he spends time with his nonsmoker fiancé.

Questions and Activities

1. On the basis of the patient's presentation and drug therapy, identify the drug- or disease-related problem, and state the current drug therapy for the problem.

2. What are the goals of pharmacotherapy for this patient?

3. Identify available treatment alternatives for the drug therapy problem.

4. Identify the intervention(s) to solve the problem(s) and the anticipated outcome(s).

5. What drug(s), dosage form(s), schedule(s), and duration(s) of therapy are optimal for the treatment of this patients' problem?

6. What intervention (e.g., patient recommendation, call to provider or family member, contact emergency medical services, etc.) is necessary for implementing this treatment?

7. What monitoring parameters available in the community pharmacy setting should be used to evaluate therapy in this patient, including efficacy and adverse effects?

8. What nondrug therapies or lifestyle modifications might be useful in managing this patient's problem? Identify barriers and triggers.

9. Using the 5 A's, develop an action plan for the patient; include short-term and long-range goals.

10. What are the pertinent topics to address during patient education?

11. How do the prescription medications bupropion and varenicline differ from nicotine replacement therapy?

12. List possible barriers to smoking cessation that a clinician might encounter, and propose action plans to eliminate them.

13. Develop an action plan for someone who has started smoking again after a cessation attempt.

14. List possible smoking triggers and actions to alleviate them.

Additional Activities

1. What are the risks of long-term use of smoking cessation products (i.e., a patient "cannot live" without putting a patch on every day)?

2. Patients who try to quit smoking often substitute food for cigarettes; develop an action plan to help patients maintain a healthy weight while trying to quit smoking.

3. Investigate how the treatment recommendations would change if:

   a. The patient was a pregnant female.

   b. The patient had failed multiple quit attempts.

Information Sources

1. University of California, San Francisco Schools of Pharmacy and Medicine. Rx for Change: Clinician-Assisted Tobacco Cessation. Available at: http://rxforchange.ucsf.edu. Last accessed October 25, 2008.

2. US Department of Health and Human Services. Treating Tobacco Use and Dependence: 2008 Update—Clinical Practice Guideline. Available at: http://www.surgeongeneral.gov/tobacco. Last accessed October 25, 2008.

3. Suchanek-Hudmon K, Kroon LA, Corelli RL. Smoking cessation. In: Berardi RR, McDermott JH, Newton GD, et al., eds. *Handbook of Nonprescription Drugs*. 14th ed. Washington, DC: American Pharmaceutical Association; 2004:1149–75.

20 Obesity

Renee Ahrens Thomas

Objectives

1. Identify the different body mass index categories to define underweight, normal weight, overweight, and obesity.

2. Apply the goals of therapy for an obese patient to a specific patient case.

3. Describe the different nondrug and drug treatments used for obesity.

4. Summarize monitoring guidelines for obesity therapy.

Scenario

You are one of three pharmacists employed by the Corner Drug Store, a small store that has been part of the community for 50 years. You know most of your patients well and have noticed that a growing portion of your population is becoming overweight or obese. Recently, you have had weekly questions about the best diet to use or whether a nonprescription weight loss product is effective. Because you have always been interested in the area of weight management, you decide to start a program to help patients lose weight.

Kara Brown is a 33-year-old female who noticed your advertisement for a weight management program in the local newspaper. She would like to enroll in the program because she has struggled with her weight for the last 10 years. Mrs. Brown gained weight with each of her three pregnancies and would now like to take off the extra weight.

You schedule an appointment with her and give her a patient history form, which includes a section on weight history, to take home and complete before she returns.

On her first visit for your weight management program, you note the following information on her completed form:

- *Medical conditions.* Hypertension for 3 years; occasional knee and joint pain.

- *Medications.* Hydrochlorothiazide 50 mg every day; occasional Motrin or Tylenol for knee and joint pain.

- *Allergies.* Penicillin.

- *Family history.* Father has heart problems and mother died young of breast cancer. Her younger brother and sister are both healthy.

- *Social history.* She does not smoke but occasionally drinks with friends on social occasions.

- *Weight history.* She has tried various diets with varying degrees of success in the past.

She lost 25 pounds with a high-protein diet but has since gained back the weight. The fad diets that she tried, such as the cabbage soup diet and the juice diet, did not work for her. She currently weighs about 50 pounds more than she did in her early 20s.

You sit down with Mrs. Brown to talk more about her history and lifestyle habits. She does not have much time or motivation to exercise. Her three children (ages 8, 5, and 3 years) keep her extremely busy with various activities. Because of their on-the-go schedule, they eat out on average 3 days a week. She does not mind cooking but generally makes foods that are easy to prepare such as "Meals-in-a-Bag." Her knee and joint pain has developed in the last few years; she has noticed the pain more as she has gained more weight. Her high blood pressure also developed when she started gaining weight, but her doctor told her it is currently controlled. When asked about her social drinking, Mrs. Brown says that she drinks probably once a month with friends. She generally has a couple of beers with them when they have dinner together. She has tried diets in the past to lose weight but has always had a hard time "sticking to them." The high-protein diet worked for awhile, but she got tired of eating only meat and cheese. She then tried some fad diets and a chitosan product, but they did not help her to lose any weight.

Mrs. Brown would like to lose the 50 pounds that she has gained since her first pregnancy. If possible, she would like to lose it before her sister's wedding, which is in 6 months. She asks whether there are any nonprescription medications that she can take to help her lose weight.

At today's session, you weigh Mrs. Brown and measure her height. She is 5 feet 6 inches tall and weighs 190 pounds. From that data, you calculate a body mass index of 30.7. Her waist circumference (over clothing) is 37 inches. Her blood pressure is 124/86 (large cuff, right arm, sitting).

Questions and Activities

1. On the basis of the patient's presentation, identify the medical condition that she is seeking help for today.

2. What are the goals of therapy for the patient?

3. Identify the interventions needed to solve the problem and the anticipated outcomes.

4. Identify the treatment alternatives available for the patient's condition.

5. What nondrug therapies or lifestyle modifications might be useful in managing this patient's condition?

6. Is this patient a candidate for drug therapy? Why or why not?

7. If drug therapy is used, what drugs, dosage forms, schedules, and duration of therapy are optimal for the treatment of this patient's condition?

8. Should nonprescription weight loss medications be used in this patient? Why or why not?

9. What intervention (e.g., patient recommendation, call to provider or family member, contact emergency services, etc.) is necessary for implementing this treatment?

10. What monitoring parameters available in the community pharmacy setting should be used to evaluate therapy in this patient, including efficacy and adverse effects?

11. Develop an action plan for the patient; include short-term and long-range goals.

12. What are the pertinent topics to address during patient education?

13. Develop a follow-up plan for this patient; include time to follow up and method of contact.

Additional Activities

1. Take the "Portion Distortion" quizzes found at the National Heart, Lung, and Blood Institute's Web site (hp2010.nhlbihin.net/portion).

2. List which medications can cause or contribute to weight gain.

3. Research the safety and efficacy of alternative treatments for weight loss.

4. Compare and contrast the different popular diets (e.g., Atkins, South Beach, Grapefruit, etc.).

5. Develop a counseling plan, including diet option, for the weight management product alli.

Information Sources

1. National Heart, Lung, and Blood Institute. *Obesity Education Initiative. Clinical Guidelines on the Identification, Evaluation, and Treatment of Overweight and Obesity in Adults: The Evidence Report.* Bethesda, Md: National Institutes of Health; 1998. NIH Publication No. 98-4083.

2. Mypyramid.com. United States Department of Agriculture. Steps to a Healthier You. Available at: http://www.mypyramid.gov. Last accessed October 25, 2008.

3. Institute of Medicine Food and Nutrition Board. *Dietary Reference Intakes for Energy, Carbohydrate, Fiber, Fat, Fatty Acids, Cholesterol, Protein, and Amino Acids.* Washington, DC: The National Academies Press; 2006. Available at: http://www.iom.edu/CMS/3788/4576/4340.aspx. Last accessed October 25, 2008.

4. US Department of Health and Human Services, US Department of Agriculture. *Dietary Guidelines for Americans 2005.* 6th ed. Washington, DC: US Government Printing Office; January 2005. HHS Publication number: HHS-ODPHP-2005-01-DGA-A. USDA Publication number: Home and Garden Bulletin No. 232. Available at: http://www.health.gov/dietaryguidelines/dga2005/document/pdf/DGA2005.pdf. Last accessed October 25, 2008.

5. Facts and Comparisons 4.0 [database online]. Drug monographs for sibutramine, orlistat, and the class monograph for anorexiants. St Louis: Facts and Comparisons. Available for subscribers at: http://online.factsandcomparisons.com/ index.aspx?. Last accessed October 2, 2006.

Section 4

Cardiovascular Disorders

21 Hypertension

Michael E. Ernst

Objectives

1. Develop a patient-centered care plan to optimize antihypertensive regimens to achieve goal blood pressure in patients with uncomplicated hypertension or hypertension accompanied by comorbidities.

2. Design a monitoring plan, including laboratory assessments and home blood pressure monitoring, for assessing therapeutic efficacy and safety of antihypertensive regimens.

3. Detect and resolve drug therapy problems in patients with hypertension, including barriers to patient adherence to therapy, occurrence of adverse drug reactions, and use of coexisting inappropriate therapies.

4. Evaluate the role of nonpharmacologic therapies and combination antihypertensive therapy regimens to achieve goal blood pressure.

5. Develop a strategy for communicating the efficacy and safety of a patient's antihypertensive regimen to other health care providers participating in the care of the patient.

Scenario

Marcy Jones, a 52-year-old white woman with known hypertension, comes to your community pharmacy today (9/15) with a prescription for a new potassium dose. When she gives the prescription to you, she says, "My doctor increased my potassium pills. These things are like horse pills and they smell and taste terrible. I don't know how I'm going to take all of them."

You have an interest in hypertension and have worked with several other patients of the pharmacy to help get their blood pressures under control. You offer to sit down with Ms. Jones and find out more information about how she is doing. She agrees.

Case Table 21–1 provides a printout of her prescription drug profile. In addition to her prescription medications,

Ms. Jones reports taking the following nonprescription medications on a regular basis:

- Naproxen 500 mg three times daily as needed for knee pain

- Loratadine 10 mg/day for allergies

- Pseudoephedrine 60 mg twice daily as needed for stuffy nose

- Tums three times daily

- Multivitamin every day

While discussing Ms. Jones's conditions and medications with her, you offer to check her blood pressure. You check her blood pressure and record a reading of 144/96 mm Hg and a heart rate of 86 beats/min. When inquiring about whether she has checked her blood pressure levels elsewhere, she tells you that she checks it occasionally on the machine at the grocery store because she does not have her own blood pressure cuff. The last three measurements she wrote down during the past month were 145/90 mm Hg, 130/92 mm Hg, and 152/88 mm Hg.

Other information you obtain from Ms. Jones is that she is 5 feet 3 inches tall and weighs 170 pounds. She smokes one-half pack/day, which is reduced from the one pack/day that she smoked for many years. She drinks two to four alcoholic beverages per week. She has been on her current antihypertensive regimen for several months with the doses of the medications gradually increased during that time. She was previously on verapamil, which made her legs swell, and she tried benazepril, which was discontinued because of intolerable cough. In the course of discussing her blood pressure medications, you find out that Ms. Jones takes her hydrochlorothiazide in the evening. She usually has to get up at least twice at night to urinate. Since the medication was increased to 50 mg/day, she purposefully skips her dose from time to time.

Questions and Activities

1. On the basis of the patient's drug therapy, identify the medical problem(s) and the current drug therapy to solve the problem(s).

CASE Table 21–1   Prescription Medication Profile

Marcy Jones
811 10th Street
Anytown, IA 52242

Phone: 319-555-1212   **DOB:** 12/9/54   **Insurer:** Medicaid

Allergies/Intolerances: NKDA

Rx No	Drug Name	Directions	Date	R/F	Prescriber	Qty	RPh
621937	Hydrochlorothiazide 50 mg	1 tablet every day	9/1	1	Drury	30	SJJ
630120	Atenolol 25 mg	1 tablet every day	9/1		Drury	30	SJJ
621936	Dilacor XR 240 mg	1 tablet every day	9/1	3	Drury	30	SJJ
621451	Potassium chloride ER 20 mEq	1 tablet twice daily	8/8	5	Drury	60	SJJ
621937	Hydrochlorothiazide 50 mg	1 tablet every day	8/8	2	Drury	30	SJJ
630120	Atenolol 25 mg	1 tablet every day	7/24		Drury	30	SJJ
621936	Dilacor XR 240 mg	1 tablet every day	7/24	4	Drury	30	SJJ
621451	Potassium chloride ER 20 mEq	1 tablet twice daily	7/16	6	Drury	60	SJJ
621937	Hydrochlorothiazide 50 mg	1 tablet every day	6/28	3	Drury	30	SJJ
621936	Dilacor XR 240 mg	1 tablet every day	6/28	5	Drury	30	SJJ
621451	Potassium chloride ER 10 mEq	1 tablet twice daily	5/25	4	Drury	60	SJJ
621453	Hydrochlorothiazide 25 mg	1 tablet every day	5/25	2	Drury	30	SJJ
621936	Dilacor XR 240 mg	1 tablet every day	5/25	6	Drury	30	SJJ
621451	Potassium chloride ER 10 mEq	1 tablet twice daily	4/25	5	Drury	60	SJJ
621453	Hydrochlorothiazide 25 mg	1 tablet every day	4/10	3	Drury	30	SJJ
621452	Dilacor XR 120 mg	1 tablet every day	4/10	6	Drury	30	SJJ
620338	Verapamil SR 240 mg	1 tablet every day	3/9	2	Drury	30	SJJ
614598	Benazepril 10 mg	1 tablet every day	2/18	2	Drury	30	SJJ

2. Identify drug-related or disease-related problem(s), the intervention(s) to solve the problem(s), and anticipated outcome(s).

3. What are the goals of pharmacotherapy for this patient?

4. Identify treatment alternatives available for the drug therapy problem(s).

5. What drug(s), dosage form(s), schedule(s), and duration(s) of therapy are optimal for the treatment of this patient's hypertension? For her hypokalemia?

6. What intervention (e.g., patient recommendation, call to health care provider or family member, con-

tact emergency medical services, etc.) is necessary for implementing this treatment?

7. What monitoring parameters available in the community pharmacy setting should be used to evaluate therapy in this patient, including efficacy and adverse effects? What laboratory monitoring parameters (and frequency) should be recommended? What monitoring parameters should be recommended to the patient for self-monitoring?

8. What nondrug therapies or lifestyle modifications might be useful in the management of this patient's hypertension? For her hypokalemia?

9. How would you advise the patient on her nonprescription medications?

10. During your discussion with the patient, she mentions that she does not understand why she just cannot take one drug to control her blood pressure. How would you respond to this comment?

11. What suggestions can be made to improve adherence with her medications?

12. Develop a medication action plan (MAP) for this patient; include short-term and long-range goals.

13. Suppose the patient also had diabetes. How would this affect your goals of therapy and MAP?

14. What are the pertinent topics to address during patient education?

15. Develop a follow-up plan for this patient; include time to follow up and method of contact.

16. In the course of working with the patient, she asks you about continuing to check her blood pressures. How would you advise her on differences in readings taken at home, a clinic, and a health kiosk with an automated blood pressure machine? What advice would you give her when selecting a home blood pressure monitor?

17. Suppose the patient's blood pressure reading in the pharmacy was 200/110 mm Hg. What questions should you ask when interpreting her blood pressure in the pharmacy? When and how would you triage elevated blood pressure readings obtained in the pharmacy?

18. Discuss the role of community pharmacists in the detection and management of hypertension.

Information Sources

1. Moser M, Setaro JF. Resistant or difficult-to-control hypertension. N Engl J Med. 2006;355:385–92.

2. Carter BL, Ernst ME, Cohen JD. Hydrochlorothiazide versus chlorthalidone: evidence supporting their interchangeability. Hypertension. 2004;43:49.

3. Chobanian AV, Bakris GL, Black HR, et al. The Seventh Report of the Joint National Committee on the Detection, Evaluation, and Treatment of High Blood Pressure: the JNC 7 report. JAMA. 2003;289:2560–72.

4. Calhoun DA, Jones D, Textor S, et al. Resistant hypertension: diagnosis, evaluation, and treatment. A scientific statement from the American Heart Association Professional Education Committee of the Council for High Blood Pressure Research. Hypertension. 2008;117:e510–26.

5. Trewet CB, Ernst ME. Resistant hypertension: identifying causes and optimizing treatment regimens. South Med J. 2008;101:166–73.

6. Williams B, Poulter NR, Brown MJ, et al. British Hypertension Society guidelines for hypertension management 2004 (BHS-IV): summary. BMJ. 2004;328:634–40.

7. Ouzan J, Pèrault C, Lincoff AM, et al. The role of spironolactone in the treatment of patients with refractory hypertension. Am J Hypertens. 2002;15:333–9.

8. Nishizaka MK, Zaman MA, Calhoun DA. Efficacy of low-dose spironolactone in subjects with resistant hypertension. Am J Hypertens. 2003;16:925–30.

9. Chapman N, Dobson J, Wilson S, et al. Effect of spironolactone on blood pressure in subjects with resistant hypertension. Hypertension. 2007;49:839–45.

10. Carlberg B, Samuelsson O, Lindholm LH. Atenolol in hypertension: is it a wise choice? Lancet. 2004;364:1684–9.

11. Ernst ME, Goerdt CJ, Carter BL, et al. Comparative antihypertensive effects of hydrochlorothiazide and chlorthalidone on ambulatory and office blood pressure. Hypertension. 2006;47:352–8.

12. Khosla N, Chua DY, Elliott WJ, Bakris GL. Are chlorthalidone and hydrochlorothiazide equivalent blood-pressure-lowering medications? J Clin Hypertens. 2005;7:354–6.

13. Chabot I, Moisan J, Gregoire JP, Milot A. Pharmacist intervention program for control of hypertension. Ann Pharmacother. 2003;37:1335–7.

14. Zillich AJ, Sutherland JM, Kumbera PA, Carter BL. Hypertension outcomes through blood pressure monitoring and evaluation by pharmacists (HOME study). J Gen Intern Med. 2005;20:1091–6.

15. Carter BL, Zillich AJ, Elliott WJ. How pharmacists can assist physicians with controlling blood pressure. J Clin Hypertens. 2003;5:31–7.

16. Yarows SA, Julius S, Pickering TG. Home blood pressure monitoring. Arch Intern Med. 2000;160:1251–7.

17. Staessen JA, Den Hond E, Celis H, et al. Antihypertensive treatment based on blood pressure measurement at home or in the physician's office. A randomized controlled trial. JAMA. 2004;291:955–64.

18. Pickering TG, Miller NH, Ogedegbe G, et al. Call to action on use and reimbursement for home blood pressure monitoring: a joint scientific statement from the American Heart Association, American Society of Hypertension, and Preventive Cardiovascular Nurses Association. Hypertension. 2008;52:1–9.

19. Fries E. Hypertension treatment: contributions and comments on challenges. J Clin Hypertens. 2004;6:45–6.

20. Pickering TG, Hall JE, Appel LJ, et al. Recommendations for blood pressure measurement in humans and experimental animals, part 1: blood pressure measurement in humans. Hypertension. 2005;45:142–61.

21. Pickering TG. Measurement of blood pressure in and out of the office. J Clin Hypertens. 2005;7:123–9.

22. Jula A, Puukka P, Karanko H. Multiple clinic and home blood pressure measurements versus ambulatory blood pressure monitoring. Hypertension. 1999;34:261–6.

23. Pickering T. Recommendations for the use of home (self) and ambulatory blood pressure monitoring. American Society of Hypertension Ad Hoc Panel. Am J Hypertens. 1996;9:1–11.

24. Graves JW. Blood pressure measurement in public places. Am Fam Physician. 2005;71:851–2.

25. Van Durme DJ, Goldstein M, Pal N, et al. The accuracy of community-based automated blood pressure machines. J Fam Pract. 2000;49:449–52.

26. Mangum SA, Kraenow KR, Narducci WA. Identifying at-risk patients through community pharmacy-based hypertension and stroke screening projects. J Am Pharm Assoc. 2003;43:50–5.

22 Congestive Heart Failure

Stefanie Ferreri

Objectives

1. Recognize the signs and symptoms of heart failure.
2. Identify medications that may exacerbate heart failure symptoms.
3. Counsel patients about appropriate use and monitoring parameters of medications.
4. Describe methods to establish collaborative relationships to help patients with heart failure.

Scenario

Earl Franklin, a 68-year-old white male with a 20-year history of type 2 diabetes mellitus and hypertension, asks to speak with the pharmacist. He says that he is not feeling "quite right" and wants to know what nonprescription products you can recommend to help him. You ask him what seems to be the problem, and he says that he is having shortness of breath (SOB) that may be due to his 8-pound weight gain over the past 2 weeks. You ask him if he started taking any new medications, and he says that his doctor added Avandia to his current insulin regimen for diabetes.

Questions and Activities

1. What do you suspect has happened over the past 2 weeks to cause the patient's SOB and weight gain?
2. What risk factors does the patient have that could cause heart failure?

3. What are some common drugs that can exacerbate heart failure or should be avoided in patients with heart failure?
4. The pharmacist advises the patient to go to his physician for a workup. Two days later the patient comes in and gives you a prescription for furosemide 80 mg taken by mouth daily. He also has prescriptions for lisinopril 5 mg taken by mouth daily, metoprolol XL 25 mg taken by mouth daily, and digoxin 0.25 mg taken by mouth daily. Is this optimal therapy for newly diagnosed heart failure?

You call Mr. Franklin to the pharmacy counter so you can counsel him about his prescriptions. When he approaches, you can visibly tell that he is still short of breath. You have some extra time to assess his symptoms, so you take him to your semi-private counseling area and use the SCHOLAR method to quickly assess the patient (Case Figure 22–1).

You conduct a quick assessment of his vital signs and note the following: sitting (for 3–5 minutes) blood pressure: 135/83 mm Hg, heart rate: 69 bpm; standing (for 1 minute) blood pressure 130/80 mm Hg, heart rate: 71 bpm.

5. On the basis of the patient's presentation, what is your assessment of the severity of his heart failure symptoms? Are the signs and symptoms indicative of right- or left-sided failure?
6. How would you counsel the patient about his medications related to heart failure?

Symptoms:	He gets "tired easily" and has to often stop walking to "catch his breath." He gets short of breath going up two flights of stairs, while shaving, and retrieving the newspaper; these tasks had once been effortless. He reports a nagging dry cough and difficulty sleeping.
Characteristics:	He often feels full before finishing meals, yet he reports an 8-pound increase in weight.
History:	One week ago, he had a flare-up of his osteoarthritis and began nonprescription ibuprofen. Since that time, he has noticed swelling around his ankles.
Onset:	These symptoms started about 4 days ago.
Location:	Weight gain is mostly in the periphery. You notice 1+ pitting ankle edema present bilaterally.
Aggravating factors:	Lying down makes his SOB worse.
Remitting factors:	Using two extra pillows helps him sleep.

CASE Figure 22–1 SCHOLAR method of assessing patient's symptoms.

7. What other suggestions about nonprescription products can you make?

8. This is the fourth patient that you have seen in the past 2 weeks with heart failure symptoms. You decide that it may be best to develop a service in your pharmacy to help meet the needs of this patient population. Describe your plan to develop a heart failure clinic at your community pharmacy.

9. As you begin marketing your service to patients, physicians and other pharmacists are skeptical about your ability to succeed. What evidence exists about the involvement of community pharmacists in the care of patients with heart failure?

10. Describe how you plan to contact the patient's physician to make a recommendation for the treatment intervention.

11. What monitoring parameters available in the community pharmacy setting should be used to evaluate the patient's therapy, including efficacy and adverse effects?

12. What nondrug therapies or lifestyle modifications might be useful in managing the patient's problem(s)?

13. How do you plan to charge for your heart failure program, and what evidence exists for pharmacist compensation?

Information Sources

1. Tang WH. Do thiazolidinediones cause heart failure? A critical review. *Cleve Clin J Med.* 2006;73:390–7.

2. Hollenberg NK. Considerations for management of fluid dynamic issues associated with thiazolidinediones. *Am J Med.* 2003;115(suppl 8A):111S–5S.

3. Nesto RW, Bell D, Bonow RO, et al. Thiazolidinedione use, fluid retention, and congestive heart failure: a consensus statement from the American Heart Association and American Diabetes Association. *Diabetes Care.* 2004;27:256–63.

4. Kahn SE, Haffner SM, Heise MA, et al. Glycemic durability of rosiglitazone, metformin, or glyburide monotherapy. *N Engl J Med.* 2006;355:2427–43.

5. Gerstein HC, Yusuf S, Bosch J, et al. Effect of rosiglitazone on the frequency of diabetes in patients with impaired glucose tolerance or impaired fasting glucose: a randomised controlled trial. *Lancet.* 2006;368:1096–105.

6. Slordal L, Spigset O. Heart failure induced by non-cardiac drugs. *Drug Saf.* 2006;29:567–86.

7. Cohn JN, Hohnson G, Ziesche S, et al. A comparison of enalapril with hydralazine-isosorbide dinitrate in the treatment of chronic congestive heart failure. *N Engl J Med.* 1991;325:303–10.

8. Effect of enalapril on survival in patients with reduced left ventricular ejection fractions and congestive heart failure. The SOLVD Investigators. *N Engl J Med.* 1991;325:293–302.

9. Effect of enalapril on mortality and the development of heart failure in asymptomatic patients with reduced left ventricular ejection fractions. The SOLVD Investigators. *N Engl J Med.* 1992:327: 685–91.

10. Packer M, Coats AJ, Fowler MB, et al. Effect of carvedilol on survival in severe chronic heart failure. *N Engl J Med.* 2001;344:1651–8.

11. Effect of metoprolol CR/XL in chronic heart failure: Metoprolol CR/XL Randomised Intervention Trial in Congestive Heart Failure (MERIT-HF). *Lancet.* 1999:353:2001–7.

12. Rathore SS, Curtis JP, Wang Y, et al. Association of serum digoxin concentration and outcomes in patients with heart failure. *JAMA.* 2003;289:871–8.

13. The effect of digoxin on mortality and morbidity in patients with heart failure. The Digitalis Investigation Group. *N Engl J Med.* 1997;336:525–33.

14. Pitt B, Waters D, Brown WV, et al. The effect of spironolactone on morbidity and mortality in patients with severe heart failure. Randomized Aldactone Evaluation Study Investigators. *N Engl J Med.* 1999;341:709–17.

15. Hagel H. Developing a practice implementation plan. In: Rovers JP, ed. *A Practical Guide to Pharmaceutical Care.* 2nd ed. Washington, DC: American Pharmaceutical Association; 2003:287–93.

16. Bouvy ML, Heerdink ER, Urquhart J, et al. Effect of a pharmacist-led intervention on diuretic compliance in heart failure patients: a randomized controlled study. *J Card Fail.* 2003:9:404–11.

17. Turner CJ, Parfrey P, Ryan K, et al. Community pharmacist outreach program directed at physicians treating congestive heart failure. *Am J Health Syst Pharm.* 2000;57:747–52.

18. Phillips SM, Marton RL, Tofler GH. Barriers to diagnosing and managing heart failure in primary care. *Med J Aust.* 2004;181:78–81.

19. Patel K, Sansgiry SS, Miller L. Pharmacist participation in home health heart-failure programs. *Am J Health Syst Pharm.* 2003;60: 2259–60.

20. Capo KM, Rutledge DR. Applying managed care performance measures in community pharmacy-based outcomes research. *J Am Pharm Assoc* (Wash). 1999;39:388–94; quiz 423–4.

23 Managing Hyperlipidemia in the Community Pharmacy

Marialice S. Bennett

Objectives

1. Recognize the resources needed to develop and implement a cholesterol management service.

2. Use the National Cholesterol Education Program's nine-step process to identify cardiovascular risks and establish treatment goals for patients.

3. Select an initial therapeutic regimen based on individualized patient information and the patient's current and target goal for low-density lipoprotein cholesterol.

4. Modify the therapeutic regimen on the basis of new information and progress toward the goals.

5. Communicate therapeutic interventions effectively to other health care providers.

6. Identify and be able to resolve common community pharmacy issues involving medications to treat hyperlipidemias.

Scenario 1

You practice in Buckeye Pharmacy, a busy independent pharmacy that provides retail pharmacy services and nursing home consultant services in the local area. You were selected to develop and implement a cholesterol screening and management program for your pharmacy. You create a mission statement, policy, and procedures, and determine that the pharmacy will provide point-of-care testing.

Questions and Activities

1. What resources, furnishings, and supplies will you need in your patient care center to provide the new cholesterol screening and management programs?

2. What regulations of the Clinical Laboratory Improvement Amendments (CLIA) of 1988 will you need to meet to provide point-of-care testing?

3. What Occupational Safety and Health Administration (OSHA) regulations will you need to meet to provide point-of-care testing?

You schedule your first wellness screening in your pharmacy. The marketing materials indicate the patient will receive a cardiovascular risk assessment; measurements of weight, blood pressure, and a fasting lipid profile; education; and any necessary referrals for a set fee.

Peggy Yetter is a walk-in patient for your screening service. The pharmacy technician has Ms. Yetter sign the consent form (Case Figure 23–1) and complete the cardiovascular risk assessment tool (Case Figure 23–2). The patient care pharmacy technician measures her height, weight, and blood pressure, and records the results on the cholesterol flow chart (Case Figure 23–3, first visit).

4. According to the guidelines of the National Cholesterol Education Program Adult Treatment Panel III (NCEP ATP III), what lipoproteins should ideally be measured during a cholesterol screening?

5. Ms. Yetter last ate 4 hours ago. What lipoproteins would you measure today for her cholesterol screening?

The patient care technician performs the point-of-care testing for the lipoproteins to be measured today and records the values in the cholesterol flow sheet (Case Figure 23–3).

You begin your encounter by reviewing the cholesterol flow sheet and the cardiovascular risk assessment tool (Case Figure 23–2) with the patient, clarifying any unclear points.

6. Does Ms. Yetter have any evidence of coronary heart disease (CHD) or a CHD equivalent?

7. What NCEP countable risk factors does Ms. Yetter have to determine her risk category?

8. Assess Ms. Yetter's 10-year CHD risk.

9. What additional risk factors for cardiovascular disease does Ms. Yetter have?

10. What advice would you give Ms. Yetter today about her results?

11. Compose a letter or fax to report Ms. Yetter's results to her primary care physician.

Patient Consent Form

During the CHOLESTEROL SCREENING, a pharmacist or student pharmacist under the direct supervision of a pharmacist or nurse will:

1.   Measure your cholesterol and/or blood sugar with a small sample of blood collected by means of a fingerstick.
2.   Discuss the results of your cholesterol test and answer any questions you may have about the results.
3.   Evaluate your risk factors for developing coronary disease.
4.   Discuss with you which risk factors you can change and which ones you cannot change.

The pharmacist may also follow up with your doctor if necessary to discuss the results of the program. No one else will be told about your results.

I understand the above information and I consent to participate in the cholesterol screening. I release any claim against any party in connection with this program.

Peggy Yetter   Peggy Yetter
—————————————   —————————————
Signature   Print Name

1st visit
—————————————
Date

CASE Figure 23–1 Patient consent form for cholesterol screening.

Ms. Yetter returns to the pharmacy in 10 weeks with a new prescription (Case Figure 23–4). She indicates that she made an appointment with her physician after the cholesterol screening at your pharmacy 8 weeks ago. She had fasting blood work completed 1 week after her appointment with her physician. Dr. May sent her a copy of her laboratory values (Case Figure 23–5) and this prescription in the mail. She is not sure what it all means.

12.   How would you advise Ms. Yetter today?

When Ms. Yetter arrives for her cholesterol management program appointment, the pharmacy technician obtains her insurance information and has her sign a consent form for release of medical information, assignment of benefits, and her responsibility for payment if her insurance company does not cover the service. The pharmacy technician explains the program's costs; measures the patient's weight, blood pressure, and waist circumference; and documents the information on the cholesterol flow chart (Case Figure 23–3, second visit).

In Ms. Yetter's chart you have the cardiovascular risk assessment tool, the cholesterol flow chart, and the return fax from her physician (Case Figure 23–6) with his goals for the patient. You request the food diary that Ms. Yetter has kept for the past several days (Case Figure 23–7). After providing an overview and goals of the cholesterol management program, you collect the following additional information.

Ms. Yetter is a busy professional woman who works approximately 60 hours a week. She is married with two grown children who no longer live at home. She has little time to incorporate physical activity into her busy schedule. When she has tried to walk 30 minutes a day in the past, her knees hurt so much that she just quit. She has three to five business meals a week and tends to carry in food rather than cook. She admits to a rich diet and a need for portion control. She has one to two glasses of wine every evening and smokes one pack of cigarettes a day. She has tried unsuccessfully to quit smoking three times before.

13.   What is Ms. Yetter's NCEP ATP III risk category?

14.   What is Ms. Yetter's goal for low-density lipoprotein (LDL) cholesterol? Justify the goal you have chosen.

15.   What percentage decrease in LDL cholesterol does Ms. Yetter need to reach her LDL cholesterol goal?

16.   What therapeutic lifestyle changes would you initiate today?

Cholesterol Screening Assessment Tool

Name:_____ Peggy Yetter_____**Today's Date:**__10/5/__

Address: ____ 2528 1st Street _____

City: ___ Columbus ___ **State:** __ Ohio____ **Zip Code:** _ 43210

Phone (day): _294-9090__ **Phone (evening):** _458-9078

Date of Birth: __9/28/50_ **Occupation:**___ investment banker__

Primary care physician: ___Dr. Fred May_____

Are you currently being treated for high cholesterol?
__ yes _x_ no

Do you currently exercise at least 30 minutes a day 3 times a week?
__ yes _x_ no

Do you eat a low-fat, low-cholesterol diet? __ yes _x_ no

Do you have, or have you had, any of the following:			
	Yes	No	When
Heart attack		X	
Angina		X	
Angioplasty		X	
Coronary artery surgery		X	
Abdominal aortic aneurysm		X	
Peripheral arterial disease		X	
Carotid artery disease		X	
Diabetes		X	

CASE Figure 23–2 Sample cholesterol screening assessment tool.

Risk Factors	Yes	No	Comments
I have smoked cigarettes within the past month.	X		
I have high blood pressure.	X		
I am a man 45 years or older.		X	
I am a woman 55 years of age or older.	X		
I have a close male relative (father, child, brother) who has had heart disease before the age of 55.		X	
I have a close female relative (mother, child, sister) who has had heart disease before the age of 65.	X		My mother had a heart attack at age 51. She also has diabetes.

Please list all the medications you are currently taking.		
Medication and Strength	**How often do you take it?**	**Start Date**
Lisinopril 10 mg	Once a day	About 10 years ago
Water pill	Once a day	About 10 year ago
Generic Claritin	Once a day	About 5 years ago
Generic Prilosec	Two times a day	About 5 years ago

Results of today's test (date _Ist visit_):
Total cholesterol ___260___ mg/dL HDL ___38___ mg/dL
Triglycerides _____ mg/dL LDL _____ mg/dL

BP 138/92

BMI = 29

CASE Figure 23–2 (Continued).

Patient Information

Name: Peggy Yetter	Patient ID:
Physician: Fred May	

Evidence of Atherosclerotic Disease

Coronary Heart Disease	Peripheral Vascular Disease	Carotid Artery Disease
☐ Myocardial infarction	☐ Arteriosclerotic occlusive disease	☐ TIA
☐ Myocardial ischemia	☐ Arteriosclerosis obliterans	☐ Stroke
☐ Coronary artery bypass grafts	☐ Renal artery stenosis	☐ Carotid bruit
☐ Coronary angioplasty		
☐ Angiographic evidence	☐ Diabetes	☐ >20% 10-year risk of CHD

CHD Risk Factors

☐ Male > 45 years old

☐ Female > 55 years old or premature menopause without estrogen replacement therapy

☐ Family history of premature CHD

☐ Current cigarette smoker

☐ Hypertension (>140/90 or on antihypertensive drugs)

☐ Low HDL cholesterol (<40 mg/dL)

Negative Risk Factor

☐ High HDL cholesterol (>60 mg/dL)

Risk Equivalent for CHD _____

Treatment Criteria	Diet	Drug	NCEP Goal
☐ No CHD with <2 risk factors	>160	>190	<160
☐ No CHD with ≥2 risk factors	>130	>160	<130
☐ With CHD or risk equivalent	>100	>130	{100

Monitoring

Date	TC	LDL	HDL	TG	TC/HDL	10-year risk%	Wt	Ht	BP	FPG	LFTs	Waist circumference
1st visit	260		38				180	5 ft 6 in	138/92			
2nd visit	268	180	38	250	7		168		135/90			37 inches
3rd visit	200	122	38	200	5.3		162		132/88		29	36.5 inches

CASE Figure 23–3 Cholesterol flow sheet.

CASE Figure 23–4 Prescription for patient Peggy Yetter.

Lipid Studies	From Doctor's Appointment
Cholesterol (<200 mg/dL)	268
HDL cholesterol (>60 mg/dL)	38
Triglycerides (<150 mg/dL)	250
LDL cholesterol, calculated (0–99 mg/dL)	180
Ratio TC/HDL (<4.5)	7
Chemistry	
ALT (8–35 U/L)	28
AST (5–34 U/L)	22
CK (0–189 U/L)	23
BUN (6–20 mg/dL)	14
Creatinine (0.6–1.1 mg/dL)	0.8
Glucose (74–106 mg/dL)	88
Endocrinology	
TSH (0.5–4.7 µg/mL)	2.2

Peggy, your cholesterol numbers are high—start the enclosed prescription.

Dr. Fred May

CASE Figure 23–5 Laboratory report with physician's note.

Cholesterol Management Service
Patient Care Pharmacy
College of Pharmacy
456 W. 10th. Ave., Columbus, OH 43210
Phone: 614-293-5585/Fax: 614-293-3170

Statement of Medical Need

Patient Name: __Peggy Yetter__   **Medical Number:** _____

Diagnosis: __Hyperlipidemia__   **ICD-9 Code:** _____272.0_____

Goals of Intervention: *Check one of the following.*

/ **X** / Please set target levels for total cholesterol, LDL, HDL, Triglycerides, and Total Cholesterol to HDL Ratio according to National Cholesterol Education Program (NCEP) Guidelines

or

/   / Please assist patient in working to achieve the following desired levels:

    Total Cholesterol: _____   LDL: _____   HDL: _____

    Triglycerides: _____   Total Cholesterol/HDL Ratio: _____

Other Goals: _____
_____
_____

/ **X** / Please refer patient to dietitian for diet assessment and management if needed.

Anticipated Duration of Therapy: *Each visit includes a lipid profile.*

/ **X** / 1st Year: Intensive therapy (1 visit every month for 3 months, then 1 visit every 3 months) Total: 6 sessions.

/   / Follow-Up Year: Maintenance therapy (1 visit every 3 months) Total: 4 sessions

_____

I am referring this patient to the Patient Care Pharmacy to monitor his/her therapy regarding cholesterol management.
I consider this program to be a necessary part of this patient's medical care.

Referring Physician's Signature: __*Dr. Fred May*__   Date: _____

Referring Physician's Printed Name: __Dr. Fred May__

Address: _____4808 N. High St._____   City/State/Zip: _____Columbus, OH 43214_____

Phone: _____268-1161_____   Pager: _____   Fax: ____268-1162____

CASE Figure 23–6 Return fax from physician.

Date	Breakfast	Lunch	Dinner	Snacks
Day 2	*Out:* 3-egg omelet 3 bacon strips Hash browns Coffee with cream	*At my desk:* Big Mac Large fries Milk shake	*Out:* Fried calamari 16-ounce steak Baked potato with sour cream and butter 2 glasses of wine 3 rolls	One-half cup nuts Chocolate bar
Day 4	*Out:* 3 waffles with syrup and whipped cream 2 sausage patties Juice Coffee with cream	*At my desk:* 3 slices of pizza Salad with ranch dressing Large cola	*Out:* Spaghetti Salad 2 pieces of garlic bread Chocolate cake 3 glasses of wine	Chocolate bar Popcorn
Day 6	*Out:* Bagel with cream cheese Juice Café mocha	Skipped	*Out:* Shrimp cocktail Pasta with alfredo sauce Green beans 3 rolls Crème brûlée 2 glasses of wine	One-half cup nuts Chocolate bar
Day 7	*Out:* Bagel with cream cheese Juice Café mocha	*At my desk:* 3 pieces of fried chicken Cole slaw Mashed potatoes and gravy Large cola	*Out:* Egg roll Sweet and sour soup Chicken almond with fried rice 2 glasses of wine	Potato chips 2 cookies Chocolate bar

CASE Figure 23–7 Patient's food diary.

17. What will be your monitoring plan for the next visit?

18. When would you have Ms. Yetter return for her next visit?

At the end of the visit, you summarize the visit and the goals Ms. Yetter has set. You direct her to the pharmacy technician to complete the billing process and schedule the next appointment.

Ms. Yetter returns for her follow-up appointment. The patient care technician measures the patient's weight, waist circumference, and blood pressure; the technician then documents these measurements and the results of her fasting lipid profile and liver function tests (LFTs) on the cholesterol flow chart (Case Figure 23–3, third visit).

You review Ms. Yetter's goals with her and determine what is going well. She claims to have made changes in her diet and to be decreasing her portion sizes, especially when she has business dinners. She is walking about 15 minutes three times a week. She has not yet decided to stop smoking.

19. A friend told Ms. Yetter that she should not drink grapefruit juice while taking cholesterol-lowering medication. How would you advise the patient?

20. List the therapeutic options you would choose from today to enhance Ms. Yetter's cholesterol management.

21. Choose the plan that you feel is most appropriate and justify your answer.

22. You call the physician with your recommendation. You are able to leave a message with the nurse, but you cannot get through to the physician right now. How do you advise Ms. Yetter today?

23. One month later Ms. Yetter brings a prescription to the pharmacy for clarithromycin 500 mg by mouth twice daily for 10 days. The computer indicates a drug interaction with the statin. What would you do?

24. Ms. Yetter has been reading on-line that statins can cause muscle pain and related kidney problems. From her research she thinks it would be a good idea to take coenzyme Q10 to avoid developing muscle pain. How would you advise her?

Scenario 2

Mrs. Jones is a new patient to your cholesterol management program. She is taking rosuvastatin 40 mg every day and has reached her LDL-cholesterol goal of less than 100 mg/dL.

Her triglyceride concentration is still at 350 mg/dL and her high density lipoprotein concentration is 35 mg/dL.

Questions

1. What are Mrs. Jones' therapeutic options?

2. Which option would you choose and why?

3. Mrs. Jones would like to switch to a generic HMG-CoA reductase inhibitor because of the significant cost savings from her health plan. What would you suggest?

Scenario 3

Tony Danko is a long-standing patron at your pharmacy. He comes to you today with a new prescription from his primary care physician.

Questions

1. At first glance you are not sure if the prescription is for Omacor or Amicar. How can you avoid these and other easy look-alike errors with cholesterol medications (e.g., simvastatin and sertraline or Zocor and Zoloft)?

Mr. Danko was taking pravastatin 40 mg every day for the past year. In past years he has experienced muscle pain on both atorvastatin and simvastatin. His triglyceride concentrations are still greater than 500 mg/dL after weight loss, diet restrictions, and increased physical activity. His new prescription is for Omacor, which you update to Lovaza.

2. When Mr. Danko realizes how expensive Lovaza is, he wants to know if it is worth it. He wants to know the difference between Lovaza and nonprescription herbal fish oil supplements that appear to cost less. Can he just take the fish oil supplements instead?

Scenario 4

Peter Holmes brings a new prescription for Niaspan to your pharmacy.

Questions

1. How would you counsel Mr. Holmes to take his Niaspan, including how to titrate the dose?

2. Mr. Holmes returns for his second refill of Niaspan. He has changed jobs and has new insurance coverage that does not cover the Niaspan. Can he substitute nonprescription niacin for the Niaspan? If so, how would you advise him to pick a product and then titrate the dose?

Information Sources

1. *American Pharmacists Association Pharmacy-Based Lipid Management Self-Study Learning Program, Module 7.* Washington, DC: American Pharmacists Association; 2005:11–2.

2. *American Pharmacists Association Pharmacy-Based Lipid Management Self-Study Learning Program, Module 6.* Washington, DC: American Pharmacists Association; 2005:3–7.

3. Centers for Medicare and Medicaid Services. Clinical Laboratory Improvement Amendments Overview. Available at: http://www.cms.hhs.gov/clia. Last accessed November 7, 2008.

4. US Food and Drug Administration Center for Devices and Radiological Health. Information on CLIA Waivers. Available at: http://www.fda.gov/cdrh/clia/cliawaived.html. Last accessed November 7, 2008.

5. US Department of Labor Occupational Safety and Health Information. OSHA Regulations. Available at: http://www.osha.gov/pls/oshaweb/owasrch.search_form?p_doc_type=STANDARDS&p_toc_level=0&p_keyvalue=. Last accessed November 7, 2008.

6. National Cholesterol Education Program. *Third Report of the National Cholesterol Education Program (NCEP) Expert Panel on Detection, Evaluation, and Treatment of High Blood Cholesterol in Adults (Adult Treatment Panel III).* Bethesda, Md: National Institutes of Health; 2001. NIH Publication No. 02-5215. Available at: http://www.nhlbi.nih.gov/guidelines/cholesterol. Last accessed November 7, 2008.

7. National Cholesterol Education Program. Implications of recent clinical trials for the National Cholesterol Education Program Adult Treatment Panel III guidelines *Circulation.* 2004;110:227–39.

8. Potential drug interactions with grapefruit. *Pharm Lett.* 2007;23: 230204.

9. Lilja JJ, Kivisto KT, Neuvonen PF. Grapefruit juice increases serum concentrations of atorvastatin and has no effect on pravastatin. *Clin Pharmacol Ther.* 1999;66:118–27.

10. Talbert RL. Safety issues with statin therapy. *J Am Pharm Assoc.* 2006;46:479–90.

11. Statin-associated myopathy. *Pharm Lett.* 2006;22:220310.

12. Graham DJ, Staffa JA, Shatin D, et al. Incidence of hospitalized rhabdomyolysis in patients treated with lipid-lowering drugs. *JAMA.* 2004;292:2585–90.

13. Institute for Safe Medication Practices. Confusion between Omacor and Amicar Letter. November 2005. Available at: http://www.ismp.org/ Newsletters/acutecare/articles/20051103_1.asp. Last accessed November 7, 2008.

14. Omacor and Amicar mix-ups. *Pharm Lett.* 2006;22;220405.

15. New drug: Omacor (omega-3 acid ethyl esters). *Pharm Lett.* 2005; 21:211003.

16. Niacin use: an update. *Pharm Lett.* 2005;21:211207.

24 Coronary Artery Disease

Kimberly M. Crosby and Jonathan D. Ference

Objectives

1. Identify the main risk factors for coronary artery disease.

2. Describe the role of antiplatelet therapy in patients with coronary artery disease.

3. Outline the proper use of sublingual and transdermal nitroglycerin.

4. Evaluate therapeutic options for the treatment of a patient with coronary artery disease.

5. Design a therapeutic plan for a patient with coronary artery disease.

Scenario

You have been working as a staff pharmacist in a rural community pharmacy for 3 years and have developed strong relationships with the patients you serve as well as the physicians in your community. Today, a well-known pharmacy customer, Karl Roberts, a 66-year-old white man comes to your pharmacy with a new prescription (Case Figure 24–1). You realize that you have not seen Mr. Roberts in the pharmacy for about 3 months. Mr. Roberts is here to purchase his new prescription and pick up refills for his other prescriptions. You are able to access his prescription drug profile in the pharmacy (Case Table 24–1).

During the visit, you find out the following information. The reason Mr. Roberts has not been in the pharmacy in 3 months is that he had a heart attack that required his cardiologist to place a stent. He spent 3 months in a subacute long-term care facility in a local metropolitan area undergoing a supervised cardiac rehabilitation program. Before being rushed to the emergency department, Mr. Roberts used his sublingual nitroglycerin 5 times in a half hour without relief before his wife called the ambulance. Mr. Roberts has had type 2 diabetes and hypertension for 5 years. His diabetes is well controlled at this time. When you check his blood pressure and heart rate, it is 153/92 mm Hg and 70 beats/min, respectively, which the patient states is consistent with his home readings. After his heart attack Mr. Roberts was told that he has high cholesterol and that his "bad cholesterol" is 150 mg/dL. He has smoked 1 pack of

cigarettes per day for the past 40 years and has now cut back to one-half pack per day on the advice of his physician. He has picked a quit date for next week. He does not drink any alcohol and has started following a low-fat diet provided for him during rehabilitation.

Questions and Activities

1. On the basis of the patient's presentation and drug therapy, identify the medication-related problems in this patient's therapy.

2. On the basis of the patient's presentation and drug therapy, identify the disease-related problems in this patient's therapy, including any untreated diseases.

Patricia Klatt, MD
Tulsa Cardiology Group
4502 E. 41st St.
Tulsa, OK 47135

Patient: Karl Roberts
Address: _____ Date: 9/15

Plavix 75 mg
#30
S&i̅ PO daily

Refill 5 Times Dr. P. Klatt

DEA NO _____

CASE Figure 24–1 Prescription for patient Karl Roberts.

CASE Table 24–1   Prescription Medication Profile

Karl Roberts
127 Mockingbird Lane
Skiatook, OK 74122

Phone: 918-253-4472   **DOB:** 7/7/1940   **Insurer:** CIGNA

Allergies/Intolerances: Norvasc (severe edema)

Notes: OTC products include aspirin 81 mg, multivitamin

Rx No.	Drug Name	Directions	Date	R/F	Prescriber	Qty	RPh
677869	Lisinopril 10 mg	1 tablet by mouth daily	6/6	1	Middleton	30	KC
677868	Toprol XL 25 mg	1 tablet by mouth daily	6/6	1	Middleton	30	KC
677867	Metformin 1000 mg	1 tablet by mouth twice daily	6/6	1	Middleton	60	KC
677869	Lisinopril 10 mg	1 tablet by mouth daily	5/3	2	Middleton	30	KC
677868	Toprol XL 25 mg	1 tablet by mouth daily	5/3	2	Middleton	30	KC
677867	Metformin 1 000 mg	1 tablet by mouth twice daily	5/3	2	Middleton	60	KC
677866	Nitro-Dur 0.1 mg/hour	Apply 1 patch daily	4/7	2	Middleton	30	KC
677869	Lisinopril 10 mg	1 tablet by mouth daily	4/7	3	Middleton	30	KC
677868	Toprol XL 25 mg	1 tablet by mouth daily	4/7	3	Middleton	30	KC
677867	Metformin 1000 mg	1 tablet by mouth twice daily	4/7	3	Middleton	60	KC
677866	Nitro-Dur 0.1 mg/hour	Apply 1 patch daily	4/7	3	Middleton	30	KC
677865	NitroQuick 0.4 mg	1 tablet sublingually as needed	4/7	3	Middleton	30	KC

3. On the basis of the problems identified in questions 1 and 2, what are the goals of pharmacotherapy for this patient?

4. Identify the interventions(s) to solve the drug-therapy problem(s), and identify the anticipated outcome(s).

5. How should this patient be instructed to use his sublingual nitroglycerin and topical nitroglycerin patch?

6. Identify appropriate therapeutic interventions for the disease-related problems in this patient, including suggested agent, dose, and duration of therapy.

7. What drug(s), dosage form(s), schedule(s), and duration(s) of therapy are optimal for the treatment of this patient's hypertension?

8. What low-density lipoprotein goal would be appropriate for this patient?

9. What monitoring parameters available in the community pharmacy setting should be used to evaluate therapy in this patient, including efficacy and adverse effects?

10. What nondrug therapies or lifestyle modifications might be useful in managing this patient's problems?

11. Develop a medication action plan for the patient; include short-term and long-range goals.

12. List important issues to address during patient education.

13. Develop a follow-up plan for this patient; include time to follow up and method of contact.

Information Sources

1. Gibbons RJ, Abrams J, Chatterjee K, et al. ACC/AHA 2002 guideline update for the management of chronic stable angina-summary article: a report of the American College of Cardiology/American Heart Association Task Force on Practice Guidelines (Committee on the Management of Patients with Chronic Stable Angina. Circulation. 2003;107:149–58.

2. American Diabetes Association. Standards of medical care in diabetes–2007. *Diabetes Care.* 2007;30(suppl 1):S4–S41.

3. Anand SS, Yusuf S. Oral anticoagulant therapy in patients with coronary artery disease: a meta-analysis. JAMA. 1999;282:2058–67.

4. Smith SC, Allen J, Blair SN, et al. AHA/ACC Guidelines for secondary prevention for patients with coronary and other atherosclerotic vascular disease: 2006 Update. *J Am Coll Cardiol.* 2006;47:2130–9.

5. Steinhubl SR, Berger PB, Mann JT III, et al. Early and sustained dual oral antiplatelet therapy following percutaneous coronary intervention: a randomized controlled trial. JAMA. 2002;288:2411–20.

6. Mehta SR, Yusuf S, Peters RJ, et al. Effects of pretreatment with clopidogrel and aspirin followed by long-term therapy in patients

undergoing percutaneous coronary intervention: the PCI-CURE study. *Lancet.* 2001;358:527–33.

7. Bhatt DL, Fox KAA, Hacke W, et al. Clopidogrel and aspirin versus aspirin alone for the prevention of atherothrombotic events. *N Engl J Med.* 2006;354:1706–17.

8. Grundy SM, Cleeman JI, Merz CN, et al. Implications of recent clinical trials for the national Cholesterol Education Program Adult Treatment Panel III guidelines. *Circulation.* 2004;110: 227–39.

9. Studer M, Briel M, Leimenstoll B, et al. Effect of different antilipidemic agents and diets on mortality. *Arch Intern Med.* 2005;165:725–30.

10. Chonbanian AV, Bakris GL, Black HR, et al. Seventh Report of the Joint National Committee on Prevention, Detection, Evaluation, and Treatment of High Blood Pressure. *Hypertension.* 2003;42:1206–52.

11. American Heart Association. Heart disease and stroke statistics–2006 update: a report from the American Heart Association Statistics Committee and Stroke Statistics Committee. *Circulation.* 2006;113:85–151.

12. Critchley J, Capewell S. Smoking cessation for the secondary prevention of coronary heart disease. *Cochrane Database Syst Rev.* 2004;1:CD003041.

13. Russell LB, Carson JL, Taylor WC, et al. Modeling all-cause mortality: projections of the impact of smoking cessation based on the NHEFS. NHANES I Epidemiologic Follow-up Study. *Am J Public Health.* 1998;88:630–6.

14. National Cholesterol Education Program (NCEP) Expert Panel on Detection, Evaluation, and Treatment of High Blood cholesterol in Adults (Adult Treatment Panel III). Third Report of the National Cholesterol Education Program (NCEP) Expert Panel on Detection, Evaluation, and Treatment of High Blood Cholesterol in Adults (Adult Treatment Panel III: Final Report. *Circulation.* 2002;106:3143–421.

15. Fiore MC, Bailey WC, Cohen SJ, et al. *Treating Tobacco Use and Dependence, Clinical Practice Guideline.* Rockville, Md: US Department of Health and Human Services, Public Health Service; 2000.

16. Talbert RL. Ischemic heart disease. In: DiPiro JT, Talbert RL, Yee GC, et al, eds. *Pharmacotherapy: A Pathophysiologic Approach.* New York; McGraw-Hill; 2005:261–90.

17. Stamler J. Diabetes, other risk-factors and 12-year cardiovascular mortality for men screened in the multiple risk factor intervention trial. *Diabetes Care.* 1993;16;434–44.

18. Atkinson W, Hamborsky J, Mcintyre L, Wolfe S, eds. *Centers for Disease Control and Prevention. Epidemiology and Prevention of Vaccine-Preventable Diseases.* 9th ed. Washington, DC: Public Health Foundation; 2006:233–53.

Endocrine Disorders

25 Type 1 Diabetes Mellitus

James R. Taylor

Objectives

1. Identify goals of therapy for diabetes mellitus.

2. Evaluate treatment regimens for type 1 diabetes mellitus.

3. Compose treatment regimens for type 1 diabetes mellitus.

4. Perform appropriate patient counseling for a patient with type 1 diabetes mellitus.

5. Assess necessary monitoring and patient follow-up.

Scenario

You are a pharmacist working at the Plaza Pharmacy. Mary James, a 24-year-old white woman comes to your pharmacy with the prescription shown in Case Figure 25–1. Her prescription drug profile is available in Case Table 25–1.

Ms. James indicates that she has a new insulin prescription. You inquire as to how her blood glucose readings have been. She says that they are still a little high, mostly in the morning, so her doctor gave her a new prescription.

John Lyle, MD
Community Practice Clinic
121 North Main Street
Gainesville, FL

FOR *Mary James*

ADDRESS_____ DATE *6/27*

Lantus
24U sq qd

REFILL *3* DR. *Lyle*

DEA NO_____

CASE Figure 25–1 Prescription for patient Mary James.

She is unable to give specific numbers because she checks her glucose at home only on occasion, although she says she adheres to her medication regimen. She indicates that she just found out she had diabetes a few months ago. She is not sure why she is having trouble controlling her diabetes and now has to take another form of insulin (she is currently mixing the Humulin N and R in the same syringe). On appearance, Ms. James is not overweight. She indicates that she weighed 127 pounds at the doctor's office this morning. On questioning, she reports that she does not follow any specific diet, she normally eats 2 to 3 meals a day (chicken, salads, sandwiches, pasta, etc.) with 1 to 2 snacks a day (fruit, crackers, etc.), although her meals are not always at the same time because she works as a secretary in a busy office and has breakfast and lunch when, and if, she has time. She denies tobacco use but does have a mixed drink once or twice a month. One reason she does not check her glucose regularly is that she is afraid her fingertips will become sore, and she has to type much of the time at work. She also was not sure that it was that important to do anyway.

Questions and Activities

1. On the basis of the patient's presentation and drug therapy, identify the disease- and drug-related problems, and state the current drug therapy for the problem.

2. What are the goals of pharmacotherapy for this patient?

3. Identify the treatment alternatives available for this patient's disease- and drug-related problems.

4. Identify the intervention(s) to solve the problem(s) and the anticipated outcome(s).

5. What drug(s), dosage form(s), schedule(s), and duration(s) of therapy are optimal for the treatment of this patient's problem?

6. What monitoring parameters available in the community pharmacy setting should be used to evaluate therapy in this patient, including efficacy and adverse effects?

CASE Table 25–1   Prescription Drug Profile

Mary James
6128 SW 121st Avenue
Gainesville, FL 22696

Phone: 854-555-7845   **DOB:** 01/05/82   **Insurer:** Blue Cross Blue Shield

Allergies/Intolerances: Codeine

Rx No.	Drug Name	Directions	Date	R/F	Prescriber	Qty	RPh
789726	Humulin R	Inject 10 units twice daily before meals	6/12	1	Lyle	10	MT
785698	Humulin N	Inject 10 units twice daily	6/12	1	Lyle	10	MT
789726	Humulin R	Inject 10 units twice daily before meals	5/1	2	Lyle	10	MT
785698	Humulin N	Inject 10 units twice daily	5/1	2	Lyle	10	MT
781212	Yasmin	Take 1 tablet once daily	5/1	2	Lyle	84	MT
785699	Humulin R	Inject 5 units twice daily before meals	3/12	3	Lyle	10	JG
785698	Humulin N	Inject 10 units twice daily	3/12	3	Lyle	10	JG
782997	Cephalexin 500 mg	Take 1 capsule twice daily until gone	2/15	0	Lyle	28	JG
781212	Yasmin	Take 1 tablet once daily	1/31	3	Lyle	84	MT

CASE Table 25–2   Recent Home Glucose Values (mg/dL)

Date	Morning	Afternoon	Evening	Bedtime	Medications
7/30	195	180		165	Humulin R 10 units in morning and evening Lantus 18 units at bedtime
7/31	205	178			Same
8/1	162		170		Same
8/2	182	190	150		Same
8/3	190	182		150	Same
8/4		170	165	140	Same
8/5	185				Humulin R 12 units in morning and 10 units in evening Lantus 18 units at bedtime
8/6	170	145			Same
8/7	195	160		155	Same
8/8	185	178	160		Same
8/9	210		155	140	Same
8/10		165			Same
8/11	184		145	138	Same
8/12	180	145			Same
8/13	192				Same

All morning values are fasting; afternoon and evening values are 2 hours postprandial.

7. What nondrug therapies or lifestyle modifications might be useful in managing this patient's problem?

8. How would you counsel this patient on the following issues: administration of new insulin regimen (including injection technique and appropriate syringe size) and storage of insulin?

9. Explain why it is important for this patient to perform self-monitoring of blood glucose and how often she

should test. Also discuss the potential role of alternate site testing in this patient.

Ms. James returns to your pharmacy about 6 weeks later because she needs a refill on her Humulin R. She also reports that she has begun to monitor her glucose at home more regularly (2–3 times a day). Case Table 25–2 contains her home glucose readings from the past 2 weeks. She reports seeing her physician 1 week ago, at which point her insulin regimen was changed. You go to fill the Humulin R and discover that she is out of refills.

10. What intervention would you recommend for solving the problem of no refills for her Humulin R?

11. On the basis of the recent glucose readings given in Case Table 25–2, develop a medication action plan for the patient; include short-term and long-range goals.

12. How would you educate the patient on the signs and symptoms of hypoglycemia and how it should be treated?

13. Develop a follow-up plan for this patient; include time to follow up and method of contact.

Additional Activities

1. Should Ms. James's physician decide to change the patient's Humulin R to another injectable insulin, what would be reasonable alternatives? Include a discussion on the potential advantages of these insulins.

2. Newer medications such as pramlintide (Symlin) are available for the treatment of type 1 diabetes mellitus. Discuss the potential role of these agents, including efficacy, dosing, and adverse effects.

3. Compare and contrast the features of blood glucose meters.

Information Sources

1. American Diabetes Association. Standards of medical care in diabetes. *Diabetes Care*. 2008;31:S12–54.

2. Levien TL, Baker DE, White JR, et al. Insulin glargine: a new basal insulin. *Ann Pharmacother*. 2002;36:1019–27.

3. Mooradian AD, Bernnaum M, Albert SG. Narrative review: a rational approach to starting insulin therapy. *Ann Intern Med*. 2006;145:125–34.

4. Briggs AL, Cornell S. Self-monitoring blood glucose (SMBG): now and the future. *J Pharm Pract*. 2004;17:29–38.

5. White JR, Campbell RK, Yarborough PC. Pharmacologic therapies. In: Franz MJ, ed. *A CORE Curriculum for Diabetes Education: Diabetes Management Therapies*. 4th ed. Chicago: American Association of Diabetes Educators; 2001:91–150.

6. Gonder-Frederick LA. Hypoglycemia. In: Franz MJ, ed. *A CORE Curriculum for Diabetes Education: Diabetes Management Therapies*. 4th ed. Chicago: American Association of Diabetes Educators; 2001:231–60.

7. Kleppinger EL, Vivian EM. Pramlintide for the treatment of diabetes mellitus. *Ann Pharmacother*. 2003;37:1082–9.

26 Type 2 Diabetes Mellitus

Magaly Rodriguez de Bittner and Heather Brennan Congdon

Objectives

1. Define the pathophysiologic and metabolic changes present in type 2 diabetes and metabolic syndrome.

2. Explain the interrelation between glycemic control and diabetic complications.

3. Define pharmacologic and nonpharmacologic strategies for the management and monitoring of glycemic control in a patient with type 2 diabetes.

4. For a patient with type 2 diabetes, develop a pharmaceutical care plan (including drug, dosage form, duration, and frequency) for the patient that considers the patient's characteristics and health beliefs.

5. Discuss the role of the community pharmacist in providing patient education to patients with diabetes.

Scenario

Mrs. Gutierrez is a 52-year-old Hispanic woman who comes to see you (the pharmacist) for medication management services at the Pharmacy Care Center. When you sit down with the patient for the interview, she says, "My doctor sent me here to learn about my diabetes and medications." You obtain the following information.

With regard to the history of her present illness, Mrs. Gutierrez was referred by her primary care physician for assessment and follow-up of her diabetes medications. Her type 2 diabetes was diagnosed 2 days ago during a physician visit. She had attended a health fair at the Hispanic Community Center, where her blood glucose was found to be "high, around 230." The patient was told to make an appointment to see a physician. She admits that she was feeling tired for a while, but she attributed her symptoms to working two jobs. Mrs. Gutierrez also admits that she had increased urination, was feeling thirsty, and was having blurred vision but did not know that diabetes can cause these symptoms. She still has polyuria, polydipsia, and polyphagia, and admits to having some tingling in her feet and decreased sensation. At night she needs to sleep with socks because her feet are always cold. In the past 3 years, the patient has gained 30 pounds and has decreased

her physical activity. Her mother had bilateral below-the-knee amputations 3 years ago because of diabetes, and the patient had to quit her job to take care of her. The patient had just started working again about 3 months ago, which has created a lot of anxiety and has impaired her ability to engage in physical activity. She is the only daughter in her family (she has three brothers), and she is expected to take care of her mother. Mrs. Gutierrez is really concerned and has asked her relatives, who have diabetes, about dietary modifications and the best medications to take. She is upset about this diagnosis because she "does not want to end up like her mom." She admits adherence with her blood pressure medicine, but at times she has difficulty buying the medication because of financial constraints.

Her past medical history (major illnesses and surgeries) from the physician's referral form includes type 2 diabetes diagnosed 2 weeks ago and hypertension for 3 years. Mrs. Gutierrez denies a history of heart attack, stroke, deep vein thrombosis or pulmonary embolus, heart disease, dyslipidemia, thyroid disease, peptic ulcer disease, bleeding problems, seizures, vertigo, difficulty with balance, or falling. She has had no surgeries. Her last menstrual period was 5 years ago.

The patient's prescription drug profile is shown in Case Table 26–1. You also conduct a medication history, including nonprescription and herbal products, and discover that Mrs. Gutierrez is using the following nonprescription medications: acetaminophen 325 mg by mouth three to four times daily as needed for headaches and an herbal tea (Savila tea) three times daily for her nerves. After speaking with Mrs. Gutierrez, you discover that she has no health insurance and pays cash for her medications, but she states adherence to her medications. She works as a receptionist at a Hispanic business and as a waitress at a local restaurant. She understands basic conversational English but has difficulty at times understanding and answering your questions.

You take the patient's blood pressure; her blood pressure is 150/93 mm Hg and her pulse is 80 beats/min. She is 5 feet 2 inches tall, weighs 187 pounds, and has a body mass index (in kg/m^2) of 34.2. You also review the laboratory results that the physician sent to you in the referral form:

CASE Table 26–1 Prescription Medication Profile

Maria Gutierrez
1111 Oak St.
Baltimore, MD 21075

Phone: 410-555-1212   **DOB:** 3/5/56   **Insurer:** Self-pay

Allergies/Intolerances: NKA

Rx No.	Drug Name	Directions	Date	R/F	Prescriber	Qty	RPh
688588	Hydrochlorothiazide 50 mg	1 tablet every morning	5/21	3	Smith	30	MB
688588	Hydrochlorothiazide 50 mg	1 tablet every morning	2/21	4	Smith	30	HC

- Potassium: 45 mmol/L
- Chloride: 102 mmol/L
- Carbon dioxide: 22 mmol/L
- Blood urea nitrogen: 16 mg/dL
- Serum creatinine: 1.0 mg/dL
- Glucose: 200 mg/dL
- Hemoglobin A1c: 8.9%
- AST: 14 U/L
- ALT: 191 U/L
- Total cholesterol: 210 mg/dL
- Low-density lipoprotein: 120 mg/dL
- High-density lipoprotein: 39 mg/dL
- Triglycerides: 360 mg/dL

Her urinalysis was negative for ketones, blood, nitrates, and leukocyte esterase and was 1+ for protein and 3+ for glucose.

Questions and Activities

1. On the basis of the patient's history, drug therapy, and the information you have from the physician's referral, identify the drug- or disease-related problem(s).

2. What are the goals of pharmacotherapy for this patient?

3. Identify the treatment alternatives available for the drug- or disease-related problems.

4. What drug(s), dosage forms, schedules, and duration of therapy are optimal for the treatment of this patient's problems?

5. What monitoring parameters available in the community pharmacy setting should be used to evaluate therapy for this patient, including efficacy and adverse effects?

6. What nondrug therapies or lifestyle modifications might be useful in managing this patient's problem?

7. Develop a medication action plan for this patient; include short-term and long-range goals.

8. What are the important areas of self-management that should be addressed during the patient education sessions?

9. Develop a follow-up plan for this patient; include time to follow up and method of contact.

Two weeks after her first visit with the pharmacist, Mrs. Gutierrez returns to the pharmacy care center for follow-up. She informs you that she was reading about diabetes and that she is interested in testing her glucose at home. She was told by her cousin that she should buy a glucometer called "OneTouch Ultra."

10. What additional questions do you need to ask Mrs. Gutierrez to make a recommendation about a glucometer and the patient's monitoring of her blood glucose?

11. As a result of counseling Mrs. Gutierrez and other patients with diabetes, you decide to develop a diabetes care program in the community pharmacy for patients with diabetes. What steps would you follow to implement these services?

Additional Activities

1. Investigate what credentials a pharmacist might want to obtain if interested in educating and managing patients with diabetes.

2. Create a plan-o-gram in a community pharmacy of products for patients with diabetes.

3. Research the safety and efficacy of alternative treatments for diabetes.

4. How would the treatment plan change if this patient were a child or adolescent with type 2 diabetes mellitus?

Information Sources

1. American Diabetes Association. Diabetes Statistics. Available at: http://diabetes.org/diabetes-statistics.jsp. Last accessed October 26, 2008.

2. American Diabetes Association. Standards of medical care in diabetes–2007. *Diabetes Care.* 2007;30(suppl):S4–41.

3. American Diabetes Association. Diagnosis and classification of diabetes mellitus. *Diabetes Care.* 2007;30(suppl):S42–7.

4. American Diabetes Association. Type 2 diabetes complications. Available at: http://diabetes.org/type-2-diabetes/complications.jsp. Last accessed October 26, 2008.

5. JNC 7 complete report: prevention, detection, evaluation, and treatment of high blood pressure. *Hypertension.* 2003;42:1206.

6. National Cholesterol Education Program Expert Panel on Detection, Evaluation, and Treatment of High Blood Cholesterol in Adults. Executive Summary of the Third Report of the National Cholesterol Education Program (NCEP) Expert Panel on Detection, Evaluation, and Treatment of High Blood Cholesterol in Adults (Adult Treatment Panel III). JAMA. 2001;285: 2486–97.

7. *Clinical Guidelines on the Identification, Evaluation, and Treatment of Overweight and Obesity in Adults.* Bethesda, Md: National Heart, Lung, and Blood Institute; 1998.

8. American Diabetes Association. Nutrition recommendations and interventions for diabetes: a position statement of the American Diabetes Association. *Diabetes Care.* 2007;30(suppl): S48–S65.

9. Grundy SM, Cleeman JI, Merz NB, et al. Implications of recent clinical trials for the National Cholesterol Education Program Adult Treatment Panel III guidelines. *Circulation.* 2004;110: 227–39.

10. Stumvoll M, Nurjhan N, Perriello G, et al. Metabolic effects of metformin in non-insulin-dependent diabetes mellitus. *Diabetes Care.* 1995;333:550–4.

11. Lacy CF, Armstrong LL, Goldman MP, et al. *Drug Information Handbook: A Comprehensive Resource for All Clinicians and Healthcare Professionals.* 15th ed. Washington, DC: American Pharmacists Association; 2007.

12. Taylor JR, Campbell KM. Home monitoring of glucose and blood pressure. *Am Fam Physician.* 2007;76:255–60.

27 Thyroid Disease

Nicole Paolini Albanese

Objectives

1. Describe and replicate the thyroid feedback loop and its importance in understanding the use of thyroid supplementation.

2. Apply pathophysiologic knowledge of the thyroid gland to patient care.

3. Develop a stepwise approach to reviewing a patient profile for specific drug–drug and drug–disease interaction related to hypothyroid treatment.

4. Understand the importance of patient communication and data collection in providing patient care.

Scenario

You are a community pharmacist who has worked at Buffalo Pharmacy for 12 years. You know almost all your patients on a first-name basis, which is why you were looking forward to hearing about Mrs. Biltmore's grandson's wedding. She looks obviously fatigued when she comes to the pharmacy today; she is wearing a heavy sweater even though it is unseasonably warm in Buffalo for October. She confirms that she "hasn't been herself these past few weeks," and is feeling tired and run down. She relays that she was too tired to stay until the end of her grandson's wedding, which upset her. After the urging of her daughter, she went to her health care provider this morning. She presents a prescription to be filled but tells you that she was not able to see her own physician, Dr. White; she saw his partner Dr. Brass. The prescription is for levothyroxine 0.175 mg by mouth once daily. Case Table 27–1 lists her other medications.

On reviewing Mrs. Biltmore's prescription drug profile, you immediately realize that a phone call to the physician may be warranted.

Questions and Activities

1. On the basis of the patient's presentation and drug therapy, identify the drug- or disease-related problem, and state the current drug therapy for the problem.

CASE Table 27–1　Prescription Medication Profile

Maria Biltmore
1234 Parkside Ave.
Buffalo, NY 12345

Phone: 716-987-6543　　　**DOB:** 07/08/1932　　　**Insurer:** BCBS

Allergies/Intolerances: Statins (muscle cramps)

Rx No.	Drug Name	Directions	Date	R/F	Prescriber	Qty	RPh
643888	Pepcid AC 40 mg	1 tablet every day as needed	9/14	1	White	30	NMP
652318	Synthroid 0.15 mg	1 tablet every day	9/21	1	White	30	NMP
652308	Hydrochlorothiazide 12.5 mg	1 tablet every day in the morning	9/22	2	White	30	JAP
643888	Pepcid AC 40 mg	1 tablet every day as needed	8/14	2	White	30	MAP
652318	Synthroid 0.15 mg	1 tablet every day	7/30	2	White	30	TMJ
652308	Hydrochlorothiazide 12.5 mg	1 tablet every day in the morning	7/30	3	White	30	TMJ
652318	Synthroid 0.15 mg	1 tablet every day	7/13	3	White	30	PAM
652308	Hydrochlorothiazide 12.5 mg	1 tablet every day in the morning	7/14	4	White	30	PAM
652318	Synthroid 0.15 mg	1 tablet every day	6/24	4	White	30	NMP
652308	Hydrochlorothiazide 12.5 mg	1 tablet every day in the morning	6/25	5	White	30	NPA
652318	Synthroid 0.15 mg	1 tablet every day	4/30	5	White	30	NPA
652308	Hydrochlorothiazide 12.5 mg	1 tablet every day in the morning	4/30	6	White	30	NPA

During the call to Dr. Brass to verify the current prescription, he provides you with Mrs. Biltmore's thyroid-stimulating hormone (TSH) concentration of 25 mcU/mL. You thank him for verifying the prescription and return to Mrs. Biltmore. You explain to Mrs. Biltmore that Dr. Brass has authorized a change to levothyroxine (a generic for Synthroid) and that he has also increased her dose, because of her laboratory values. Mrs. Biltmore insists on staying on Synthroid because that is what Dr. White always prescribes for her.

2. How would you handle Ms. Biltmore's refusal to change to a new medication? Also, explain why a dosage increase is warranted because of specific patient measures (Hint: Describe the thyroid feedback loop).

Mrs. Biltmore is concerned about her TSH value. She confides to you that she is not sure Dr. Brass knows what he is doing because her TSH has always been normal (usually around 2–3 mcU/mL). This remark prompts you to ask Mrs. Biltmore how and when she usually takes her Synthroid and if she has started taking any other medications (such as a vitamin or herbal product). Mrs. Biltmore admits that her daughter told her to eat more dairy, so she has been taking all her medications with a cup of yogurt in the morning.

3. Describe all possible drug–drug, drug–disease, or drug–food interactions that may be the cause of Mrs. Biltmore's current symptoms and presentation.

4. What are the goals of pharmacotherapy for the problem?

5. Identify the treatment alternatives available for the drug therapy problem.

6. Identify the intervention(s) to solve the problem(s) and the anticipated outcome(s).

7. What drug(s), dosage form(s), schedule(s), and duration(s) of therapy are optimal for the treatment of this patient's problem?

8. What intervention (e.g., patient recommendation, call to health care provider or family member, contact emergency medical services, etc.) is necessary for implementing this treatment?

9. What monitoring parameters available in the community pharmacy setting should be used to evaluate therapy in this patient, including efficacy and adverse effects?

10. What nondrug therapies or lifestyle modifications might be useful in managing this patient's problem?

11. Develop a medication action plan for the patient; include short-term and long-range goals.

12. What are the pertinent topics to address during patient education?

13. Develop a follow-up plan for this patient; include time to follow up and method of contact.

Additional Activities

1. List the signs and symptoms of hypo- and hyperthyroidism.

2. Research which medications might interfere with thyroid function.

3. Investigate how the management of this patient would change if she were a pregnant 29-year-old with hypothyroidism.

4. Research the safety and efficacy of dietary supplements and alternative medications for the treatment of hypo- and hyperthyroidism.

5. Develop a business plan for a patient care service in a community pharmacy focused on thyroid screening and management.

Information Sources

1. Clinical Pharmacology Web site. Available at: http://clinicalpharmacology-ip.com/. Last accessed November 11, 2006.

2. Talbert RL. Thyroid disorders. In: DiPiro JT, et al., eds. *Pharmacotherapy: A Pathophysiologic Approach*. 6th ed. New York: McGraw-Hill; 2005.

3. Blackwell J. Evaluation and treatment of hyperthyroidism and hypothyroidism. *J Am Acad Nurse Pract*. 2004;16:422–5.

4. Chen YF, Avery AJ, Neil KE, et al. Incidence and possible causes of prescribing potentially hazardous/contraindicated drug combinations in general practice. *Drug Saf*. 2005;28:67–80.

5. Escobar-Morreale HF, Botella-Carretero JI, Gomez-Bueno M, et al. Thyroid hormone replacement therapy in primary hypothyroidism: a randomized trial comparing L-thyroxine plus liothyronine with L-thyroxine alone. *Ann Intern Med*. 2005;142:412–24.

6. Medical Letter Inc. Drugs for hypothyroidism and hyperthyroidism. *Treat Guidel Med Lett*. 2006;4:17–24.

7. Jordan S. Prescription drugs: uses and effects. Thyroid disorders: symptom control. *Nurs Stand*. 2005;19:2 p following 56.

8. Synthroid [package insert]. Chicago: Abbott Laboratories; 2005.

9. Escobar-Morreale HF, Botella-Carretero JI, Escobar del Rey F, Morreale de Escobar G. REVIEW: treatment of hypothyroidism with combinations of levothyroxine plus liothyronine. *J Clin Endocrinol Metab*. 2005;90:4946–54.

10. Laurberg P, Andersen S, Bulow Pedersen I, Carle A. Hypothyroidism in the elderly: pathophysiology, diagnosis and treatment. *Drugs Aging*. 2005;22:23–38.

11. TSH Home Test Kit. Available at: http://www.healthhometest.com. Last accessed October 26, 2008.

12. Hamburger JI, Meier DA. How to use modern thyroid function tests. *Am Fam Physician*. 1971;3:72–80.

13. Kisch E, Segall HS. Interaction between simvastatin and L-thyroxine [letter]. *Ann Intern Med*. 2005;143:547.

14. Lilja JJ, Laitinen K, Neuvonen PJ. Effects of grapefruit juice on the absorption of levothyroxine. *Br J Clin Pharmacol*. 2005;60:337–41.

15. Roos A, Linn-Rasker SP, van Domburg RT, et al. The starting dose of levothyroxine in primary hypothyroidism treatment: a prospective, randomized, double-blind trial. *Arch Inter Med*. 2005;165:1714–20.

28 Metabolic Syndrome

Michael Hogue

Objectives

1. Define metabolic syndrome.

2. List the relevant practice standards that apply to patients with metabolic syndrome.

3. Identify appropriate drug therapies for each of the diseases that represent the metabolic syndrome.

4. Identify appropriate primary prevention therapies for patients with metabolic syndrome.

5. Provide cost-effective and therapeutically sound recommendations for drug therapy for the patient with complex metabolic syndrome when presented with income and insurance coverage information.

6. Create a medication action plan for the patient with metabolic syndrome.

Scenario

Mary Smith, a 29-year-old white female who is 64 inches tall and weighs 180 pounds, comes to your community pharmacy regularly. She comes to your pharmacy today for refills on her maintenance medications and with a new prescription for an oral contraceptive (Case Figure 28–1). Her current medication regimen is available in Case Table 28–1.

Ms. Smith has enrolled today in your medication therapy management (MTM) program after referral by her insurance carrier, and she has brought her blood glucose log with her. Her fasting morning blood glucose values have ranged from 118 to 260 mg/dL during the past 30 days, with an average morning blood glucose of 220 mg/dL. You have determined her adherence with all existing therapies to be good through verbal questioning, with only 2 missed medication doses over the past month. You measure her blood pressure today to be 180/95 mm Hg, pulse 72 beats/min, and a respiratory rate of 16 beats/ min. Although you have not tested her cholesterol in the pharmacy, she did bring a copy of her most recent laboratory results from her primary care provider (2 months ago), which shows total cholesterol of 220 mg/dL, low-density lipoprotein of 140 mg/dL, high-density lipoprotein of 35 mg/dL, and triglycerides of 280 mg/dL. She was started on simvistatin by her physician

as a result of these findings. Social history is significant for tobacco use for 5 years, although she stopped smoking 1 year ago. She denies use of alcohol or illicit drugs. She works as a medical technician at a local hospital and is married with 2 children (grava 2, para 2).

She has a brand-name prescription co-payment of $40 per 30-day supply, a generic co-payment of $0 for a 30-day supply, and a $150 annual deductible that she has already met for this year. Her insurance company provides for a one-time medication therapy review per year, with a quarterly MTM session of up to 30 minutes with a community pharmacist in either a face-to-face or electronic environment.

Family History

Her mother died of a stroke at age 68; her father is living. Family history is significant for hypertension and diabetes on the maternal side and colorectal cancer on the paternal side. She has no siblings.

Medication History

A review of Ms. Smiths's refill history shows that she is consistently 7 to 10 days late in getting her routine medications

---

Xuan-Dao Thi Pham, MD
Jefferson County Department of Health
30th Avenue North
Birmingham, Alabama

FOR_____Mary Smith_____
ADDRESS_____ DATE ___ 1/6_____

Ortho-Novum 1/35
Disp: 3 packs
Sig: Take one tablet every day as directed.

REFILL ___3____ TIMES   DR. ___Pham_____
DEA NO._____BP1234567_____

CASE Figure 28–1 New prescription for patient Mary Smith.

CASE Table 28–1   Prescription Medication Profile

Mary Smith
1001 29th Court South, Apt. 36
Birmingham, AL 35201

Phone: 203-561-7788   **DOB:** 06/15/36   **Insurer:** Blue Cross Blue Shield of Alabama

Allergies/Intolerances: NKDA

Rx No.	Drug Name	Directions	Date	R/F	Prescriber	Qty	RPh
698504	Metformin XR 500 mg	2 tablets twice daily	12/07	10	Pham	120	MH
698503	Glyburide ER 10 mg	1 tablet twice daily	12/07	10	Pham	60	MH
698501	Simvastatin 20 mg	1 tablet every day	12/07	10	Pham	30	MH
698500	Atenolol 25 mg	1 tablet twice daily	12/07	10	Pham	60	MH
669304	Citalopram 20 mg	1 tablet every morning	11/07	10	Pham	30	MH
669303	Naproxen 550 mg	1 tablet three times daily as needed for menstrual cramps	11/07	10	Pham	30	MH
669302	BG Test Strips	Use as directed	11/07	10	Pham	100	MH
6695301	Nateglinide 60 mg	1 tablet three times daily before meals	11/07	10	Pham	90	MH

refilled. Current medications are those listed in Case Table 28–1. She has no known drug allergies. She was prescribed and completed therapy 10 months ago with bupropion SR 150 mg twice daily for 2 months and nicotine replacement patch taper for smoking cessation. In addition to her listed medications, she takes acetaminophen 500 mg 2 capsules every 4 hours as needed for aching in her knees; she requires this therapy about 3 days each week.

Questions and Activities

1. This is a case of metabolic syndrome. What information presented supports this fact, and is any further information needed to definitively state that the patient has metabolic syndrome according to generally accepted criteria?

2. Is the patient being appropriately treated for each of the primary conditions (hypertension, diabetes, and dyslipidemia) according to current clinical guidelines?

3. Is this patient receiving appropriate cardiovascular primary prevention therapy according to current clinical guidelines?

4. What are the goals of therapy for this patient?

5. Identify the existing medication-related problems present in this patient and create a medication action plan (MAP) to be shared with both the patient and her primary care provider.

6. What nondrug recommendations would you make to this patient, her primary care provider, or both at this time?

7. What immunizations does this patient need to receive, given her medical conditions and age?

Additional Activities

1. This patient's insurance also covers diabetes self-management education and training provided by an American Diabetes Association (ADA)–recognized program. What are the steps to providing an ADA-recognized program for diabetes self-management education?

2. Consider your actions if the patient's hepatic enzymes were three or more times the upper limit of normal. Would any of her medications need to be discontinued? How could you now treat the condition(s) for which those medications were intended?

3. Chronic renal failure is a common complication for patients with uncontrolled diabetes and hypertension and thus metabolic syndrome. How would this patient's renal function potentially affect her medication regimen?

4. If this patient were to become pregnant, how would her drug therapy have to be adjusted from the MAP you designed?

Information Sources

1. American Dietetic Association. Metabolic Syndrome: What Is It and What Are the Symptoms. Available at: http://www.eatright.org/cps/rde/xchg/ada/hs.xsl/home_4505_ENU_HTML.htm. Last accessed October 26, 2008.

2. Ford E, Giles W, Dietz W. Prevalence of the metabolic syndrome among US adults: findings from the Third National Health and Nutrition Examination Survey. *JAMA*. 2002;287:356–9.

3. Centers for Disease Control and Prevention. The Weight Management Research to Practice Series. Available at: http://www.cdc.gov/nccdphp/dnpa/nutrition/health_professionals/practice/index.htm. Last accessed October 26, 2008.

4. National Cholesterol Education Program Expert Panel on Detection, Evaluation, and Treatment of High Blood Cholesterol in Adults (Adult Treatment Panel III). Bethesda, Md: National Heart, Lung, and Blood Institute; May 2001. Available at: www.nhlbi.nih.gov/guidelines/cholesterol/atp3xsum.pdf. Last accessed October 26, 2008.

5. The Seventh Report of the Joint National Committee on Prevention, Detection, Evaluation, and Treatment of Hypertension. Bethesda, Md: National Heart, Lung, and Blood Institute; August 2004. Available at: www.nhlbi.nih.gov/guidelines/hypertension/jnc7full.pdf. Last accessed October 26, 2008.

6. American Diabetes Association. Clinical Practice Guidelines 2008. *Diabetes Care*. 2008;31(suppl 1) S1–S108. Available at: http://care.diabetesjournals.org/content/vol31/Supplement_1/. Last accessed October 26, 2008.

7. Sowers JR. Effects of statins on the vasculature: implications for aggressive lipid management in the cardiovascular metabolic syndrome. *Am J Cardiol*. 2003;91(suppl):14B–22B.

8. US Preventive Services Task Force. Aspirin for the primary prevention of cardiovascular events: recommendation and rationale. *Ann Int Med*. 2002;136:157–60.

9. Prevention of pneumococcal disease: recommendations of the Advisory Committee on Immunization Practices (ACIP). *MMWR Recomm Rep*. 1997;46(RR-8):1–24.

10. Kretsinger K, Broder KR, Cortese MM, et al. Preventing tetanus, diphtheria, and pertussis among adults: use of tetanus toxoid, reduced diphtheria toxoid and acellular pertussis vaccine recommendations of the Advisory Committee on Immunization Practices (ACIP) an recommendation of CIP, supported by the Healthcare Infection Control Practices Committee (HICPAC), for use of Tdap among health-care personnel. *MMWR Recomm Rep*. 2006;55(RR-17):1–37.

11. Fiore AE, Shay DK, Broder K, et al. Prevention and control of influenza. Recommendations of the Advisory Committee on Immunization Practices (ACIP), 2007. *MMWR Recomm Rep*. 2008;57(RR-7):1–60.

12. Weiss R, Dziura J, Burgert T, et al. Obesity and the metabolic syndrome in children and adolescents. *N Engl J Med*. 2004;350:2362–74.

13. Hayden M, Pignone M, Phillips C, Mulrow C. Aspirin for the primary prevention of cardiovascular events: a summary of the evidence for the U.S. Preventive Services Task Force. *Ann Int Med*. 2002;136:161–72.

Section

Respiratory Disorders

6

29 Adult Asthma

Sarah Parnapy

Objectives

1. Identify common signs and symptoms of asthma.

2. Describe a management plan for improvement of asthma control.

3. Educate patients on the proper use of inhaled medications and common concerns that are seen in the community pharmacy setting.

4. Recommend a comprehensive approach to management of adult asthma, including therapeutic endpoints, dosage regimens, monitoring measures, and follow-up.

Scenario

Joyce Thomas, a 54-year-old female comes to the community pharmacy for assistance with her current symptoms. She just finished walking to the pharmacy, and you notice that she has shortness of breath (SOB) and pronounced wheezing. She started with these symptoms about 30 minutes ago. Usually, when she walks, she gets SOB and wheezes within 20 minutes of walking, and it continues for a couple of hours. Ms. Thomas has noticed that her symptoms are lasting longer each time she exercises. Her asthma was diagnosed 20 years ago, but her symptoms have increased over the past few months. She has started using her peak flow meter for the past week. Her peak flow readings have ranged from 350 to 380 (personal best 380) before exercise and 270 to 280 after exercise. She is worried that she is not taking her medications properly or that they do not have enough time to work before she exercises. Ms. Thomas is nonadherent with her controller medication and uses her reliever medication on a daily basis (for the past 3 months). The pharmacist spoke to her previously about overuse of her albuterol inhaler, but she stated that she needed to have two of them because she uses them fast.

She has moderate persistent asthma and has been treated for 20 years; she was hospitalized three times in the past 2 years for asthma exacerbations and was in the emergency department three times in the past year. She also has hypertension, diagnosed 8 years ago.

She is married, lives with husband who smokes, and has 3 children who are now healthy adults. She has worked as a secretary at a university for the past 25 years. She denies use of tobacco and alcohol.

Her father and mother have hypertension (both are still alive); she has one sister with osteoporosis and one brother with asthma.

Ms. Thomas's prescription medication profile is shown in Case Table 29–1.

When asked about current nonprescription medications, she states that she takes the following: acetaminophen 500 mg as needed and calcium + vitamin D 500 mg 1 tablet twice daily.

She also wakes up in the night (at least three times/week) with SOB and chest tightness. She took her albuterol inhaler 1 hour ago, so the pharmacist recommends that she use it now. As she does this, the pharmacist watches her technique, which is poor.

Questions and Activities

1. On the basis of the patient's presentation and drug therapy, identify the disease-related problem and state the current drug therapy for the problem.

2. How would you properly manage exercise-induced bronchospasm? Did Ms. Thomas treat herself properly?

3. What stage of asthma is Ms. Thomas classified as having, and what is the preferred treatment?

4. How can you assess asthma control?

5. What are some signs and symptoms of poor asthma control?

6. Identify intervention(s) to solve the problem and the anticipated outcome.

7. What is the difference between the onset of action and duration with inhaled bronchodilators?

CASE Table 29–1 Prescription Medication Profile

Joyce Thomas
509 West Main Street
New Town, VA 12345

Phone: 555-123-4567   **DOB:** 03/09/1954   **Insurer:** CIGNA Prescription Insurance

Allergies/Intolerances: NKDA

Rx No.	Drug Name	Directions	Date	R/F	Prescriber	Qty	RPh
622569	Albuterol inhaler	Inhale 2 puffs every 6 hours as needed	6/25	6	Hall	1	MJ
622569	Albuterol inhaler	Inhale 2 puffs every 6 hours as needed	5/23	7	Hall	1	SG
622573	Hydrochlorothiazide 25 mg	1 tablet every day	5/25	8	Young	30	MJ
622567	Flovent HFA 44 mcg inhaler	Inhale 2 puffs twice daily	5/2	10	Hall	1	SG
622573	Hydrochlorothiazide 25 mg	1 tablet every day	4/23	9	Young	30	MJ
622573	Hydrochlorothiazide 25 mg	1 tablet every day	3/25	10	Young	30	MJ
622567	Flovent HFA 44 mcg inhaler	Inhale 2 puffs twice daily	3/25	11	Hall	1	SG
622569	Albuterol inhaler	Inhale 2 puffs every 6 hours as needed	3/25	8	Hall	1	MJ
622573	Hydrochlorothiazide 25 mg	1 tablet every day	2/13	11	Young	30	SG
622569	Albuterol inhaler	Inhale 2 puffs every 6 hours as needed	2/5	9	Hall	1	MJ
622573	Hydrochlorothiazide 25 mg	1 tablet every day	1/15	12	Young	30	SG
622569	Albuterol inhaler	Inhale 2 puffs every 6 hours as needed	1/15	10	Hall	1	SG
622567	Flovent HFA 44 mcg inhaler	Inhale 1 puff twice daily	1/15	12	Hall	1	SG

8. What are the goals of pharmacotherapy for this patient?

9. List nonpharmacologic options available for patients with asthma.

10. What drug(s), dosage forms, and schedule(s) of therapy are optimal for the treatment of this patient?

11. What are the brand and generic names of the inhaled corticosteroids, and what are the differences in potencies?

12. What are some other pharmacotherapy options for this patient?

13. What are key counseling points for the use of Advair Diskus?

14. What are the proper steps for use of a DPI (dry powder inhaler) and metered-dose inhaler (MDI)?

15. Ms. Thomas is a little confused about why she has two inhalers. She thinks that they do the same thing in her lungs. How would you explain to her how controller and reliever medications work?

16. During the counseling session Ms. Thomas asks about using the "float test" to tell if there is still some medication in her inhaler. How do you counsel on this, including the most accurate way to estimate the amount of medication left in the inhaler?

17. The MDIs that are still available are coming out as HFA (hydrofluoroalkane). What does that mean, and are they different from the older MDIs?

18. What is peak flow monitoring, and why is it important?

19. How would you counsel a patient on the use of a peak flow meter?

20. When should Mrs. Thomas use her peak flow meter?

21. Ms. Thomas is concerned that she will not remember these readings and what she would need to do. So you decide to develop an asthma action plan for her, including her green, yellow, and red zones for peak flow readings, and what she should do when she is in those zones.

22. What monitoring parameters can a community pharmacist use to evaluate therapy in this patient?

23. What nondrug therapies or lifestyle modifications might be useful in managing this patient's problem?

24. Ms. Thomas has heard a lot in the news about proper immunization. What are the specific vaccinations for patients with asthma?

25. Ms. Thomas is currently using Tylenol for the treatment of headaches. Would she be able to use aspirin or an NSAID instead?

26. Ms. Thomas is also concerned about what she has heard in the news about the long-acting beta$_2$-agonist causing death. How would you address her concern?

27. What key topics need to be addressed during patient education?

28. Develop a follow-up plan for this patient; include time to follow up and method of contact.

Additional Activities

1. Compare and contrast the proper demonstration and counseling points of an MDI and other DPIs (e.g., Pulmicort Turbohaler and Spiriva Handihaler), peak flow meters, and spacers.

2. Develop a business plan for an asthma disease management program in a community pharmacy

Information Sources

1. *National Asthma Education and Prevention Program Expert Panel Report 3: Guidelines for the Diagnosis and Management of Asthma.* Bethesda, Md: National Institutes of Health; 2007. NIH Publication No. 08-4051. Also available at: www.nhlbi.nih.gov/guidelines/asthma/asthgdln.htm. Last accessed October 26, 2008.

2. O'Mara NB. The safety of long-acting beta-2 agonist in patients with asthma. Therapeutic Research Center. *Pharm Lett.* 2005;21:210907.

3. Woelfel JA. Proper use of inhaler devices. Therapeutic Research Center. *Pharm Lett.* 2005;21:210303.

4. U.S. Food and Drug Administration Center for Drug Evaluation and Research. Your Metered-Dose Inhaler Is Changing to Help Improve the Environment. Available at: http://www.fda.gov/Cder/consumerinfo/metered-dose-inhaler-2pge.htm. Last accessed August 4, 2008.

Objectives

1. Identify signs from a community pharmacy medication list that may point to diagnosis of asthma.

2. Identify barriers to providing counseling for patients or patient representatives through a drive-thru window, and learn techniques to overcome these barriers.

3. Determine the severity level of asthma.

4. Identify and make recommendations to change possible asthma triggers.

5. List self-assessment skills patients need to better control asthma.

6. Develop a patient care plan for a pediatric patient with asthma.

7. Discuss limitations that finances have on asthma care and asthma-related outcomes.

Scenario

You were hired at the community pharmacy to identify, enroll, and manage patients in the care programs at the pharmacy. One way to identify patients is evaluation of the current medication profile when the prescription is brought to the pharmacy. Interactions during consulting at prescription pickup are also essential in gathering information and identifying patients for the program.

At the drive-thru window, a woman drops off prescriptions for her son (Case Figure 30–1). The prescriptions are for a young patient whom you have not encountered previously. His profile may be found in Case Table 30–1.

As you carefully evaluate the prescription medication profile, information within the profile indicates recurrent health problems with this patient. On the basis of the prescriptions presented at this pharmacy visit, this patient may have a diagnosis of asthma. The diagnosis was confirmed with the prescribing physician; therefore, Jonathan would be an excellent candidate for the newly developed asthma program offered at your pharmacy.

Jonathan's mother arrives at the drive-thru window to pick up the prescriptions and appears to be in a hurry and does not want to discuss anything at this time. She admits being interested in the information you can provide about her child's asthma and new medications; however, she cannot spend the time needed because she left Jonathan with a friend so she could come to the pharmacy. She made an appointment with you for later that day to review the new prescriptions and devices.

Questions and Activities

1. How would you counsel the patient through the drive-thru window? List some barriers and benefits of a drive-thru window.

2. How do you calculate the dosing for the Zithromax? Which formulation of Zithromax would you use for this patient?

Jonathan's mother returned with Jonathan later that same day for the asthma consult. The following information was collected: Jonathan has never been diagnosed with asthma previously, but he has had difficulty with "lung and ear infections" for a long time. He wakes sometimes at night coughing, and this recurs about one time per week, especially in the past 6 months. Quietly, Jonathan's mother admits that she is a single mother, has no job, and relies solely on welfare for her income. Often, she has not gone to the physician when Jonathan has been sick because of the cost of gas and because her car is not reliable. Therefore, Jonathan's physician will call in a prescription without an office visit after she calls the office to let them know Jonathan is sick. Usually a neighbor picks up the prescription for Jonathan's mother.

No other children are in the home. Jonathan's mother smokes about one pack of cigarettes per day; she tries to go outside or open a window, but it gets cold and she finds herself smoking more and more indoors. She has a dog that stays indoors. Jonathan's family lives in the public housing building on the outskirts of town. Another woman in Jonathan's building has noticed some cockroaches in her kitchen, but Jonathan's mother has not seen any in their apartment. Allergies were diagnosed this past summer which are treated with "syrup." The new medication helps most of the time with his constant runny nose.

Rebecca Stevens
5931 Cold Stone Ave
North Pole, Alaska 99675
907-897-5879

Name _Jonathan Mustard_

Address_____ Date_____

Nebulizer c̄ albuterol
for neb #1 box
use Q4h PRN asthma

☐ May not substitute
☐ May Substitute

Refill _12_ Dr._____

Rebecca Stevens
5931 Cold Stone Ave
North Pole, Alaska 99675
907-897-5879

Name _Jonathan Mustard_

Address_____ Date_____

Albuterol MDI
1-2 puffs Q4h PRN
#2

☐ May not substitute
☐ May Substitute

Refill _12_ Dr._____

Rebecca Stevens
5931 Cold Stone Ave
North Pole, Alaska 99675
907-897-5879

Name _Jon Mustard_

Address_____ Date_____

Zithromax Susp
per weight normal
dosing 40 lbs

☐ May not substitute
☐ May Substitute

Refill_____ Dr._____

Rebecca Stevens
5931 Cold Stone Ave
North Pole, Alaska 99675
907-897-5879

Name _Jonathan Mustard_

Address_____ Date_____

Spacer
with

☐ May not substitute
☐ May Substitute

Refill_____ Dr._____

CASE Figure 30–1 Prescriptions for patient Jonathan Mustard.

CASE Table 30–1   Prescription Medication Profile

Jonathan Mustard
500 South Polar Bear Street
North Pole, Alaska 99669

Phone: 907-555-5555   **DOB:** 6 years old (3/7/02)   **Insurer:** Medicaid

Allergies/Intolerances: PCN

DX: None marked in patient profile   **Notes:** None

Rx No.	Drug Name	Directions	Date	R/F	Prescriber	Qty	RPh
630521	Nasonex 50 mcg/spray (120 sprays)	1 spray in each nostril daily	09/18	10	Johnson	17 grams	JKM
629901	Elidel cream 1%	Apply to affected areas twice daily	09/18	8	Johnson	60 grams	JKM
631005	Cephalexin 250 mg/5 mL	1 teaspoon by mouth four times daily for 10 days	09/18	0	Stevens	150 mL	JKM
630522	Zyrtec 1 mg/mL	1 teaspoon by mouth daily	09/10	10	Johnson	150 mL	JKM
630994	Azithromycin 200 mg/mL	1 teaspoon by mouth daily for 5 days	09/10	0	Johnson	25 mL	JKM
630800	Azithromycin 200 mg/mL	1 teaspoon on day 1, 1/2 teaspoon on days 2–5 until gone	09/05	0	Johnson	25 mL	JKM
629901	Elidel cream 1%	Apply to affected areas twice daily	08/28	9	Johnson	60 grams	JKM
630521	Nasonex 50 mcg/spray (120 sprays)	1 spray in each nostril daily	07/15	11	Johnson	17 gm	JKM
630522	Zyrtec 1 mg/mL	1 teaspoon by mouth daily	08/15	11	Johnson	150 mL	JKM
630752	Hydroxyzine 10 mg/5 mL	1 teaspoon four times daily as needed for itching	08/15	0	Johnson	120 mL	JKM
630700	Amoxicillin 250 mg/5mL	1 teaspoon three times daily for 10 days	08/13	0	Johnson	150 mL	JKM
629901	Elidel cream 1%	Apply to affected areas twice daily	08/01	10	Johnson	60 grams	JKM
630603	Amoxicillin 250 mg/5 mL	1 teaspoon three times daily for 10 days	08/01	0	Johnson	150 mL	JKM
630522	Zyrtec 1 mg/mL	1 teaspoon by mouth daily	07/15	12	Johnson	150 mL	JKM
630521	Nasonex 50 mcg/spray (120 sprays)	1 spray in each nostril daily	07/15	12	Johnson	17 grams	JKM
630420	Amoxicillin 250 mg/5 mL	1 teaspoon three times daily for 10 days	07/15	0	Johnson	150 mL	JKM
629901	Elidel cream 1%	Apply to affected areas twice daily	07/01	11	Johnson	60 grams	JKM
630250	Amoxicillin 250 mg/5 mL	1 teaspoon three times daily for 10 days	07/01	0	Johnson	150 mL	JKM
630101	Amoxicillin 250 mg/5 mL	1 teaspoon three times daily for 10 days	06/13	0	Johnson	150 mL	JKM
629902	Amoxicillin 250 mg/5 mL	1 teaspoon three times daily for 10 days	06/01	0	Johnson	150 mL	JKM
629901	Elidel cream 1%	Apply to affected areas twice daily	05/31	12	Johnson	60 grams	JKM
629769	Hydrocortisone Cream 2.5%	Apply to affected area three times daily	05/21	2	Johnson	30 grams	JKM

(continued)

CASE Table 30–1 Prescription Medication Profile (continued)

Rx No.	Drug Name	Directions	Date	R/F	Prescriber	Qty	RPh
629805	Elimite Cream 1%	Apply a generous amount of cream from head to feet, leave on for 8–14 hours, and wash with soap/water, repeat in 14 days if needed	05/15	12	Johnson	30 grams	JKM
629769	Hydrocortisone Cream 2.5%	Apply to affected area three times daily	05/14	3	Johnson	30 grams	JKM
629782	Amoxicillin 250 mg/5 mL	1 teaspoon three times daily for 10 days	05/14	0	Johnson	150 mL	JKM
629769	Hydrocortisone Cream 2.5%	Apply to affected area three times daily	04/21	4	Johnson	30 grams	JKM
629700	Amoxicillin 250 mg/5 mL	1 teaspoon three times daily for 10 days	04/21	0	Johnson	150 mL	JKM
629600	Amoxicillin 250 mg/5 mL	1 teaspoon three times daily for 10 days	04/13	0	Johnson	150 mL	JKM

Recently, Jonathan developed a different rash while taking his usual antibiotic. The physician prescribed some syrup for itching and a new antibiotic. Finally, Jonathan has had problems with "skin rashes" since the time he was young and currently uses a cream that helps "a little." Mom notes that Jonathan weighs about 50 pounds and is within normal body weight for his age, according to the physician. Mom is most appreciative of the time you are spending to talk with her because she is concerned about her child. Review the patient's current condition; consider education points and appropriate medication for the condition.

3. What are the risk factors for asthma in children? What indicators do you have from the profile that the patient may have or be at risk of asthma?

4. What are the pharmacotherapy goals for this patient?

5. Identify the alternative (complementary) therapies and treatments available for the drug therapy problem.

6. List the education topics that should be addressed with this patient and the patient's caregiver.

7. What is the pharmacist's role in the education of patients and caregivers of patients with asthma? What educational points can be used to enhance this role?

8. Describe the components of an asthma diary, and provide education on how the patient should use the asthma diary.

9. Describe the components of an asthma action plan, and develop one for this patient.

10. Identify aggravating factors for asthma. What are the educational points for this patient so he can avoid or minimize aggravating factors and their effects?

11. What drug(s), dosage form(s), schedule(s), and duration(s) of therapy are optimal for the treatment of this patient's problem?

12. What intervention (e.g., patient recommendation, call to provider or family member, contact emergency medical services, etc.) is necessary for implementing this treatment?

13. What monitoring parameters available in the community pharmacy setting should be used to evaluate therapy in this patient, including efficacy and adverse effects?

14. What nondrug therapies or lifestyle modifications might be useful in managing this patient's problem? Develop a medication action plan for the patient; include short-term and long-range goals.

15. Develop a follow-up plan for this patient; include time to follow up and method of contact.

16. What barriers do the limited financial resources place on asthma care for this patient?

17. Should this patient use a peak flow meter? Why or why not?

18. Identify any previous, current, or potential medication-related problems. Develop counseling points for current or potential medication-related problems.

19. How is the use of Elidel indicative of a possible problem with asthma? Is Elidel indicated for long-term use? What intervention should be made, if any, about Elidel use in this patient?

Additional Activities

1. Discuss appropriate and inappropriate antibiotic prescribing.

2. Identify or develop educational materials for children with asthma.

3. Discuss how to present educational material in a way that patients can relate to and understand.

4. Discuss barriers with different cultures and language to educating patients.

5. Role-play an educational session.

6. Discuss with learners obstacles that must be overcome to change habits in the home of children with asthma. How would the learners overcome these obstacles?

7. Compare and contrast the different nebulizers. When should inhalers or nebulizers be used in pediatric patients?

8. Develop strategies for dealing with financial problems. In addition, research which states have programs in which Medicaid will pay for pharmacy services.

9. Research whether the learners' state Medicaid program covers peak flow meters. Discuss with the group if peak flow meters are generally covered on health care plans in the area.

Information Sources

1. Berger TG, Duvic M, Van Voorhees AS, et al. The use of topical calcineurin inhibitors in dermatology: safety concerns. Report of the American Academy of Dermatology Association Task Force. *J Am Acad Dermatol.* 2006;54: 818–23.

2. FDA Public Health Advisory. Elidel (pimecrolimus) cream and Protopic (tacrolimus) ointment. March 10, 2005. Available at: http://www.fda.gov/cder/drug/advisory/ elidel_protopic.htm. Last accessed October 26, 2008.

3. FDA Talk Paper. FDA issues public health advisory informing health care providers of safety concerns associated with the use of two eczema drugs, Elidel and Protopic. March 10, 2005. Available at: http://www.fda.gov/bbs/ topics/ANSWERS/2005/ANS01343. html. Last accessed October 26, 2008.

4. Eichenfield LF. Consensus guidelines in diagnosis and treatment of atopic dermatitis. *Allergy.* 2004;59(suppl 78): 86–92.

5. Schatz R, Belloto RJ Jr, White DB, Bachmann K. Provision of drug information to patients by pharmacists: the impact of the Omnibus Budget Reconciliation Act of 1990 a decade later. *Am J Ther.* 2003;10:93–103.

6. National Heart, Lung, and Blood Institute; National Asthma Education and Prevention Program, Expert Panel Report 3: Guidelines for the Diagnosis and Management of Asthma. Bethesda, Md.: U.S. Department of Health and Human Services; 2007. NIH Publication No. 08-5846.

7. Nazir Z, Razaq S, Mir S, et al. Revisiting the accuracy of peak flow meters: a double-blind study using formal methods of agreement. *Respir Med.* 2005:5;592–5.

8. Dolovich MA, MacIntyre NR, Shand R, et al. Consensus conference on aerosols and delivery devices. *Respir Care.* 2000;45:589–96.

9. Williams DM, Self TH. Asthma. In: Berardi RR, McDermott JH, Newton GD, et al, eds. *Handbook of Nonprescription Drugs.* 14th ed. Washington DC: American Pharmacists Association; 2006:287–313.

10. Stepwise Approach to Managing Asthma Long Term for Adults and Children More than 5 years of Age. Bethesda, Md: National Institutes of Health; 1997. NIH Publication No. 99-4055A.

11. Raissy HH, Marshi PL, Kelly WHH. Drug-induced pulmonary diseases. In: Dipiro JT, Talbert RL, Yee GC, et al, eds. *Pharmacotherapy: A Pathophysiologic Approach.* 5th ed. New York: McGraw-Hill; 2002:519–61.

12. Barrett BP, Brown RL, Locken K, et al. Treatment of the common cold with unrefined echinacea: a randomized, double-blind, placebo-controlled trial. *Ann Intern Med.* 2002; 137:939–46.

13. Taylor JA, Weber W, Standish L, et al. Efficacy and safety of echinacea in treating upper respiratory tract infections in children: a randomized controlled trial. *JAMA.* 2003;290: 2824–30.

14. Natural Medicines Comprehensive Database. Natural medicines in clinical management of colds and flu. Available at: http://www. naturaldatabase.com/(S(tybfjk55xewqe5inqajbr255))/ce/ceCourse. aspx?s=ND&cs=&st=0&li=0&pc=03%2D27&cec=1&pm=5. Last accessed October 26, 2008.

15. Mullins RJ, Heddle R. Adverse reactions associated with echinacea: the Australian experience. *Ann Allergy Asthma Immunol.* 2002;88:42–51.

16. Bielory L. Complementary and alternative interventions in asthma, allergy, and immunology. *Ann Allergy Asthma Immunol.* 2004;93(2 suppl 1):S45–S54.

17. Riccioni G, D'Orazio N. The role of selenium, zinc and antioxidant vitamin supplementation in the treatment of bronchial asthma: adjuvant therapy or not? *Expert Opin Investig Drugs.* 2005;14:1145–55.

18. Primatene Mist Consumer Information Web Wyeth Pharmaceutical Consumer Healthcare. Available at: http://www. primatene.com/ products/primatene_mist.asp. Last accessed October 26, 2008.

19. Bunting BA, Cranor CW. The Asheville Project: long-term clinical, humanistic, and economic outcomes of a community-based medication therapy management program for asthma. *J Am Pharm Assoc.* 2006;46:133–47.

20. Stergachis A, Gardner JS, Anderson MT, Sullivan SD. Improving pediatric asthma outcomes in the community setting: does pharmaceutical care make a difference? *J Am Pharm Assoc.* 2002;42:743–52.

21. Kamps AW, Roorda RJ, Brand PL. Peak flow diaries in childhood asthma are unreliable. *Thorax.* 2001;56(3): 180–2.

22. Eid N, Yandell B, Howell L, et al. Can peak expiratory flow predict airflow obstruction in children with asthma? *Pediatrics.* 2000;105: 354–8.

23. Reed CH. The natural history of asthma. *J Allergy Clin Immunol.* 2006;118:543–8.

24. Drazen JM, Weinberger. Disorders of the respirator system. In: Brawnwald E, Fauci AS, Kasper DL, et al. *Harrison's Principles of Internal Medicine.* 15th ed. New York: McGraw-Hill; 2001:1443–75.

25. GlaxoSmithKline. How to Use the Advair Diskus. Available at: http://www.advair.com/kids/asthma_inhaler.html. Last accessed October 26, 2008.

31 Chronic Obstructive Pulmonary Disease

Kristin Kouski and Michelle Herbert Thomas

Objectives

1. Describe optimal pharmacologic therapy for chronic obstructive pulmonary disease.

2. Outline community-monitoring measures for chronic obstructive pulmonary disease.

3. Identify important patient education points for patients with chronic obstructive pulmonary disease.

4. Develop a medication action plan for both pharmacologic and nonpharmacologic therapies; include short-term and long-term goals.

Scenario

Bob Wallace is a 67-year-old man who comes as a new patient to your community pharmacy. He has recently moved to the area, and his sister recommended that he transfer his prescriptions to your pharmacy. Today, he complains of an intermittent cough, clear sputum production, and persistent shortness of breath that worsens during activity. He mentions that recently he has not been able to walk down the street to the store without resting. You sit down with Mr. Wallace to fill out a patient profile and to answer any questions that he may have. His new prescription medication profile is found in Case Table 31–1. From your conversation, you collect the following information.

CASE Table 31–1 Prescription Medication Profile

Bob Wallace
100 Main Rd.
Richmond, VA 23235

Phone: 804-555-1000   **DOB:** 6/13/39   **Insurance:** Humana

Allergies/Intolerances: NKDA

Past Medical History: COPD, hyperlipidemia

Social History: Alcohol, none; tobacco, 2 ppd × 45 years

Medications: Transferred from Across Town Pharmacy

Rx No.	Drug Name	Directions	Date	R/F	Prescriber	Qty	RPh
645789	Combivent	Inhale 2 puffs four times a day; may inhale up to 12 puffs in 24 hours if needed	10/25 Last fill 7/17	5	Smith	14.7	KEF
645788	Serevent 50 mcg	Inhale 1 puff twice daily	10/25 Last fill 8/10	5	Smith	60	KEF
645787	Prednisone 40 mg	1 tablet daily for 14 days	10/25 Last fill 2/04	0	Jacobs	10	KEF
645786	Lipitor 40 mg	1 tablet at bedtime	10/25 Last fill 9/25	2	Smith	30	KEF

On inquiring about his inhaler use, Mr. Wallace says that he cannot remember to use the "inhaler that comes in the green and orange box" four times a day, and instead he uses it twice a day. Mr. Wallace says that he is not sure that he "gets all the medicine out" of the round inhaler. His condition was diagnosed as chronic obstructive pulmonary disease 2 years ago, and he was hospitalized at least three times for exacerbations, with the most recent being approximately 6 months ago. Mr. Wallace has smoked 2 packs of cigarettes per day (ppd) for 45 years, but about a month ago he cut back to 1 ppd because his breathing had gotten worse and his activity level had decreased. You stress the importance of quitting smoking as soon as possible to protect his health, and you tell him that many methods are available to aid in smoking cessation. He understands that his lung function will never go back to "normal," but he wants to prevent it from getting worse. He is also worried about the risk of lung cancer and wants to be around to see his grandchildren grow up. The patient tells you that when he is ready to quit, he will come back to discuss products to help him "kick the habit."

Questions and Activities

1. What are the stages of chronic obstructive pulmonary disease (COPD)? How do you differentiate between stages? What are the symptoms associated with each stage?

2. On the basis of Mr. Wallace's explanation of symptoms and medication profile, identify the drug- or disease-related problem, and state the current drug therapy for this problem.

3. What is the stage of this patient's COPD? What drug(s), dosage form(s), schedule(s), and duration(s) of therapy are optimal to improve his quality of life?

4. What could the community pharmacist do to solve Mr. Wallace's drug therapy problem? What would be the anticipated benefits of the intervention(s)?

5. What are the goals of pharmacotherapy for this patient?

6. Identify the pharmacologic treatment alternatives for managing COPD.

7. What nondrug therapies or lifestyle modifications could the pharmacist recommend to help in managing this patient's COPD?

8. After assessing Mr. Wallace's symptoms and medication profile, the pharmacist recognizes interventions to be made. What can the pharmacist do (e.g., patient recommendation, call to provider or family member, etc.) to accomplish these interventions?

9. What are important counseling points or education topics to address before Mr. Wallace leaves the pharmacy?

10. What monitoring parameters available in the community pharmacy setting should be used to evaluate efficacy of therapy in this patient?

11. Develop a follow-up plan for this patient; include time to follow up and method of contact.

12. Develop a medication action plan for the patient; include short-term and long-range goals.

13. Identify the risk factors associated with the development of COPD.

14. What symptoms of a COPD exacerbation would indicate a need for hospital admission?

15. Discuss the use of antibiotics for COPD exacerbations in the community setting.

16. When discussing vaccines, the patient says that he got a "shot" about 12 years ago when he was in car accident. What vaccines would you administer to this patient on the basis of this information and his medical history?

Additional Activities

1. Discuss the Treatment for Change Model for smoking cessation (the five A's). Ask about tobacco use.[1]

2. Research the smoking cessation medication varenicline (Chantix), including mechanism of action, dosage, contraindications and precautions, common adverse effects, and patient education.[2–4]

3. Create a business plan for a COPD disease management program.

Information Sources

1. Sin DD, McAlister FA, Man SF, Anthonisen, NR. Contemporary management of chronic obstructive pulmonary disease. *JAMA*. 2003;290:2301–12.

2. van der Molen T, Willemse BWM, Schokker S, et al. Development, validity, and responsiveness of the clinical COPD questionnaire. *Health Qual Life Outcomes*. 2003;1: 13. Available at: http://www.hqlo.com/content/1/1/13. Last accessed October 26, 2008.

3. Hudmon KS, Corelli RL, Berger BA. Treating tobacco use and dependence. *Rx Consult*. 2001;10(9):1–7.

4. American Pharmacists Association, National Association of Chain Drug Stores Foundation. *Medication Therapy Management in Pharmacy Practice. Core Elements of an MTM Service Model. Version 2.0.* Washington, DC: American Pharmacists Association; March 2008.

5. Berger, B. Effective patient counseling. *US Pharm*. Available at: http://www.uspharmacist.com/oldformat.asp?url=Newlook/files/

Phar/ACF59D.cfm&pub_id=8&article_id=157. Last accessed October 26, 2008.

6.   van der Molen T, Willemse BWM, Schokker S, et al. Clinical COPD questionnaire. 1999. Available at: http://www. ccq.nl. Last accessed October 26, 2008.

7.   Tovar JM, Gums JG. Monitoring pulmonary function in asthma and COPD: point-of-care testing. *Ann Pharmacother*. 2004;38:126–33.

8.   Brennan KJ. Pulmonary rehabilitation and oxygen in the treatment of COPD. *COPD Case Rev Q*. 2005;1:2–5.

9.   NHLBI/WHO Global Initiative for Chronic Obstructive Lung Disease (GOLD). Executive Summary: Global Strategy for the Diagnosis, Management, and Prevention of COPD. 2006. Available at: http://www.goldcopd.org/Guidelineitem.asp?l1=2&l2=1&intId=996. Last accessed October 26, 2008.

10.   Hunter MH, King DE. COPD: management of acute exacerbations and chronic stable disease. *Am Fam Physician*. 2001;64:603–12.

11.   Center for Disease Control. Recommended adult immunization schedule October 2007–September 2008. Available at: http://www.cdc.gov/vaccines/recs/schedules/adult-schedule.htm. Last accessed October 26, 2008.

12.   Centers for Disease Control and Prevention. Preventing tetanus, diphtheria, and pertussis among adults: use of tetanus toxoid, reduced diphtheria toxoid and acellular pertussis vaccine. Recommendations of the Advisory Committee on Immunization Practices (ACIP). *MMWR Morb Mortal Wkly Rep*. 2006;55(RR-17):1–35.

13.   Harpez R, Ortega-Sanchez IR, Seward J. Centers for Disease Control and Prevention. Prevention of Herpes Zoster. Recommendations of the Advisory Committee on Immunization Practices (ACIP). *MMWR Morb Mortal Wkly Rep*. 2008;57(RR-5):1–30.

32 Pediatric Cough, Cold, and Fever

Macary Weck Marciniak and Kristin W. Weitzel

Objectives

1. List key questions that a pharmacist can use to quickly and accurately assess a patient seeking self-treatment for cough, cold, and fever.

2. Describe cough and cold symptoms that can be self-treated and those that require referral to a physician.

3. Identify treatment goals and available alternatives to treat symptoms of the common cold.

4. Use available evidence to select appropriate nondrug and nonprescription medication therapy for a child for with cough, cold, and fever.

5. Provide counseling on proper use, side effects, and monitoring measures of medications used for the self-treatment of cough and cold.

Scenario

Mrs. Johns, a regular customer in your pharmacy, is standing in the nonprescription cough and cold product aisle. She appears to be staring at a few products and reading the front of the packages. After a few moments, you step out from behind the pharmacy counter and ask her if you can be of assistance. She looks a bit frazzled but smiles and says, "Yes, my daughter is not feeling well and I am trying to find something to make her feel more comfortable. Are these Triaminic Thin Strips Cold (phenylephrine 2.5 mg/strip) any good? Will they work for her?"

"Well, that depends. How old is your daughter and what symptoms does she have?"

"She is 7 years old and she has a cold."

"Tell me more about her cold; how long has it been going on?"

"Well, it has sort of 'creeped up' on her over the last few days. It started with her feeling a little out of sorts and having a sore throat. She felt kind of warm, but I didn't take her temperature; we couldn't find the thermometer at home."

"You say that her illness started with a sore throat. Does she have more symptoms than that right now?"

"Today, she started getting a runny nose and a cough."

"Is the cough wet and productive, where she coughs up mucus, or is it dry and tickly?"

"It is a dry cough."

"Does she have any congestion, either in her nose or in her chest?"

"She does have a stuffy nose. It is stuffy and runny."

"Does anyone else in your household have these symptoms?"

"Thankfully, no, and, I'd like to keep it that way. I have a husband and a 10-month-old son at home, and I don't want a sick household."

"What products have you tried for her symptoms so far?"

"Not much. I gave her a few lozenges that we had, and it might have helped her throat a little. I didn't have too much at home so, when she started feeling worse, I thought I should stop by the pharmacy and pick up some things."

"Before I make a recommendation for her, I have just a few last questions. Does your daughter have any chronic medical conditions?"

"No, she is a pretty healthy girl."

"Does she take any prescription medications?"

"No, she doesn't."

"And, does she take any over-the-counter medications or herbal products on a regular basis?"

"No. Well, I do give her a multivitamin every day, other than that, no."

"Okay, sounds good. I think I have all the information that I need to help your daughter get back on the road to recovery."

Questions and Activities

1. On the basis of the patient's presentation, identify the drug- or disease-related problem, and state the current drug therapy for the problem.

2. On the basis of the patient's presentation, is the patient a self-care candidate?

3. If the patient is not a self-care candidate, what symptom(s) or information indicate(s) the need for referral to a physician?

4. What are the goals of pharmacotherapy for this patient?

5. Identify the treatment alternatives available for this patient's cold symptoms. Include the place in therapy and efficacy or toxicity considerations for treatments modalities for each of the following symptoms in children:

   - Sore throat
   - Fever
   - Rhinorrhea
   - Nasal congestion
   - Nonproductive cough

6. Mrs. Johns asked you about a cold product that contains the decongestant phenylephrine. What can you tell her about phenylephrine and how it compares with pseudoephedrine for relief of cold symptoms?

7. The product she mentioned is also available in a "thin filmstrip," rather than a traditional syrup or chewable tablet. What are advantages and disadvantages of thin filmstrip dosage forms for children?

8. What drug(s), dosage form(s), schedule(s), and duration(s) of therapy are optimal for the treatment of this patient's problem?

9. Mrs. Johns is happy that you are able to make a recommendation for her, but she says she would really rather buy just one product instead of multiple single-ingredient products. She wants to know if there is a combination product you can recommend instead. How do you respond to her question?

10. How would you advise Mrs. Johns to monitor for improvement or worsening of symptoms once she gets home? What symptoms would make you recommend that she contact her pediatrician rather than continuing to self-treat her child at home?

11. What nondrug therapies can you recommend?

12. What else would you need to address during patient education?

13. One of the products that she may purchase today is in a liquid dosing form. What advice can you give Mrs. Johns about safely and accurately measuring and administering medications in a liquid dosage form for children?

14. In the past, Mrs. Johns has gotten her daughter's antibiotics "flavored" at the pharmacy. She says she has a much easier time getting her daughter to take something when it tastes like bubble gum. She would like to know whether you are able to flavor her nonprescription medicines too.

15. Mrs. Johns is grateful for your help, but she does have a couple of other questions. Because she does not have a thermometer at home, she would like to purchase one. She would specifically like to know about the accuracy of the "ear thermometers" compared with the newer temporal artery or standard digital thermometers. What advice can you give her on purchasing a new thermometer (keep in mind the ages of both of her children when making your recommendation)?

16. Many caregivers are often confused about when a child's fever should or should not be treated. What is "fever phobia?" How would you counsel a patient about treating a fever in a child?

17. Mrs. Johns also confesses she has always wondered whether there are any differences between children's acetaminophen and ibuprofen for treating fever or aches and pains. What advice can you give her about the comparative efficacy and safety of these agents? When would you recommend one agent over the other?

18. Mrs. Johns says that her friend who is a nurse has recommended that for a high fever she give acetaminophen, followed by ibuprofen 2 hours later, followed by another dose of acetaminophen in another 2 hours. How would you counsel Mrs. Johns about this practice? Is there any benefit to alternating acetaminophen and ibuprofen in the case of a high fever to provide relief more quickly?

19. Now that Mrs. Johns has made her product selections for her daughter, she confesses she is worried that her 10-month-old son may be coming down with the same thing. She does not want to take any more of your time, so she asks if she can just "use the same medicine" for her son if he develops similar symptoms. How would you counsel Mrs. Johns?

20. Develop a follow-up plan for Mrs. Johns and her daughter; include time to follow up and method of contact.

Additional Activities

1. Research natural products and dietary supplements (e.g., Airborne) promoted for cold prevention in children and adults. Would you recommend these to parents or caregivers to prevent cold or flu? What are the most effective measures to prevent a cold?

2. Review and compare efficacy and safety of natural products promoted or used to treat cold symptoms in children (e.g., echinacea, zinc, vitamin C, etc.). When would you recommend these in children?

3. Review and differentiate among different types of humidifiers. When would you recommend these devices? What type would you recommend? What precautions should be taken in cleaning, using, and storing humidifiers?

4. Research and review poison prevention techniques in children. What are the most common nonprescription causes of poisonings in children and toddlers? What is the National Poison Control hotline telephone number?

Information Sources

1. American Pharmacists Association. *Assisting Self-Treating Patients Quickly and Effectively.* Partners in Self-Care Continuing Education Monograph. Washington, DC: American Pharmacist Association; 2003.

2. Simasek M, Blandino DA. Treatment of the common cold. *Am Fam Physician.* 2007;75:515–520, 522.

3. Scolaro KL. Disorders related to cold and allergy. In: Berardi RR, Kroon LA, McDermott JH, et al., eds. *Handbook of Nonprescription Drugs: An Interactive Approach to Self-Care.* 15th ed. Washington, DC: American Pharmacists Association; 2006:201–28.

4. DeSutter AIM, Lemiengre M, Campbell H. Antihistamines for the common cold. *Cochrane Database Syst Rev* 2003; 3:CD001267.

5. US Department of Justice, Drug Enforcement Administration, Office of Diversion Control. Combat Methamphetamine Epidemic Act 2005. Available at: http://www.deadiversion.usdoj.gov/meth. Last accessed October 26, 2008.

6. Hendeles L, Hatton RC. Oral phenylephrine: an ineffective replacement for pseudoephedrine? *J Allergy Clin Immunol.* 2006;118:279–80.

7. Irwin RS, Baumann MH, Bolser DC, et al. Diagnosis and management of cough executive summary: ACCP evidence-based clinical practice guidelines. *Chest.* 2006;129 (suppl);1S–23S.

8. Centers for Disease Control and Prevention. Infant deaths associated with cough and cold medications: two states, 2005. *MMWR Morb Mortal Wkly Rep.* 2007;56:1–4.

9. Changes to OTC cough and cold products. *Pharmacists Lett Prescribers Lett.* 2006;22:221207.

10. National Institutes of Health, National Institute of Allergies and Infectious Diseases. Common Cold. Available at: http://www3.niaid.nih.gov/healthscience/healthtopics/colds. Last accessed October 26, 2008.

11. National Council for Patient Information and Education. Uses and Attitudes About Taking Over-the-Counter Medicines: Findings of a 2003 National Opinion Survey Conducted for The National Council on Patient Information and Education. Available at: http://www.bemedwise.org/survey/summary_survey_findings.pdf. Last accessed October 26, 2008.

12. FLAVORx. Columbia, Md: FLORVORx Inc. Available at: http://www.flavorx.com. Last accessed October 26, 2008.

13. Dew PL. Is tympanic membrane thermometry the best method for recording temperature in children? *J Child Health Care.* 2006;10:96–110.

14. Canales AE. OTC device: temporal scanner TAT-2000C. *J Am Pharm Assoc.* 2007;47:112.

15. Devrim I, Kara A, Ceyhan M, et al. Measurement accuracy of fever by tympanic and axillary thermometry. *Pediatr Emerg Care.* 2007;23:16–9.

16. Crocetti M, Moghbeli N, Serwint J. Fever phobia revisited: have parental misconceptions about fever changed in 20 years? *Pediatrics.* 2001;107:1241–6.

17. O'Neill-Murphy K, Liebman M, Barnsteiner JH. Fever education: does it reduce parent fever anxiety? *Pediatr Emerg Care.* 2001;17:47–51.

18. Dlugosz CK, Chater RW, Engle JP. Appropriate use of nonprescription analgesics in pediatric patients. *J Pediatr Health Care.* 2006;20:316–25.

19. American Academy of Pediatrics Committee on Drugs. Acetaminophen toxicity in children. *Pediatrics.* 2001;108: 1020–4.

Gastrointestinal Disorders

Section

7

33 Peptic Ulcer Disease

Kimberly D. Mitchell

Objectives

1. List the common symptoms of peptic ulcer disease and risk factors for peptic ulcer disease.

2. Compare the symptoms related to duodenal ulcer and gastric ulcer.

3. Classify patient symptoms, and construct an outline of treatment options for the patient.

4. Design treatment strategies in conjunction with the patient, and develop lifestyle modification guidelines for patient education.

5. Evaluate treatment effectiveness through appropriate follow-up consultations.

Scenario

You have recently obtained licensure in your home state of Texas and secured a position with Super S Drug and Food. Your long-time friend has recently returned to the area as well, after college graduation, and comes to your pharmacy late one evening to say hello and also to purchase some nonprescription items, including two bottles of Titralac.

You ask him about his large purchase, and he says he uses the Titralac for his "nervous stomach," which, on further questioning, he describes as a burning pain in his stomach. He tells you he uses Titralac almost every day, three to four times daily. The symptoms are usually worse between meals, at night, and in the mornings; they began last month when he started his new job.

You encourage him to see his family physician but are met with a negative response. His insurance and prescription coverage have not yet gone into effect under the new company plan, and he is still paying for recent physician visits. He insists he will not be able to seek care until later next month when his insurance becomes available and his finances stabilize. You tell your friend you have some thoughts on what will help his condition in the meantime. He agrees to provide you with some additional information on his health while you review his prescription medication profile (Case Table 33–1) and compile your information:

*   Nonprescription medications: Titralac tablets, 2 tablets as needed for stomach pain; ibuprofen 200 mg tablets, 5 tablets at bedtime as needed for knee pain (3–4 nights per week); One-A-Day Weight Smart 1 tablet daily

CASE Table 33–1   Prescription Medication Profile

James Bentley
1234 Sandy Lane
Lookmore, Texas 75555

Phone: 940-555-5555   **DOB:** 09/03/1977   **Insurer:** BlueCross BlueShield of Texas

Allergies/Intolerances: NKDA

Notes: Height: 74 inches tall; weight: 220 lb

Past Medical History: Right knee injury 1998; sports related

Rx No.	Drug Name	Directions	Date	R/F	Prescriber	Qty	RPh
92856	Azithromycin 250 mg	1 tablet daily	6/1	0	Decker	30	AJD
92855	Celebrex 200 mg	1 capsule twice daily	6/1	3	Decker	30	AJD
49465	Hydrocodone/acetaminophen 7.5/500	1 tablet four times daily	6/1	0	Decker	30	LAG
91824	Naproxen 500 mg	1 tablet twice daily	5/28	0	Decker	30	KLG
91824	Naproxen 500 mg	1 tablet twice daily	5/1	1	Decker	60	CLU

- Supplements: Protein powder daily
- Social history: 8 to 10 beers per week, no tobacco, no illicit drug use, regular cardiovascular exercise and weight training sessions each week, most meals away from home, on and off the Atkins Diet

Questions and Activities

1. On the basis of the patient's symptom history, identify the likely medical problem.

2. Identify the possible sources of the patient's symptoms and medical problem.

3. What are the goals of therapy for this patient?

4. What barriers to care exist in this patient?

5. Identify reasonable drug treatment options for this patient.

6. What drug(s), dosage form(s), schedule(s), and duration(s) of therapy are optimal for the treatment of this patient's problem?

7. What monitoring parameters available in the community practice setting should be used to evaluate therapy in this patient, including efficacy and adverse effects?

8. What nondrug therapies or lifestyle modifications might be useful in managing this patient's problem?

9. Develop a follow-up plan for this patient; include time to follow up and method of contact.

Additional Activities

1. What are the symptoms of a gastric ulcer, and how does treatment differ from a duodenal ulcer? In addition, what is the prevalence of *Helicobacter pylori* in patients with gastric ulcer?

2. Develop a business plan for your pharmacy clinic that includes testing patients for *H. pylori*.

3. Compare and contrast available treatments regimens for *H. pylori*.

Information Sources

1. Berardi RR. Peptic ulcer disease. In: Dipiro JT, Talbert RL, Yee GC, et al., eds. *Pharmacotherapy: A Pathophysiologic Approach.* 4th ed. New York: McGraw-Hill; 1999:548–70.

2. Hoogerwerf WA, Pasricha PJ. Pharmacotherapy of gastric acidity, peptic ulcers and gastroesophageal reflux disease. In: Bruton LL, Lazo JS, Parker KL, eds. *Goodman and Gilman: The Pharmacological Basis of Therapeutics.* 11th ed. New York: McGraw-Hill; 2005:978–80.

3. Lexi-Comp Online Drug Database. Hudson, Ohio: Lexi-Comp.

4. Zweber A, Berardi RR. Heartburn and dyspepsia. In: Berardi RR, Kroon LA, McDermott JH, et al., eds. *Handbook of Nonprescription Drugs.* 15th ed. Washington, DC: American Pharmacists Association; 2006:265–82.

34 Gastroesophageal Reflux Disease

Nimita Thekkepat

Objectives

1. Outline the major signs and symptoms that a person with gastroesophageal reflux disease might experience.

2. Identify the pharmaceutical agents that may contribute to gastroesophageal reflux disease.

3. Analyze the different prescription and nonprescription therapies available for the treatment of gastroesophageal reflux disease.

4. Outline the important counseling points that are necessary with gastroesophageal reflux disease therapy.

5. Describe the lifestyle modifications that are necessary for a patient with gastroesophageal reflux disease.

Scenario

Mr. Tom Robert comes to your pharmacy counter huffing and sweating, "Hey, how are you? My wife and I went to this excellent Italian restaurant that opened just down and the street. I loved it! But now my heartburn is so bad, and my Tums isn't just kicking it like it use to. I almost went through the whole pack of 24! You think you can recommend something that will get me through the night because I seem not to be able to sleep when this happens? I feel like I need to spit up every time I lie down. Lately, this has been happening almost every day. Here are three prescriptions I got from the doc yesterday (Case Figures 34–1, 34–2, and 34–3). Can you fill them now? I think one might be for my stomach and the other a refill. I can't remember what the other one was for. I will wait for the

CASE Figure 34–2 Prescription #2 for patient Tom Robert.

CASE Figure 34–1 Prescription #1 for patient Tom Robert.

CASE Figure 34–3 Prescription #3 for patient Tom Robert.

stomach one. I am in too much in pain to come back later."

As Mr. Robert waits for his prescription, he engages in light conversation. "I really need to quit smoking and lose some weight. I can barely breathe walking from the parking lot to the drop-off counter. I really want to quit smoking, and I have dropped down from a pack and a half to a pack a day. My daughter is getting married in a month and I need to fit into my tuxedo. I bet the financial stress will make me lose weight altogether."

Before you recommend anything for Mr. Robert, you decide to review his prescription medication profile (Case Table 34–1). The two new prescriptions that Dr. Mills ordered are for AcipHex and Reglan.

Mr. Robert's allergy profile shows that he is allergic to codeine because it made him "drowsy" and amoxicillin because it gave him a "bright red rash" all over his chest.

Questions and Activities

1. On the basis of Mr. Robert's presentation, identify the medical problem and the current drug therapy for the problem.

2. What are the goals of pharmacotherapy for Mr. Robert?

3. Mr. Robert asks you how long the medication will take to work. On the basis of the new prescription that Mr. Robert was given and the past drug therapies he used, identify any other possible treatment alternatives available for him.

4. What drug(s), dosage form(s), schedule(s), and duration(s) of therapy are optimal for the treatment of this patient's problem?

5. Mr. Robert has health insurance through his employer, a local power company. After entering the prescription for AcipHex, you find that only Protonix is preferred under his plan. What intervention (e.g., patient recommendation, call to provider or family member, contact emergency medical services, etc.) is necessary for implementing this treatment?

6. Describe how you will counsel Mr. Robert on the change in his medication?

7. Why do you think Dr. Mills prescribed Reglan 15 mg for Mr. Robert? How do you think the doctor told Mr. Robert to take this medication?

8. What monitoring parameters available in the community pharmacy setting should be used to evaluate therapy and change in therapy in this patient, including efficacy and adverse effects?

9. What nondrug therapies or lifestyle modifications might be useful in managing this patient's problem?

CASE Table 34–1 Prescription Medication Profile

Tom Robert
3500 Pacific Drive
Pleasantville, Virginia 22601

Phone: 556-793-3311   **DOB:** 02/09/1949   **Insurer:** United Health Care

Rx No.	Drug Name	Directions	Date	R/F	Prescriber	Qty	RPh
18434	Metformin 1000 mg	1 tablet by mouth twice daily	9/2	5	Mills	60	PJ
18432	Albuterol inhaler	Inhale 2 puffs every 4 to 6 hours as needed	9/2	4	Mills	1	PJ
18430	Lipitor 40 mg	1 tablet by mouth at bedtime	9/2	5	Mills	30	PJ
18431	Hydrochlorothiazide 25 mg	1 tablet by mouth every morning	8/30	5	Mills	30	BH
18429	Lisinopril 10 mg	1 tablet by mouth once daily	8/30	5	Mills	30	BH
18428	Verapamil 240 mg SA	1 tablet by mouth every morning	8/30	0	Mills	30	PJ
18432	Albuterol inhaler	Inhale 2 puffs every 4 to 6 hours as needed	8/15	5	Mills	1	PJ
18434	Metformin 1000 mg	1 tablet by mouth twice daily	8/3	6	Mills	60	PJ
18430	Lipitor 40 mg	1 tablet by mouth at bedtime	8/3	6	Mills	30	PJ
18431	Hydrochlorothiazide 25 mg	1 tablet by mouth every morning	8/1	6	Mills	30	BH
18429	Lisinopril 10 mg	1 tablet by mouth once daily	8/1	6	Mills	30	BH
18428	Verapamil 240 mg SA	1 tablet by mouth every morning	8/1	1	Mills	30	BH
18432	Albuterol inhaler	Inhale 2 puffs every 4 to 6 hours as needed	7/15	6	Mills	1	PJ

10. Develop a medication action plan for the patient; include short-term and long-range goals.

11. On the basis of Mr. Robert's profile, what major counseling points or patient education would you provide Mr. Robert about his new prescriptions?

12. Identify medications that may contribute to gastroesophageal reflux disease (GERD).

13. On the basis of Mr. Robert's albuterol refill history, what can you tell about his asthma and how is this related to GERD?

14. Does Mr. Robert have a real allergy to codeine or amoxicillin?

15. Develop a follow-up plan for Mr. Robert; include time to follow up and method of contact.

Additional Activities

1. What are the exclusion criteria for self-treatment of heartburn?

2. Develop a business plan for a pharmacy service that provides education, management, and monitoring for heartburn.

3. How is GERD treated in infants? List the advantages and disadvantages of available therapies, including compounded omeprazole suspension and alcohol-free ranitidine suspension.

Information Sources

1. Siepler JK, Smith-Scott C. Upper gastrointestinal disorders. In: Koda-Kimble MA, Young LY, Kradjan WA, eds. *Applied Therapeutics: The Clinical Use of Drugs*. 8th ed. Baltimore: Lippincott Williams & Wilkins; 2005: 27-1 to 27-23.

2. DeVault KR, Castell DO. Updated guidelines for the diagnosis and treatment of gastroesophageal reflux disease. *Am J Gastroenterol*. 2005;100:190–200.

3. Smith L. Updated ACG guidelines for diagnosis and treatment of GERD. *Am Fam Physician*. 2005;71:2376–82.

4. Fass R. Treatment of gastroesophageal reflux disease. *Clin Cornerstone*. 2003;5(4):18–29.

5. Williams DB. Gastroesophageal reflux disease. In: Dipiro JT, Talbert RL, Yee GC, eds. *Pharmacotherapy: A Pathophysiologic Approach*. 6th ed. New York: McGraw-Hill; 2005:613–27.

6. Lacy CF, Armstrong LL, Goldman MP, et al. *Drug Information Handbook*. 12th ed. Hudson, Ohio: Lexi-Comp; 2004:957–8.

7. Harding SM. Gastroesophageal reflux: a potential asthma trigger. *Immunol Allergy Clin North Am*. 2005;25:131–48.

35 Diarrhea

Kara M. Carruthers

Objectives

1. Accurately describe the characteristics/causes of diarrhea.

2. Determine whether a person is a candidate for self-treatment.

3. Use a formulary to determine most cost-effective treatment options.

4. Describe the mechanism of action of common OTC treatment options for diarrhea.

5. Describe the signs, symptoms, and treatment options for dehydration.

Scenario

Paul Taylor is a 53-year-old white man who appears to have poor hygiene. He comes to your pharmacy today with a complaint of diarrhea, which he states has persisted despite use of Loperamide 2 mg capsules, #20 (40 mg), as needed to treat this condition. He wondered if you could recommend something else to treat his diarrhea or recommend a change for his Nexium (he believes this is what is causing the diarrhea) to his physician. He wants to avoid an office visit with his doctor. He is a Medicaid patient who lives alone in a one-room efficiency apartment with only a bathroom and microwave as amenities. He receives most meals from the local soup kitchen, and once a week receives a meal from the local Meals On Wheels program.

Questions and Activities

1. What questions could you ask to determine the cause of the diarrhea?

2. What are the characteristics of antibiotic-induced diarrhea, food-borne infectious diarrhea, and food-induced (intolerant) diarrhea?

Mr. Taylor responds to your questioning and states that his diarrhea is watery and of a large amount, and has occurred 3 to 4 times every Friday for the past 2 years. He takes his Loperamide as stated above, which helps, but the diarrhea persists for 2 days,

gradually receding and returning the following week. He denies the presence of fever, weakness, loss of appetite, presence of blood, tenesmus, and dizziness, but he admits to abdominal pain, cramps, fatigue, nausea, and occasional vomiting. He also admits to thirst and xerostomia. Mr. Taylor states that he gets his Meals On Wheels meal on Wednesday afternoon, but the soup kitchen is open on Wednesday and closed Thursday, so he eats that meal Thursday evening. The meals vary but usually contain a protein (ham, chicken, or beef), a vegetable (cole slaw, corn, or green beans), a fruit (peaches, pears, or an apple), and a slice of bread and occasionally some type of casserole.

He denies the use of multivitamins or herbal supplements, except for the occasional glass of tea. He denies illicit drug use; occasionally he uses caffeinated products. Mr. Taylor has a 40-year smoking history, but he has not smoked since February 2001, when COPD was diagnosed. Review of his pharmacy profile shows reported allergies to penicillin (coma), sulfa (hives and swelling), and latex (dermatitis), and he reports lactose intolerance. Mr. Taylor has good adherence, per refill history, to prescribed medications. His current medications are listed in Case Table 35–1 Upon further questioning you find out the following information about Mr. Taylor's medications: He takes only 1 methocarbamol and 1 nabumetone at night, and uses the albuterol inhaler 2 puffs every block while walking, >24 puffs daily He also mentions getting metoclopramide filled at another pharmacy. While helping him to a chair so you could examine his pharmacy record, you note a minor loss in his skin turgor.

3. What medication(s) may possibly contribute to Mr. Taylor's diarrhea? What other causes may be present?

4. What is the mechanism of action of loperamide (Imodium) and bismuth subsalicylates (Pepto-Bismol), and what are their maximum daily doses? How would you counsel a patient to use them?

5. Create a list of the patient's drug-related problems.

6. What signs and symptoms are present to suggest dehydration? What is an appropriate treatment for this patient's dehydration?

7. Is Mr. Taylor's current complaint of diarrhea acute or chronic? How do you know?

CASE Table 35–1   Prescription Medication Profile

Paul Taylor
5575 Willow Blvd
Davenport, IA 52803

Phone: 319-555-1641   **DOB:** 7-24-1965   **Insurer:** IA Medicaid

Allergies/Intolerances: Sulfonamides (rash/hives), penicillin (coma), latex (dermatitis)

Rx No.	Drug Name	Directions	Date	R/F	Prescriber	Qty	RPh
607276	Methocarbamol 750 mg	3 times daily as needed for shoulder pain or arthritis	08/05/06	11	Ward	90 tablets	KC
624284	Nabumetone 750 mg	Twice daily as needed for shoulder pain or arthritis	07/06/07	11	Ward	60 tablets	KW
607275	ProAir HFA 90 mcg	2 puffs 4 times daily as needed for COPD	08/05/06	11	Jackson	8.5 grams	KC
607278	Nexium 40 mg	Once daily for GERD	08/05/06	11	Ward	30 capsules	KC
629523	Micardis 40 mg	Once daily for hypertension	11/05/07	5	Grey	30 tablets	KW
614285	Norvasc 10 mg	Once daily for hypertension	07/06/07	11	Grey	30 tablets	KW
629594	Lunesta 3 mg	Every night for increased sleep latency	11/06/07	2	Ward	30 tablets	KC
612483	Zyprexa 7.5 mg	Every night for schizophrenia	12/14/06	11	Patel	30 tablets	LG
612484	Loperamide 2 mg	Twice daily as needed for diarrhea	12/14/06	11	Ward	60 capsules	LP
612485	Lamisil 250 mg	Once daily for onychomycosis of right toe	12/14/06	11	Ward	30 tablets	LP
607277	Selenium 2.5% shampoo	As directed for psoriasis of scalp	08/05/06	11	Ward	120 mL	KC

8.   Is self-treatment appropriate for Mr. Taylor's diarrhea?

9.   What are the therapeutic goals for diarrhea treatment?

You consult your local Medicaid preferred drug plan and discover the following medications to be covered: diphenoxylate/atropine (Lomotil), Sandostatin (octreotide), and loperamide (Imodium).

10.   Develop a medication action plan based on this patient's insurance.

11.   Develop a follow-up plan for this patient; include time to follow up and method of contact.

The new prescription is denied because the claim was processed after coverage was terminated. You discover that Mr. Taylor has dual eligibility because of a disability and he now has Medicare Part D (MPD) insurance. He was unaware that he had been automatically assigned to an MPD plan. After determining his coverage, you consult your third-party references and discover the following medications are covered entities on his MPD plan: Sandostatin Tier 3, Motofen (difenoxin/atropine) Tier 3, loperamide Tier 1, bismuth subsalicylate Tier 1, diphenoxylate/atropine Tier 1.

12.   Does your choice of therapy change because of the patient's new insurance formulary?

Additional Activities

1.   Investigate what prescription medications can cause diarrhea.

2.   How should a patient treat medication-induced diarrhea?

3.   What diet is recommended for patients who have diarrhea?

4. How do sports drinks fit into a plan for rehydration for diarrhea?

Information Sources

1. Spruill WJ, Wade WE. Diarrhea, constipation, and irritable bowel syndrome. In: DiPiro JT, Talbert RL, Yee GC, et al., eds. *Pharmacotherapy: A Pathophysiologic Approach.* 6th ed. New York: McGraw-Hill; 2005:677–84.

2. Walker PC. Diarrhea. In: Berardi RR, McDermott J, Newton GD, et al., eds. *Handbook of Nonprescription Drugs: An Interactive Approach to Self-Care.* 14th ed. Washington, DC: American Pharmaceutical Association; 2004:405–32.

3. Bonis PAL, LaMont JT. Approach to the adult; in the United States and other developed countries; with acute diarrhea. Available at: http://www.uptodate.com. Last accessed September 27, 2006.

4. Aranda-Michel J, Giannella RA. Acute diarrhea: a practical review. *Am J Med.* 1999;106:670–6.

5. Clinical Pharmacology Online. Available at: http://www.clinical pharmacology.com. Monographs: Loperamide; Loperamide/Simethicone; Bismuth Subsalicylate; Albuterol. Last accessed October 2, 2006.

6. Wanke CA. Travelers' diarrhea. Available at: http://www. uptodate.com. Last accessed September 27, 2006.

7. Acheson DWK. Differential diagnosis of microbial foodborne disease. Available at: http://www.uptodate.com. Last accessed October 5, 2006.

Case

36 Constipation

Jeffery D. Evans

Objectives

1. Compare available medicinal agents that may treat or prevent constipation.

2. Evaluate patients to determine whether nonprescription therapy is appropriate and safe.

3. Develop a management plan (including lifestyle changes, medication, and herbals) for constipation that is patient specific and effective.

4. Provide complete patient education for the treatment of constipation at a level the patient is able to understand.

Scenario

You are a busy pharmacist at a chain, community pharmacy in a middle-sized town. You have been at the store for more than 4 years and recently became the pharmacy manager. You are familiar with both employees of the store and the regular customers of the store. Nancy Dimagho is a 44-year-old-woman who has been coming to the phar-macy since before you arrived. She has been taking pain medications for about 2 years and frequently tries to have the medication filled early (generally 2 or 3 days). She is having an escalation of the number of tablets that she takes to control her pain. She comes at the end of your shift on a Thursday with two prescriptions for two pain medications. You reluctantly take the prescriptions because they are both for oxycodone-containing products (Case Figures 36-1 and 36-2). She also asks that you include two boxes of Dulcolax tablets with her prescrip-tions. You recall that you have seen her purchasing these tablets every time she comes into the pharmacy. You decide to question her about the medications.

Initially, you interview her at the drop-off window but quickly realize that she would like more privacy, so you move her into the patient counseling area. She tells you that she is buying Dulcolax because she has been consti-pated for about 5 months. She has considered using supposi-tories or enemas but feels they would make her sick so she will not use them. You question her about what does it mean to her to be constipated, and she states that she some-times will go 3 or 4 days without having a bowel movement.

Philip R. Autry, MD
Pain Management Associates, Inc.
567 West Circle Drive
Jacksonville, FL 37757

FOR NANCY DIMAGHO

ADDRESS _____ DATE 2/20

OXYCONTIN 20MG
ĪĪĪ po QAM
ĪĪ po QPM   #150

REFILL Ø TIMES DR. Autry

DEA NO BA1424326

CASE Figure 36–1 Prescription #1 for patient Nancy Dimagho.

Philip R. Autry, MD
Pain Management Associates, Inc.
567 West Circle Drive
Jacksonville, FL 37757

FOR NANCY DiNAGHO

ADDRESS _____ DATE 2/20

PERCOCET #120
Ī po Q4-6H PRN PAIN

REFILL Ø TIMES DR.

DEA NO BA1424326

CASE Figure 36–2 Prescription #2 for patient Nancy Dimagho.

She discusses that she often feels dirty if she waits to have a bowel movement naturally, so she will take a Dulcolax tablet. She reports that she eats mostly meat and potatoes and little fruit and vegetables.

You question her about her medical history, and she tells you that she had breast cancer 5 years ago and received radiation. From that time she has had to take pain medication for progressively worse, in her opinion, bone pain. She states that she frequently has to take more medication than was prescribed for her because her pain is worse at certain times. She also has hypertension and is currently going through menopause. She does not smoke and reports to be a "social" drinker. She reports that with her insurance she does not have any problems affording her medications and likes to have generic medications if they are available. When asked about herbal medications, she initially denies usage of any herbal therapies, but then asks if St. John's wort is considered an herbal therapy. She states that she has been using it off and on for about two months for her hot flashes.

She denies having painful bowel movements, although occasionally after eating certain foods she feels bloated and will need medication to remove the pain (Dulcolax). She reports that she exercises about three times a week, walking on a treadmill, but has gained about 40 pounds since having cancer.

You review her prescription medication profile (Case Table 36–1).

CASE Table 36–1	Prescription Medication Profile

Nancy Dimagho
3578 Flamingo Street
Jacksonville, Florida 37757

Phone: 555-555-3567 **DOB:** 02/18/1950 **Insurer:** Blue Cross Blue Shield

Allergies/Intolerances: None

Rx No.	Drug Name	Directions	Date	R/F	Prescriber	Qty	RPh
600930	Zoloft 50 mg	1 tablet once daily for depression	02/18	3	Autry	30	RA
600929	Verapamil 240 mg	1 tablet once daily for blood pressure	02/18	4	Smith	30	JS
699234	Tamoxifen 20 mg	1 tablet once daily	02/05	10	Wong	30	RA
203494	Oxycodone/APAP 7.5/325	1 tablet every 4 hours as needed for pain	02/01	0	Autry	180	JS
203495	OxyContin 40 mg	1 tablet every 12 hours	02/01	0	Autry	60	JS
600930	Zoloft 50 mg	1 tablet once daily for depression	01/17	4	Autry	30	RA
600929	Verapamil 240 mg	1 tablet once daily for blood pressure	01/17	5	Smith	30	RA
699234	Tamoxifen 20 mg	1 tablet once daily	01/05	11	Wong	30	JS
202998	Oxycodone/APAP 7.5/325	1 tablet every 4 to 6 hours as needed for pain	01/05	0	Autry	180	JS
202999	OxyContin 40 mg	1 tablet every 12 hours	01/05	0	Autry	60	JS
443093	Hydrocodone/Ibuprofen 5/200	1 tablet every 4 hours as needed for pain; must make appointment with primary care provider	01/01	0	Johnson	15	KJ
600930	Zoloft 50 mg	1 tablet once daily for depression	12/15	5	Autry	30	KJ
600929	Verapamil 240 mg	1 tablet once daily for blood pressure	12/15	6	Smith	30	KJ
202440	Oxycodone/APAP 7.5/325	1 tablet every 4 to 6 hours as needed for pain	12/08	0	Autry	150	JS
202441	OxyContin 20 mg	2 tablet every morning and 1 tablet every evening	12/08	0	Autry	90	JS
695443	Tamoxifen 20 mg	1 tablet once daily	12/02	0	Wong	30	RA

Questions and Activities

1. Create a problem list for this patient.

2. On the basis of the patient's presentation and interview, what disease or physiologic issues might be causing this patient's primary complaint?

3. On the basis of the patient's prescription history, which of her medications may be worsening or causing her constipation?

4. What are some lifestyle modifications that Mrs. Dimagho could make that would decrease her symptoms of constipation?

5. What are the goals of therapy for the treatment of constipation?

6. What changes could be made to Mrs. Dimagho's medication regimen that would reduce her chances of having constipation?

7. What will you tell Mrs. Dimagho about her use of Dulcolax?

8. Which nonprescription medications may be used to treat Mrs. Dimagho's constipation on the basis of her preferences for therapy? How often may she use these agents, and how should they be administered?

9. What are common side effects of each of the recommendations in question 8?

10. Which nonprescription medications may be used to prevent constipation in Mrs. Dimagho? What dosages should be used and what are common side effects of each?

11. What herbal therapies may treat Mrs. Dimagho's complaints of constipation?

12. What may be used to determine whether the recommendations in question 8 are working?

13. Mrs. Dimagho mentions that as a kid her grandmother gave her castor oil or mineral oil for constipation; she states that she would like to try one of these. What do you tell her?

14. Develop a medication action plan for the patient that includes short- and long-term goals, side effect management, and when and how to follow up to determine whether the treatment is working.

15. What are the key points of education that the pharmacist should provide to Mrs. Dimagho? (Include information about the causes, prevention [lifestyle modification and nonprescription, prescription, and herbal products]), treatment, and monitoring of the disease.)

16. What concerns or questions do you have about the two new prescriptions Mrs. Dimagho dropped off?

17. What are indicators of drug-seeking behavior? Which ones does Mrs. Dimagho exhibit?

Mrs. Dimagho returns after three months (she did not follow the treatment plan that you recommended) with a question about a new medication. She states that she was watching television when a commercial for a new drug called Zelnorm came on. She heard it was good for chronic constipation, which is what she says she has. She would like to know if you think this medication would be good for her.

18. Create a benefit and risk analysis, and decide whether Zelnorm would be an appropriate therapy for this patient?

Additional Activities

1. How would you counsel a parent who says her 2-year-old child is constipated? What would be appropriate treatment for a child?

2. How does GlycoLax work and who should use this medication?

3. What is cathartic colon and which medications are usually the culprit? How do you treat cathartic colon?

Information Sources

1. Hseih C. Treatment of constipation in adults. *Am Fam Physician.* 2005;72:2277–84.

2. Curry CE, Butler DM. Constipation. In: Berardi RR, Kroon LA, McDermott JH, et al., eds. *Handbook of Nonprescription Drugs.* 13th ed. Washington DC: American Pharmacists Association; 2006: 305–34.

3. Joint National Committee on Prevention, Detection, Evaluation, and Treatment of High Blood Pressure. National Heart, Lung, and Blood Institute, National High Blood Pressure Education Program Coordinating Committee. Seventh Report of the Joint National Committee on Prevention, Detection, Evaluation, and Treatment of High Blood Pressure (JNC 7). Available at: www.nhlbi.nih.gov/guidelines/hypertension/jnc7full.pdf. Last accessed August 15, 2008.

4. Müller-Lissner SA, Kamm MA, Scarpignato C, et al Myths and misconceptions about chronic constipation. *Am J Gastroenterol.* 2005;100:232–42.

5. American College of Gastroenterology Chronic Constipation Task Force. An Evidence-based approach to the management of chronic constipation in North America. *Am J Gastroenterol.* 2005;100 (suppl):S1–22.

6. Ramkumar D, Rao SS. Efficacy and safety of traditional medical therapies for chronic constipation: systematic review. *Am J Gastroenterol.* 2005;100:936–71.

7. Hurdon V, Viola R, Schroder C. How useful is docusate in patients at risk for constipation? A systematic review of the evidence in the chronically ill. *J Pain Symptom Manage.* 2000; 9:130–6.

8. Kienzle-Horn S, Vix JM, Schuijt C, et al. Efficacy and safety of bisacodyl in the acute treatment of constipation: a double-blind, randomized, placebo-controlled study. *Aliment Pharmacol Ther.* 2006;23:1479–88.

9. Schiller LR. Review article: the therapy of constipation. *Aliment Pharmacol Ther.* 2001;15:749–63.

10. Hansen GR. The drug-seeking patient in the emergency room. *Emerg Med.* 2005;23:349–65.

11. Kamm MA, Müller-Lissner S, Talley NJ, et al. Tegaserod for the treatment of chronic constipation: a randomized, double blind, placebo-controlled multinational study. *Am J Gastroenterol.* 2005;100:362–72.

Objectives

1. State signs and symptoms of irritable bowel syndrome (IBS), including factors that may exacerbate symptoms.

2. Recognize demographics of people who typically have IBS. Implement Rome III criteria for IBS constipation predominant (IBS-C), IBS diarrhea predominant (IBS-D), and intermittent symptoms of IBS-C and IBS-D.

3. Differentiate between IBS and other gastrointestinal problems (i.e., inflammatory bowel disease, gastroesophageal disease).

4. Identify treatment options for IBS-associated constipation, diarrhea, abdominal discomfort, and pain.

5. Compose a management plan for patients with IBS, including both pharmacologic and nonpharmacologic modalities.

6. Monitor the safety and efficacy of treatment regimen for the patient with IBS.

7. Evaluate for necessary changes that could be adapted to the overall care of a patient with IBS.

Scenario

Mary Malone, a 32-year-old woman comes into the pharmacy to purchase Maalox. She witnesses you taking a customer's blood pressure and seeks your advice about a complaint of abdominal pain and constipation. As the community pharmacy resident, you do an extensive medication history on Ms. Malone. She explains that ever since she started graduate school, her "body just does not feel right." She states "my stomach is always bloated and gassy. Even when I do go to the bathroom, I feel as if I never went." Mary also mentions that her stools look really strange, "like little hard balls." She has even missed a few classes because of her stomach problems. Her diet includes vegetables and legumes because she is a vegetarian and likes to have a healthy diet. Until recently, she never really spoke to anyone about her stomach problems and basically "lived off Maalox." However, she feels quite comfortable talking to you because you seem like you really care.

You ask Ms. Malone to wait a few minutes as you look up her medication profile.

After reviewing Ms. Malone's prescription medication profile (Case Table 37–1), you ask her a few more questions about her other medications. You particularly notice the prescription for diphenoxylate/atropine (Lomotil). Ms. Malone tells you that sometimes she gets diarrhea and that about a month ago it was really bad. "I don't have insurance so I went to the student clinic on campus because I was in a lot of pain and my stomach felt very uncomfortable. They basically told me that it was probably food poising from the Mexican restaurant that I went to the other night. The medicine they gave me really helped!" You also mention to her that a symptom of hypothyroidism is constipation, and by correcting this health problem with Levoxyl, it can sometimes cause symptoms of hyperthyroidism, such as diarrhea. She says that she has remained on the same dose of Levoxyl for almost a decade and that these stomach problems started about 6 months ago. Coincidentally, she started taking Ambien around 6 months ago. You ask her the reason for taking Ambien. She confides in you that she started taking the pills because her mother bumped into her stepfather at a New Year's party earlier this year and has stayed in touch with him ever since. It makes Ms. Malone really nervous because he was quite abusive to both of them, and it took a lot to restart their lives after leaving him many years ago.

Questions and Activities

1. On the basis of the patient's drug therapy, identify the disease-related problem and state the current drug therapy to solve the problem.

2. After interviewing Ms. Malone further about her specific bowel movements, you suspect that she may have IBS. Identify signs and symptoms associated with IBS and tools that can aid in diagnosing it on the basis of her specific symptoms.

3. What are the goals of pharmacotherapy for this patient?

4. Identify the treatment alternatives available for the drug therapy problem.

CASE Table 37–1 Prescription Medication Profile

Mary Malone
895 Clinton St
Somerset, NJ 08823

Phone: 908-454-7892   **DOB:** 07/21/1974   **Insurance:** None

Allergies/Intolerances: NKDA

Rx No.	Drug Name	Directions	Date	R/F	Prescriber	Qty	RPh
2320382	Yasmin	1 tablet by mouth once daily	7/02	5	Brown	28	JM
1909078	Levoxyl 75 mcg	1 tablet by mouth every morning	7/02	5	Brown	30	JM
6783439	Ambien 10 mg	1 tablet by mouth every night	7/02	5	Brown	30	JM
2320382	Yasmin	1 tablet by mouth once daily	6/05	5	Brown	28	JM
1909078	Levoxyl 75 mcg	1 tablet by mouth every morning	6/05	5	Brown	30	JM
6783439	Ambien 10 mg	1 tablet by mouth every night	6/05	5	Brown	30	JM
5345844	Diphenoxylate HCl/ atropine 2.5/.025 mg	2 tablets every 6 hours as needed	6/01	0	Brown	56	JM
2320382	Yasmin	1 tablet by mouth once daily	5/08	5	Brown	28	JM
1909078	Levoxyl 75 mcg	1 tablet by mouth every morning	5/08	5	Brown	30	JM
6783439	Ambien 10 mg	1 tablet by mouth every night	5/08	5	Brown	30	JM
2320382	Yasmin	1 tablet by mouth once daily	4/11	5	Brown	28	JM
1909078	Levoxyl 75 mcg	1 tablet by mouth every morning	4/11	5	Brown	30	JM
6783439	Ambien 10 mg	1 tablet by mouth every night	4/11	5	Brown	30	JM
2320382	Yasmin	1 tablet by mouth once daily	3/14	5	Brown	28	JM
1909078	Levoxyl 75 mcg	1 tablet by mouth every morning	3/14	5	Brown	30	JM
6783439	Ambien 10 mg	1 tablet by mouth every night	3/14	5	Brown	30	JM
2320382	Yasmin	1 tablet by mouth once daily	2/15	5	Brown	28	JM
1909078	Levoxyl 75 mcg	1 tablet by mouth every morning	2/15	5	Brown	30	JM
6783439	Ambien 10 mg	1 tablet by mouth every night	2/15	5	Brown	30	JM
2320382	Yasmin	1 tablet by mouth once daily	1/18	5	Brown	28	JM
1909078	Levoxyl 75 mcg	1 tablet by mouth every morning	1/18	5	Brown	30	JM

5. Using Case Figure 37–1, identify the interventions(s) to solve Ms. Malone's problem(s) and the anticipated outcome(s).

6. What drug(s), dosage form(s), and duration(s) of therapy are optimal for the treatment of this patient's problem?

7. Ms. Malone mentions to you that she read somewhere about taking alternative medications for stomach problems. She would like to know your opinion about the use of herbal and alternative medications for IBS.

8. What intervention (e.g., patient recommendation, call to provider or family member, contact emergency medical services, etc.) is necessary for implementing the treatment?

9. What monitoring parameters available in the community pharmacy setting should be used to evaluate therapy in this patient, including efficacy and adverse effects?

10. What nondrug therapies or lifestyle modifications might be useful in managing this patient's problem?

11. Develop a medication action plan for the patient; include short-term and long-range goals.

12. What are the pertinent topics to address during patient education?

13. Develop a follow-up plan for this patient; include time to follow up and method of contact.

Which of the following symptoms do you have?
- Abdominal cramps
- Bloating
- Constipation
- Diarrhea   *Sometimes*
- Anxiety
- Nausea
- Tiredness

Do the above symptoms recur? If so, how frequently?
I get the symptoms at least once a week.

If you have abdominal cramps, how bad are they on a scale from 1 to 5 (five being the worst)?   *3*

Does the pain subside after a bowel movement?   *Yes*

When you have a bowel movement, do you have a feeling of incomplete evacuation?   *Yes*

Do you locate the nearest toilet wherever you go?   *No*

When you have a bowel movement, do you have to strain?   *Yes*

Which of the following describe your stools?
Hard, lumpy and painful to pass   *Mainly*
Solid but soft and easy to pass
Watery and difficult to control   *Sometimes*

When you have an "attack," does the appearance of your bowel change?
Yes, usually it becomes hard—like pellets.

When did you first experience the above symptoms?   *About 6 months ago*

Can you relate it to any big event in your life (change of job, house, divorce, bereavement)?
Actually yes, I started graduate school this year and it is hard to go back to school full-time after working for so many years.

Does stress appear to bring it on?
Yes, especially when my mom talks to my stepfather.

Can you relate it to any change in your eating habits?
I don't think so. I always try to eat healthy.

Have you experienced any rectal bleeding, fever, night sweats or weight loss since you have had these problems?   *None at all*

CASE Figure 37–1 Symptom questionnaire for irritable bowel syndrome.

Additional Activities

1. Compare and contrast clinical presentation and treatments of IBS, Crohn's disease, and ulcerative colitis.

2. Compare and contrast the different probiotics and their role in improving symptoms of IBS.

3. Research the alternative medicine therapies for the treatment and prevention of IBS.

4. Develop a business plan for implementing an education and monitoring service for patients with IBS.

Information Sources

1. Drossman DA, LI Z, Andruzzi E, et al. US householder survey of functional gastrointestinal disorders. Prevalence, sociodemography, and health impact. *Dig Dis Sci.* 1993;38:1559–80.

2. Drossman DA, Camilleri M, Mayer EA, et al. AGA technical review on irritable bowel syndrome. *Gastroenterology.* 2002;123:2108–31.

3. Manning AP, Thompson WG, Heaton KW, et al. Towards positive diagnosis of the irritable bowel. *Br Med J.* 1978;2:653–4.

4. Drossman DA. The functional gastrointestinal disorders and the Rome III process. *Gastroenterology.* 2006;130:1377–90.

5. Hammer J, Eslick GD, Howell SC, et al. Diagnostic yield of alarm features in irritable bowel syndrome and functional dyspepsia. *Gut.* 2004;53:666–72.

6. Drossman DA, Leserman J, Nachman G, et al. Sexual and physical abuse in women with functional or organic gastrointestinal disorders. *Ann Intern Med.* 1990;113:828–33.

7. Whitehead WE, Bosmajian L, Zonderman AB, et al. Symptoms of psychologic distress associated with irritable bowel syndrome. Comparison of community and medical clinic samples. *Gastroenterology.* 1988;95:709–14.

8. Drossman DA, Sandler RS, McKee DC, et al. Bowel patterns among subjects not seeking health care. Use of a questionnaire to identify a population with bowel dysfunction. *Gastroenterology.* 1982;83:529–34.

9. Gralnek IM, Hays RD, Kilbourne A, et al. The impact of irritable bowel syndrome on health-related quality of life. *Gastroenterology.* 2000;119:654–60.

10. van Dulmen AM, Fennis J, Mokkink HG, et al. The relationship between compliant-related cognitions in referred patients with irritable bowel syndrome and subsequent health care–seeking behavior in primary care. *Fam Pract.* 1996;13:12–7.

11. Jailwala J, Imperiale TF, Kroenke K. Pharmacologic treatment of the irritable bowel syndrome: a systematic review of randomized, controlled trials. *Ann Intern Med.* 2000;133:136–47.

12. Brandt LJ, Bjorkman D, Fennerty MB, et al. Systematic review on the management of irritable bowel syndrome in North America. *Am J Gastroenterol.* 2002;97(11 suppl):S7–26.

13. Bueno L, Fioramonti J, Delvaux M, Frexinos J. Mediators and pharmacology of visceral sensitivity: from basic to clinical investigations. *Gastroenterology.* 1997;112:1714–43.

14. Jackson JL, O'Malley PG, Tomkins G, et al. Treatment of functional gastrointestinal disorders with antidepressant medications: a meta-analysis. *Am J Med.* 2000;108:65–72.

15. Bensoussan A, Talley NJ, Hing M, et al. Treatment of irritable bowel syndrome with Chinese herbal medicine: a randomized controlled trial. *JAMA.* 1998;280:1585–9.

16. Pittler MH, Ernst E. Peppermint oil for irritable bowel syndrome: a critical review and meta-analysis. *Am J Gastroenterol.* 1998; 93:1131–5.

17. Spanier JA, Howden CW, Jones MP. A systematic review of alternative therapies in the irritable bowel syndrome. *Arch Intern Med.* 2003; 163:265–74.

38 Inflammatory Bowel Disease

Margie E. Snyder and Melissa A. Somma

Acknowledgments: Mark Hahn, PharmD, and Thomas Willoughby, PharmD Candidate, for their assistance in the preparation of this case.

Objectives

1. Describe similarities and differences in patient presentation and diagnostic tests in patients with Crohn's disease and ulcerative colitis.

2. List goals of therapy for inflammatory bowel disease (IBD).

3. Formulate drug and nondrug treatment alternatives for a patient with IBD.

4. Identify common challenges encountered by pharmacists in the community setting when providing patient care, and suggest possible solutions.

5. Design a patient-specific medication-related action plan with monitoring and follow-up.

6. Provide appropriate patient education.

Scenario

At 8 pm on August 27, you are working as a student pharmacist at a community pharmacy alongside a pharmacist preceptor in a dispensing role. A patient, Rachel Thompson, approaches the drop-off window of your pharmacy. You introduce yourself as a student pharmacist and the patient presents the following prescription: prednisone 20 mg #10 take as directed.

You gather her basic information (address, date of birth, phone number, and allergies) and then ask the patient to step to the side of the counter for privacy. You proceed to ask her what the medication is to be used for and if she understands how she is to take it. She explains the medication is for a flare-up of her Crohn's disease and that she was just seen about an hour earlier at a nearby emergency department. However, her abdominal discomfort had made it difficult to focus on what the physician was saying, and she does not remember how she was instructed to take the medication. You explain that your preceptor will need to contact the prescribing physician, and you proceed to ask the patient to sit in the waiting area.

You present the information you gathered from the patient to your pharmacist preceptor. The pharmacist proceeds to call the emergency department seeking the dosage instructions from the physician resident who wrote the prescription. On calling, the pharmacist learns the resident has left for the evening and will need to be paged. While you and your preceptor wait for a call back, you notice the patient take out a pack of cigarettes and step outside for a few minutes.

The physician resident returns the call after approximately 20 minutes. The instructions are provided and you proceed to fill the prescription and counsel the patient.

Questions and Activities

1. What are the appropriate counseling points for a patient with Crohn's disease taking prednisone as prescribed in the scenario?

As you are speaking with the patient, you begin to realize she has a number of questions about her medications and her disease. You also note she has some concerns about the cost of all of her medications. You and your preceptor suggest to the patient that she may benefit from a one-to-one session with the pharmacist, which is called a medication therapy management appointment. You explain the service and suggest that an appointment is available for the next day.

2. How would you explain a medication therapy management service (MTMS) to a patient?

The patient agrees to an appointment, mentioning that her physician had recently encouraged her to quit smoking. The next morning, you begin preparing for Ms. Thompson's visit by printing her prescription medication profile (Case Table 38–1) from the pharmacy's dispensing software.

3. On the basis of the patient's presentation and drug therapy, identify the drug- or disease-related problems, and state the current drug therapy for each problem.

CASE Table 38–1   Prescription Medication Profile

Rachel Thompson
324 Oak Blvd.
Pittsburgh, PA 15211

Phone: 412-231-8990   **DOB:** 4-18-1984   **Insurer:** None

Allergies/Intolerances: Sulfa drugs

Rx No.	Drug Name	Directions	Date	R/F	Prescriber	Qty	Day Supply	Price[a]	Customer Paid	RPh
124414	Prednisone 20 mg	2 tablets daily	8/27	0	Williams	10	5	7.99	7.99	DR
123457	Ortho Tri-Cyclen	1 tablet daily	8/23	2	Charles	28	28	48.07	48.07	FT
123457	Ortho Tri-Cyclen	1 tablet daily	7/23	3	Charles	28	28	48.07	48.07	FT
124210	Pentasa 250 mg cap	4 capsules four times daily	7/23	0	Charles	240	14	169.86	169.86	FT
123457	Ortho Tri-Cyclen	1 tablet once daily	6/27	4	Charles	84	90	129.96	40.00	DR
123457	Ortho Tri-Cyclen	1 tablet once daily	5/26	5	Charles	84	90	129.96	40.00	DR
123456	Pentasa 250 mg cap	4 capsules four times daily	4/25	0	Charles	1440	90	916.24	40.00	DR
123457	Ortho Tri-Cyclen	1 tablet once daily	4/25	6	Charles	84	90	129.96	40.00	DR
123810	Ranitidine 150 mg	1 tablet daily	4/25	4	Charles	90	90	14.99	14.99	DR
123457	Ortho Tri-Cyclen	1 tablet daily	3/25	7	Charles	84	90	129.96	40.00	FT
123457	Ortho Tri-Cyclen	1 tablet daily	2/25	8	Charles	84	90	129.96	40.00	FT
123457	Ortho Tri-Cyclen	1 tablet daily	1/25	9	Charles	84	90	129.96	40.00	FT
123456	Pentasa 250 mg cap	4 capsules four times daily	1/25	1	Charles	1440	90	916.24	40.00	FT

[a] Prices from http://www.drugstore.com. Last accessed November 6, 2006.

4. What are the goals of pharmacotherapy for this patient?

5. What are the treatment alternatives available for each drug therapy problem?

6. What nondrug therapies or lifestyle modifications might be useful in managing this patient's problems?

7. What are pertinent topics to address during patient education?

8. Before seeing this patient, what other information will you try to collect by contacting her physician? How will this contact be made?

9. What questions will you need to ask the patient during her appointment?

During her visit, you learn that her Crohn's disease was diagnosed as mild-to-moderate approximately 4 years ago, and she has been a patient at your pharmacy for about 1 year. She last had active Crohn's disease symptoms approximately 2 years ago. She tells you that she recently graduated from college and was removed from her father's insurance plan. She is getting married in 3 months and will be covered by her husband's insurance at that time; however, her current position does not offer prescription drug benefits. Because of the cost, she has been taking her Pentasa as one 250 mg capsule four times daily to extend the time between refills while "still getting some medication." Fortunately, her symptoms of gastroesophageal reflux disease have been mostly well controlled, although she has noticed increased frequency of heartburn since she stopped taking the ranitidine.

In addition, she smokes approximately 1 pack per day and is interested in quitting. She mentions that both her physician and her fiancé support her decision to quit. Unfortunately, quitting has been difficult because she is under a lot of stress lately between losing her health insurance and making plans for her wedding.

After asking about nonprescription and herbal product use, you add the following to her medication profile:

- *Ibuprofen 200 mg, 1 to 2 capsules every 6 to 8 hours as needed for menstrual cramps*
- *Loperamide 2 mg, 1 tablet as needed for diarrhea*
- *Ferrous sulfate 325 mg, 1 tablet three times daily for anemia (purchases OTC)*

Physical assessment measures included:

- *Height: 62 inches tall*
- *Weight: 112 pounds*
- *Blood pressure: 114/76 mm Hg*
- *Heart rate: 74 beats/min*

Review of systems revealed:

- *Patient complained of moderate abdominal pain (4 on 10-point scale) and had 2 loose stools this morning.*
- *Patient denied headache, dizziness, changes in vision, shortness of breath, chest pain, and lower-extremity edema.*
- *Laboratory data (faxed from the physician's office) was within normal limits, except hemoglobin concentration of 11 g/dL, hematocrit of 35%, and mean corpuscular volume of 70 μm^3.*
- *Diagnostic reports showed mild-to-moderate ileocolonic Crohn's disease.*

10. With this information about her presentation and laboratory values, how would the patient's disease- and drug-related problem list change?

11. How might Ms. Thompson's presentation, laboratory information, or both change if she had mild-to-moderate ulcerative colitis?

12. Identify the interventions necessary to solve the problems and the anticipated outcomes.

13. What drugs, dosage forms, schedules, and durations of therapy are optimal for the treatment of this patient's problems? In all cases, what do you monitor for efficacy and toxicity?

14. What interventions are necessary for implementing this treatment?

15. How would your responses to questions 12, 13, and 14 change if you were unable to obtain Ms. Thompson's laboratory information from her physician before her MTMS appointment?

16. What monitoring parameters available in the community pharmacy setting should be used to evaluate therapy in this patient, including efficacy and adverse effects?

17. Develop a personal medication record and medication action plan for Ms. Thompson; include short-term and long-term goals.

18. Develop a follow-up plan for Ms. Thompson; include time to follow up and method of contact.

19. Develop a consultation letter for the patient's physician, and describe how you will follow up with the physician.

20. When speaking with the patient, she mentions her upcoming wedding and that she and her husband wish to have children in the future. How would your response to question 13 change if this patient were pregnant?

21. How might this patient's drug therapy and medication action plan be different if she had mild-to-moderate ulcerative colitis?

Additional Activities

1. Investigate new therapies for Crohn's disease.

2. Research the efficacy and safety of alternative medications for the treatment of IBD.

3. Develop a business plan for a new patient care service focused on managing and educating patients with IBD.

4. When do patients usually present with IBD, and what signs and symptoms lead to diagnosis?

Information Sources

1. Micromedex Healthcare Series [database online]. Greenwood Village, Colo: Thomson Micromedex. Updated periodically. Available at: http://www.micromedex.com (subscription required). Last accessed September 2008.

2. Bluml BM. Definition of medication therapy management: development of professionwide consensus. *J Am Pharm Assoc.* 2005;45:566–72.

3. American Pharmacists Association and National Association of Chain Drug Stores Foundation. Medication therapy management

in community pharmacy practice: core elements of an MTM service (version 1.0). *J Am Pharm Assoc.* 2005;45:573–9.

4. Hanauer SB, Sandborn W. Management of Crohn's disease in adults. *Am J Gastroenterol.* 2001;96:635–43.

5. DeVault KR, Castell DO. Updated guidelines for the diagnosis and treatment of gastroesophageal reflux disease. *Am J Gastroenterol.* 2005;100:190–200.

6. Frishman WH, Mitta W, Kupersmith A, Ky T. Nicotine and non-nicotine smoking cessation pharmacotherapies. *Cardiol Rev.* 2006;14:57–73.

7. Surgeon General Guide: treating tobacco use and dependence. Available at: http://www.surgeongeneral.gov/tobacco. Last accessed August 16, 2008.

8. Knutson D, Greenburg G, Cronau H. Management of Crohn's disease: a practical approach. *Am Fam Physician.* 2003; 68:707–14.

9. Hanauer SB. Inflammatory bowel disease: epidemiology, pathogenesis, and therapeutic opportunities. *Inflamm Bowel Dis.* 2006;12(suppl):S3–9.

10. Bruno M. Irritable bowel syndrome and inflammatory bowel disease in pregnancy. *J Perinat Neonat Nurs.* 2004;18:341–50.

11. Friedman S, Blumberg R. Inflammatory bowel disease. In: Kasper DL, Braunwald E, Fauci A, et al., eds. *Harrison's Principles of Internal Medicine.* 16th ed. New York: McGraw-Hill; 2005: 1776–88.

12. Umbreit J. Iron deficiency: a concise review. *Am J Hematol.* 2005;78:225–31.

13. Best WR, Becktel JM, Singleton JW. Rederived values of the eight coefficients of the Crohn's Disease Activity Index (CDAI). *Gastroenterology.*1979;77:843–6.

14. Kornbluth A, Sachar DB. Ulcerative colitis practice guidelines in adults (update). *Am J Gastroenterol.* 2004;99:1371–85.

39 Nausea and Vomiting

Denise L. Glasser

Objectives

1. Provide nonpharmacologic therapy recommendations for nausea and vomiting.

2. Describe the pharmacologic therapy for nausea and vomiting; include medication names, medication classes, mechanisms of action, and adverse effects.

3. Given an individual patient case, design an optimal treatment regimen for a patient with nausea and vomiting.

4. Develop a plan for monitoring the efficacy of a treatment regimen for a patient with nausea and vomiting.

Scenario

A family of four approaches the counseling counter at the local pharmacy. The family is leaving tomorrow for a cruise to Bermuda. The mother has heard that the waters to Bermuda are usually rough, and she is worried about motion sickness for her two children. She would like to consult the pharmacist on available preventive measures for motion sickness. The children are 3 and 10 years of age.

Questions and Activities

1. On the basis of the patient's presentation and drug therapy, identify the drug- or disease-related problem and state the current drug therapy for the problem.

2. What are the goals of pharmacotherapy for this family?

3. Identify the treatment alternatives available for the drug therapy problem.

4. Identify the intervention(s) to solve the problem(s) and the anticipated outcome(s).

5. What drug(s), dosage form(s), schedule(s), and duration(s) of therapy are optimal for the treatment of this family's problem?

6. What intervention (e.g., patient recommendation, call to provider or family member, contact emergency medical services, etc.) is necessary for implementing this treatment?

7. What monitoring parameters available in the community pharmacy setting should be used to evaluate therapy in this family, including efficacy and adverse effects?

8. What nondrug therapies or lifestyle modifications might be useful in managing this family's problem?

9. Develop a medication action plan for the family; include short-term and long-range goals.

10. What are the pertinent topics to address during patient education?

11. Develop a follow-up plan for this family; include time to follow up and method of contact.

12. The mother is purchasing a bottle of liquid Pepto-Bismol to take on the trip. What counseling should the pharmacist perform?

13. List exclusions for self-treatment of nausea and vomiting in adults.

14. List exclusions for self-treatment of nausea and vomiting in children.

15. How is chemotherapy-induced nausea and vomiting treated differently?

16. What herbal products have evidence for the treatment of nausea and vomiting?

Additional Activities

1. What medications and treatment alternatives would be appropriate for pregnancy-induced nausea and vomiting?

2. Develop a fluid rehydration plan; include the types of fluids for the following patients:

   a. 75-kg man with mild dehydration and four vomiting episodes per day

   b. 10-kg child with no dehydration but three vomiting episodes per day

3. Create a plan-o-gram in a community pharmacy for products to prevent and treat motion sickness and nausea and vomiting.

Information Sources

1. Shane-McWhorter L, Fermo J. Nausea and vomiting. In: Berardi RR, McDermott JH, Newton, GD, et al., eds. *Handbook of Nonprescription Drugs*. 15th ed. Washington, DC: American Pharmacists Association; 2006:381–401.

2. Jewell D, Young G. Interventions for nausea and vomiting in early pregnancy. *Cochrane Database Syst Rev.* 2003;4:CD000145.

3. Taketomo CK, Hodding JH, Kraus DM. *Pediatric Dosage Handbook.* 13th ed. Hudson, Ohio: Lexi-Comp; 2006.

4. Jewell D, Young G. Interventions for nausea and vomiting in early pregnancy. *Cochrane Database Syst Rev.* 2003;4:CD000145.

Section

8

Rheumatology and Immunologic Disorders

40 Osteoarthritis

Holly Hurley

Objectives

1. Recognize the pathophysiology and clinical presentation of osteoarthritis.

2. Identify risk factors and goals of therapy for a patient with osteoarthritis.

3. Discuss nonpharmacologic therapy that is pertinent for patients with osteoarthritis.

4. Discuss pharmacotherapeutic options for patients with osteoarthritis, and include dose, schedule, duration of therapy, and patient education.

5. Reevaluate the patient's osteoarthritis therapy after follow-up with the patient.

Scenario

You are working on a Saturday at your community pharmacy practice and are busy dispensing medications. A patient comes to the counter and asks to speak to you, the pharmacist. She needs your advice about a nonprescription medication her neighbor mentioned that can help with arthritis pain. She believes it is called "Gluco something" plus another drug that starts with a "C," but she cannot remember the medication's name.

On speaking with the patient, you learn that she is experiencing tenderness and dull, aching pain in her hands and knees. She tells you that the pain worsens at night, and she has not been able to sleep for months. The patient appears to be obese and tired. She has been taking Tylenol PM (gelcaps) every night to help with insomnia. She also states that her knee tends to crackle when she gets up from a chair. In addition, her knee tends to buckle, and 1 month ago she fell in the shower. The patient was sent to the emergency department; she sustained no major injuries from the fall. However, the patient had some soreness from the event for a couple of days; therefore, the physician was giving her some pain medication.

She does not know the name of the prescription medications she is taking, but she does know she has diabetes, osteoporosis, and a thyroid issue. You find out that the

patient, Sarah Adams, a 66-year-old white woman, is an existing customer at your pharmacy. You decide to step up to the prescription counter and check the computer for a list of her current prescription medications (Case Table 40–1).

Questions and Activities

1. What other questions would you ask the patient before counseling her on her current drug therapy?

2. On the basis of the patient's presentation and chief complaint, identify the current disease-related problem.

3. What risk factors does the patient have for osteoarthritis?

4. Name the signs and symptoms mentioned by the patient that are consistent with osteoarthritis.

5. What are the goals of pharmacotherapy for this patient?

6. What nondrug therapies or lifestyle modifications might be useful for this patient to help manage the symptoms of osteoarthritis? Include a discussion of the role of weight loss and physical activity programs, assistive medical devices, and alternative therapies such as massage, acupuncture, and so forth in your answer.

7. What product was probably recommended by Ms. Adams' friend? What information can you give her about this product's efficacy and safety in osteoarthritis treatment?

8. Would you recommend glucosamine and/or chondroitin for Ms. Adams today? If so, what information can you give Ms. Adams on selecting a product, dosing, duration of therapy, and so forth?

9. Ms. Adams understands a bit more about glucosamine but is concerned about her diabetes because this medicine has the word "glucose" in it. She wants to know if it can increase her blood glucose concentrations.

10. What other prescription or nonprescription drug(s), dosage form(s), schedule(s), and duration(s) of

CASE Table 40–1   Prescription Medication Profile

Sarah Adams
187 Larson St.
Bristol, VA 24202

Phone: 276-766-7234   **DOB:** 09/08/40   **Insurer:** Medicare-Humana

Allergies/Intolerances: PCN

Rx No.	Drug Name	Directions	Date	R/F	Prescriber	Qty	RPh
617243	Synthroid 137 mcg	1 tablet by mouth every morning	09/04	2	Clemmons	30	TY
412423	Darvocet N-100	1 tablet by mouth every 4 hours as needed for pain	08/18	3	Clemmons	60	HH
614323	Glyburide 10 mg	1 tablet by mouth every morning	08/15	3	Adkins	30	TY
814323	Diabetic Test Strips	Use as directed for testing blood glucose concentration	08/15	As needed	Adkins	50	TY
617243	Synthroid 137 mcg	1 tablet by mouth every morning	08/03	0	Clemmons	30	HH
614323	Glyburide 10 mg	1 tablet by mouth every morning	07/14	1	Adkins	30	TY
612646	Fosamax 70 mg	1 tablet by mouth once weekly on the same day of the week	02/15	10	Clemmons	4	HH

therapy are recommended as first-line treatment for Ms. Adam's osteoarthritis symptoms?

11. Ms. Adams is also interested in learning more about topical osteoarthritis therapies. Discuss efficacy and safety of topical products. Which treatment(s) would you recommend if Ms. Adams would like to try a topical therapy?

12. What potential drug therapy problem(s) do you identify from Ms. Adams' complaints today and the information in her medication profile?

13. Identify the treatment alternatives available for the drug therapy problems.

14. What would you recommend for Ms. Adams today on the basis of her questions? Please include dose and duration of therapy with all recommendations.

15. What intervention (e.g., patient recommendation, call to provider or family member, contact emergency services, etc.) is necessary to solve the patient's medication problems?

16. Develop a follow-up plan for this patient; include time to follow up and method of contact.

17. The patient returns to the pharmacy about 3 months after the first visit. The drug therapy is helping to manage the patient's knee pain on most days of the week. However, she is now having some inflammation of the knee joint as well. What therapy approach would you now recommend to the patient?

18. The patient returns to the pharmacy about 9 months after the first visit. The drug therapy instituted is no longer helping to manage the patient's knee pain. She has tried acetaminophen, NSAIDs, and most other osteoarthritis drug therapies. The patient is complaining of severe joint pain, buckling, and crackling of the knee. She describes the crackling sound as "bone grinding on bone." What therapy approach would you now recommend to the patient?

Additional Activities

1. Review the medication guide for NSAIDs. What information in this medication guide do you think is most important for patients to know? How would you obtain a large number of NSAID medication guides for distribution in a busy community pharmacy? Discuss methods to ensure medication guides are dispensed for each intended patient and to increase awareness of medication guide information among patients.

2. Look over the natural supplement area in a community pharmacy and select products that promote "joint health" or other related claims. What common ingredients are listed in these products? Would you recommend any of these products for your patients?

Information Sources

1. *Osteoarthritis*. Atlanta, Ga: Arthritis Foundation; 2002:2–20. Publication No. 835–5265/7.02.

2. Hinton R, Moody RL, Davis AW, et al. Osteoarthritis: diagnosis and therapeutic considerations. *Am Fam Physician*. 2002;65:841–8.

3. Hanson KE, Elliott, ME. In: DiPiro JT, Talbert. RL, et al., eds. *Pharmacotherapy: A Pathophysiologic Approach*. 6th ed. New York: McGraw-Hill; 2002:1685–703.

4. Recommendations for the medical management of osteoarthritis of the hip and knee: 2000 update. *Arthritis Rheum*. 2000;43:1905–15.

5. Centers for Disease Control and Prevention. Arthritis Intervention Programs. Available at: http://www.cdc.gov/arthritis/intervention. Last accessed August 11, 2008.

6. Arthritis Foundation. Arthritis Self-Help Course. Available at: http://www.arthritis.org/events/getinvolved/ProgramsServices/arthritisselfhelp.asp. Last accessed August 18, 2008.

7. Felson DT. Osteoarthritis. *Rheum Dis Clin North Am*. 1990;16:499–512.

8. Arthritis Foundation. Exercise Program. Available at: http://www.arthritis.org/events/getinvolved/ProgramsServices/afep.asp. Last accessed August 18, 2008.

9. Ettinger W, Burns R, Messier P, et al. A randomized trial comparing aerobic exercise and resistance exercise with a health education program in older adults with knee osteoarthritis: the Fitness Arthritis and Seniors Trial. *JAMA*. 1997;277:25–31.

10. Arthritis Foundation. Aquatic Program. Available at: http://www.arthritis.org/events/getinvolved/ProgramsServices/aquaticprogram.asp. Last accessed August 18, 2008.

11. Messier SP, Loeser RF, Miller GD, et al. Exercise and dietary weight loss in overweight and obese older adults with knee osteoarthritis: the Arthritis, Diet, and Activity Promotion Trial. *Arthritis Rheum*. 2004;50:1501–10.

12. *The Effect of Reducing Falls on Long-Term Care Expenses: Literature Review*. Washington, DC: US Department of Health and Human Services; 2004:1–100. Publication No. HHS-100-03-0008.

13. Morelli V, Naquin C, Weaver V, et al. Alternative therapies for traditional disease states: osteoarthritis. *Am Fam Physician*. 2003;67:339–44.

14. Clegg DO, Reda DJ, Harris CL, et al. Glucosamine, chondroitin sulfate, and the two in combination for painful knee osteoarthritis. *N Engl J Med*. 2006;354:795–808.

15. Marshall PD, Poddar S, Tweed EM. Do glucosamine and chondroitin worsen blood sugar control in diabetes? *J Fam Pract*. 2006;55:1091–3.

16. Deal CL, Schnitzer TJ, Lipstein E. Treatment of arthritis with topical capsaicin: a double-blind trial. *Clin Ther*. 1991;13:383–95.

17. Kirkwood CK, Melton ST. In: Berardi RR, Kroon LA, McDermott JH, et al., eds. *Handbook of Nonprescription Drugs: An Interactive Approach to Self-Care*. 15th ed. Washington, DC: American Pharmacists Association; 2006:995–1007.

18. Manek NJ, Lane NE. Osteoarthritis: current concepts in diagnosis and management. *Am Fam Physician*. 2000;61:1795–804.

19. Altman R, Alarcon G, Appelrouth D, et al. The American College of Rheumatology criteria for the classification and reporting of osteoarthritis of the hand. *Arthritis Rheum*. 1990;33:1601–10.

20. Hilaire ML, Treatment of osteoarthritis. *US Pharm*. 2006;31:49–55.

21. DeAngelo NA, Gordin V. Treatment of patients with arthritis-related pain. *J Am Osteopath Assoc*. 2004;104(suppl):S2–S5.

22. Yu JG, Boies SM, Olefsky JM. The effect of oral glucosamine sulfate on insulin sensitivity in human subjects. *Diabetes Care*. 2003;26:1941–2.

23. Easton, BT. Evaluation and treatment of the patient with osteoarthritis. *J Fam Pract*. 2001;50:791–7.

24. Runkel DR, Cupp MJ. Glucosamine sulfate use in osteoarthritis. *Am J Health Syst Pharm*. 1999;56:267–9.

41 Rheumatoid Arthritis

Amy L. Whitaker

Objectives

1. List treatment alternatives for rheumatoid arthritis, their mechanism of action, and place in therapy.

2. Evaluate the drug regimen of a patient with rheumatoid arthritis for appropriateness of care.

3. Recommend appropriate nonpharmacologic options for managing patients with rheumatoid arthritis.

4. Counsel patients about the drug therapy used to treat rheumatoid arthritis.

5. Identify medication and therapy issues in the care of patients with rheumatoid arthritis specific to community pharmacy practice.

Scenario

Anna Montgomery is a 58-year-old white woman well known to you in your pharmacy. She comes to the pharmacy today with two new prescriptions (Case Figures 41–1 and 41–2).

At the drop-off counter, the patient expresses concern about giving herself injections. She does not know how to give herself a shot. She also asks you if she will need to continue to take that "little yellow pill" every day because the doctor is changing her arthritis medicine from tablets to a shot. You are able to review her prescription records in your pharmacy computer (Case Table 41–1).

Questions and Activities

1. What are the goals of pharmacotherapy for this patient?

2. Identify the treatment alternatives available to treat this patient, their mechanism of action, and place in therapy.

3. Will the patient need to continue with her folic acid? Why or why not?

4. You realize that you do not have the injectable methotrexate in stock. You would like to verify that you can order it while you are talking to Mrs. Montgomery. You pull up your pharmacy wholesaler's order

CASE Figure 41–1 Prescription for patient Anna Montgomery.

CASE Figure 41–2 Prescription for patient Anna Montgomery.

CASE Table 41–1   Prescription Medication Profile

Anna Montgomery
12204 Bridgeview Circle
Richmond, VA 23296

Phone: 804-555-3237   **DOB:** 08/22/1950   **Insurer:** Anthem

Allergies/Intolerances: NKDA

Rx No.	Drug Name	Directions	Date	R/F	Prescriber	Qty	RPh
696872	Rheumatrex 2.5 mg	Take 6 tablets as directed each week	9/4	0	Bombay	24	GC
696871	Folic acid 1 mg	1 tablet every day	9/4	0	Bombay	30	GC
692888	Prednisone 10 mg	Take as directed	8/9	0	Bombay	48	CT
694027	Rheumatrex 2.5 mg	Take 6 tablets as directed each week	8/2	1	Bombay	24	CT
694026	Folic acid 1 mg	1 tablet every day	8/2	1	Bombay	30	CT
694027	Rheumatrex 2.5 mg	Take 6 tablets as directed each week	7/10	2	Bombay	24	CT
694026	Folic acid 1 mg	1 tablet every day	7/10	2	Bombay	30	CT
694027	Rheumatrex 2.5 mg	Take 6 tablets as directed each week	6/12	3	Bombay	24	CT
694026	Folic acid 1 mg	1 tablet every day	6/12	3	Bombay	30	CT
693145	Rheumatrex 2.5 mg	Take 4 tablets as directed each week	5/5	0	Bombay	16	GC
693144	Folic acid 1 mg	1 tablet every day	5/5	0	Bombay	30	GC
692888	Prednisone 10 mg	Take as directed	4/24	1	Bombay	48	MC
683218	Rheumatrex 2.5 mg	Take 4 tablets as directed each week	4/9	1	Bombay	16	CT
683217	Folic acid 1 mg	1 tablet every day	4/9	1	Bombay	30	CT
683218	Rheumatrex 2.5 mg	Take 4 tablets as directed each week	3/10	2	Bombay	16	GC
683217	Folic acid 1 mg	1 tablet every day	3/10	2	Bombay	30	GC
683218	Rheumatrex 2.5 mg	Take 4 tablets as directed each week	2/12	3	Bombay	16	GC
683217	Folic acid 1 mg	1 tablet every day	2/12	3	Bombay	30	GC

page and notice that injectable methotrexate is available as a multidose vial and in single-dose vials. Which product should you order for Mrs. Montgomery today? Why does this matter?

5. How would you counsel Mrs. Montgomery on administering the methotrexate injection?

6. What monitoring tools could be used in the community pharmacy setting to evaluate therapy in this patient, including efficacy and adverse effects?

7. What nondrug therapies or lifestyle modifications might be useful in the management of this patient's rheumatoid arthritis?

8. While talking with the patient, she tells you that she is having difficulty doing tasks around the house that require manual dexterity (turning on lights, opening cans, tying her shoes, etc.). What might you be able to recommend to this patient to help with this issue?

9. When evaluating drug interactions and implications of long-term treatment, what are some of the issues that would need to be considered with NSAID therapy?

10. Many of the newer agents for the treatment of rheumatoid arthritis are quite expensive. What are some strategies community pharmacists could use to manage their pharmacy's inventory and meet the needs of their patients?

11. Develop a follow-up plan for this patient; include time to follow up and method of contact.

Additional Activities

1. Compare and contrast the various biologic agents used to treat rheumatoid arthritis. Note mechanism of action, route of administration, dosing, and cost of treatment. When would you consider using biologic agents in patients with rheumatoid arthritis?

2. Evaluate the various assistance devices designed for patients with arthritis, and select several (6–8) that you think should be available in a community pharmacy.

3. Review the following information sources on specialty pharmacies. Are specialty pharmacies helpful in meeting patients' needs for expensive biologic drug

therapies? What effect do you think specialty pharmacies will have on community pharmacy practice?

- Stern D, Reissman D. Specialty pharmacy cost management strategies of private health care payers. *J Manag Care Pharm.* 2006;12:736–44.

- Dong X, Fetterolf D. Specialty pharmacy: an emerging area of interest for medical management. *Dis Manag.* 2005;8:73–85.

- Morrow TJ. Designing and implementing an effective specialty pharmacy service program. *Manag Care Interface.* 2003;16:50–3.

Information Sources

1. Hamilton RA, Kremer JM. Why intramuscular methotrexate may be more efficacious than oral dosing in patients with rheumatoid arthritis. *Br J Rheumatol.* 1997;36:86–90.

2. Weinblatt ME. Efficacy of methotrexate in rheumatoid arthritis. *Br J Rheumatol.* 1995;34(suppl 2):43–8.

3. Methotrexate sodium for injection [package insert]. Florence, Ky: Xanodyne Pharmacal; 2006.

4. Arthur V, Jubb R, Homer D. A study of parenteral use of methotrexate in rheumatic conditions. *J Clin Nurs.* 2002;11:256–63.

5. American College of Rheumatology Subcommittee on Rheumatoid Arthritis Guidelines. Guidelines for the management of rheumatoid arthritis: 2002 update. *Arthritis Rheum.* 2002;46:328–46.

42 Osteoporosis

Gilbert A. Steiner

Objectives

1. Define osteoporosis and list the non-modifiable and modifiable risk factors associated with it.

2. Compare the two primary densitometry technologies, dual-energy X-ray absorptiometry and quantitative ultrasound, commonly available to community pharmacists for screening for low bone density.

3. Explain the diagnosis of osteoporosis as defined by the World Health Organization, while describing the derivation and use of the T-score.

4. Develop a nonprescription and lifestyle treatment plan that the pharmacist could recommend to enhance a patient's bone health, relating this plan to the patient's risk factors.

5. Develop an osteoporosis therapeutic plan that combines approved prescription and nonprescription medications and lifestyle measures.

Scenario

Rose Wong, a 47-year-old Asian American woman comes to the health center in the Community Clinical Pharmacy where you are the clinical coordinator. Ms. Wong says that because of some recent television commercials about osteoporosis, she has been thinking about her potential risk of developing the disease. When she came to the pharmacy for a prescription today, she noticed that your health center offers bone mineral density testing and would like some information on the test. You inform her that a decision to screen for osteoporosis is based on an assessment of risk factors and that you would be happy to assess those factors if she would fill out an assessment form. After asking if her insurance would cover the cost of the test, you inform her that currently pharmacists cannot bill her health insurance. As a result, she would be required to pay the usual fee of $40. You also inform her that if this screening procedure indicates a high risk of osteoporosis, this result may trigger her insurance to pay for a much more expensive diagnostic test available at the hospital. She is now willing to pay your fee and completes the risk assessment and consent form.

While the patient is completing her risk assessment form, you review her prescription medication profile (Case Table 42–1).

In reviewing Ms. Wong's completed assessment (Case Figure 42–1), you note that she has at least four risk factors for osteoporosis; therefore, it is reasonable to conduct a

---

CASE Table 42–1   Patient Prescription Medication Profile

Rose Wong
157 Herring Ave.
Buies Creek, NC 27506

Phone: 910-555-1234   **DOB:** 07/10/59   **Insurance:** BC/BS

Allergies/Intolerances: NKA

Rx No.	Drug Name	Directions	Date	R/F	Prescriber	Qty	RPh
622500	Prednisone 5 mg	As directed for asthma	08/16	1	Johnson	100	GS
622501	Albuterol inhaler	2 puffs four times daily as needed	08/16	2	Johnson	34 grams	GS
622501	Albuterol inhaler	2 puffs four times daily as needed	07/06	3	Johnson	34 grams	GS
622501	Albuterol inhaler	2 puffs four times daily as needed	05/28	4	Johnson	34 grams	GS
622500	Prednisone 5 mg	As directed for asthma	05/28	2	Johnson	100	GS

Community Clinical Pharmacy
Buies Creek, NC

Osteoporosis Risk Assessment and Bone Density Measurement Consent Form

In order to determine whether you could benefit from a bone mineral density screening procedure, it is recommended that you have at least three risk factors for osteoporosis. Please answer the following questions to determine your risk. Place a check on all lines that apply. Each check represents a risk.

Group A Risk Factors (Non-Modifiable)

_____ Someone in my family has/had osteoporosis? If so, who? _____

__X__ I am of Asian or Caucasian (white) race

_____ I have fractured a bone after the age of 40

_____ I have a small body frame (ask us how to determine this)

__X__ I weigh less than 127 pounds

_____ If female, I have started/completed menopause or had a complete hysterectomy

_____ If past menopause, I am taking/have taken (circle one) estrogen

_____ I have: rheumatoid arthritis__, thyroid disease__, diabetes__, lung disease__

_____ I take the following medicines: _____

Group B Risk Factors (Modifiable)

__X__ I DO NOT eat a diet high in calcium containing foods (dairy, green vegetables)

_____ I DO NOT take a calcium supplement

__X__ I DO NOT do weight-bearing exercise, 30 minutes/day, 3-5 days/week

__X__ I drink more than 24oz (about 4 cups) of caffeine-containing beverages/day

_____ On average, I drink more than 7 alcohol-containing beverages/week

_____ I (currently/used to) use tobacco products. If you have quit, how long ago?_____

Consent

I understand that the results and assessment discussed with me today as a result of this screening procedure do not constitute a diagnosis. Likewise, I understand that it would be in my best interest to discuss the results and assessment with my primary care physician and/or other provider interested in my bone health (e.g., OB/GYN). I understand also that the pharmacists here at Community Clinical Pharmacy may discuss my results and assessment with my medical provider.

Signature _Rose Wong_____ Date _10/6_____

Print Name _Rose Wong_____ DOB _7/10/59_ Age _47_ M/(F)

Address _157 Herring Ave_ City _Buies Creek_ State _NC_ Zip _27506_

Race: White/Caucasian __ Black/African-American __ Hispanic __ Asian _X_ Other _____

Right handed _____ Left handed _X_

Results: t-Score _-2.8_ Risk Assessment for Osteoporosis: High _X_ Moderate _____ Low _____

Assessing Pharmacist: Name _Gil Steiner_____ Signature _Gil Steiner_____

Figure 1: Completed risk assessment and consent form   Source: Author

CASE Figure 42–1 Sample completed risk assessment and consent form.

screening bone mineral density test. As such, you ask Ms. Wong to have a seat in the testing area, immediately in front of the Norland McCue Ultrasound Densitometer, and to remove her right shoe and sock. After positioning her foot for optimum scanning of the calcaneus, you conduct the test. The results indicate a T-score of −2.8.

1. Why is it necessary for Ms. Wong to complete a risk factor assessment?

2. What are the risk factors for osteoporosis? How does risk of low bone mass relate to fracture risk? Describe non-modifiable factors as well as those that can be affected by lifestyle, disease, and medications.

3. What are the two most commonly used technologies available to pharmacists for screening for bone mineral density? Please compare these two technologies with regard to cost, utility, portability, contraindications, and regulatory control.

4. From a business standpoint, what variables must be considered in deciding to offer a bone density screening service?

The patient's T-score, combined with her risk assessment, indicates that she is at high risk of developing osteoporosis. You explain to her once again that this is a screening procedure and that you are not making a diagnosis of osteoporosis. However, you strongly recommend that she see her primary care physician as soon as possible for further evaluation and diagnosis. You offer to call and make an appointment with her physician, but first you fax her results to the physician. After reviewing your fax, Dr. Johnson calls you, somewhat indignant, to reproach you for "practicing medicine" and questioning the value of your "service."

5. How do you respond to Dr. Johnson and validate your service? Please include primary literature citations to support your answer.

After hearing your explanation, Dr. Johnson agrees to see Ms. Wong. You tell her that she has an appointment to see Dr. Johnson in 2 weeks.

6. Pending Ms. Wong's medical appointment, what suggestions could you make that would have a positive effect on risk factor reduction, regardless of the diagnostic result? What nondrug therapies or lifestyle modifications might be useful in managing this patient's problem?

7. After hearing these recommendations, Ms. Wong says that she has heard Paul Harvey advertising Citracal on the radio. She asks if that would be a good brand to take.

8. Because it would be more convenient for her to do so, Ms. Wong asks if she can take all of her daily calcium at once before bedtime.

Ms. Wong agrees to try your suggestions.

9. Following World Health Organization guidelines, what further diagnostic steps will Dr. Johnson consider in evaluating Ms. Wong? How will she interpret the results of the tests she orders?

10. Define osteoporosis and summarize the clinical, epidemiologic, and economic implications of this disease in women and men.

11. Assuming that Dr. Johnson does, in fact, diagnose osteoporosis, what are the goals of pharmacotherapy for this patient?

12. Identify the treatment alternatives available for Ms. Wong. Please consider first- and second-line therapy. Pay particular attention to recommendations for steroid-induced osteoporosis.

13. Keeping in mind the discussion in question 12, what would you recommend for treatment of Ms. Wong's osteoporosis?

Ms. Wong returns to the pharmacy after her appointment with Dr. Johnson with a new prescription (Case Figure 42–2).

J. Johnson, MD
Family Practice Associates
2205 Main Street
Buies Creek, NC
FOR ROSE WONG
ADDRESS_____DATE_____

BONIVA 150 mg
#1
T PO ONE
DAY OF EACH
MONTH

REFILL 11 TIMES   DR. J Johnson

CASE Figure 42–2 Prescription for patient Rose Wong.

14. Is this an appropriate choice for Ms. Wong? Why or why not? What intervention (e.g., patient recommendation, call to provider or family member, contact emergency medical services, etc.) is necessary for implementing any changes, if necessary?

15. When counseling Ms. Wong on her therapy, she asks you how long you expect her to be on this regimen. How do you respond?

16. Ms. Wong acknowledges these instructions but is concerned about a serious adverse reaction with this type of drug. Her neighbor told her that she heard people can "lose their jaws" with this medicine. Ms. Wong asks, "Is this true?"

17. What monitoring parameters available in the community pharmacy setting should be used to evaluate therapy in this patient, including efficacy and adverse effects? Develop a follow-up plan for this patient; include time to follow up and method of contact.

18. Develop a medication action plan to which the patient can refer for various contingencies such as adverse reactions, missed doses, and so forth. Include short-term and long-term goals.

19. What are the pertinent topics to address during patient education?

Additional Activities

1. Go to a community pharmacy and review calcium supplement options to determine what brands, strengths, and dosage forms are available. Determine what your first-tier brand or generic product recommendation would be for different patient populations (e.g., the elderly, patients with diabetes, etc.).

2. Contact your state Board of Pharmacy to see if bone density screening is allowable under your Pharmacy Practice Act. Identify and contact the appropriate state regulatory agency to see which devices and screening tests are permissible for use by pharmacists.

3. Do research to determine pricing options for approved testing devices in your state. What funds might be available to a community pharmacist to purchase this device? Break into groups and brainstorm about how you could seek alternative funding sources for purchasing a bone density screening device in the community pharmacy setting.

4. Develop a business plan for developing and implementing an osteoporosis screening program in the community pharmacy setting.

5. Prepare a patient education brochure on calcium that provides information on dietary sources of calcium, the different types of calcium preparations, daily requirements for calcium based on age and menopausal status, administration tips, and so forth.

Information Sources

1. Nelson HD, Helfand M, Woolf SH. Screening for postmenopausal osteoporosis: a review of the evidence for the US Preventive Services Task Force. *Ann Intern Med.* 2002;137:529–41.

2. American Association of Clinical Endocrinologists medical guidelines for clinical practice for the prevention and treatment of postmenopausal osteoporosis: 2001 edition, with selected updates for 2003. *Endocr Pract.* 2003;9:545–64.

3. Clinician's Guide to Prevention and Treatment of Osteoporosis. Available at: http://www.nof.org/professionals/nof_clinicians_guide.htm. Last accessed October 27, 2008.

4. US Preventive Services Task Force. Screening for osteoporosis in postmenopausal women: recommendations and rationale. *Ann Intern Med.* 2002;137:526–8.

5. O'Connell MB, Seaton TL. Osteoporosis and osteomalacia. In: DiPiro JT, Talbert RL, Yee GC, et al., eds. *Pharmacotherapy: A Pathophysiologic Approach.* 6th ed. New York: McGraw-Hill; 2005:1645–69.

6. Al Attia H, Adams B. Osteoporosis in men: are we referring enough for DXA and how? *Clin Rheumatol.* 2007;26:1123–6.

7. Bagger YZ, Tanko LB, Alexandersen P, et al. The long-term predictive value of bone mineral density measurements for fracture risk is independent of the site of measurement and the age at diagnosis: results from the Prospective Epidemiological Risk Factor study. *Osteoporos Int.* 2006;17:471–7.

8. Neuner JM, Binkley N, Sparapani MS, et al. Bone density testing in older women and its association with patient age. *J Am Geriatr Soc.* 2006;54:485–9.

9. Writing Group for the Women's Health Initiative Investigators. Risks and benefits of estrogen plus progestin in healthy postmenopausal women. *JAMA.* 2002;288:321–33.

10. The Women's Health Initiative Steering Committee. Effects of conjugated equine estrogen in postmenopausal women with hysterectomy. *JAMA.* 2004;291:1701–12.

11. Pothiwala P, Evans EM, Chapman-Novakofski KM. Ethnic variation in risk for osteoporosis among women: a review of biological and behavioral factors. *J Womens Health.* 2006;15:709–19.

12. Cerulli J, Zeolla M. Impact and feasibility of a community pharmacy bone mineral density screening and education program. *J Am Pharm Assoc.* 2004;44:161–7.

13. Grabe DW, Cerulli J, Stroup J, et al. Comparison of the Achilles Express Ultrasonometer with central dual-energy x-ray absorptiometry. *Ann Pharmacother.* 2006;40:830–5.

14. Kent K, McDonough RP, Dinges B, et al. Retrospective financial analysis of wellness center from an independent community pharmacy perspective. *J Am Pharm Assoc.* 2006;46:447–52.

15. Goode J, Swiger K, Bluml B. Regional osteoporosis screening, referral, and monitoring program in community pharmacies: findings from Project ImPACT: Osteoporosis. *J Am Pharm Assoc.* 2004;44:152–60.

16. Feldstein A, Elmer PJ, Orwoll E, et al. Bone mineral density measurement and treatment for osteoporosis in older individuals with fractures. *Arch Intern Med.* 2003;163:2165–72.

17. Rohr CI, Clements JM, Sarkar A. Treatment and prevention practices in postmenopausal women after bone mineral density screening

at a community-based osteoporosis project. *J Am Osteopath Assoc.* 2006;106:396–401.

18. Elliott ME, Meek PD, Kanous NL, et al. Osteoporosis screening by community pharmacists: use of National Osteoporosis Foundation resources. *J Am Pharm Assoc.* 2002;42:101–10.

19. Carmona RH. Bone Health and Osteoporosis: A Report of the Surgeon General. Washington, DC: US Department of Health and Human Services; 2004:1–29. Publication No. WE 225 B71259 2004 suppl.

20. Heaney RP. Calcium, dairy products and osteoporosis. *J Am Coll Nutr.* 2000;19(suppl):83S–99S.

21. Shea B, Wells G, Cranney A, et al. Meta-analysis of calcium supplementation for the prevention of postmenopausal osteoporosis. *Endocr Rev.* 2002;23:552–9.

22. Reid IR, Mason B, Horne A, et al. Randomized controlled trial of calcium in healthy older women. *Am J Med.* 2006;119:777–85.

23. Peris P, Monega A, Martinez MA, et al. Bone mineral density evolution in young premenopausal women with idiopathic osteoporosis. *Clin Rheumatol.* 2007;26:958–61.

24. Going S, Lohman T, Houtkooper L, et al. Effects of exercise on bone mineral density in calcium-replete postmenopausal women with and without hormone replacement therapy. *Osteoporos Int.* 2003:14:637–43.

25. Orwoll E, Ettinger M, Weiss S, et al. Alendronate for the treatment of osteoporosis in men. *N Engl J Med.* 2000;343:604–10.

26. Nakamura T, Liu JL, Morii H, et al. Effect of raloxifene on clinical fractures in Asian women with postmenopausal osteoporosis. *J Bone Miner Metab.* 2006;24:414–8.

27. Gallagher JC, Rosen CJ, Chen P, et al. Response rate of bone mineral density to teriparatide in postmenopausal women with osteoporosis. *Bone.* 2006;39:1268–75

28. Neer RM, Arnaud CD, Zanchetta JR, et al. Effect of parathyroid hormone (1–34) on fractures and bone mineral density in postmenopausal women with osteoporosis. *N Engl J Med.* 2001;344: 1434–41.

29. Black DM, Greenspan SL, Ensrud KE, et al. The effects of parathyroid hormone and alendronate alone or in combination in postmenopausal osteoporosis. *N Engl J Med.* 2003;349:1207–15.

30. Finkelstein JS, Hayes A, Hunzelman JL, et al. The effects of parathyroid hormone, alendronate, or both in men with osteoporosis. *N Engl J Med.* 2003;349:1216–26.

31. Black DM, Schwartz AV, Ensrud KE, et al. Effects of continuing or stopping alendronate after 5 years of treatment. *JAMA.* 2006;296:2927–38.

32. Krueger CD, West PM, Sargent M, et al, Bisphosphonate-induced osteonecrosis of the jaw. *Ann Pharmacother.* 2007;41:276–84.

43 Allergic Rhinitis

Catrina Schwartz

Objectives

1. Identify key allergic rhinitis symptoms noted by affected persons.

2. Analyze physical examination findings, and determine whether they are significant for allergic rhinitis.

3. Assess patient profile and presentation to identify presence of comorbid conditions associated with allergic rhinitis.

4. Evaluate the patient's current pharmacologic and non-pharmacologic therapy for allergic rhinitis, develop an appropriate treatment plan, and include patient education for allergic rhinitis to improve outcomes.

5. Summarize available pharmacologic and nonpharmacologic treatment options for allergic rhinitis.

Scenario

You are working as a pharmacy manager in a local community pharmacy over a 3-day holiday weekend when Andrea Jones, a regular customer, approaches the counter with her 12-year-old son Joey. She is interested in purchasing a nonprescription herbal medication for Joey's congestion, coughing, sneezing, and runny nose but is not sure which product to buy.

While you are speaking with Mrs. Jones, you note that Joey appears to be tired, he has dark circles around his eyes, and his nose is reddened with creases from rubbing. When you ask him how he is feeling, he says, "OK." You further inquire about how well he is sleeping. He replies, "Not a lot." Mrs. Jones adds that Joey has recently been taking care of his new puppy Peanut, which has affected his sleep during the past few weeks. On further questioning, Joey denies having fever, muscle aches, or pain. However, he notes that his eyes have been feeling itchy and watery. You ask Joey how long he has had his symptoms. He thinks it has been about a month. Mrs. Jones nods in agreement. During your brief conversation with Joey, you observe that his breathing appears a bit labored. He is breathing through his mouth and nose. You also note that he has been rubbing his nose upward with the palm of his hand during the course of your conversation.

You assure Mrs. Jones that you will help her find the best product for Joey but you would like to review his prescription medication profile first (Case Table 43–1).

You confirm Joey's only current medication is albuterol and determine that fluticasone is used only when Joey's asthma worsens. His asthma has been well controlled for about 2 years. You also ask Mrs. Jones about any nonprescription or herbal medications that Joey may be taking. She says he currently takes a multivitamin daily. He does not take any herbal products.

You then ask Joey how he is doing with managing his asthma. How frequently is he using his albuterol? He confesses about 2 to 4 puffs per day recently. Before he was using only 2 puffs weekly. Mrs. Jones looks surprised to learn this. You also inquire about his use of a peak flow meter. He looks at you and his mom with a confused look. Mrs. Jones admits that Joey had a prescription for a peak flow meter, but she did not obtain one because it was not covered by insurance.

Questions and Activities

1. Evaluate Joey's symptoms. Do they support or rule out a viral or bacterial infection?

2. What physical signs or symptoms is Joey showing that are consistent with a diagnosis of allergic rhinitis?

3. Describe the factors that may have contributed to Joey's symptoms.

4. Discuss Joey's current medication regimen. How well is this regimen managing his condition(s)? On the basis of current practice guidelines, is his therapy appropriate? What modifications, if any, are needed?

5. What are the goals of pharmacotherapy for this patient?

6. Evaluate the nonprescription treatment options available for allergic rhinitis, and compare and contrast the appropriateness of the drugs and dosage forms for antihistamines, decongestants, and nonmedicated products.

CASE Table 43–1   Prescription Medication Profile

Joey Jones
3637 West Elm St.
Spokane, WA 99999

Phone: 509-123-4567   **DOB:** 3/20/1997   **Insurer:** Blue Cross

Allergies/Intolerances: Bee sting

Rx No.	Drug Name	Directions	Date	R/F	Prescriber	Qty	RPh
687214	Albuterol HFA	Inhale 1–2 puffs every 4–6 hours as needed for shortness of breath, wheezing; not to exceed 12 puffs in 24 hours	7/6	10	Cordova	1	CRS
684322	Fluticasone HFA 44 mcg	Inhale 1 puff twice daily when asthma worsens; rinse mouth after each use	3/20	0	Cordova	1	CRS
684321	EpiPen	Inject as directed into thigh for treatment of allergic reaction to bee sting	3/20	10	Cordova	1	LGM

7. Joey's mom is interested in using a nonprescription herbal product to treat Joey's symptoms. Evaluate the herbal treatment alternatives available for allergic rhinitis, and discuss the appropriateness of the herbal products available.

8. List the prescription treatment alternatives available for allergic rhinitis, and briefly discuss their place in therapy for allergic rhinitis, including oral acute and preventive agents, ocular medications, and intranasal agents.

9. Should long-term corticosteroids be used in children? What about intranasal corticosteroids?

10. Why is it important to effectively treat allergic rhinitis with children?

11. What prescription drugs are appropriate for the treatment of Joey's condition if nonprescription products do not adequately control or prevent his symptoms?

12. On the basis of Joey's symptoms, what would you recommend to his mom today?

13. What nondrug therapies or lifestyle modifications would be useful in managing Joey's condition(s)?

14. Joey returns to the pharmacy 2 weeks later after seeing his physician for his allergic rhinitis. Dr. Cordova would like Joey to continue taking loratadine 5 mg daily and start Flonase (fluticasone) nasal spray 1 spray into each nostril daily. How would you counsel Joey to use this nasal spray?

15. What monitoring parameters available in the community pharmacy setting should be used to evaluate Joey's therapy, including efficacy and adverse effects?

16. What are the pertinent topics to address during patient education?

17. Develop a follow-up plan for Joey; include time to follow up and method of contact. What are short-term and long-term goals of treatment?

Information Sources

1. Quillen DM, Feller DB. Diagnosing rhinitis: allergic vs. nonallergic. Am Fam Physician. 2006;73:1583–90.

2. Stroebel R, Graft D, Takahashi M, et al. Health Care Guideline: Rhinitis. 5th ed. Bloomington, Minn: Institute for Clinical Systems Improvement (ICSI); 2003:1–35.

3. Blaiss M. Current concepts and therapeutic strategies for allergic rhinitis in school-age children. Clin Ther. 2004;26:1876–89.

4. Long A, McFadden C, DeVine D, et al. Management of Allergic and Nonallergic Rhinitis (Evidence Report/Technology Assessment No. 54). Rockville, Md: Agency for Healthcare Research and Quality; 2002:1–195. AHRQ Publication No. 02-E024.

5. Bousquet J, Van Cauwenberge P, Khaltaev N. Allergic rhinitis and its impact on asthma. J Allergy Clin Immunol. 2001;108(5 suppl):1–205.

6. National Asthma Education and Prevention Program Expert Panel Report 3: Guidelines for the Diagnosis and Management of Asthma. Bethesda, Md: National Institutes of Health; 2007. NIH Publication No. 08-4051. Also available at: http://www.nhlbi.nih.gov/guidelines/asthma/asthgdln.htm. Last accessed November 8, 2008.

7. Blaiss MS. Allergic rhinitis and impairment issues in schoolchildren: a consensus report. *Curr Med Res Opin.* 2004;20:1937–52.

8. Baena-Cagnani CE. Safety and tolerability of treatments for allergic rhinitis in children. *Drug Saf.* 2004;27:883–98.

9. Johansson SGO, Haahtela T. World Health Organization guidelines for prevention of allergy and allergic asthma. *Int Arch Allergy Immunol.* 2004;135:83–92.

10. Plaut, M, Valentine MD. Allergic rhinitis. *N Engl J Med.* 2005;353:1934–44.

11. Covington TR. *Nonprescription Drug Therapy Guiding Patient Self Care.* St Louis: Facts and Comparisons; 1999:553–64, 771–86.

12. Zaditor [full prescribing information]. East Hanover, NJ: Novartis Pharmaceutical; December 2006.

13. NasalCrom product information. Available at: http://www.pfizerch.com/product.aspx?id=419. Last accessed November 8, 2008.

14. Guo R, Pittler MH, Ernst E. Herbal medicines for the treatment of allergic rhinitis: a systematic review. *Ann Allergy Asthma Immunol.* 2007;99:483–95.

15. Abelson MB, George MA, Garofalo C, et al. An effective treatment for allergy sufferers. *Contact Lens Spectr.* 1995;28–32.

16. Noble S. Daily application of the homeopathic remedy Zicam allergy relief significantly improves the quality of life and impairment in patients with seasonal allergic rhinitis. *Internet J Fam Pract.* 2000;1(1).

17. Ten Eick AP, Blumer JL, Reed MD. Safety of antihistamines in children. *Drug Saf.* 2001;24:119–47.

18. Wahn U, Meltzer EO, Fin AF Jr, et al. Fexofenadine is efficacious and safe in children (aged 6–11 years) with seasonal allergic rhinitis. *J Allergy Clin Immunol.* 2003;111:763–9.

19. Astelin [full prescribing information]. Somerset, NJ: MedPointe Healthcare; February 2006.

20. Dykewicz MS, Fineman S, Skoner DP, et al. Diagnosis and management of rhinitis: complete guidelines of the Joint Task Force on Practice Parameters in Allergy, Asthma, and Immunology. American Academy of Allergy, Asthma, and Immunology. *Ann Allergy Asthma Immunol.* 1998;81(5 pt 2):478–518.

21. Murphy K, Uryniak T, Simpson B, et al. Growth velocity in children with perennial allergic rhinitis treated with budesonide aqueous nasal spray. *Ann Allergy Asthma Immunol.* 2006;96:723–30.

22. Claritin [full prescribing information]. Kenilworth, NJ: Schering Corp; September 2000.

23. Clarinex [full prescribing information]. Kenilworth, NJ: Schering Corp; April 2005.

24. Allegra [full prescribing information]. Kansas City, Mo: Aventis Pharmaceuticals; May 2003.

25. Zyrtec [full prescribing information]. New York: Pfizer Labs; July 2004.

26. Crolom [full prescribing information]. Bristol, Tenn: King Pharmaceuticals; May 1999.

27. Livostin [full prescribing information]. Duluth, Ga: Novartis Ophthalmics; March 2002.

28. Patanol [full prescribing information]. Fort Worth, Tex: Alcon Laboratories. December 2003.

29. Elestat [full prescribing information]. Irvine, Calif: Allergan; August 2004.

30. Alomide [full prescribing information]. Fort Worth, Tex: Alcon Laboratories; 2002.

31. Alocril [full prescribing information]. Irvine, Calif: Allergan; 2000.

32. Alamast [full prescribing information]. Rochester, Mich: Parkedale Pharmaceuticals; September 1999.

33. Optivar [full prescribing information]. Somerset, NJ: MedPointe Healthcare; July 2003.

34. Emadine [full prescribing information]. Fort Worth, Tex: Alcon Laboratories; August 2002.

35. Flonase [full prescribing information]. Research Triangle, NC: GlaxoSmithKline; March 2004.

36. Nasonex [full prescribing information]. Kenilworth, NJ: Schering Corp; September 2005.

37. Rhinocort Aqua [full prescribing information]. Wilmington, Del: AstraZeneca LP; January 2005.

38. Nasacort AQ [full prescribing information]. Bridgewater, NJ: Aventis Pharmaceuticals; September 2006.

39. Beconase AQ [full prescribing information]. Research Triangle Park, NC: GlaxoSmithKline; April 2005.

40. Nasarel [full prescribing information]. Mississauga, Ontario, Canada: Ivax Laboratories; May 2000.

Hematologic Disorders

44 Anticoagulation

Christine Lee and Stuart T. Haines

Objectives

1. Given an anticoagulation case, confirm that the initial treatment plan for a patient who presents with an acute deep vein thrombosis is appropriate; include medications, dose, length of therapy, and monitoring parameters.

2. List the purpose, proper administration, and most common side effects of anticoagulation therapy.

3. Given an anticoagulation case, ask appropriate questions to be able to make a recommendation if a patient needs to seek immediate care.

4. Given an anticoagulation case, identify possible drug–drug interactions and provide possible alternative therapies that are safer to use.

Scenario

Mrs. Page is a 56-year-old African American obese woman who brings two new prescriptions to the pharmacy to be filled (Case Figure 44–1). After speaking with Mrs. Page, you determine that she was discharged from the hospital this morning. She was admitted 3 days ago with a deep vein thrombosis. Mrs. Page informs you that she was driving with her husband from Florida to Maryland when she began to experience pain and swelling in her left leg. When she returned home, she called her daughter and mentioned the pain; her daughter decided to take her to the emergency department. The physician ordered a venous ultrasonography, and the results were positive for deep vein thrombosis. She was then admitted to the hospital for treatment.

Mrs. Page was told by the nurse in the hospital that both the Lovenox (enoxaparin) and Coumadin (warfarin) were "blood thinners." She was told the Lovenox was "very expensive" and needed to be injected. She does not like the idea of giving herself an injection. She would prefer to take only the oral medication and would like to know if it would be a big problem if she chooses not to fill the Lovenox. You review Mrs. Page's pharmacy records (Case Table 44–1).

Questions and Activities

1. What risk factors contributed to the development of Mrs. Page's deep vein thrombosis (DVT)?

2. What are the goals of pharmacotherapy for Mrs. Page?

3. What are the recommended initial treatment options for patients with DVT? Please list advantages and disadvantages of each therapy.

4. In the case of Mrs. Page, what drug(s), dosage forms, schedules, and duration of therapy would be the best choice?

CASE Figure 44–1 Prescriptions for patient Elena Page.

CASE Table 44–1   Prescription Medication Profile

Elena Page
111 Main Street
Baltimore, MD 21201

Phone: 410-555-5555   **DOB:** 3/15/54   **Insurer:** Blue Cross/Blue Shield of Maryland (co-pay: $7/$10/$25)

Allergies/Intolerances: NKDA

Notes: Height: 5 feet 4 inches tall; weight: 178 lb

Rx No.	Drug Name	Strength	Date	R/F	Prescriber	Qty	RPh
620307	Fluoxetine 20 mg	1 capsule every day	10/15	1	Porter	90	DKM
620306	Hydrochlorothiazide 25 mg	1 tablet every day	10/15	1	Porter	90	DKM
621098	Premarin 0.625 mg	1 tablet every day	10/15	0	Smith	90	DKM
620307	Fluoxetine 20 mg	1 capsule every day	7/17	2	Porter	90	DKM
620306	Hydrochlorothiazide 25 mg	1 tablet every day	7/17	2	Porter	90	DKM
621098	Premarin 0.625 mg	1 tablet every day	7/17	1	Smith	90	DKM
620307	Fluoxetine 20 mg	1 tablet every day	4/13	3	Porter	90	DKM
620306	Hydrochlorothiazide 25 mg	1 tablet every day	4/13	3	Porter	90	DKM
620098	Premarin 0.625 mg	1 tablet every day	4/13	2	Smith	90	DKM
620307	Fluoxetine 20 mg	1 capsule every day	01/18	4	Porter	90	DKM
620306	Hydrochlorothiazide 25 mg	1 tablet every day	1/18	4	Porter	90	DKM

5. Are there any potential issues that need to be brought to the prescribing physician's attention? How should the pharmacist handle this situation?

6. Why do patients taking Coumadin therapy require frequent monitoring? What test is used to monitor this therapy? How often should a patient on this therapy be monitored?

7. What nondrug therapies and lifestyle changes might be useful in managing this patient's problem?

8. What are the pertinent topics to address during patient education? What is the Coumadin MedGuide? Who should receive it? What does it contain?

9. How should the pharmacist address Mrs. Page's concern about injecting a medication?

10. What important points should pharmacists include when counseling patients on how to use either low-molecular-weight heparin or fondaparinux?

11. What monitoring parameters can be collected in the community pharmacy setting?

12. What information is needed to evaluate therapy in this patient, including efficacy and adverse effects?

Two days after dispensing the prescription for Coumadin and Lovenox, Mrs. Page calls the pharmacy and asks to speak with

you. She is concerned because she noticed bruising on her abdomen and wants to know if she should call her physician or go to the emergency department.

13. What additional questions do you need to ask Mrs. Page to determine whether she should go to the emergency department?

Ten days after starting anticoagulant therapy Mrs. Page's international normalized ratio (INR) value is 1.5. The physician would like to continue on Lovenox therapy until she reaches her goal INR. She used her last Lovenox prefilled syringe this morning. The physician calls in a new prescription to the pharmacy for Lovenox 120 mg once daily, inject as directed; quantity 10; no refills.

The pharmacist begins to fill the prescription and realizes that he has only Lovenox 60, 100, and 150 mg syringes in stock. If the pharmacist orders Lovenox 120 mg syringes from the wholesaler today (Friday), the medication will arrive in 3 days (Monday).

14. Given that the pharmacy is temporarily out of stock, would it be acceptable for Mrs. Page to be off Lovenox (enoxaparin) therapy for 3 days? If not, what can you do to ensure that Mrs. Page continues therapy over the weekend?

One week later the physician reports that Mrs. Page's INR is now 6.4. The physician gives you a verbal order for a single Mephyton (phytonadione) 5 mg tablet to be taken as soon as possible and to instruct the patient to hold the next two doses of her Coumadin before restarting her new dose: 5 mg on Sundays, Mondays, Wednesdays, and Fridays; 2.5 mg (1/2 tablet) on Tuesdays, Thursdays, and Saturdays.

15. According to the American College of Chest Physicians' North American Conference on Antithrombotic and Thrombolytic Therapy (the Chest Guidelines), is a single 5 mg dose of phytonadione (oral vitamin K) an appropriate treatment of an elevated INR?

16. Is intravenous vitamin K a more appropriate option?

17. What changes in therapy, if any, should you recommend to the prescribing physician to most appropriately manage Mrs. Page's elevated INR?

Mrs. Page comes to the pharmacy to refill her hydrochlorothiazide, fluoxetine, and warfarin. She hands you a new prescription for Bactrim DS (sulfamethoxazole/trimethoprim). She explains she was prescribed this antibiotic because she was experiencing frequent urination with burning. She was told she has a urinary tract infection.

18. Is sulfamethoxazole/trimethoprim a safe and effective choice for Mrs. Page to take for urinary tract infection?

19. Are there alternative medications that may be safer options for Mrs. Page?

20. Does the pharmacist need to inform the prescribing physician about the possible drug interaction? What and how should the pharmacist document the intervention, regardless of whether the physician accepts or refuses the recommendation to change the initially prescribed antibiotic?

21. What is the difference between pharmacokinetic and pharmacodynamic drug–drug interactions? List two warfarin drug–drug interactions from each category.

Mrs. Page also mentions that she has been experiencing hot flashes since stopping her conjugated estrogen (Premarin) therapy and that a coworker recommended black cohosh.

22. Is black cohosh a safe and effective choice for Mrs. Page to take for relief of her hot flashes?

23. Are there alternative medications that would be better options for Mrs. Page?

24. What herbal medications should be avoided by patients who are taking Coumadin?

Several weeks later, Mrs. Page comes into the pharmacy to refill her Coumadin prescription. She says that she is doing well. She denies unexplained bruising; blood in her urine or stool; leg swelling, warmth, or pain; chest pain; and shortness of breath.

She has been within her goal INR range at her last two visits. When Mrs. Page receives her new prescription bottle, she notices that she has been given generic warfarin instead of brand-name Coumadin. She asks to speak with the pharmacist to find out the difference(s) between the two products.

25. Are there any known differences between brand-name Coumadin and generic warfarin regarding bioequivalence, efficacy, or adverse effects?

Information Sources

1. Buller HR, Agnelli G, Hull RD, et al. Antithrombotic therapy for venous thromboembolic disease: the Seventh ACCP Conference on Antithrombotic and Thrombolytic Therapy. *Chest.* 2004;126 (suppl):S401–28.

2. Turpie AG, Chin BS, Lip GY. ABC of antithrombotic therapy: venous thromboembolism: treatment strategies. *BMJ.* 2002;325: 948–50.

3. Tillman DJ, Charland SL, Witt DM. Effectiveness and economic impact associated with a program for outpatient management of acute deep vein thrombosis in a group model health maintenance organization. *Arch Intern Med.* 2000;160:2926–32.

4. Haines ST, Zeolla M, Witt DM. Venous thromboembolism. In: DiPiro JT, Talbert RL, Yee GC, et al., eds. *Pharmacotherapy: A Pathophysiologic Approach.* 6th ed. New York: McGraw-Hill; 2005:373–413.

5. Lovenox ckage insert]. Available at: http://www.lovenox.com/ consumer/aboutLovenox/main.aspx. Last accessed August 22, 2008.

6. Micromedex. Available at: http://www.thomsonhc.com. Last accessed August 22, 2008.

7. Mismetti P, Quenet S, Merli G, et al. Enoxaparin in the treatment of deep vein thrombosis with or without pulmonary embolism: an individual patient data meta-analysis. *Chest.* 2005;128:2203–10.

8. Bishop B, Wilson AG, Post D. et al. A pilot study of home treatment of deep vein thrombosis with subcutaneous once-daily enoxaparin plus warfarin. *J Managed Care Pharm.* 2006;12:70–5.

9. Kearon C, Ginsberg JS, Julian JA, et al. Comparison of fixed-dose weight-adjusted unfractionated heparin and low-molecular weight heparin for acute treatment of venous thromboembolism. *JAMA.* 2006;296:935–42.

10. Ansell J, Hirsh J, Poller L, et al. The pharmacology and management of the vitamin K antagonists. The Seventh ACCP Conference on Antithrombotic and Thrombolytic Therapy. *Chest.* 2004; 126(suppl):S204–33.

11. Menenedez-Jandula B, Carols Souto J, Oliver A, et al. Comparing self-management of oral anticoagulant therapy with clinic management. *Ann Intern Med.* 2005;142:1–10.

12. Amruso NA. Ability of clinical pharmacists in a community pharmacy setting to manage anticoagulation therapy. *J Am Pharm Assoc.* 2004;44:467–71.

13. Calis KA, Davis SR, Kalantaridou SN. Hormone therapy in women. In: DiPiro JT, Talbert RL, Yee GC, et al., eds. *Pharmacotherapy: A Pathophysiologic Approach.* 6th ed. New York: McGraw-Hill; 2005:373–413.

14. Curb D, Prentice RL, Bray PF, et al. Venous thrombosis and conjugated equine estrogen in women without a uterus. *Arch Intern Med.* 2006;166:772–80.

15. Partsch H, Kaulich M, Mayer W. Immediate mobilization in acute vein thrombosis reduces post-thrombotic syndrome. *Int Angiol.* 2004;23:206–12.

16. Bauer LA. Clinical pharmacokinetics and pharmacodynamics. In: DiPiro JT, Talbert RL, Yee GC, et al., eds. *Pharmacotherapy: A Pathophysiologic Approach.* 6th ed. New York: McGraw-Hill; 2005:60–73.

17. Fitzmaurice DA, Blann AD, Lip GY. ABC of antithrombotic therapy: bleeding risks of antithrombotic therapy. *BMJ*. 2002;325:828–31.

18. Greenblatt DJ, Von Moltke LL. Interaction of warfarin with drugs, natural substances, and foods. *J Clin Pharmaco*. 2005;45:127–32.

19. Wittkowky AK. A systematic review and inventory of supplement effects on warfarin and other anticoagulants. *Thromb Res*. 2005; 117:81–6.

20. Holbrook AM, Pereira JA, Labiris R, et al. Systematic overview of warfarin and its drug and food interactions. *Arch Intern Med*. 2005;165:1095–106.

21. Carroll DG. Nonhormonal therapies for hot flashes in menopause. *Am Fam Physician*. 2006;73:457–64.

22. Haines ST. Reflections on generic warfarin. *Am J Health Syst Pharm*. 1998;55:729–33.

23. Swenson CN, Fundak G. Observational cohort study of switching warfarin sodium products in a managed care organization. *Am J Health Syst Pharm*. 2000;57:452–5.

24. Weibert RT, Yeager BF, Wittkowsky AK, et al. A randomized, crossover comparison of warfarin products in the treatment of chronic atrial fibrillation. *Ann Pharmacother*. 2000;34:981–8.

45 Anemias

Annie Lam

Objectives

1. Describe the goals of treatment and the signs and symptoms of iron deficiency anemia.

2. List the risk factors and treatment strategy for iron deficiency anemia.

3. Discuss monitoring measures of the drug therapy and treatment alternatives for the drug therapy for iron deficiency anemia.

4. Compare four common types of anemia and their blood indexes.

5. Compare the elemental iron contents, cost, and product selection of different ferrous salts.

6. Review the common side effects and potential drug–drug and drug–food interactions of oral iron therapy, and suggest strategies to avoid the interactions.

7. Develop a medication action plan and a follow-up plan for the patient with iron deficiency anemia.

Scenario

Joyce Nabor is the owner-pharmacist of an independent community pharmacy located adjacent to a community health center. Many health center patients have their prescriptions filled in this pharmacy. One morning, Julie Smith came to the pharmacy with three new prescriptions (Case Figures 45–1 and 45–2). Ms. Smith was also holding a bottle of a generic multivitamin and Mylanta for cash purchase. While processing the prescription orders, pharmacist Nabor reviewed Ms. Smith's prescription medication profile on her computer (Case Table 45–1).

On reviewing Ms. Smith's profile, pharmacist Nabor decided to have an in-depth discussion with the patient about her concerns for potential drug interactions between the patient's current medications and the new prescriptions. During their conversation, Ms. Smith told pharmacist Nabor about her most recent health problems.

CASE Figure 45–1 Prescription #1 for patient Julie Smith.

The patient has recently had unusually heavy menstrual blood loss, a decrease in her energy level, unusual fatigue, frequent feelings of shortness of breath, and headache. She went to the clinic 2 weeks ago to have a checkup. Blood and urine tests were ordered, and today she went in for a follow-up visit. She was told she has iron deficiency anemia and a urinary tract infection. She denied feeling any symptoms of urinary tract infection, and said her doctor told her the iron deficiency anemia could be a result of decreased dietary intake of iron and heavy menstrual blood loss. She expressed feelings of guilt and was upset because she thought she might have caused the anemia by not maintaining a well-balanced diet for almost 6 months in an effort to lose weight. She wanted to start taking better care of herself, so she decided to begin taking a multivitamin in addition to the iron that her doctor prescribed for her. She also explained the Mylanta is for an upset stomach. She explained she was prescribed pantoprazole (Protonix) for the upset stomach, but she suspected this medication might have caused her recent fatigue, so she stopped taking the Protonix about 2 weeks ago.

R. Winston, MD
Family Practice Group

FOR _Julie Smith_

ADDRESS_____ DATE_____

Ciprofloxacin 500mg

T BID x 7 days

REFILL _Ø_ TIMES

DR. _RWin_

R. Winston, MD
Family Practice Group

FOR _Julie Smith_

ADDRESS_____ DATE_____

Fosamax 35mg
#4
T Qweek

REFILL _Ø_ TIMES

DR. _RWust_

CASE Figure 45–2 Prescriptions #2 and #3 for patient Julie Smith.

Questions and Activities

1. On the basis of the conversation, what are some of the signs and symptoms of iron deficiency anemia the patient has exhibited?

2. How can the pharmacist identify other patients who may be at risk of iron deficiency? Does the patient have any of these risk factors?

3. Before discussing the patient's therapy any further, the pharmacist wants to make sure to talk to the patient about her immediate concerns. How should the pharmacist address the patient's distress over "causing" her anemia by dieting?

4. The patient is starting to feel better now that she understands a little more about the anemia. She also wants to make sure that she is on the right path for treating it. What are the goals of treatment for iron deficiency anemia? What is the usual treatment dose?

5. On the basis of the information about treatment goals and dosing, is the patient receiving the appropriate amount of iron supplement?

6. List two treatment strategies in addition to iron salts for the patient's anemia.

7. The patient would also like more information on how her physician will know when her anemia is improving. How is iron deficiency anemia treatment monitored?

8. When can the patient expect to see improvements in her condition?

9. What are some potential interactions between medications in the patient's medication profile and her new prescriptions?

10. What can the pharmacist tell the patient about dietary iron absorption and potential food–drug interactions?

11. During the discussion of potential food–drug interactions, the patient notices this statement on her prescription bottle: "Take medication on an empty stomach." She is confused by this instruction because she had heard that iron supplements can cause stomach upset and assumed they should be taken with food. What can the pharmacist tell the patient about this issue?

12. How can the pharmacist advise the patient about the common side effects of iron and counsel her about taking the ferrous sulfate?

13. Identify some of the common nonprescription iron salts currently available. What are the elemental contents of the common iron salts?

14. What advice can the pharmacist give the patient about selecting the most appropriate iron products available in the marketplace?

15. As the pharmacist is ringing up the patient's purchases and finishing her consultation, the patient notices that her co-pay for the iron prescription is pretty expensive. She asks if she can just get a non-

CASE Table 45–1   Prescription Medication Profile

Julie Smith
3567 Pleasant Valley Drive
Manakin Sabot, VA 23103

Phone: 804-876-9888   **DOB:** 04/15/1960   **Insurer:** Basic Health

Allergies/Intolerances: NKDA

Rx No.	Drug Name	Directions	Date	R/F	Prescriber	QTY	RPh
606333	Ibuprofen 400 mg	1 tablet every 4–6 hours as needed for pain or headache	8/1	2	Winston	30	JN
606332	Levothyroxine 0.125 mg	1 tablet every day	8/1	4	Winston	30	JN
608678	Protonix 40 mg	1 tablet every day for gastric discomfort	8/1	0	Winston	30	JN
606332	Levothyroxine 0.125 mg	1 tablet every day	7/1	5	Winston	30	JN
606333	Ibuprofen 400 mg	1 tablet every 4–6 hours as needed for pain or headache	7/1	3	Winston	30	JN
606332	Levothyroxine 0.125 mg	1 tablet every day	6/1	6	Winston	30	JN
601789	Ibuprofen 400 mg	1 tablet every 4–6 hours as needed for pain or headache	5/1	0	Winston	30	JN
601789	Ibuprofen 400 mg	1 tablet every 4–6 hours as needed for pain or headache	4/2	1	Winston	30	JN
601789	Ibuprofen 400 mg	1 tablet every 4–6 hours as needed for pain or headache	3/6	2	Winston	30	JN

prescription iron supplement instead. If so, which one would you recommend?

16. Name three other types of anemia. How are they different from iron deficiency anemia?

17. How can the pharmacist help the patient with her medications to make sure she avoids potential drug interactions?

18. How can the pharmacist advise the patient today about her recent complaints of stomach pain, and her choice to stop her Protonix and use Mylanta instead?

19. What other interventions can the pharmacist make on behalf of the patient with her provider to improve her current medication profile?

20. Help the pharmacist make a follow-up plan with the patient.

Ms. Smith returned to the pharmacy a week later to buy chewable vitamins for her 3-year-old son. She thanked pharmacist Nabor for warning her about the dark-colored stool, which she noticed. She also reported having problems with constipation and needed some advice. She described her bowel movements as being difficult (because of hard crusty stool) and less frequent (from once every 1–2 days to once every 3–4 days). She asked if she should take some Metamucil to help alleviate the problem.

21. What advice can the pharmacist give the patient about the constipation side effect of oral iron therapy?

22. What storage precautions about iron products should the pharmacist mention to the patient?

Information Sources

1. O'Bryant C, Bestul D. Hematopoietic disorders. In: Young LY, Koda-Kimble MA, eds. *Applied Therapeutics: The Clinical Use of Drugs.* 8th ed. Vancouver, Wash: Applied Therapeutics Inc; 2004:86.1–21.

2. Quan DJ. Iron deficiency and megaloblastic anemias. In: Helms RA, Herfinal ET, Quan DJ, et al., eds. *Textbook of Therapeutics Drugs and Disease Management.* 8th ed. Philadelphia: Lippincott Williams and Wilkins; 2006: 771–98.

3. Spruill WJ, Wade WE. Hematologic disorders. In: Dipiro JT, Talbert RL, Hayes PE, et al., eds. *Pharmacotherapy: A Pathophysiologic Approach.* 2nd ed. Norwalk, Conn: Appleton & Lange; 1992: 1423–42.

4. Biskupial JE, Brixner DI, Howard KB, Doerda GM. Gastrointestinal complications of over-the-counter nonsteroidal anti-inflammatory drugs. *J Pain Palliat Care Pharmacother.* 2006;20:7–14.

5. Regula J, Butruk E, Dekkers CP, de Boer SY, et al. Prevention of NSAID-associated gastrointestinal lesions: a comparison study pantoprazole versus omeprazole. *Am J Gastroenterol.* 2006;101:1747–55.

6. Rufer A, Criblez D, Wuillemin WA. Iron-deficiency anemia and gastrointestinal bleeding. *Ther Umsch.* 2006;63:339–43.

7. Jordan NS. Hematology: red and white blood cell tests. In: Lee M, ed. *Basic Skills in Interpreting Laboratory Data.* 3rd ed. Bethesda, Md: American Society of Health-Systems Pharmacists; 2004:441–67.

8. de Paz R, Hernandez-Navarro R. Management, prevention and control of anemia secondary to iron deficiency. *Nutr Hosp.* 2005;20:364–7.

9. Trace elements iron. In: Kastrup EK, Horenkamp JR, McCarron SM, et al., eds. *Drug Facts and Comparisons.* Updated monthly. Conshohocken, Pa: Wolters Kluwer Health; 2006:31–3.

10. Huckleberry Y, Rollins CJ. Essential and conditionally essential nutrients. In: Berardi RR, Kroon LA, McDermott JH, et al., eds. *Handbook of Nonprescription Drugs: An Alternative Approach to Self-Care.* 15th ed. Washington, DC: American Pharmacists Association; 2006:441–74.

11. Wong PY, Zhu M, Li RC. Pharmacokinetic and pharmacodynamic interactions between intravenous ciprofloxacin and oral ferrous sulfate. *J Chemother.* 2000;12:286–93.

12. Marchbanks CR. Drug-drug interactions with fluoroquinolones. *Pharmacotherapy.* 1993;13(2 pt 2):23S–8S.

13. O'Neil-Cutting MA, Crosny WH. The effects of antacids on the absorption of simultaneously ingested iron. *JAMA.* 1986;255: 1468–70.

14. D'Arey PF, McElnay JC. Drug-antacid interactions: assessment of clinical importance. *Drug Intell Clin Pharm.* 1987;21:607–17.

15. Shakir KM, Chute JP, Aprill BS, et al. Ferrous sulfate-induced increase in requirement for thyroxine in a patient with primary hypothyroidism. *South Med J.* 1997;90:637–9.

16. Curry CE Jr, Butler DM. Constipation. In: Berardi RR, Kroon LA, McDermott JH, et al., eds. *Handbook of Nonprescription Drugs: An Alternative Approach to Self-Care.* 15th ed. Washington, DC: American Pharmacists Association; 2006:299–326.

17. Rimon E, Kagansky N, Kagansky M, et al. Are we giving too much iron? Low-dose iron therapy is effective in octogenarians. *Am J Med.* 2005;118:1142.

18. Bar-Oz B, Levichek Z, Koren G. Medications that can be fatal for a toddler with one tablet or teaspoonful: a 2004 update. *Paediatr Drugs.* 2004;6:123–6.

19. Consumer Product Safety Commission. Child-resistant packaging for certain over-the-counter drug products. Final rule. *Fed Regist.* 2001;66:40111–6.

20. Food and Drug Administration, Department of Health and Human Services. Iron-containing supplements and drugs; label warning statements and unit-dose packaging requirements; removal of regulations for unit-dose packaging requirements for dietary supplements and drugs. Final rule; removal of regulatory provisions in response to court order. *Fed Regist.* 2003;68:9714–5.

Infectious Diseases

Section

10

46 Acute Otitis Media

Margaret Tomecki and Jennifer McFee

Objectives

1. Understand the epidemiology, etiology, and pathophysiology of acute otitis media.

2. Recognize the clinical presentation of acute otitis media.

3. Determine if a patient is a self-care candidate for treatment of acute otitis media.

4. Describe the appropriate use of various pharmacotherapeutic choices to treat acute otitis media, including dosing, administration, adverse effects, and precautions.

5. Identify an appropriate treatment regimen and its corresponding monitoring plan, given a patient's case.

Scenario

You are a community pharmacist in an urban chain pharmacy. You have just opened the pharmacy for the day, and the first call you receive is from a regular patient. Mrs. Xavier is calling because she is concerned about her children. She says that when she picked up her children from daycare yesterday, the owner said that both children seemed irritable. Joshua, her 8-month-old infant, had been pulling on his left ear and crying throughout the day. Joshua's 30-month-old sister, Chloe, had been complaining that her right ear hurt and that she felt a little warm. Unfortunately, the daycare center did not have a thermometer to check to see if the children had a fever.

When Mrs. Xavier called the pediatrician's office, it had already closed for the day. As the night went on, Joshua continued to cry and developed a fever of 103°F. Chloe was restless throughout the night, and she had a temperature of 100°F. She continued to complain about her ear hurting.

Mrs. Xavier called the pediatrician's office before calling the pharmacy. However, because of the Thanksgiving holiday, the office was overbooked and could not see the children until late afternoon today. At this time, Mrs. Xavier would like to know what she can do to make her children more comfortable until they see their pediatrician.

Questions and Activities

1. What questions would you need to ask Mrs. Xavier to obtain more information?

2. What (if any) recommendations would you make at this time?

3. If you suggested drug therapy, what drug therapy and dose would you recommend for each child? What patient counseling would you provide? (Joshua weighs 20 pounds, and Chloe weighs 29 pounds.)

Later that evening, Mrs. Xavier returns to the pharmacy with a prescription for Joshua (Case Figure 46–1). She tells you that the doctor said Joshua had an ear infection. You can access Joshua's patient profile in your computer system (Case Table 46–1).

4. What other information about Joshua would you need from Mrs. Xavier before filling the prescription?

5. Is the prescribed antibiotic appropriate for Joshua's acute otitis media (AOM)?

    a. If yes, is the antibiotic dosed appropriately for Joshua's AOM?

    b. If your answer is no, what would you recommend and why?

6. How would you counsel Mrs. Xavier regarding the prescription?

7. If Mrs. Xavier were to forget and not refrigerate the medication overnight, would this problem alter the effectiveness of the medication?

8. What common risk factors are associated with AOM?

After obtaining all the necessary information on Joshua, you ask Mrs. Xavier if she also has a prescription for Chloe. She replies that the physician suggested only Tylenol and to call the office if Chloe does not feel better in 2 days. Mrs. Xavier asks what she should do if the Tylenol does not relieve the fever. She also mentions that her friend recommends giving the children an antihistamine and/or decongestant to help relieve the "ear pressure"

CASE Figure 46–1 Prescription #1 for patient Joshua Xavier.

CASE Table 46–1 Prescription Medication Profile for Joshua Xavier

Joshua Xavier
92200 Presidential Lane
Chicago, IL 91403

Phone: 312-810-1999 **DOB:** 03/15/06 **Insurer:** Blue Cross Blue Shield HMO

Allergies/Intolerances: NKDA

Rx No.	Drug Name	Directions	Date	Qty	R/F	Prescriber	RPh
623457	Azithromycin 100 mg/5 mL	Take as directed	9/20	15 mL	0	Dennis	HJT

that they are experiencing. She wants to know if you agree and if you can recommend a medication to try.

9. Why do you think the physician did not prescribe any antibiotic therapy for Chloe?

10. What other nonprescription medication(s) could you recommend that Mrs. Xavier use to help relieve Chloe's fever?

11. In addition to nonprescription medication(s), what nonpharmacologic measures can Mrs. Xavier use to help relieve the fever?

12. Are antihistamines and/or decongestants beneficial in resolving the signs and symptoms associated with AOM? Would you recommend an antihistamine and/or decongestant for Joshua and Chloe? If yes, list the agent, dose, and duration of therapy that you would recommend.

After counseling Mrs. Xavier on Joshua's prescription and Chloe's Tylenol, you mention the Antibiotic Call Back Program

that you have implemented at your pharmacy. You offer to call Mrs. Xavier in 2 days to see how the children are feeling. Mrs. Xavier agrees to participate in the program.

Two days later, during your shift, you call Mrs. Xavier to follow up on Joshua and Chloe. Mrs. Xavier is happy to hear from you because she has another dilemma. Today, she noticed that Joshua is developing a rash on his chest. Chloe is still complaining about her ear and continues to have a low-grade fever. She is wondering what she should do.

13. What other information would you need to better assist Mrs. Xavier with Joshua?

14. What other information would you need to better assist Mrs. Xavier with Chloe?

At this time, you suggest that Mrs. Xavier follow up with the pediatrician. Mrs. Xavier agrees and decides to call the pediatrician's office. Later that afternoon, Mrs. Xavier returns to the pharmacy with two new prescriptions for Joshua and Chloe (Case Figures 46–2 and 46–3). You can access a printout of Chloe's patient profile in your pharmacy computer (Case Table 46–2).

CASE Figure 46–2 Prescription #2 for patient Joshua Xavier.

CASE Figure 46–3 Prescription #1 for patient Chloe Xavier.

CASE Table 46–2 Prescription Medication Profile for Chloe Xavier

Chloe Xavier
92200 Presidential Lane
Chicago, IL 91403

Phone: 312-810-1999   **DOB:** 02/30/04   **Insurer:** Blue Cross Blue Shield HMO

Allergies/Intolerances: NKDA

Rx No.	Drug Name	Directions	Date	Qty	Refills	Prescriber	RPh
623389	Amoxicillin 400 mg/5 mL	One teaspoonful by mouth twice daily	4/05	100 mL	0	Dennis	HJT
623268	Amoxicillin 400 mg/5 mL	One teaspoonful by mouth twice daily	1/18	100 mL	0	Dennis	HJT

15. Is there any additional information you need from Mrs. Xavier at this time?

16. Is cefdinir an appropriate alternative for Joshua's AOM? If no, what would you recommend and why?

17. Are the cefdinir dosage and duration appropriate for Joshua? If no, what would you recommend and why?

18. Is amoxicillin an appropriate choice of therapy for Chloe's AOM? Why or why not?

19. Are the amoxicillin dosage and duration appropriate for Chloe? If no, what would you recommend and why?

Upon receiving all of the necessary information, you dispense the appropriate medication to each patient and remind Mrs. Xavier that you will be calling her again in 2 days to see how the children are doing on their antibiotic medications.

Two days later, you call Mrs. Xavier to see how Joshua and Chloe are doing. She is relieved to report that things are going well. Joshua no longer has his rash and is sleeping better through the night. Chloe has stopped complaining about her ear and is back to her "usual self."

Additional Activities

1. If Joshua had a type 1 reaction to cefdinir, what antibiotic therapy would you recommend and why?

2. In what AOM case would you use parenteral ceftriaxone? How long would you use this therapy and at what dose?

3. Does flavoring affect the stability of antibiotic medications? In addition to flavoring, what else can caregivers do to help increase palatability and adherence?

4. What mechanisms can pharmacists use in the community setting to assess and improve antibiotic therapy outcomes?

Information Sources

1. American Academy of Pediatrics Subcommittee on Management of Acute Otitis Media. Diagnosis and management of acute otitis media. *Pediatrics.* 2004;13:1412–29.

2. American Academy of Pediatrics. Committee on Psychosocial Aspects of Child and Family Health; Task Force on Pain in Infants, Children, and Adolescents. The assessment and management of acute pain in infants, children, and adolescents. *Pediatrics.* 2006;108:793–7.

3. Hoberman A, Paradise JL, Reynolds EA, Urkin J. Efficacy of Auralgan for treating ear pain in children with acute otits media. *Arch Ped Adolesc Med.* 1997;151:675–8.

4. Sarrell EM, Mandelberg A, Cohen HA. Efficacy of naturopathic extracts in the management of ear pain associated with acute otitis media. *Arch Ped Adolesc Med.* 2001;155:796–9.

5. Sarrell EM, Cohen HA, Kahan E. Naturopathic treatment for ear pain in children. *Pediatrics.* 2003;111(5 pt 1):e574–9.

6. Taketomo CK, Hodding JH, Kraus DM. *Lexi-Com's Pediatric Dosage Handbook.* 12th ed. Hudson, Ohio: Lexi-Comp; 2005.

7. McCormick DP, Chonmaitree R, Pittman C, et al. Non-severe acute otitis media: a clinical trial comparing outcomes of watchful waiting versus immediate antibiotic treatment. *Pediatrics.* 2005;115:1455–65.

8. Spiro DM, Tay KY, Arnold DH, et al. Wait-and-see prescription for the treatment of acute otitis media. *JAMA.* 2006;296:1235–41.

9. O'Mara NB. Antipyretics in fever in children. *Pharm Lett.* 2006;22(220409):2–5.

10. Mayoral CE, Marino RV, Rosenfeld W, Greensher J. Alternating antipyretics: is this an alternative? *Pediatrics.* 2000:105:1009–12.

11. Liza Takiya. Fever. In: Berardi RR, Kroon LA, McDermott JH, et al., eds. *Handbook of Nonprescription Drugs: An Interactive Approach to Self-Care.* 15th ed. Washington DC: American Pharmacists Association; 2006.

12. Bhambhani K, Foulds DM, Swamy KN, et al. Acute otitis media in children: are decongestants or antihistamines necessary? *Ann Emerg Med.* 1983 January;12:13–16.

13. Schnore SK, Sangster JF, Gerace RM, Bass MJ. Are antihistamine-decongestants of value in the treatment of acute otitis media in children? *J Fam Pract.* 1986;22:39–43.

14. Centers for Disease and Control. Infant deaths associated with cough and cold medications—two states, 2005. *MMWR Morb Mortal Wkly Rep.* 2007;56:25–9.

15. Food and Drug Administration. Cold, cough, allergy, bronchodilator, and antiasthmatic drug products for over-the-counter human use. 21 CFR Part 341; 2006.

16. Bell EA. Improving tastes of liquid antibiotics [Infectious Diseases in Children Web site]. July 2004. Available at: http://www.idin children.com/200407/frameset.asp?article=pharmconsult.asp. Last accessed November 8, 2008.

47 Human Immunodeficiency Virus

Lisa D. Inge

Objectives

1. Identify the criteria for use of antiretroviral therapy in the treatment-naive patient.

2. Construct an appropriate treatment regimen taking into account specific indications or contraindications for particular medications.

3. Detect common drug–drug interactions and drug–food interactions.

4. Assess the effectiveness and toxicities associated with current antiretroviral therapy.

5. Describe the factors that are necessary to promote treatment success in the HIV patient population.

6. Summarize the modes of HIV prevention that may be implemented.

Scenario

Susan Parker is a 38-year-old African American woman who frequents your pharmacy for her prescription needs, as well as your occasional lipid screening clinic, offered this past year. Today she approaches the counter in tears and asks if her doctor called in any new medication. She looks exhausted, appears to be shaking, and has a rash that is barely visible without proper lighting. Concerned that she may be having a drug reaction, you decide to investigate her prescription medication profile (Case Table 47–1) and ask a few questions. Her symptoms of a sore throat, fever, and rash prompted the visit to her primary care doctor. These symptoms started about a week ago.

The patient's lipid screening (total cholesterol) values are as follows:

- August 5: 230 mg/dL
- September 5: 200 mg/dL
- December 5: 190 mg/dL

She begins to sob and says that she thought it was the flu. Her doctor requested an HIV test as part of the assessment. It was explained that this HIV test was recommended by the CDC for all patients between the ages of 13 and 64 years regardless of risk. The blood work showed she has HIV. The doctor called her condition acute retroviral syndrome. She does not know what all those terms mean, or how long these symptoms will last.

CASE Table 47–1	Prescription Medication Profile						

Susan Parker
24 Blue Street
Tampa, Florida 32267

Phone: 813-230-4587 **DOB:** 10/23/69 **Insurer:** Blue Cross Blue Shield

Allergies/Intolerances: None

Rx No.	Drug Name	Directions	Date	R/F	Prescriber	Qty	RPh
659788	Famciclovir 500 mg	1 tablet by mouth twice daily for 10 days as needed for HSV outbreaks	4/25	6	Johnson	14	GH
655678	Ortho-Novum 7/7/7	1 tablet by mouth every day	2/5	5	Johnson	28	TP
655678	Ortho-Novum 7/7/7	1 tablet by mouth every day	1/5	6	Johnson	28	TP
655679	Atorvastatin 20 mg	1 tablet by mouth every day	1/5	3	Johnson	30	TP
655679	Atorvastatin 20 mg	1 tablet by mouth every day	1/5	2	Johnson	30	TP

Questions and Activities

1. Define the term *acute retroviral syndrome* along with the typical presentation and duration of this syndrome.

2. Looking confused, the patient begins by asking you the difference between HIV and AIDS. Explain the difference between HIV and AIDS.

Ms. Parker continues, "The doctor mentioned there were drugs to treat this infection. Did he call them in for me? I have a follow-up appointment for more testing in the next couple weeks."

3. What therapeutic options are currently available for those patients whose condition is diagnosed as acute HIV infection?

"Why would the doctor want me to come back for more testing if he is not going to start medications? What do you think he wants to find out from these tests?"

4. What are the recommended components of an initial patient evaluation and assessment according to the guidelines?

5. Ms. Parker's physician has decided not to start antiretroviral treatment at this time. List the current monitoring measures and recommended cutoffs that assist in determining when antiretroviral therapy should be started on a patient. Identify any exceptions to these recommendations.

6. What are the goals of pharmacotherapy for patients prescribed highly active antiretroviral therapy (HAART)?

7. Explain how a pharmacist could assist an HIV-positive patient in obtaining these treatment goals?

8. Six months later Ms. Parker has a $CD4^+$ cell count of 280 cells/mm^3 and a viral load of 50,000 copies/mL. She asks you if you think she should start medications. What is your recommendation? Why or why not?

9. What assessments should be made by the health care team before prescribing antiretroviral therapy that will assist in identifying the most appropriate HAART regimen for a particular patient?

10. List and explain why certain treatment options or combinations are not to be offered at any time. (A review of guidelines from the Department of Health and Human Services [DHHS] is available at aidsinfo.nih.gov/guidelines.)

Through continuing discussion with Ms. Parker, you identify that she has no problem swallowing pills but prefers not to consume a large number of pills. She travels for business and does not want to carry or take a large number of medications on these trips because she often shares a room with a coworker. Her physician has informed her that all of her previous laboratory screening tests came back normal. She denies any history of kidney or liver disease. Although she is still of childbearing age, she states that she is not pregnant nor does she plan on getting pregnant in the near future.

11. Using the January 29, 2008, DHHS recommendations for preferred regimens for treatment-naive patients, what therapeutic options might work best for this patient if the number of pills is her primary concern? How many pills would be included in each of these options for treatment-naive patients?

12. Although the number of pills remains Ms. Parker's primary concern, she would like to know the common side effects and potential toxicities of the preferred HAART regimens recommended for treatment-naive patients. She plans on discussing this with her doctor also. Please describe the more common side effects and toxicities for each of the preferred medications.

Ms. Parker's physician has prescribed Atripla, according to the guidelines. Although your pharmacy routinely stocks most of these medications, you are missing this one. You were able to get the physician to switch the prescription to emtricitabine/tenofovir (Truvada) and efavirenz (Sustiva) for the prescribed "cocktail," only to find that you are also out of the Sustiva 600 mg tablet until tomorrow afternoon.

13. Ms. Parker is extremely anxious about starting medications and would prefer to get started on her antiretroviral medications today. She asks if she could take the Truvada today and just start the Sustiva tomorrow when it is in stock. What recommendation would you give to Ms. Parker about the scheduled starting time for this therapy?

14. While counseling Ms. Parker on her new antiretrovirals, Sustiva and Truvada, you review her prescription medication profile for drug–drug interactions. Provide a list of your findings, and describe possible intervention(s) that you could make to resolve any potential problem(s).

15. Account for any potential interactions with herbs, alcohol, recreational agents, and dietary changes that should be assessed with your patient at this time. Provide examples of potential interactions, and include how these interactions could affect therapy.

16. What counseling recommendations could you make to assist in increasing the effectiveness and decreasing the side effects with Ms. Parker's new antiretroviral regimen?

Four weeks later Ms. Parker returns to your pharmacy with complaints of feeling "drunk" all the time. She states that she is still not able to concentrate at work and is unsure if she can continue with this regimen. Ms. Parker would like to discuss other medication options with you before her next doctor's visit.

17. Knowing your patient's symptoms are probably attributable to efavirenz and that she has a history of lipid abnormalities, what other preferred antiretroviral agents would you recommend be added to Ms. Parker's regimen to replace efavirenz? Explain the reason for each drug choice, and give the appropriate dose and schedule.

18. What effect, if any, will this change in Ms. Parker's antiretroviral regimen have on her hyperlipidemia?

19. Ms. Parker returns to your pharmacy to collect her newly prescribed antiretroviral medication. While waiting for her prescription, she places a box of Prilosec OTC on the counter, which she plans on using for her occasional heartburn. What effect, if any, will her treatment choice for heartburn have on this new antiretroviral regimen? If necessary, provide treatment alternative(s) for this occasional heartburn?

20. Ms. Parker has continued to have her prescriptions filled at your private pharmacy. You notice that each month Ms. Parker is a few days late in picking up her medications. When you question her about this, she admits that she has been missing some of her doses. What type of education should be provided to Ms. Parker about adherence to therapy?

21. Ms. Parker has come to depend on you for answers to a lot of her questions. Today, she would like you to educate her about how to prevent viral transmission to her new HIV-negative partner. Summarize the components involved in HIV prevention.

Additional Activities

1. Identify what types of assistance your pharmacy could offer the local health department by implementing a community prevention campaign or serving as a community education resource.

2. Ascertain the effectiveness of different types of condoms (male and female) in preventing sexually transmitted diseases, including HIV transmission.

3. Investigate the recommended immunization protocol for this patient population, along with those vaccines that are contraindicated.

4. Develop an adherence program that assesses barriers to medication adherence, and propose different strategies or aids to overcome barriers. Methods of communication with the other members of the health care team should be included.

5. Discuss the types of services a community pharmacist could offer patients with HIV when developing a medication therapy management program.

Information Sources

1. US Department of Health and Human Services (DHHS) and National Institutes of Health (NIH). The Living Document: Guidelines for the Use of Antiretroviral Agents in HIV-infected Adults and Adolescents. Available at: http://www.aidsinfo.nih.gov. Last accessed October 28, 2008.

2. Zetola NM, Pilcher CD. Diagnosis and management of acute HIV infection. *Infect Dis Clin North Am.* 2007:21:19–48.

3. Brenner BG, Roger M, Routy JP, et al. High rates of forward transmission events after acute/early HIV-1 infection. *J Infect Dis.* 2007;195:951–9.

4. Schackman BR, Gebo KA, Walensky RP, et al. The lifetime cost of current human immunodeficiency virus care in the United States. *Med Care.* 2006;44:990–7.

5. Hammer SM, Eron JJ, Reiss P, et al. Antiretroviral treatment of adults HIV infection: 2008 recommendations of the International AIDS Society–USA panel. *JAMA.* 2008;300:555–70.

6. Mallal S, Phillips E, Carosi G, et al. HLA-B*5701 screening for hypersensitivity to abacavir. *N Engl J Med.* 2008;358:568–79.

7. ASHP statement on the pharmacist's role in care of patients with HIV infection. *Am J Health Syst Pharm.* 2003;60:1998–2003.

8. March K, Mak M, Louie SG. Effects of pharmacists' interventions on patient outcomes in an HIV primary care clinic. *Am J Health Syst Pharm.* 2007;64:2574–8.

9. Koziel MJ, Peters MG. Viral hepatitis and HIV infection. *N Engl J Med.* 2007;356:1445–54.

10. Iser DM, Sasadeusz JJ. Current treatment of HIV/hepatitis B virus coinfection. *J Gastroenterol Hepatol.* 2008;23:699–706.

11. Atripla. *Med Lett Drugs Ther.* 2006;48:78–9.

12. Prezista (darunavir) [package insert]. Bridgewater, NJ: Tibotec Pharmaceuticals; 2008.

13. Antioniou T, Tseng AL. Interactions between recreational drugs and antiretroviral agents. *Ann Pharmacother.* 2002:6:1598–613.

14. Sax PE. Strategies for management and treatment of dyslipidemia in HIV/AIDS. *AIDS Care.* 2006;18:149–57.

15. Guidelines for the evaluation and management of dyslipidemia in human immunodeficiency virus (HIV)–infected adults receiving antiretroviral therapy. *Clin Infect Dis.* 2003;37:613–27.

16. Reyataz (atazanavir) [package insert]. Princeton, NJ: Bristol-Myers Squibb; 2008.

17. Branson BM, Handsfield HH, Lampe MA, et al. Revised recommendations for HIV testing of adults, adolescents, and pregnant women in health-care settings. *MMWR Recomm Rep.* 2006;55(RR-14):1–17.

18. Centers for Disease Control and Prevention. Incorporating HIV prevention into the medical care of persons living with HIV. *MMWR Morb Mortal Wkly Rep.* 2003; 52(RR-12):1–24.

19. Nagot N, Quedraogo A, Foulongne V, et al. Reduction of HIV-1 RNA levels with therapy to suppress herpes simplex virus. *N Engl J Med.* 2007;356:790–9.

48 Respiratory Infections

Roger D. Lander and Hind I. Hamid

Objectives

1. Classify and describe upper and lower respiratory tract infections, be able to delineate the type of pneumonia found in this patient, and provide the symptoms present that support your answer.

2. Analyze a patient's total medication regimen, and include how to detect and resolve medication-related problems.

3. Develop a medication action plan for a patient.

4. Justify your reasoning behind any recommended changes made in a patient's drug therapy plan.

5. Create a monitoring plan for the patient presented.

Scenario

You are the pharmacist on duty today at Coffee's Pharmacy. You have provided patient counseling and information services since you started working there 3 years ago. Recently, you completed training offered by your state pharmacy association to help you in your quest to offer medication therapy management (MTM) services to your patients. This morning, a patient who is well known to you has brought in several prescriptions. Mr. Harvey Tuttle is a 68-year-old white man who visits your store each month to get his regular medications. Today, his wife and daughter accompany him, and he is coughing and having trouble breathing. His wife Margaret explains that he was just discharged from the local hospital, where he was admitted 5 days ago for pneumonia. She hands you the following prescriptions, which are reproduced in Case Figures 48–1, 48–2, and 48–3. Mr. Tuttle also would like to purchase a bottle of Tylenol PM.

To evaluate the appropriateness of today's therapy, you inquire about Mr. Tuttle's hospitalization and receive the following information. Mr. Tuttle became ill 6 days ago, when he woke with chills in the middle of the night. By that morning, he was coughing frequently, felt feverish, and had two episodes of alternating chills and heavy perspiration. He called his physician's office and spoke to Dr. Johnson's nurse, who told him that Dr. Johnson was out of town.

She told him to come into the office and the practice's newest partner, Dr. Hill, would try to work him in. In the doctor's office, Mr. Tuttle recalls giving the nurse a sputum sample and having a chest X-ray done. He was then instructed to go down the street to the local hospital, where

CASE Figure 48–1 Prescription #1 for patient Harvey Tuttle.

CASE Figure 48–2 Prescription #2 for patient Harvey Tuttle.

```
            Phillip Hill, M.D.
             1221 Main Street
          COFFEETOWN, AL 35227
              (205) 931-7161

Name    Harvey Tuttle

Address  327 Main Street  35227   Date  6/2

           Cipro 500 mg
                #20
              ī BID


Refill  NR  1 2 3 4 5  Void after _____

   Phillip Hill
Dispense as Written           May Substitute
```

CASE Figure 48–3 Prescription #3 for patient Harvey Tuttle.

he was admitted that afternoon. Mrs. Tuttle relates to you that Mr. Tuttle was given fluids and antibiotics into his veins for the next 4 days and that Dr. Hill said that he had acute pneumonia. Yesterday afternoon, Dr. Hill had come by the hospital room and told them that Mr. Tuttle could go home in the morning. Dr. Hill told them he would leave some prescriptions with the nurses and instructed Harvey that it was important for him to take all the medication when he was discharged.

The prescription medication profile for Mr. Tuttle is available in Case Table 48–1. After evaluating Mr. Tuttle's prescriptions and patient profile, you decide that he qualifies for an MTM consultation under the guidelines of his insurance carrier. You explain this to him and his wife, and they are agreeable to return in 2 days if he is feeling better so that you can spend some time with them to perform the consultation.

Today, in your pharmacy, Mr. Tuttle is moderately short of breath and states that he feels tired, but that he is much better than he was when he went to the hospital.

Questions and Activities

1. What types of organisms are found in community-acquired pneumonia? Make a list of these, and include the medication of choice to treat each one.

2. Compare and contrast the signs and symptoms of influenza, pneumonia, and the common cold.

3. On the basis of the patient's symptoms and drug therapy, identify the medical problem, and state the current drug therapy for the problem.

4. Identify the treatment alternatives available for the infectious problem diagnosed in Mr. Tuttle.

5. What are the goals of pharmacotherapy for this patient?

CASE Table 48–1   Prescription Medication Profile

Harvey Tuttle
1247 W. Harrison Drive
Hoover, AL 35226

Phone: 205-418-2726   **DOB:** 3/17/1938   **Insurer:** BCBS of AL

Allergies/Intolerances: PCN (developed a rash when he was given PCN by his dentist; approximate date: 1960s); codeine (he had nausea and vomiting from a Tylenol #3 prescription about 10 years ago)

Rx No.	Drug Name	Directions	Date	R/F	Prescriber	Qty	RPh
606143	Hydrochlorothiazide 25 mg	1 tablet by mouth each morning	10/2	3	Johnson	30	MH
606142	Monopril 10 mg	1 tablet by mouth each morning	10/2	3	Johnson	30	MH
606141	Lipitor 20 mg	1 tablet by mouth at bedtime	10/2	3	Johnson	30	MH
606140	Dilantin 100 mg	3 capsules by mouth at bedtime	10/2	3	Johnson	90	MH
615738	Avandamet 2/500	1 tablet by mouth twice daily	10/1	5	Johnson	60	MH
613172	Naproxen 375	1 tablet twice daily as needed for hip pain	9/14	0	Johnson	30	MH
606143	Hydrochlorothiazide 25 mg	1 tablet by mouth each morning	8/30	4	Johnson	30	MH
606142	Monopril 10 mg	1 tablet by mouth each morning	8/30	4	Johnson	30	MH
606141	Lipitor 20 mg	1 tablet by mouth at bedtime	8/30	4	Johnson	30	MH
606140	Dilantin 100 mg	3 capsules by mouth at bedtime	8/30	4	Johnson	90	MH
606143	Hydrochlorothiazide 25 mg	1 tablet by mouth each morning	7/28	5	Johnson	30	MH
606142	Monopril 10 mg	1 tablet by mouth each morning	7/28	5	Johnson	30	MH
606141	Lipitor 20 mg	1 tablet by mouth at bedtime	7/28	5	Johnson	30	MH
206140	Dilantin 100 mg	3 capsules by mouth at bedtime	7/28	5	Johnson	90	MH

6. What drug(s), dosage form(s), schedule(s), and duration of therapy are optimal for the treatment of this patient's problem?

7. What intervention (e.g., patient recommendations, call to provider, contact emergency services, etc.) is necessary for implementing this treatment?

8. What monitoring parameters available in your community pharmacy setting should be used to evaluate therapy in the patient, including efficacy and adverse effects?

Two days later, Mr. and Mrs. Tuttle return to your pharmacy for the MTM consultation. Mr. Tuttle has more strength today, with good color in his cheeks, and seems to be doing better. During this consultation, you collect the following information.

When you go over his medication history with Mr. Tuttle, he relates that Dr. Johnson started him on the diabetes medicine at his last visit because his sugar was too high. Dr. Johnson recommended that he buy a blood glucose monitor and testing supplies, but he has not gotten them yet because he was in too big of a rush when he came in the pharmacy the last time and got his medications filled. He states that he takes his medication and rarely misses any doses. He takes Tylenol extra strength tablets occasionally for pain in his right hip. He seldom has headaches. He did not sleep well in the hospital and relates that this is why he wants to buy the Tylenol PM. You take his blood pressure and it is 143/88 mm Hg (left arm, regular cuff, sitting) and his peripheral pulse is 82 beats/min.

9. What nondrug therapies or lifestyle modifications might be useful in managing the patient's problem?

10. Develop a medication action plan for the patient; include short-term and long-range goals.

11. What are the pertinent topics to address during patient education?

12. During your patient education discussion with Mr. and Mrs. Tuttle, you mention that they should return to the pharmacy 1 week from today. They ask why they need to come back in a week. Explain what you would tell them about the need for follow-up and what your plan for that visit would involve, and include what, if anything, they should bring with them.

Additional Activities

1. What immunizations are indicated for patients older than 65 years?

2. Research the common organisms that cause upper respiratory tract infections. How do these differ from the organisms that cause lower respiratory tract infections, like Mr. Tuttle had?

3. Develop a business plan for an antibiotic monitoring program in a community pharmacy, perhaps the pharmacy in which you work.

Information Sources

1. Gelone SP, Donnell JO. Respiratory tract infections. In: Koda-Kimble MA, Young LY, Kradjan WA, et al., eds. *Applied Therapeutics: The Clinical Use of Drugs*. 8th ed. Philadelphia: Lippincott Williams & Wilkins; 2006:60:1–17.

2. Glover ML, Reed MD. Lower respiratory tract infections. In: DiPiro JT, Talbert RL, Yee GC, et al., eds. *Pharmacotherapy: A Pathophysiologic Approach*. 6th ed. New York: McGraw-Hill; 2005:1943–62.

3. Donowitz GR, Mandell GL. Acute pneumonia. In: Mandell GL, Bennett JE, Dolin R, eds. *Mandell, Douglas, and Bennett's Principles and Practice of Infectious Disease*. 6th ed. Philadelphia: Elsevier; 2005:819–45.

4. Mandell LA, Wunderink RG, Anzueto A, et al. Infectious Diseases Society of America/American Thoracic Society consensus guidelines on the management of community-acquired pneumonia in adults. *Clin Infect Dis*. 2007;44(suppl 2):S27–S72.

5. Treanor JJ. Influenza virus. In: Mandell GL, Bennett JC, Dolin R, eds. *Mandell, Douglas, and Bennett's Principles and Practice of Infectious Disease*. 6th ed. Philadelphia: Elsevier; 2005:2060–85.

6. Gwaltney JW. The common cold. In: Mandell GL, Bennett JC, Dolin R, eds. *Mandell, Douglas, and Bennett's Principles and Practice of Infectious Disease*. 6th ed. Philadelphia: Elsevier; 2005:747–52.

7. Humibid. Facts & Comparisons. Available at: http://www.factsandcomparisons.com/. Last accessed December 15, 2007.

8. Graham NMH, Douglas RM, Ryan P. Stress and acute respiratory infection. *Am J Epidemiol*. 1986;124:389–401.

9. Kardas P. Patient compliance with antibiotic treatment for respiratory tract infections. *J Antimicrob Chemother*. 2002;49:897–903.

10. Klentrou P, Cieslak T, MacNeil M, et al. Effect of moderate exercise on salivary immunoglobulin A and infection risk in humans. *Eur J Appl Physiol*. 2002;87:153–8.

11. American Pharmacists Association, National Association of Chain Drug Stores Foundation. *Medication Therapy Management in Pharmacy Practice. Core Elements of an MTM Service*. Version 2.0. 2007. Available at: http://www.pharmacist.com/AM/Template.cfm?Section=Pharmacist_Practitioners&TEMPLATE=/CM/ContentDisplay.cfm&CONTENTID=17031. Last accessed September 24, 2008.

12. Chobanian AV, Bakris GL, Black HR, et al. The seventh report of the Joint National Committee on Prevention, Detection, Evaluation, and Treatment of High Blood Pressure: The JNC 7 Report. *JAMA*. 2003;289:2560–72.

13. Expert Panel on Detection, Evaluation, and Treatment of High Blood Cholesterol in Adults (Adult Treatment Panel III). Third report of the National Cholesterol Education Program (NCEP) Expert Panel on Detection, Evaluation, and Treatment of High Blood Cholesterol in Adults (Adult Treatment Panel III) final report. *Circulation*. 2002;106:3143–421.

14. Talbert RL. Role of the National Cholesterol Education Program Adult Treatment Panel III guidelines in managing dyslipidemia. *Am J Health Syst Pharm*. 2003;60(suppl 2):S3–S8.

15. Qaseem A, Vijan S, Snow V, et al. Glycemic control and type 2 diabetes mellitus: the optimal hemoglobin A1c targets. A guidance statement from the American College of Physicians. *Ann Intern Med*. 2007;147:417–22.

Objectives

1. Define and recognize symptoms of various types of conjunctivitis.

2. Identify the treatment alternatives available for conjunctivitis.

3. Analyze various treatment methods, and describe the optimal choice for the treatment of ocular herpes simplex virus.

4. Design a therapeutic plan for a patient with ocular herpes simplex, and include short-term and long-range goals.

Scenario

You are working a weekend night shift at your local pharmacy when a middle-aged woman steps to your counter with visibly noticeable swollen eyes. You ask her, "How may I help you?" She starts complaining of painful, red, watery eyes that started 2 weeks ago. She continues, "It almost feels like I placed a handful of sand in my left eye. I've been using Visine for several days, but it is not working."

You notice that Kristin Bath's right eye has a bright red appearance and is tearing continuously. Her eyelids are also slightly swollen. You inquire about any recent trauma to the eye as well as past medical history and allergies. She states that she has chronic allergies during this portion of the year, but she is concerned that she has "pink eye" because one of her kids had this about a month ago. She continued, "High blood pressure (diagnosed in May), hypothyroidism (diagnosed in September), and chronic allergies. I hate to go to the ER about my eye because I don't have insurance. I lost my job about 1 month ago, and I don't know how I will pay for this or my other medications. Isn't there something you can recommend that is over-the-counter?"

Questions and Activities

1. On the basis of the patient's presentation and drug therapy, identify the disease-related problem.

2. Describe the different types of conjunctivitis and the symptoms involved.

3. How should the pharmacist in this case determine whether Ms. Bath can be treated with nonprescription remedies and self-care or be referred to a physician?

4. Should Visine be continued to reduce redness? What other nonpharmacologic recommendations could be suggested to reduce Ms. Bath's symptoms?

5. What clinical information should be obtained from the patient to distinguish the type of conjunctivitis?

After further discussion of symptoms and evaluation of past medical history and the patient's prescription medication profile (Case Table 49–1), you advise her to seek medical attention from her primary care physician.

Ms. Bath returns to your pharmacy the next day and states she was diagnosed with bacterial conjunctivitis. She states she was given a prescription (Case Figure 49–1) to help with the infection and her symptoms, and she inquires about the cost of the prescription (she is on a fixed budget and her insurance is not yet active). While she waits for you to fill her prescription, she checks her blood pressure and finds that it is 174/98 mm Hg.

6. If this patient has bacterial conjunctivitis, what organisms should be targeted for treatment?

7. What are the goals of pharmacotherapy for this patient?

After filling the prescription for Ms. Bath you realize that the cost of the prescription may not be in her budget. After discussing the situation with the patient, you leave a message for the doctor asking for a more economical alternative.

8. Identify treatment options available for bacterial conjunctivitis, and include the generic and brand names, dose, dosage form, schedule, and duration of therapy. Identify which option you will suggest to Dr. Brown that will be equally efficacious and economical, and will be easy for the patient to remain adherent to.

CASE Table 49–1   Prescription Medication Profile

Kristin Bath
7 Dorset Place
Roanoke, VA24018

Phone: 540-998-7765   **DOB:** 10/15/69   **Insurer:** Anthem

Allergies/Intolerances: None

Rx No.	Drug Name	Directions	Date	R/F	Prescriber	Qty	RPh
615041	Hyzaar 100/12.5 mg	1 tablet by mouth every day	9/27	2	Dyson	30	GK
609695	Synthroid 50 mg	1 tablet by mouth every day	9/26	2	Powell	30	GK
609696	Spironolactone 25 mg	1 tablet by mouth every day	9/26	3	Powell	30	GK
608791	Norvasc 10 mg	1 tablet by mouth every day	9/26	2	Wade	30	GK
607714	Toprol XL	1 tablet by mouth every day	8/23	1	Rathore	60	NT
603543	Hyzaar 50/12.5 mg	1 tablet by mouth every day	5/27	3	Martinez	30	GK

CASE Figure 49–1 Prescription for patient Kristin Bath.

Dr. Brown's nurse calls in a prescription for Zymar. You place another call to Dr. Brown's office for a change in therapy and find that he is out of the country for the next week (he works in a solo practice). His nurse states that he just left for the airport and you may be able to contact him on his cellular phone. You follow the nurse's suggestion and call Dr. Brown to discuss an alternative treatment. However, Dr. Brown is less than pleased that you are calling him now that he has started his vacation and states that he would prefer keeping the prescription for Zymar for Ms. Bath. It appears that your only alternative now is to obtain the medication through a patient assistance program.

9. Describe how you would obtain and complete the designated forms for Ms. Bath.

10. How would you counsel this patient on using eyedrops, ointments, or multiple drops?

11. If Ms. Bath were a child, when would you recommend that she return to school?

Ms. Bath returns to your pharmacy a week later stating that her symptoms have worsened despite using Zymar every 2 hours as directed. She mentions that she was also careful not to spread the infection by washing her hands carefully and did not contaminate the applicator tip. She exclaimed, "My symptoms have worsened, and now I have blurry vision, sensitivity to light, and crusting of the eyes when I wake up in the morning." She inquired about other options for treatment. You call Dr. Brown, and he advises you to have Ms. Bath see Dr. Xavier (an ophthalmologist) at 3 pm today.

12. Which type of herpes simplex virus is probably the most common cause in this case?

13. How would you distinguish between herpes zoster ophthalmicus and herpes simplex?

14. What is the treatment of choice for this patient? What are other options for therapy?

15. What nondrug therapies or lifestyle modifications might be useful in the management of this patient's eye infection?

16. Suggest a plan to follow up with the patient. What will be the focus of the contact?

17. What are Ms. Bath's other drug-related problems. Please suggest options for modifying therapy.

Additional Activities

1. Discuss any precautions that should be taken when treating eye infections for patients who wear contact lenses.

2. Describe any differences in signs and symptoms if the patient had allergic conjunctivitis.

3. Discuss the treatment for allergic conjunctivitis; include nonprescription and prescription medications.

4. Investigate alternative medications that patients might use to treat eye infections.

Information Sources

1. American Academy of Ophthalmology. Cornea/External Disease Panel, Preferred Practice Patterns Committee Conjunctivitis. San Francisco, Calif: American Academy of Ophthalmology; 2003. Available at: http://www.aao.org/ppp. Last accessed September 12, 2008.

2. A controlled trial of oral acyclovir for the prevention of stromal keratitis or iritis in patients with herpes simplex virus epithelial keratitis. The Epithelial Keratitis Trial. The Herpetic Eye Disease Study Group. *Arch Ophthalmol.* 1997;115:703–12.

3. Pepose JS, Keadle TL, Morrison LA. Ocular herpes simplex: changing epidemiology, emerging disease patterns, and the potential of vaccine prevention and therapy. *Am J Ophthalmol.* 2006; 141:547–57.

4. Kaiserman I, Kaiserman N, Nakar S. Herpetic eye disease in diabetic patients. *Ophthalmology.* 2005;112:2184–8.

5. Acyclovir for the prevention of recurrent herpes simplex virus eye disease. Herpetic Eye Disease Study Group. *N Engl J Med.* 1998; 339:300–6.

6. Sozen E, Avunduk AM, Akyol N. Comparison of efficacy of oral valacyclovir and topical acyclovir in the treatment of herpes simplex keratitis: a randomized clinical trial. *Chemotherapy.* 2006;52:29–31.

7. Tabbara KF. Treatment of herpetic keratitis [letter]. *Ophthalmology.* 2005;112:1640.

50 Urinary Tract Infections

Lisa D. Inge and Allana Mehlhorn

Objectives

1. Describe the risk factors for development of a urinary tract infection.

2. Characterize the clinical presentation of an uncomplicated and a complicated urinary tract infection.

3. Recommend common empiric treatment options and durations of therapy for cystitis and uncomplicated pyelonephritis.

4. Evaluate and design a therapeutic regimen for the treatment of a urinary tract infection in specific patient populations, and take into account contraindications, allergies, and side effects.

5. Distinguish between relapse and reinfection in recurrent infections and identify risk factors for each.

Scenario

As a community residency-trained pharmacist working on Saturday morning at a local independent pharmacy, you are approached by Sara Johns. Ms. Johns, a 40-year-old woman, appears to be having some discomfort and would like to know if you carry any home tests that screen for urinary tract infections (UTIs). She has been having frequent urination along with a slight burning, since yesterday evening. A friend told her that you carried these screening tests and that they were fairly accurate.

Her information in your computer is current. She just changed pharmacies last month to get a better price on her diabetes medication and to attend the disease state training classes offered at your store. You do a quick review of her prescription medication profile (Case Table 50–1).

While reviewing her profile, your discussion indicates that her diabetes was diagnosed about 2 years ago. Since that time, she has had one prior urinary tract infection about 18 months ago, but no other major concerns. Currently, she denies any vaginal discharge, nausea, vomiting, fever, or flank pain. Her urine has an "odor," but she states that she takes a multivitamin every day and took an extra 500 mg of vitamin C this morning. She always adds the extra vitamins to her pillbox when she feels like she is getting sick. Her general health has been much better as a result of her new physical activity class that she attends twice a week and her low-carbohydrate diet. It has even provided more "spice" in her marriage, increasing the use of her diaphragm with spermicidal gel for birth control. Her nonprescription product use includes store-brand acetaminophen as needed for occasional headaches or pain from physical activity.

Questions and Activities

1. List the common symptoms that might help you identify whether Ms. Johns has a complicated or an uncomplicated urinary tract infection (UTI).

2. Identify the more common risk factors for a UTI. Which patient populations, disease states, or medical situations pose an increased risk of having a complicated UTI? State the rationale for the classification of these risk factors.

CASE Table 50–1 Prescription Medication Profile

Sara Johns
789 Beach Street
Ft. Lauderdale, FL 33301

Phone: 954-355-9921   **DOB:** 11/5/68   **Insurer:** None (cash)

Allergies/Intolerances: Sulfa products

Rx No.	Drug Name	Directions	Date	R/F	Prescriber	Qty	RPh
611553	Glyburide 5 mg	1 tablet by mouth twice daily	11/05	3	Timmons	60	HW

3. Describe the types of home UTI screening tests currently available along with their method(s) of detection. What are the recommendations for their use?

4. When performing any screening test, the sensitivity and specificity of the test should be evaluated. What are the limitations in terms of sensitivity and specificity of some common home UTI tests? How might these UTI testing limitations affect their potential clinical use?

5. Describe the patient counseling a pharmacist should provide to any patient who is about to purchase a UTI screening kit. Include both the general information on the test kit itself and the steps involved in urine collection.

6. What is your recommendation on the use of home UTI testing for this patient?

7. List your therapeutic goals for this patient.

8. What nonprescription (pharmacologic) therapeutic recommendations could you make for this patient on the basis of your prior therapeutic goals? Identify the key counseling points for each recommendation.

9. What organisms are likely responsible for Ms. Johns' current UTI?

10. This patient would like to know if she may purchase cranberry juice to treat her infection because it could be cheaper than an antibiotic. What response would you provide the patient?

After this conversation, you recommend that Ms. Johns see her local doctor for a prescription. Later that afternoon, she returns to your pharmacy with a prescription (Case Figure 50–1).

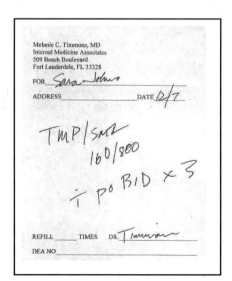

CASE Figure 50–1 Prescription for patient Sara Johns.

11. List the recommended empiric therapeutic options, doses, and durations of therapy for uncomplicated cystitis, complicated lower UTIs, and uncomplicated acute pyelonephritis.

12. Do you have any concerns about this patient's prescribed therapeutic regimen?

13. What general therapeutic considerations should be assessed before making a recommendation to her health care provider?

14. On the basis of these considerations, what recommendation would you make for your patient's empiric therapy? If the patient were pregnant, would that change your recommended regimen?

15. Describe the counseling you would provide for your recommended empiric treatment regimen?

16. What follow-up nonpharmacologic interventions might be suggested for the prevention of UTIs in this patient?

17. Identify any nonprescription products that are suggested for prevention of UTIs in patients.

18. Would you recommend a follow-up culture in this patient? Provide support for your recommendation.

19. Ms. Johns returns to your pharmacy 3 weeks later with another infection. Would you consider this a recurrent infection, a relapse, or reinfection? Why or why not?

20. If this patient's original UTI occurred 18 months ago, would you recommend that she be placed on prophylactic therapy to prevent any recurrent UTI? Why or why not?

21. What factors and management strategies need to be considered when designing a therapeutic plan for patients with recurrent UTIs? What are common medications, including dosage and duration, used in the identified management strategies?

Additional Activities

1. Plan an antibiotic monitoring program for a community pharmacy.

2. Investigate what alternative medications may be used to treat UTIs, and include their safety and efficacy.

3. Investigate other dietary factors that can be used to promote urinary tract health (i.e., yogurt) and the evidence supporting their use.

4. Develop a plan for incorporating home UTI test kits in a patient care service in your pharmacy.

Information Sources

1. Coyle EA, Prince RA. Urinary tract infections and prostatitis. In: DiPiro JT, Talbert RL, Yee GC, et al., eds. *Pharmacotherapy: A Pathophysiologic Approach.* 6th ed. New York: McGraw-Hill; 2005:2081–96.

2. Franco AV. Recurrent urinary tract infections. *Best Pract Res Clin Obstet Gynaecol.* 2005;19:861–73.

3. Sheffield JS, Cunningham FG. Urinary tract infection in women. *Obstet Gynecol.* 2005;106:1085–92.

4. Fihn SD. Acute uncomplicated urinary tract infection in women. *N Engl J Med.* 2003;349:259–66.

5. Warren JW, Abrutyn E, Hebel JR, et al. Guidelines for antimicrobial treatment of uncomplicated acute bacterial cystitis and acute pyelonephritis in women. Infectious Diseases Society of America (IDSA). *Clin Infect Dis.* 1999;29:745–58.

6. Bremnor JD, Sadovsky R. Evaluation of dysuria in adults. *Am Fam Physician.* 2002;65:1589–96.

7. Car J. Urinary tract infections in women: diagnosis and management in primary care. *BMJ.* 2006;332:94–7.

8. Hoepelman AI, Meiland R, Geerlings SE. Pathogenesis and management of bacterial urinary tract infections in adult patients with diabetes mellitus. *Int J Antimicrob Agents.* 2003;22(suppl 2):35–43

9. Ramakrishnan K, Scheid DC. Diagnosis and management of acute pyelonephritis in adults. *Am Fam Physician.* 2005;71:933–42.

10. Nicolle LE. Urinary tract infection in diabetes. *Curr Opin Infect Dis.* 2005;18:49–53

11. Scholes D, Hooton TM, Roberts PL, et al. Risk factors for recurrent urinary tract infection in young women. *J Infect Dis* 2000;182:1177–82.

12. Rosenthal WM, Briggs GC. Home testing and monitoring devices. In: Berardi RR, Kroon LA, Newton GD, et al., eds. *Handbook of Non-prescription Drugs: An Interactive Approach to Self-Care.* 15th ed. Washington, DC: American Pharmacists Association; 2006:1064–5.

13. Fox GN. Sensitivity and specificity of urinary nitrite for UTIs [letter]. *Am Fam Physician.* 2005;72:2180.

14. Nys S, van Merode T, Bartelds AI, et al. Urinary tract infections in general practice patients: diagnostic tests versus bacteriological culture. *J Antimicrob Chemother.* 2006;57:955–8.

15. Simerville JA, Maxted, Pahira JJ. Urinalysis: a comprehensive review. *Am Fam Physician.* 2005;71;1153–62.

16. Phenazopyridine. Clinical Pharmacology [subscription required]. 2007. Available at: http://www.goldstandard.com. Last accessed October 5, 2008.

17. Lowe FC, Fagelman E. Cranberry juice and urinary tract infections what is the evidence? *Urology.* 2001;57:407–13.

18. Raz R, Chazan B, Dan M. Cranberry juice and urinary tract infection. *Clin Infect Dis.* 2004;38:1413–9.

19. Lynch DM. Cranberry for prevention of urinary tract infections. *Am Fam Physician.* 2004;70:2175–7.

20. Cranberry. International Bibliographic Information on Dietary Supplements (IBIDS) Database. Available at: http://ods.od.nih.gov/Health_Information/IBIDS.aspx. Last accessed September 12, 2008.

21. Hume AL, Strong KM. Botanical medicines. In: Berardi RR, Kroon LA, Newton GD, et al., eds. *Handbook of Nonprescription Drugs: An Interactive Approach to Self-Care.* 15th ed. Washington, DC: American Pharmacists Association; 2006:1103–36.

22. Proquin XR (Ciprofloxacin extended release) [package insert]. East Brunswick, NJ: Espirit Pharma; 2005.

23. Cipro XR (Ciprofloxacin extended release) [package insert]. West Haven, Conn: Bayer Pharmaceuticals. April 2008.

24. Macejko AM, Schaeffer AJ. Asymptomatic bacteriuria and symptomatic urinary tract infections during pregnancy. *Urol Clin North Am.* 2007;34:35–42.

25. Ribera MC, Pascual R, Orozco D, et al. Incidence and risk factors associated with urinary tract infection in diabetic patients with and without asymptomatic bacteriuria. *Eur J Clin Microbiol Infect Dis.* 2006;25:389–93.

26. Nicolle LE. Asymptomatic bacteriuria: review and discussion of the IDSA guidelines. *Int J Antimicrob Agents.* 2006;28(suppl):S42–8.

27. Albert X, Heurtas I, Pereiro II, et al. Antibiotics for preventing recurrent urinary tract infection in non-pregnant women. *Cochrane Database Syst Rev.* 2004;3:CD001209.

51 Sexually Transmitted Infections

Jeffery A. Goad

Objectives

1. Describe the risk factors for acquiring gonorrhea and chlamydia infections.

2. Characterize the clinical presentation of gonorrhea and chlamydia in males and females.

3. Recommend common empiric treatment options and durations of therapy for uncomplicated gonorrhea and chlamydia infections.

4. Evaluate and design a therapeutic regimen for the treatment of gonorrhea and chlamydia infections in specific patient populations, and take into account contraindications, allergies, side effects, and resistance trends.

5. Discuss ways to prevent future infections and ongoing transmission to patients and partners.

Scenario

You are a community pharmacist in a suburb of a large metropolitan city in the Midwest.

John Roamer is a 29-year-old white man who comes to your pharmacy for the first time with prescriptions (Case Figures 51–1 and 51–2). He requests to pay cash and not use his prescription drug plan. He reports no allergies to medications and is otherwise in good health. During consultation, you determine that he was prescribed the two antibiotics for a suspected gonorrhea and chlamydia infection that he states he likely acquired on a business trip to China approximately 1 week ago. The patient is married, but he withheld this information from the physician he saw at the free clinic. His concern with the medication is how he is going to conceal 7 days of therapy and about how long he should abstain from sexual activity with his wife after starting treatment.

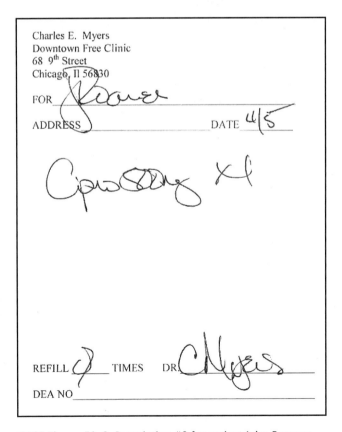

CASE Figure 51–1 Prescription #1 for patient John Roamer.

CASE Figure 51–2 Prescription #2 for patient John Roamer.

Questions and Activities

1. How common are gonorrhea and chlamydia in the United States and abroad?

2. Describe the spectrum of illness related to gonorrhea and chlamydia infection, and the association between these two bacteria.

3. Knowing the region of travel and that the patient had unprotected sexual contact, for what other sexually transmitted infections (STIs) should he be tested?

4. What are the common signs and symptoms of gonorrhea and chlamydia infections in men and in women?

5. Define syndromatic diagnosis for STIs, and describe relevant laboratory tests to confirm the presence of *Neisseria gonorrhea* and *Chlamydia trachomatis*.

6. How efficiently is gonorrhea and chlamydia transmitted? Describe risk factors for acquiring gonorrhea and chlamydia, and for developing more severe disease.

7. Evaluate whether the patient's wife should be tested or treated for presumed gonorrhea and chlamydia.

Concerned that his gonorrhea might be quinolone-resistant and that the patient is unlikely to adhere to a 7-day course of doxycycline, you phone the prescribing physician to change the prescription to cefixime 400 mg and azithromycin 1 gram, administered as a one-time dose. The physician agrees, and the patient takes both doses in your pharmacy.

8. Describe an approach to treatment that relies on microbiologic and epidemiologic characteristics.

9. How effective are the various treatment approaches mentioned in this case?

10. What alternatives could be suggested if the patient has a severe allergy to penicillins and cephalosporins?

11. How would you counsel this patient about when to resume sexual activity with his wife?

12. Should the patient return to his primary care provider after treatment for a test of cure?

13. What vaccine(s) could be recommended for this patient to protect against acquiring STIs from future extramarital sexual contacts and why?

Additional Activities

1. Investigate how the treatment of this patient would differ if the patient were a pregnant female.

2. Research other STIs, and include associated pathogens, signs and symptoms, and treatments.

3. Compare and contrast the different types of male condoms, and include efficacy for preventing STIs.

4. Compare and contrast the efficacy of different types of contraceptive methods for preventing bacterial and viral STIs.

5. Develop an educational campaign for a community pharmacy that focuses on decreasing risk for STIs in adolescents and young adults.

6. Create a plan-o-gram in a community pharmacy for products to prevent STIs.

Information Sources

1. Centers for Disease Control and Prevention. *Sexually Transmitted Disease Surveillance, 2005*. Atlanta, Ga: US Department of Health and Human Services; 2006. Available at: http://www.cdc.gov/std/stats/toc2006.htm. Last accessed October 5, 2008.

2. Weinstock H, Berman S, Cates W Jr, et al. Sexually transmitted diseases among American youth: incidence and prevalence estimates, 2000. *Perspect Sex Reprod Health*. 2004;36:6–10.

3. World Health Organization. *Trends in Sexually Transmitted Infections and HIV in the European Region, 1980–2005*. Copenhagen: World Health Organization; 2006. Available at: http://www.euro.who.int/Document/RC56/etb01b.pdf). Last accessed September 13, 2008.

4. World Health Organization. *Global Strategy for the Prevention and Control of Sexually Transmitted Infections: 2006–2015*. Geneva: World Health Organization; 2007. Available at: http://www.who.int/reproductive-health/publications/stisstrategy/stis_strategy.pdf. Last accessed October 5, 2008.

5. Meyers DS, Halvorson H, Luckhaupt S; US Preventive Services Task Force. Screening for chlamydial infection: an evidence update for the U.S. Preventive Services Task Force. *Ann Intern Med*. 2007;147:135–42.

6. Lyss SB, Kamb ML, Peterman TA, et al. Chlamydia trachomatis among patients infected with and treated for Neisseria gonorrhoeae in sexually transmitted disease clinics in the United States. *Ann Intern Med*. 2003;139:178–85.

7. Tapsall J. *Antimicrobial Resistance in Neisseria gonorrhoeae*. Geneva: World Health Organization; 2001:1–58.

8. Reed JL, Mahabee-Gittens EM, Huppert JS. A decision rule to identify adolescent females with cervical infections. *J Womens Health* (Larchmt). 2007;16:272–80.

9. Warner L, Stone KM, Macaluso M, et al. Condom use and risk of gonorrhea and chlamydia: a systematic review of design and measurement factors assessed in epidemiologic studies. *Sex Transm Dis*. 2006;33:36–51.

10. Hillis SD, Owens LM, Marchbanks PA, et al. Recurrent chlamydial infections increase the risks of hospitalization for ectopic pregnancy and pelvic inflammatory disease. *Am J Obstet Gynecol*. 1997;176(1 pt 1):103–7.

11. Centers for Disease Control and Prevention. *Fact Sheet: Gonorrhea*. Atlanta, Ga: Centers for Disease Control and Prevention; 2006.

12. Matteelli A, Carosi G. Sexually transmitted diseases in travelers. *Clin Infect Dis*. 2001;32:1063–7.

13. Ward BJ, Plourde P. Travel and sexually transmitted infections. *J Trav Med*. 2006;13:300–17.

14. Ram S, Rice PA. Gonococcal infections. In: Kasper DL, Braunwald E, Fauci AS, et al., eds. *Harrison's Principles of Internal Medicine* [electronic edition]. 16th ed. New York: McGraw-Hill; 2007: chapter 128.

15. Mehrany K, Kist JM, O'Connor WJ, et al. Disseminated gonococcemia. *Int J Dermatol.* 2003;42:208–9.

16. Geisler WM. Management of uncomplicated Chlamydia trachomatis infections in adolescents and adults: evidence reviewed for the 2006 Centers for Disease Control and Prevention sexually transmitted diseases treatment guidelines. *Clin Infect Dis.* 2007;44(suppl 3):S77–S83.

17. Darroch J, Myers L, Cassell J. Sex differences in the experience of testing positive for genital chlamydia infection: a qualitative study with implications for public health and for a national screening programme. *Sex Transm Infect.* 2003;79:372–3.

18. Johnson RE, Newhall WJ, Papp JR, et al. Screening tests to detect Chlamydia trachomatis and Neisseria gonorrhoeae infections–2002. *MMWR Recomm Rep.* 2002;51(RR-15):1–38.

19. Centers for Disease Control and Prevention. Sexually transmitted diseases treatment guidelines, 2006. *MMWR Recomm Rep.* 2006;55 (RR-11):1–94.

20. Lau C-Y, Qureshi AK. Azithromycin versus doxycycline for genital chlamydial infections: a meta-analysis of randomized clinical trials. *Sex Transm Dis.* 2002;29.497–502.

21. Mast EE, Weinbaum CM, Fiore AE, et al. A comprehensive immunization strategy to eliminate transmission of hepatitis B virus infection in the United States: recommendations of the Advisory Committee on Immunization Practices (ACIP), part II: immunization of adults. *MMWR Recomm Rep.* 2006;55(RR-16):1–33; quiz CE1–CE4.

52 Fungal Infection of the Nails

Allana Mehlhorn

Objectives

1. Design an appropriate therapeutic regimen for the treatment of toenail fungus.

2. Recognize contraindications to medications used for the treatment of toenail fungus.

3. Recommend nondrug therapies that may be useful to prevent recurrence of toenail fungus.

4. Counsel a patient who is starting a therapeutic regimen for toenail fungus.

Scenario

Today, a well-known pharmacy customer, Janet Lockwood, comes to your community pharmacy. When you greet her, she tells you that she has a toenail fungus and would like it resolved before she leaves for vacation next week. She is excited that she is going to visit her grandchildren in Florida, and she wants to wear open-toed beach sandals. She hands you her prescription (Case Figure 52–1).

Phil Stevenson, MD
Family Practice Associates
1200 Pine Street
Bridgeport, CT 06610

FOR _Janet Lockwood_

ADDRESS _2121 Maple Ave._ DATE _4/22_

Sporanox Pulse Pak
Sig: Take as directed.
_#28_

REFILL _1_ TIMES DR. _Stevenson_

DEA NO _____

CASE Figure 52–1 Prescription for patient Janet Lockwood.

Janet Lockwood would also like to purchase an OTC topical antifungal cream for "extra protection."

Case Table 52–1 is a printout of her prescription medication profile. After reviewing Ms. Lockwood's prescription medication profile, you ask her how long she has had congestive heart failure. She responds that it was diagnosed about 1 year ago. When asked if she has any other medical conditions, she says she does not but was told to follow up with her doctor next month to "recheck her blood sugars."

You also ask if she is taking any OTC or herbal products. She says she takes only one baby aspirin a day because her doctor told her it was good for her heart. You also inquire if she has ever had a problem with nail fungus in the past. She says that, fortunately, this is the first time she has ever had this problem. Because her usual doctor was so busy, she went to see a different physician so she could get a prescription for the nail fungus before the start of her vacation.

Questions and Activities

1. Ms. Lockwood also wants to know what the "Take as Directed" means. Provide patient counseling to Ms. Lockwood about her new prescription.

2. In addition, Ms. Lockwood wants to know if she should continue using the Lamisil Cream that she bought. What do you tell her?

3. On the basis of the patient's presentation and medication therapy, identify the medication-related medical problem.

4. Identify the intervention(s) to solve the problem(s) and the anticipated outcome(s).

5. Identify the available treatment alternatives for toenail fungus.

6. What drug(s), dosage form(s), schedule(s), and duration(s) of therapy are optimal for the treatment of this patient's problem?

7. Why is it important to treat toenail fungus?

CASE Table 52–1

Janet Lockwood
2121 Maple Avenue
Bridgeport, CT 06610

Phone: 203-561-7788 **DOB:** 06/15/36 **Insurer:** CIGNA

Allergies/Intolerances: PCN (rash)

Rx No.	Drug Name	Directions	Date	R/F	Prescriber	Qty	RPh
682504	Lasix 40 mg	1 tablet every day	4/01	8	Matteo	30	JK
682503	K-Dur 20 mEq	1 tablet every day	4/01	8	Matteo	30	JK
682502	Altace 5 mg	1 capsule twice daily	4/01	8	Matteo	30	JK
682501	Toprol XL 100 mg	1 tablet every day	4/01	8	Matteo	30	JK
682500	Zocor 40 mg	1 tablet every night	4/01	8	Matteo	30	JK
680304	Lasix 40 mg	1 tablet every day	3/01	9	Matteo	30	JK
680303	K-Dur 20 mEq	1 tablet every day	3/01	9	Matteo	30	JK
680302	Altace 5 mg	1 capsule twice daily	3/01	9	Matteo	30	JK
680301	Toprol XL 100 mg	1 tablet every day	3/01	9	Matteo	30	JK
680300	Zocor 40 mg	1 tablet every night	3/01	9	Matteo	30	JK
679541	Lasix 40 mg	1 tablet every day	2/01	10	Matteo	30	JK
679540	K-Dur 20 mEq	1 tablet every day	2/01	10	Matteo	30	JK
679539	Altace 5 mg	1 capsule twice daily	2/01	10	Matteo	30	JK
679538	Toprol XL 100 mg	1 tablet every day	2/01	10	Matteo	30	JK
679537	Zocor 40 mg	1 tablet every night	2/01	10	Matteo	30	JK

8. What nondrug therapies or lifestyle modifications might be useful in managing this patient's problem?

9. What are the goals of pharmacotherapy for this patient?

10. What monitoring parameters available in the community pharmacy setting should be used to evaluate therapy in this patient, including efficacy and adverse effects?

11. What are the pertinent topics to address during patient education?

12. Develop a follow-up plan for this patient; include time to follow up and method of contact.

Additional Activities

1. Identify all medication and food interactions with antifungals and the significance of each interaction.

2. Develop a monitoring program for liver function tests in a community pharmacy setting.

3. Investigate the safety and efficacy of alternative treatments for toenail fungus.

Information Sources

1. Sporanox (itraconazole) [product information]. Raritan, NJ: Ortho Biotech; October 2007.

2. Tan J, Joseph W. Common fungal infections of the feet in patients with diabetes mellitus. *Drugs Aging.* 2004;21:101–12.

3. Rodgers P, Bassler M. Treating onychomycosis. *Am Fam Physician.* 2001;63:663–72.

4. Debruyne D, Coquerel A. Pharmacokinetics of antifungal agents in onychomycoses. *Clin Pharmacokinet.* 2001;40:441–72.

5. Brown T, Chin T. Superficial fungal infections. In: DiPiro JT, Talbert RL, Yee GC, et al., eds. *Pharmacotherapy: A Pathophysiologic Approach.* 7th ed. New York: McGraw-Hill; 2008: 1957–72.

6. Penlac (ciclopirox) topical solution [product information]. Bridgewater, NJ: Dermik Laboratories (division of sanofi-aventis); July 2006.

7. Hay R. Dermatophytosis and other superficial mycoses. In: Mandell G, Bennett J, Dolin R, eds. *Principles and Practice of Infectious Diseases.* 6th ed. Philadelphia: Elsevier; 2005:3051–61.

8. Hainer B. Dermatophyte infections. *Am Fam Physician.* 2003;67:101–8.

9. Rodgers P, Bassler M. Treating onychomycosis. *Am Fam Physician.* 2001;63:663–72.

10. Pray W, Pray J. Toenail fungal infection. *US Pharm.* 2004;8:16–27.

11. Bedinghaus J, Niedfeldt M. Over-the-counter foot remedies. *Am Fam Physician.* 2001;64:791–6.

12. Lamisil (terbinafine) [product information]. East Hanover, NJ: Novartis Pharmaceuticals; September 2007.

13. Lacy CF, Armstrong LL, Goldman MP, Lance LL. *Drug Information Handbook.* 17th ed. Hudson, Ohio: Lexi-Comp; 2008.

Objectives

1. Identify and differentiate between influenza and the common cold on the basis of signs and symptoms and patient information.

2. Recommend appropriate prescription, nonprescription, and lifestyle treatment options.

3. Develop a specific treatment plan, and include monitoring and follow-up for a patient with influenza.

4. Assess other options for prevention of the influenza, and include indications and contraindications.

Scenario

Walking into your building for work, you run into John Taylor, the accountant who works across the hall from your local pharmacy. John, normally full of energy and life, today seems to be struggling to walk through the door. Upon questioning him, you find out that on arrival at home the previous day, John began to experience chills and extreme weakness.

A few hours later that same morning, Mr. Taylor enters your pharmacy looking for something to help him feel better. In his office he found a thermometer and discovered that his temperature was 102°F. For the past hour, his body has ached all over. He thought some coffee would pep him up, but he does not feel like drinking or eating anything. You immediately call upstairs to Dr. Powell's office to see if Mr. Taylor can get an appointment. However, Dr. Powell prefers that Mr. Taylor not come into his office to avoid infecting any other patients in his office. Dr. Powell decides that he is comfortable prescribing something for Mr. Taylor based on your recommendations. You review the patient's prescription medication profile (Case Table 53–1) before making a recommendation.

Questions and Activities

1. On the basis of Mr. Taylor's presentation and current drug therapy, what is your assessment of his problem and why?

2. Describe the different types of the influenza virus that can infect humans and the available treatment options.

3. Is antiviral treatment an option for Mr. Taylor? Why or why not?

4. What is your recommendation for Dr. Powell, including drug(s), dosage form(s), schedule (s), and duration(s) of therapy?

5. Identify the treatment alternatives for the drug therapy problem.

6. What nonprescription medications can be recommended for symptom relief and why?

7. What are the goals of pharmacotherapy for this patient?

8. What treatment options are available for the patient if he had presented after experiencing more than 48 hours of symptoms?

9. What lifestyle modifications might be useful in managing this patient's problem?

10. What are the pertinent topics to address during patient education?

11. What symptoms would indicate infection in the patient's children?

12. Should his children take any medications to prevent infection?

13. What is the difference between influenza and the common cold?

14. What is the best way to prevent influenza?

15. Is the patient eligible for an influenza vaccination this year? Next year?

16. Who is at risk of influenza (i.e., what patients should be recommended to receive the vaccine)?

17. Describe the types of influenza vaccinations available.

18. What monitoring parameters should be communicated about the vaccination?

CASE Table 53-1   Prescription Medication Profile

John Taylor
2415 Gimmeck Rd.
Madison, MO 12123

Phone: 573-839-2350   **DOB:** 9/28/63   **Insurer:** United Health   **Employer:** Express Busch, Inc.

Allergies/Intolerances: NKDA

Social History: Widow; 2 children (Amanda, 8 y.o.; Joey, 15 y.o.); EtOH: daily beer with dinner; Tobacco: social cigar smoker

Physical Examination: BP: 150/82 mm Hg; HR: 97 beats/min; T: 102°F; Wt: 212 lb; Ht: 5 ft 10 in

Immunizations: None to date

Rx No.	Drug Name	Directions	Date	R/F	Prescriber	Qty	RPh
650414	Hyzaar 100/12.5 mg	1 tablet by mouth every day	9/27	3	Powell	30	HP
658085	Metformin HCl ER 500 mg	1 tablet by mouth twice daily	9/26	0	Powell	60	RJ
658086	Spironolactone 25 mg	1 tablet by mouth every day	9/26	2	Powell	30	RJ
658087	Clopidogrel 75 mg	1 tablet by mouth every day	9/26	2	Powell	30	RJ
658088	Felodipine ER 10 mg	1 tablet by mouth every day	9/26	0	Powell	30	RJ
648791	Glipizide XL 10 mg	1 tablet by mouth every day	8/23	0	Powell	30	HP
648792	Cialis 20 mg	As directed	8/23	9	Powell	10	HP
648793	Toprol XL 50 mg	1 tablet by mouth every day	8/23	2	Powell	30	HP
637912	Tricor 145 mg	1 tablet by mouth every day	6/30	1	Powell	30	HP
637913	Plavix 75 mg	1 tablet by mouth every day	6/30	3	Powell	30	RJ
637914	Glipizide XL 5 mg	1 tablet by mouth every day	6/30	3	Powell	30	RJ
637915	Hyzaar 50/12.5 mg	1 tablet by mouth every day	6/30	1	Powell	30	RJ
635798	Toprol XL 50 mg	1 tablet by mouth every day	5/27	0	Powell	30	RJ

19. Which type of vaccine would you recommend for this patient? Discuss screening and contraindications to the vaccines.

20. Should the patient's children receive a vaccination? Will the vaccination prevent them from getting sick immediately?

21. What is the rapid influenza test, and how it is useful?

22. Should the pharmacist consider implementing the use of the rapid influenza test in the practice for future patients?

Additional Activities

1. Investigate how to identify and track if influenza is in your area.

2. Design promotional activities to promote National Influenza Vaccination Week in a community pharmacy.

3. Develop a collaborative practice protocol for the pharmacist to initiate influenza treatment in a community pharmacy.

Information Sources

1. Fiore AE, Shay DK, Broder K, et al. Prevention and control of influenza. Recommendations of the Advisory Committee on Immunization Practices (ACIP). *MMWR Recomm Rep*. 2008;57(RR-7): 1–60.

2. Nicholson KG. Clinical features of influenza. *Semin Respir Infect*. 1992;7:26–37.

3. Demicheli V, Jefferson T, Rivetti D, et al. Prevention and early treatment of influenza in healthy adults. *Vaccine*. 2000;18:957–1030.

4. Hayden FG, Osterhaus AD, Treanor JJ, et al. Efficacy and safety of the neuraminidase inhibitor zanamivir in the treatment of influenza virus infections. GG167 Influenza Study Group. *N Engl J Med*. 1997;337:874–80.

5. Randomised trial of efficacy and safety of inhaled zanamivir in treatment of influenza A and B virus infections. The MIST (Management of Influenza in the Southern Hemisphere Trialists) Study Group. *Lancet*. 1998;352:1877–81.

6. Makela MJ, Pauksens K, Rostila T, et al. Clinical efficacy and safety of the orally inhaled neuraminidase inhibitor zanamivir in the treatment of influenza: a randomized, double-blind, placebo-controlled European study. *J Infect*. 2000;40:42–8.

7. Matsumoto K, Ogawa N, Nerome K, et al. Safety and efficacy of the neuraminidase inhibitor zanamivir in treating influenza virus infection in adults: results from Japan. GG167 Group. *Antivir Ther*. 1999;4:61–8.

8. Monto AS, Fleming DM, Henry D, et al. Efficacy and safety of the neuraminidase inhibitor zanamivir in the treatment of influenza A and B virus infections. *J Infect Dis*. 1999;180:254–61.

9. Douglas R Jr. Influenza in man. In: Kilbourne ED, ed. *Influenza Viruses and Influenza.* New York: Academic Press; 1975:395–418.

10. Relenza (zanamivir for inhalation) [product information]. Research Triangle Park, NC: Glaxo Wellcome; 2001.

11. National Institute of Allergy and Infectious Diseases. Flu (Influenza) Treatment. Available at: http://www3.niaid.nih.gov/topics/Flu/understandingFlu/Treatment.htm. Last accessed October 5, 2008.

12. Centers for Disease Control and Prevention. Seasonal Flu: Good Health Habits for Prevention. Available at: http://www.cdc.gov/flu/protect/habits.htm. Last accessed September 13, 2008.

13. Centers for Disease Control and Prevention. Questions & Answers: Cold Versus Flu. Available at: http://www.cdc.gov/flu/about/qa/coldflu.htm. Last accessed September 13, 2008.

14. Centers for Disease Control and Prevention. Key Facts About Seasonal Flu Vaccine. Available at: http://www.cdc.gov/flu/protect/keyfacts.htm. Last accessed September 13, 2008.

15. Centers for Disease Control and Prevention. Question & Answers: Seasonal Flu Vaccine. Available at: http://www.cdc.gov/flu/about/qa/fluvaccine.htm. Last accessed September 13, 2008.

16. Hayden FG, Pavia AT. Antiviral management of seasonal and pandemic influenza. *J Infect Dis.* 2006;194(suppl):S119–26.

Section

11

Ocular Disorders

54 Contact Lens

Audrey Smith and Janelle Ruisinger

Objectives

1. Determine the effect of product formulations in selecting nonprescription ophthalmic products.

2. Evaluate eye-related symptoms and provide corresponding treatment alternatives.

3. List drug–contact lens interactions and provide specific counseling points for each.

4. Assess self-care procedures of contact lens wearers and describe appropriate lens handling.

5. Identify interventions, goals, and follow-up plans for contact lens wearers with eye problems.

Scenario

Lucy Moore is a 35-year-old white woman who comes to your pharmacy complaining of red, itchy, watering eyes that seem to be getting worse the past week. She also mentions that she has been wearing soft contact lenses for several years. Ms. Moore tells you that her eye care practitioner suggested she ask her pharmacist to recommend a nonprescription product that she can use to help alleviate her symptoms.

Questions and Activities

1. Identify possible intervention(s) to solve Ms. Moore's chief complaint.

2. What nondrug therapies or lifestyle modifications might be useful in managing Ms. Moore's red, itchy, watering eyes?

3. List your nonprescription treatment alternatives for Ms. Moore, based on her symptoms.

4. Considering the options to treat Ms. Moore's symptoms, identify indications, precautions, and counseling points for the following nonprescription ophthalmic products: rewetting solutions, artificial tears or lubricating solutions, ocular antihistamines, and ocular decongestants.

5. Summarize key counseling points about appropriate administration of nonprescription ophthalmic drops, gels, and ointments.

6. What monitoring parameters available in the community pharmacy setting should be used to evaluate selected nonprescription therapy for Ms. Moore, including efficacy and adverse effects?

7. Because Ms. Moore wears contact lenses, which nonprescription ophthalmic products should be avoided?

8. Why is it important to consider a preservative-free ophthalmic product for Ms. Moore compared with an ophthalmic product containing preservatives?

9. Develop a follow-up plan for Ms. Moore; include time to follow up and method of contact.

Because you are not aware of Ms. Moore's current self-care regimen for her contact lenses, you decide to also question her about her current contact lens self-care procedures and provide additional counseling if necessary.

10. Summarize pertinent counseling points about the following types of products for soft contact lenses: handling, disinfection, cleaning, and storage.

11. What additional recommendations should you provide Ms. Moore in relation to her contact lens self-care regimen?

12. Does the type of contact lens cleaning solution affect Ms. Moore's contact lens care? Why or why not?

About 1 month later, Ms. Moore comes to your pharmacy with two prescriptions (Case Figure 54–1 and Case Figure 54–2).

13. What counseling points are important to share with Ms. Moore about her new prescriptions because she wears contact lenses?

14. Name two additional prescription medications that require counseling points for contact lens wearers; include specific counseling points for each medication.

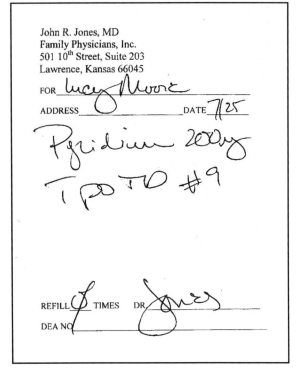

John R. Jones, MD
Family Physicians, Inc.
501 10th Street, Suite 203
Lawrence, Kansas 66045

FOR _Lucy Moore_

ADDRESS_____ DATE _7/25_

Pyridium 200mg

i po TID #9

REFILL _0_ TIMES DR _Jones_

DEA NO_____

CASE Figure 54–1 Prescription #1 for patient Lucy Moore.

John R. Jones, MD
Family Physicians, Inc.
501 10th Street, Suite 203
Lawrence, Kansas 66045

FOR _Lucy Moore_

ADDRESS_____ DATE _7/25_

Bactrim DS 800/160

i po BID x 5
_#10_

REFILL _0_ TIMES DR _Jones_

DEA NO_____

CASE Figure 54–2 Prescription #2 for patient Lucy Moore.

CASE Table 54–1	Prescription Medication Profile

Lucy Moore
10987 Cedar Hill Drive
Lawrence, Kansas 66045

Phone: 913-654-3425 **DOB:** 6/20/73 **Insurer:** Anthem

Allergies/Intolerances: NKDA

Rx No.	Drug Name	Directions	Date	R/F	Prescriber	Qty	RPh
642677	Nor-QD	1 tablet by mouth daily	07/01	1	Jones	28	ALS
642677	Nor-QD	1 tablet by mouth daily	06/05	2	Jones	28	ALS
642677	Nor-QD	1 tablet by mouth daily	05/10	3	Jones	28	ALS
643295	Allegra-D 24 Hour	1 tablet by mouth daily	04/22	3	Jones	30	ALS
643294	Patanol	Instill 1 drop in each eye 2 times daily	04/22	1	Jones	5	ALS
642677	Nor-QD	1 tablet by mouth daily	04/15	4	Jones	28	ALS
641599	Ambien 10 mg	1 tablet by mouth at bedtime as needed for insomnia	04/01	1	Jones	15	ALS

When Ms. Moore picks up her new prescriptions, you ask about her ophthalmic symptoms. She indicates that she noticed some symptomatic improvement, but her symptoms really have not improved significantly. You are aware that Ms. Moore is a regular customer at your pharmacy, so you check her prescription medication profile before making another recommendation (Case Table 54–1). Her medication profile indicates that Ms. Moore has no known medication allergies.

15. After reviewing Ms. Moore's prescription medication profile, what additional options would you discuss with Ms. Moore to help her red, itchy, and watery eyes?

16. Which medications from Ms. Moore's prescription medication profile could be causing her recurrent eye symptoms?

17. What are the short-term and long-term goals of pharmacotherapy for this patient related to treating her eye symptoms?

18. Describe specific eye symptoms or complaints that would exclude a patient from self-treatment and warrant a referral to an eye care practitioner.

Additional Activities

1. Describe the differences between soft contact lenses, hard contact lenses, and rigid gas-permeable lenses.

2. Explain the differences among the following products for each type of contact lens. In addition, provide an example of when each product would be appropriate to use:

    a. For hard contact lenses: cleaning solutions, soaking solutions, wetting solutions, and rewetting solutions

    b. For soft contact lenses: cleaning products, disinfecting products, saline products, and rewetting solutions

3. Explain the functions of multipurpose solutions. Describe the main problems with multipurpose solutions. Explain why multipurpose solutions are appropriate to use with some types of contact lenses but not others.

Information Sources

1. Engle JP. Prevention of contact lens-related disorders. In: Bready RR, Kroon LA, McDermott JH, et al., eds. *Handbook of Nonprescription Drugs: An Interactive Approach to Self-Care.* 15th ed. Washington, DC: American Pharmacists Association; 2006:605–32.

2. Fiscella RG, Jensen MK. Ophthalmic disorders. In: Beradi RR, Kroon LA, McDermott JH, et al., eds. *Handbook of Nonprescription Drugs: An Interactive Approach to Self-Care.* 15th ed. Washington, DC: American Pharmacists Association; 2006:577–603.

3. *Drug Facts & Comparisons.* Conshohocken, Pa: Wolters Kluwer Health; 2006.

Women's Health

55 Postmenopausal Hormone Therapy

Erin C. Raney

Objectives

1. Describe the current role of hormone therapy in the management of menopausal symptoms.

2. Compare and contrast the therapeutic effects of various estrogen formulations.

3. Explain the role of progestins in combined hormone therapy.

4. Recommend nonestrogen alternatives for the management of menopausal symptoms.

Scenario

You have worked as a pharmacist for Good Medicine Pharmacy for several years. During a particularly busy evening shift, you overhear a patient asking the pharmacy technician at the pick-up window if Remifemin is a good product for symptoms of menopause. You notice it is Joan Smith, a patient you have known for about 6 months. Ms. Smith appears somewhat embarrassed when you approach her to see if you can help, and she asks if she can talk with you in a more private area. As you move to the consultation room, Ms. Smith confides that she started taking "hormones" 6 months ago for symptoms of vaginal dryness and hot flashes. The medications helped with the hot flashes, but she continues to have vaginal symptoms. She mentioned this at a visit with her gynecologist 3 months ago, and it was suggested that she could increase the dose of her Premarin. At the time she did not like the idea of taking a higher dose of estrogen, so she decided to just live with the symptoms. A friend recently recommended that she try Remifemin, which she had seen advertised as a "natural" way to relieve menopause symptoms. As you make plans to address her concern, you review her prescription medication profile (Case Table 55–1).

CASE Table 55–1 Prescription Medication Profile

Joan Smith
3000 Main Ave
Phoenix, AZ 85331

Phone: 602-222-3333 **Age:** 52 years **Insurer:** Americare

Allergies/Intolerances: PCN (rash)

OTC/Herbal Medications: Calcium carbonate 500 mg 3 times daily

Rx No.	Drug Name	Directions	Date	R/F	Prescriber	Qty	RPh
A415678	Premarin 0.45 mg	1 tablet every day	10/1	1	Fenway	30	TK
A415678	Premarin 0.45 mg	1 tablet every day	8/30	2	Fenway	30	TK
A415678	Premarin 0.45 mg	1 tablet every day	7/30	3	Fenway	30	TK
A411302	Venlafaxine XR 75 mg	1 tablet every day	7/13	2	Little	90	RS
A415678	Premarin 0.45 mg	1 tablet every day	6/29	4	Fenway	30	TK
A430987	Ciprofloxacin 500 mg	1 tablet twice daily	6/7	0	Moore	20	RS
A415678	Premarin 0.45 mg	1 tablet every day	5/30	5	Fenway	30	LM
A415679	Provera 2.5 mg	1 tablet every day	5/30	5	Fenway	30	LM
A415678	Premarin 0.45 mg	1 tablet every day	4/28	6	Fenway	30	LM
A415679	Provera 2.5 mg	1 tablet every day	4/28	6	Fenway	30	LM
A411302	Venlafaxine XR 75 mg	1 tablet every day	4/15	3	Little	90	RS

As you review the prescription medication profile, you notice that Ms. Smith has not been refilling her medroxyprogesterone. On questioning her, you learn that she had not discussed this with her physician but discontinued it on her own. She found that after starting the medication she was bothered by the unpredictable "spotting" that she was having and also began to feel more "moody" than she had been before taking it. She read in the medication information provided by the pharmacy that medroxyprogesterone could cause mood changes and felt it was a good idea to stop taking it because she already was being treated for depression by Dr. Little. Since discontinuing it, she has felt her "normal" self and likes the idea of not having to worry about the bothersome bleeding.

Questions and Activities

1. On the basis of the patient's drug therapy, identify the medical problem(s) and the current drug therapy to solve the problem(s).

2. As you review Ms. Smith's prescription medication profile to further classify her drug therapy problems, you take note of the antidepressant that she is taking. What effect, if any, could the venlafaxine XR have on her menopausal symptoms?

3. Identify the drug-related or disease-related problem(s), the intervention(s) to solve the problems, and the anticipated outcomes.

4. What are the goals of pharmacotherapy for the patient?

5. Is Remifemin an appropriate alternative for treating this patient's complaints? Why or why not?

6. What drug(s), dosage form(s), schedule(s), and duration(s) of therapy are optimal for the treatment of this patient's complaints?

7. Ms. Smith decides that she would prefer to avoid another estrogen product, even if it is applied locally for her vulvovaginal symptoms. She is worried about the risks associated with estrogen. What are the current recommendations for the use of postmenopausal hormone therapy to maximize benefits and minimize risks (dosing, length of therapy, and target symptoms)?

8. You determine that a nonestrogen OTC vaginal moisturizer may be the best therapy to add to the patient's current estrogen dose for her vaginal symptoms. What is the advantage of a vaginal moisturizer over a vaginal lubricant for this patient?

9. What intervention (e.g., patient recommendation, call to provider or family member, contact emergency services, etc) is necessary for implementing these treatments?

10. What monitoring parameters available in the community pharmacy setting should be used to evaluate therapy in this patient, including efficacy and adverse effects?

11. What nondrug therapies or lifestyle modifications might be useful in managing this patient's problem?

12. Develop a medication action plan for the patient; include short-term and long-range goals.

13. What are the pertinent topics to address during patient education?

14. Develop a follow-up plan for this patient; include time to follow up and method of contact.

Additional Activities

1. Research the safety and efficacy of alternative treatments of menopause.

2. Investigate the safety and efficacy of bioidentical hormones. How should they be incorporated into the management of patients with signs and symptoms of menopause?

3. Compare and contrast home menopause test kits. Design a pharmacy patient care program that uses these to manage patients with menopausal symptoms.

Information Sources

1. AACE Menopause Guidelines Revision Task Force. American Association of Clinical Endocrinologists medical guidelines for clinical practice for the diagnosis and treatment of menopause. *Endocr Pract.* 2006;12:315–37.

2. The North American Menopause Society. Treatment of menopause-associated vasomotor symptoms: position statement of The North American Menopause Society. *Menopause.* 2004;11:11–33.

3. The North American Menopause Society. Estrogen and progestogen use in postmenopausal women: July 2008 position statement of The North American Menopause Society. *Menopause.* 2008;15:584_603.

4. The North American Menopause Society. The role of local vaginal estrogen for treatment of vaginal atrophy in postmenopausal women: 2007 position statement of The North American Menopause Society. *Menopause.* 2007;14:357–69.

5. Nedrow A, Miller J, Walker M, et al. Complementary and alternative therapies for the management of menopause-related symptoms: a systematic evidence review. *Arch Intern Med.* 2006;266:1453–65.

6. US Preventive Services Task Force. Hormone therapy for the prevention of chronic conditions in postmenopausal women: recommendations from the U.S. Preventive Services Task Force. *Ann Intern Med.* 2005;142:855–60.

7. National Institutes of Health. National Institutes of Health State-of-the-Science Conference statement: management of menopause-related symptoms. *Ann Intern Med.* 2005;142:1003–13.

8. Willhite LA, O-Connell MB. Urogenital atrophy: prevention and treatment. *Pharmacotherapy.* 2001;21:464–80.

56 Contraception

Maria Maniscalco-Feichtl and Eric Frontera-Zayas

Objectives

1. Describe the menstrual cycle.

2. Describe the therapeutic use of a combined hormonal (estrogen and progestin) pill for the purpose of contraception and decreasing duration of menses.

3. List absolute and relative contraindications for oral contraceptive pills.

4. Identify significant drug interactions with an oral contraceptive pill and be able to recommend appropriate alternatives.

5. Analyze a given patient, considering medical history, current medications, and compliance issues, to recommend an appropriate method of contraception.

6. Counsel a patient on the proper use, risks, and benefits of an oral contraceptive pill.

Scenario

As a pharmacist for University Community Pharmacy, you often fill prescriptions for college students. Your pharmacy manager contracts with a pharmaceutical manufacturer for Clinic Pack oral contraceptive pills (OCPs). The Clinic Pack OCP has a different package than the traditional brand version of the same OCP (Case Figure 56–1).

As part of the pricing agreement, the University Community Pharmacy may offer the Clinic Pack OCP to only female students with a valid student identification card from the local university. A female patient, Mia Perez, presents with a prescription (Case Figure 56–2).

Mia is thrilled to find out her oral contraceptive is available in a Clinic Pack. The Ortho Tri-Cyclen Lo Clinic Pack contracted price is $18.95 compared with the brand average wholesale price of approximately $61.50.[1,2] She says her epilepsy medication costs her a $40 co-pay per month (Case Table 56–1), and she was worried the oral contraceptive would be just as expensive. Her budget is limited because she is a college student.

After viewing the prescription and Ms. Perez's pharmacy profile, you have some concerns. You decide to speak with the patient first. She tells you that she has had epilepsy for several years now, and since starting Lamictal she has not had any seizures. She is happy with the efficacy of her Lamictal therapy. When asked why she is dropping off a prescription for an OCP, she mentions the past few months her menstrual cycle was lasting 10 to 12 days. Her physician prescribed an oral contraceptive to help regulate her period. Mia is hopeful the OCPs will work for her.

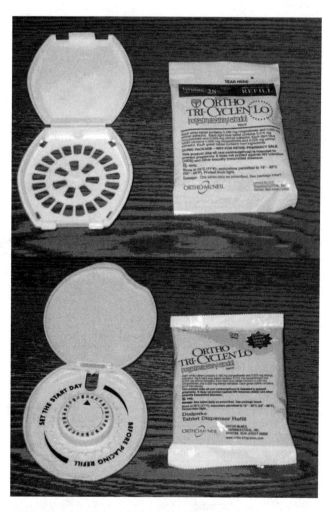

CASE Figure 56–1 Top: Clinic Pack; bottom: original brand packaging. (Photograph courtesy of authors.)

Questions and Activities

1. The patient wants to know how an oral contraceptive pill (OCP) prevents a pregnancy and why it will help shorten the duration of her period (menstruation). Explain the mechanism of action of an OCP (Case Figure 56–3).[3]

2. What characteristics or disease states increase a woman's risk of adverse effects from an OCP? Does the patient have any of these characteristics or disease states?

3. What counseling points should be discussed with the patient regarding her Lamictal prescription?

4. On the basis of the patient's presentation, identify the drug- or disease-related problem, and state the current drug therapy for the problem.

5. What are the goals of pharmacotherapy for this patient?

6. Identify the treatment alternatives available for the drug therapy problem.

7. Identify the intervention(s) to solve the problem(s) and anticipated outcomes.

8. What drug(s), dosage form(s), schedule(s), and duration(s) of therapy are optimal for the treatment of this patient's problem?

9. What monitoring parameters available in the community pharmacy setting should be used to evaluate therapy in this patient, including efficacy and adverse effects?

10. Develop a medication action plan for the patient; include short-term and long-range goals.

11. What are the pertinent topics to address during patient education?

Dr. O.B. Gwhyn
University Student Health Clinic
3200 South College Road
Ft. Lauderdale, FL 33328

09/15

Name: Mia Perez   Age: 21
Address:

ORTHO TRI-CYCLEN® Lo #28
As directed

Refill_11__
Dr.__Gwhyn_____
DEA#_____   Lic#_____

CASE Figure 56–2 Prescription #1 for patient Mia Perez.

CASE Table 56–1 Prescription Medication Profile

Mia Perez
Lehman Hall
3200 College Road
Fort Lauderdale, FL 33328

Phone: 954-555-5555   **DOB:** 06/11/1985   **Insurer:** Aetna

Allergies/Intolerances: NKDA

Rx No.	Drug Name	Directions	Date	R/F	Prescriber	Qty	RPh
604101	Lamictal 100 mg	1 tablet every day	8/18	1	Beene	30	EF
604101	Lamictal 100 mg	1 tablet every day	7/19	2	Beene	30	EF
604101	Lamictal 100 mg	1 tablet every day	6/20	3	Beene	30	EF
604101	Lamictal 100 mg	1 tablet every day	5/18	4	Beene	30	EF
604101	Lamictal 100 mg	1 tablet every day	4/22	5	Beene	30	EF
604101	Lamictal 100mg	1 tablet every day	3/19	6	Beene	30	EF
604101	Lamictal 100 mg	1 tablet every day	2/21	7	Beene	30	EF
604101	Lamictal 100 mg	1 tablet every day	1/18	8	Beene	30	EF
640981	Lamictal 25 mg	Use as directed	12/15	0	Beene	70	EF

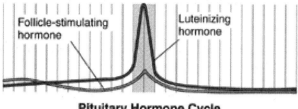

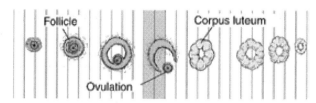

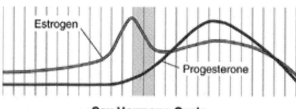

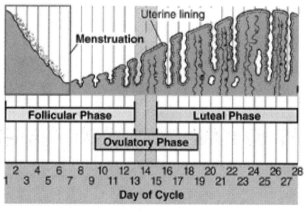

CASE Figure 56–3 Phases of the menstrual cycle. (*Source:* Reprinted with permission from reference 3.)

12. Develop a follow-up plan for this patient; include time to follow up and method of contact.

After the patient verbalizes her understanding of your directions, she takes out a tube of Oxy 10 Vanish Cream from her purse. She asks if you think it is effective for treating acne.

13. Explain the indication for Oxy 10 Vanish Cream (benzoyl peroxide).

14. Describe your counseling points and recommendations (specifically for benzoyl peroxide use).

Carole Sanford, D.M.D.
Family Medicine Associates
1668 Mario Quinton St.
Ft. Lauderdale, FL 33328

10/16

Name: Mia Perez   Age 21
Address:

Ampicillin 500mg #28
Take 1 capsule QID for 7 days

Refills: <u>PRN</u>

CASE Figure 56–4 Prescription #2 for patient Mia Perez.

15. On the basis of this presentation, describe the counseling points about Ortho Tri-Cyclen Lo and acne control.

After your recommendation is accepted, the patient goes home. About 4 weeks later, when she picks up her Ortho Tri-Cyclen Lo refill, she also brings a new prescription (Case Figure 56–4).

16. On the basis of this presentation, what drug–drug interactions may occur with the use of ampicillin?

17. Describe your counseling points and recommendations (be specific about contraceptive protection).

Additional Activities

1. Develop a contraceptive formulary that lists contraception methods of choice and the rationale for this recommendation in patients with the following characteristics:

- Older than 35 years of age with no concomitant disease states
- Older than 35 years of age with hypertension
- Menstrual migraine
- Women desiring little or no monthly menstrual bleeding
- Breast-feeding
- Women desiring transdermal or other nonoral method of contraception (list options)
- Migraine with aura

- Overweight
- Acne
- Other(s)

2. List advantages and disadvantages of monophasic, biphasic, or triphasic oral contraceptives, and provide examples of each type.

3. Research the potential increased thromboembolic potential of the Ortho-Evra contraceptive patch. List patient populations appropriate for Ortho-Evra, those that should avoid it because of the risk of thromboembolism, and patient counseling points with its use.

4. Explain the terms "bi-cycling" or "tri-cycling" oral contraceptives. List advantages and disadvantages of this practice. List examples of oral contraceptives that can be used in this manner.

5. Compare and contrast contraceptive methods other than oral contraceptives, including those for both males and females.

References

1. Ortho Tri-Cyclen Lo [package insert]. Raritan, NJ: Ortho-McNeil Pharmaceutical; 2007

2. Average wholesale price for Ortho Tri- Cyclen Lo. Available at: http://www.mckesson.com. Last accessed September 23, 2008.

3. Beers MH, ed. *Merck Manual of Medical Information, Second Home Edition.* Whitehouse Station, NJ: Merck & Co; 2003: 1347. Available at: http://www.merck.com/mmhe/sec22/ch241/ch241e.html. Last accessed August 25, 2008.

Other Information Sources

1. Chrousos GP. The gonadal hormones & inhibitors. In: Katzung BG, ed. *Basic & Clinical Pharmacology.* 8th ed. New York: McGraw-Hill; 2004:679–80.

2. Dickerson LM, Bucci KK. Contraception. In: DiPiro J, Talbert R, Yee G, et al., eds. *Pharmacotherapy: A Pathophysiologic Approach.* 6th ed. New York: McGraw-Hill; 2005:1443–64.

3. Lamictal [package insert]. Research Triangle Park, NC: DSM Pharmaceuticals or GlaxoSmithKline; 2005.

4. Sidhu J, Job S, Singh S, et al. The pharmacokinetic and pharmacodynamic consequences of the co-administration of lamotrigine and a combined oral contraceptive in healthy female subjects. *Br J Clin Pharmacol.* 2006;61:191–9.

5. Sidhu J, Bulsara S, Job S, et al. A bidirectional pharmacokinetic interaction study of lamotrigine and the combined oral contraceptive pill in healthy subjects. *Epilepsia.* 2004;45(suppl 7):330.

6. Sabers A, Ohman I, Christensen J, et al. Oral contraceptives reduce lamotrigine plasma levels. *Neurology.* 2003;61:570–1.

7. Sabers A, Buchholt JM, Uldall P, et al. Lamotrigine plasma levels reduced by oral contraceptives. *Epilepsy Res.* 2001;47:151–4.

8. O'Brien MD, Guillebaud J. Contraception for women with epilepsy. *Epilepsia.* 2006;47:1419–22.

9. Murad F, Kuret JA. Estrogens and progestins. In: Goodman LS, Gilman A, Rall TW, et al., eds. *Goodman and Gilman's: The Pharmacological Basis of Therapeutics.* 8th ed. New York: McGraw-Hill; 1993:1384–412.

10. Reimers A, Helde G, Brodtkorb E. Ethinyl estradiol, not progestogens, reduces lamotrigine serum concentrations. *Epilepsia.* 2005;46:1414–7.

11. Redmond GP, Olson WH, Lippman JS, et al. Norgestimate and ethinyl estradiol in the treatment of acne vulgaris: a randomized, placebo-controlled trial. *Obstet Gynecol.* 1997;89:615–22.

12. Lucky AW, Henderson TA, Olson WH, et al. Effectiveness of norgestimate and ethinyl estradiol in treating moderate acne vulgaris. *J Am Acad Dermatol.* 1997;37:746–54.

13. Dickinson BD, Altman RD, Nielsen NH, et al. Drug interactions between oral contraceptives and antibiotics. *Obstet Gynecol.* 2001; 98:853–60.

57 Infertility

Judy Sommers Hanson

Objective

1. List the goals of infertility pharmacotherapy treatment.

2. Identify potential drug therapy problems for a patient undergoing fertility treatment.

3. Develop a plan to resolve potential drug therapy problems for a patient undergoing fertility treatment.

4. Explain the appropriate counseling points to share with a patient concerning preconception care and ovulation induction therapy.

Scenario

Dorothy Givens is a 35-year-old white female who stops by your community pharmacy in October to pick up the medications that she had dropped off yesterday with your staff pharmacist to be filled. At the drop-off window of your pharmacy she hands the pharmacy technician a new prescription and states that she will wait for it to be filled. Ms. Givens walks away from the counter and begins to look at the family planning section in your pharmacy. As the technician begins to type in Ms. Givens' new prescription, the pharmacy's computer drug profiling system detects the following drug interaction, and the pharmacy technician brings it to your attention:

> DUR ERROR MESSAGE: Clarinex 5 mg 1 tablet every day
> ***Potential Drug–Disease Interaction: Clarinex and Pregnancy***

You examine the patient's prescription medication profile (Case Table 57–1). You see on her profile that for the past 6 months she has used a medication for the treatment of infertility. After evaluating Ms. Givens' profile, you decide to a have a conversation with her to obtain more information about her drug therapy. You explain that a potential drug interaction was identified and you want to get more information from her about the new prescription she dropped off today. She says that her physician wanted to change her allergy medication from the nasal spray to the tablets because her physician was told that the allergy tablets are safer to use in pregnancy.

Before you can continue to ask any additional questions, you see that Ms. Givens looks upset and she starts crying. You escort her to the counseling area of your pharmacy for some privacy and ask if you can help her. She apologizes for her emotions. Then she tells you that she is depressed and upset about the difficulty that she and her husband are having in becoming pregnant. The clomiphene she has been taking for the past several months has not helped them to become pregnant, and now she will be using these new medications to try to become pregnant through intrauterine insemination. Because of the limited coverage of expensive fertility medicines through her prescription drug benefit, she will have to pay for herself out of pocket. She is a little afraid of using needles and is unsure that she will be able take these new medications. She feels that it will be impossible for her and her husband to become pregnant. You assure her that you are here to help her in any way that you can.

Questions and Activities

1. On the basis of the patient's drug therapy, identify the drug-related problem and the current drug therapy for the problem.

2. What are the goals of pharmacotherapy for this patient?

3. Identify treatment alternatives for the drug therapy problem.

4. Identify the intervention(s) to solve the problem(s) and the anticipated outcome(s).

5. What drug(s), dosage form(s), schedule(s), and duration(s) of therapy are optimal for the treatment of this patient's problem?

6. What interventions (e.g., patient recommendation, call to provider or family member, contact medical services, etc.) are necessary for implementing this treatment?

7. What monitoring parameters available in the community pharmacy setting should be used to evaluate this patient, including efficacy and adverse effects?

CASE Table 57–1   Prescription Medication Profile

Dorothy Givens
19840 Cardiff Way
Prairieville, IL 69124

Phone: 224-555-1221   **DOB:** 6/24/71   **Insurer:** Superior Prescription Drug Plan

Allergies/Intolerances: No known allergies

Notes:

Medical history: perennial allergic rhinitis (confirmed by physician); unexplained infertility (inferred by medications)

Social history: nonsmoker; 1 glass of wine with dinner

Height: 5 feet 4 inches tall; weight: 185 pounds

Nonprescription medications: ibuprofen 200 mg liquid gelcaps 1–2 caps every 6 hours for headaches; calcium carbonate 500 mg chew tablets 1 tablet as needed for heartburn

Rx No.	Drug Name	Directions	Date	R/F	Qty	Prescriber	RPh	Price
6280903	Crinone 8% (90 mg)	Insert vaginally once daily as directed	10/6	2	30	Miller	ESS	399.70
6280902	Ovidrel 250 mcg syringe	Inject every day by physician	10/6	2	1	Miller	ESS	87.99
6780901	Gonal-f RFF 75 IU vials	Inject 75 IU every day for 7 days as directed	10/6	2	1	Miller	ESS	3924.79
6780900	BD Luer-Lok 25 G × 5/8" 3 ml Syringe	Use as directed	10/6	2	30	Miller	ESS	7.48
6257134	Clomiphene 50 mg	3 tablets every day on days 5 to 9 of cycle	8/27	0	15	Miller	ESS	15.00
6185832	Fluticasone propionate 50 mcg nasal spray	2 sprays in each nostril every day	7/6	9	17	Harris	KLN	15.00
6257134	Clomiphene 50 mg	3 tablets every day on days 5 to 9 of cycle	7/6	1	15	Miller	KLN	15.00
6219058	Clomiphene 50 mg	2 tablets every day on days 5–9 of cycle	5/24	0	10	Miller	EDC	15.00
6185832	Fluticasone propionate 50 mcg nasal spray	2 sprays in each nostril every day	4/26	10	17	Harris	KLN	15.00
6219058	Clomiphene 50 mg	2 tablets every day on days 5–9 of cycle	4/26	1	10	Miller	ESS	15.00
6185832	Fluticasone propionate 50 mcg nasal spray	2 sprays in each nostril every day	3/18	11	17	Harris	KLN	15.00
6185833	Clomiphene 50 mg	1 tablet every day on day 5–9 of cycle	3/18	0	5	Miller	KLN	15.00
6185833	Clomiphene 50 mg tablets	1 tablet every day on days 5–9 of cycle	2/12	1	5	Miller	ESS	15.00
6185832	Fluticasone propionate 50 mcg nasal spray	2 sprays in each nostril every day	2/12	12	17	Harris	ESS	15.00

8. The patient asks you which ovulation prediction kit she should purchase to assist her in detecting her most fertile time of her cycle. What is your response?

9. What nondrug therapies or lifestyle modifications might be useful in managing this patient's problem?

10. Develop a medication action plan for the patient; include short-term and long-range goals.

11. Describe the technique that the patient would use to administer her medications.

12. What are the pertinent topics to address during patient education?

13. While discussing the use of these new medications, the patient says that she read on a fertility Web blog that guaifenesin can help fertility. How do you respond?

14. Develop a follow-up plan for this patient; include time to follow up and method of contact.

Additional Activities

1. Investigate which drugs may contribute to or cause infertility in females.

2. Investigate which drugs may contribute to or cause infertility in males.

3. Research how the treatment would change if this patient were a male with infertility problems.

4. Compare and contrast home infertility tests for males and females.

5. Develop a business plan for a patient care service to care for patients with infertility.

Information Sources

1. Schering-Plough. Clarinex [package insert]. Available at: http://www.spfiles.com/piclarinex.pdf. Last accessed August 28, 2008.

2. Lieu CL, Yoshida T. Infertility. In: Dipiro JT, Talbert RL, Yee GC, et al., eds. *Pharmacotherapy: A Pathophysiologic Approach.* 5th ed. New York: Appleton & Lange; 2002:1431–41.

3. Akil M, Amos RS, Stewart P. Infertility may sometimes be associated with NSAID consumption. *Br J Rheumatol.* 1996;35:76–78.

4. National Institute for Clinical Excellence. Fertility: assessment and treatment for people with fertility problems. Available at: http://nice.org/nicemedia/pdf/CG011fullguideline.pdf. Last accessed September 9, 2008.

5. Lieu CL. Providing Care for Infertility Patients Terrie YC. Available at: http://www.uspharmacist.com/oldformat.asp?url=newlook/files/feat/cyp.htm. Last accessed September 9, 2008.

6. Foster KT. Common Drugs Used in Assisted Reproductive Technologies. *US Pharm.* 2005;1:HS27–HS36.

7. Fiore AE, Shay DK, Broder K et al. Centers for Disease Control and Prevention. Prevention and Control of Influenza Recommendations of the Advisory Committee on Immunization Practices. *MMWR* 2008;57(RR-7):1–60. Available at: http://www.cdc.gov/mmwr/preview/mmwrhtml/rr5510a1.htm?s_cid=rr5510a1_e. Last accessed August 28, 2008.

8. Terrie YC. Coping with infertility. Available at: http://www.pharmacytimes.com/issues/articles/2006-06_3606.asp. Last accessed September 9, 2008.

9. Loratadine. In: Briggs GG, Freeman RK, Yaffe SJ, eds. *Drugs in Pregnancy and Lactation: A Reference Guide to Fetal and Neonatal Risk.* 7th ed. Baltimore: Lippincott Williams & Wilkins; 2005:940–1.

10. Acetaminophen. In: Briggs GG, Freeman RK, Yaffe SJ, eds. *Drugs in Pregnancy and Lactation: A Reference Guide to Fetal and Neonatal Risk.* 7th ed. Baltimore: Lippincott Williams & Wilkins; 2005:7–13.

11. Ladipo OA. Nutrition in pregnancy: mineral and vitamin supplementation. Available at: http://www.ajcn.org/cgi/content/full/72/1/280S. Last accessed August 28, 2008.

12. RESOLVE: The National Infertility Association. Available at: http://www.resolve.org. Last accessed September 9, 2008.

13. Fertility Lifelines, Serono Fertility Drug Product Support. Gonal-f RFF [package insert]. Available at: http://www.fertilitylifelines.com/assets/pdfs/products/gonalf75/gonal-f.rff75iu_pi.pdf. Last accessed August 28, 2008.

14. Fertility Lifelines, Serono Fertility Drug Product Support. Ovidrel [package insert]. Available at: http://www.fertilitylifelines.com/assets/pdfs/products/ovidrel/ovidrel_pi.pdf. Last accessed August 28, 2008.

15. Crinone USA. Crinone 8% [package insert]. Available at: http://www.crinoneuse.com/professionals/prescribing_information.pdf. Last accessed September 9, 2008.

16. Munroe RW, Clark BG. Home testing and monitoring devices. In: Berardi RR, McDermott JH, Newton GD, et al., eds. *Handbook of Nonprescription Drugs: An Interactive Approach to Self-Care.* 14th ed. Washington, DC: American Pharmacists Association; 2004:1179–211.

17. Crinone USA. Applying Crinone 8%. Available at: http://www.crinoneuse.com/patients/applying_crinone.html. Last accessed September 9, 2008.

18. Check JH, Adelson HG, Wu CH. Improvement of cervical factor with guaifenesin. *Fertil Steril.* 1982;37:707–8.

58 Nonprescription Drug Use during Pregnancy and Lactation

Kristin W. Weitzel

Objectives

1. Describe the FDA pregnancy categories.

2. List helpful resources for information about nonprescription medications in pregnancy and lactation.

3. Identify appropriate nonpharmacologic and pharmacologic therapy for treatment of common self-care complaints in pregnant women.

4. List physician referral criteria for common self-care complaints in pregnant women.

5. List nonprescription medications known to be safe for use in lactating mothers.

6. When presented with a patient, determine the appropriate course of action for common self-care scenarios during pregnancy.

The purpose of this case is to review drug-related issues about common self-care needs in pregnancy, including use of analgesics and cough/cold medications, and treatment of nausea and vomiting, gastroesophageal reflux disease, and constipation. Basic principles of medication use in pregnancy are also reviewed. Data on drugs in pregnancy are dynamic; therefore, knowing where to find the information is important to ensure that pharmacists know the most current information before answering questions that may affect the health of both the mother and child. The following precase questions are intended to help identify the primary sources for information on medication use during pregnancy.

Precase Questions

1. Briefly describe the FDA drug pregnancy category ratings and how they are interpreted.

2. List resources that pharmacists may find helpful when answering questions about drugs in pregnancy.

3. List at least three universal principles about nonprescription medication selection during pregnancy (e.g., choosing among different formulations of the same drug, variable drug effects in different pregnancy trimesters, role of nondrug therapy in pregnant women, etc.).

Scenario

Darlene Wilson is a 31-year-old female who presents to your pharmacy with a question for the pharmacist. When you speak with her, she tells you she just found out that she is 8 weeks pregnant. She says that she is incredibly nauseated, although she has not thrown up, and would like to know what you recommend.

Questions and Activities

1. Before responding to the patient's questions, you realize you need some more information. What questions do you need to ask Mrs. Wilson before you can counsel her appropriately?

2. List nonpharmacologic measures that may help with pregnancy-related nausea.

3. Mrs. Wilson is concerned about using any medications in pregnancy. She heard from a friend that ginger was helpful in her pregnancy, and she also read about a "nausea wristband" on the Internet. She is interested to know if these would be helpful. How do you respond to her questions?

4. Mrs. Wilson is interested in knowing more about any nonprescription medications to help with nausea during pregnancy. What can you tell her about the nonprescription medications pyridoxine (vitamin B_6) and doxylamine, used alone or in combination?

5. What (if anything) would you recommend for her today?

Mrs. Wilson is grateful for all the information you provided. She opts not to buy anything today but, instead, to wait and see if she feels better on her own. She returns to the pharmacy 3 days later and says that she has thrown up four times in the past 24 hours. She wants to know if she should try some of the products you discussed earlier or make an appointment with her doctor.

6. How would you counsel Mrs. Wilson today? What guidelines would you use to refer pregnant patients to their physician for further evaluation before using self-care for nausea and vomiting?

Mrs. Wilson comes back to your pharmacy about a month later with a prescription for Lortab with instructions to take 1 tablet every 4 to 6 hours as needed for migraines. You are able to get additional information from her prescription medication profile (Case Table 58–1).

While you are preparing her prescription, Mrs. Wilson asks if you can answer some other questions for her. She is holding a bottle of ibuprofen. She tells you that she has had migraines off and on for the past 10 years, but they have been much worse since she became pregnant. Before pregnancy, she took 3 to 4 ibuprofen tablets as needed for her headaches. She would like to keep some on hand "just in case" the Lortab is not enough. She says that she has tried Tylenol with no relief. You recall from your earlier conversation with Mrs. Wilson that her medical history is not significant, other than migraines. She does not take any other medications except her prenatal vitamins, and her pregnancy has been without complications so far.

7. What information can you provide to Mrs. Wilson about the safety of ibuprofen in each trimester of pregnancy? How would you counsel her about purchasing ibuprofen today? Please provide data to support any recommendation(s).

Three weeks later, Mrs. Wilson returns to your pharmacy. She says her migraines responded to the Lortab and seem to be getting better now that she is beyond the first trimester. Unfortunately,

she has now developed a terrible cold, and she would like to know what she can take for her symptoms. She remembers that Tylenol is considered safe, so she has chosen a Tylenol Cold combination product that contains acetaminophen, phenylephrine, dextromethorphan, and diphenhydramine. When asked, she says her obstetrician did not make any recommendations about cold medications in pregnancy.

8. What else do you need to know before answering Mrs. Wilson's question?

9. Mrs. Wilson describes her symptoms as being predominantly congestion, runny nose, sneezing, and a nonproductive cough. She has not had a fever, but her throat is sore and she feels miserable. What nonpharmacologic treatment measures can you recommend?

10. After reviewing nondrug therapy with Mrs. Wilson, you take a look at the combination cold product she has selected and notice it contains an analgesic, decongestant, antitussive, and antihistamine. What do you know about the nonprescription medication of choice during pregnancy in each of those drug classes? Please provide supporting data.

Mrs. Wilson has said that she is well into her second trimester now. In answering your previous questions, she denied fever or any other symptoms that might exclude self-treatment.

11. What recommendation would you make for her cold symptoms today?

12. How would your recommendation(s) change if Mrs. Wilson were in her first trimester?

13. When would you refer Mrs. Wilson to her physician for her cold symptoms?

CASE Table 58–1 Prescription Medication Profile

Darlene Wilson
5000 Gator Drive
Jacksonville, FL 32244

Phone: 904-555-1098   **DOB:** 3/5/1977   **Insurer:** Anthem

Allergies/Intolerances: Amoxicillin (rash)

Rx No.	Drug Name	Directions	Date	R/F	Prescriber	Qty	RPh
423256	Hydrocodone/APAP 5/500	1 tablet every 4–6 hours as needed for migraine	10/6	1	Martin	20	RH
662189	Citracal Prenatal	1 tablet every day	9/30	1	Martin	30	PL
662189	Citracal Prenatal	1 tablet every day	8/28	2	Martin	30	RH
662189	Citracal Prenatal	1 tablet every day	7/25	3	Martin	30	RH
660105	Z-Pak 250 mg	Take as directed	7/7	0	Martin	6	PL
662189	Citracal Prenatal	1 tablet every day	6/25	4	Martin	30	RH
662189	Citracal Prenatal	1 tablet every day	5/28	5	Martin	30	PL

Mrs. Wilson returns to your pharmacy about 2 months later and asks to speak to you again. She tells you that her pregnancy is going well and she has almost reached her due date. Now that she is starting her third trimester, she is having a lot of trouble with heartburn. She would like to know what you would recommend. She says that her pregnancy has remained healthy with no complications and she continues to take her prenatal vitamins as her only regular medication. When asked to describe her heartburn symptoms, she tells you that the heartburn just started recently and her symptoms tend to come and go. She says they are worse at night and after eating a fatty meal or drinking a soda. She has not tried any medications yet, and her obstetrician did not make any recommendations for treatment of heartburn.

14. What nonpharmacologic recommendations can you make for Mrs. Wilson's reflux symptoms?

15. What do you know about the nonprescription medication of choice during pregnancy in each of the following drug classes: antacids and antisecretory medications (H_2-receptor antagonists, proton pump inhibitors)? Please provide supporting data.

16. On the basis of this information, what would you recommend for Mrs. Wilson today?

Mrs. Wilson returns about a month later and says she has only a few weeks before her due date. Her heartburn seems to be under control since she made some of the changes you suggested. Her only problem now is frequent constipation. She asks you if there are any dietary measures she can try to prevent this from happening.

17. What dietary measures would you recommend for Mrs. Wilson's constipation?

Mrs. Wilson says she has actually tried everything you mentioned. She is having an acute problem right now and may need to try something that has a quicker onset of action.

18. What do you know about the following nonprescription medications and their use in pregnancy? Please provide supporting data.

- Bulk-forming laxatives (e.g., psyllium, methylcellulose)
- Stimulant laxatives (e.g., bisacodyl, senna, castor oil)
- Saline or osmotic laxatives (e.g., milk of magnesia, MiraLAX)
- Lubricant laxatives (e.g., mineral oil, castor oil)
- Stool softeners (e.g., docusate)

19. On the basis of this information, what would you recommend for Mrs. Wilson today?

20. When would you refer Mrs. Wilson to her physician for constipation?

Mrs. Wilson returns to the pharmacy about a month later. She says that everything went great with her pregnancy and delivery. She says she is still nursing the baby for most of her feedings and would like to know a little bit more about what nonprescription medications are safe to take while she is breast-feeding.

21. What do you tell Mrs. Wilson about the safety of nonprescription medications during breast-feeding?

Additional Activities

1. List five prescription drugs that should absolutely be avoided during pregnancy and explain the rationale for avoiding each one.

2. Significant changes were made in recent years about the safety of medications used to treat depression during pregnancy. Research and review this topic. When is treatment for depression indicated during pregnancy? What medications can be recommended for patients? What medications should be avoided and why?

3. List nonprescription medications of choice for treating vaginal yeast infections during pregnancy. When would you refer a pregnant patient to her physician for treatment of a yeast infection during pregnancy?

4. Spend time exploring the Internet resources listed below. When would you use these in practice? Which sites would you recommend for patients? Which of the sites below would you recommend for a patient who is concerned about a drug she took before finding out she was pregnant?

- Motherisk (www.motherisk.org/index.jsp)
- Perinatology.com (www.perinatology.com)
- Organization of Teratology Information Specialists (www.otispregnancy.org)
- OBfocus (www.obfocus.com)
- LactMed (toxnet.nlm.nih.gov/cgi-bin/sis/htmlgen? LACT)
- Safe Fetus (www.safefetus.com)
- Breastfeeding Online, Breastfeeding and Medications section (www.breastfeedingonline.com/meds.shtml)

Information Sources

1. The use of newer asthma and allergy medications during pregnancy. Position Statement. The American College of Obstetricians and Gynecologists (ACOG) and the American College of Allergy, Asthma and Immunology (ACAAI). *Ann Allergy Asthma Immunol.* 2000;84:475–80.

2. Briggs GG. Freeman RK, Yaffe SJ. *Drugs in Pregnancy and Lactation.* 7th ed. Philadelphia: Lippincott Williams & Wilkins; 2005.

3. Cough and cold medicine use in pregnancy. *Pharm Lett Prescr Lett.* 2006;22:221112.

4. Ibuprofen. Available at: http://www.perinatology.com/exposures/ druglist2.htm#Ibuprofen. Last accessed November 4, 2006.

5. Ofori B, Oraichi D, Blais L, et al. Risk of congenital anomalies in pregnant users of non-steroidal anti-inflammatory drugs. A nested case-control study. *Birth Defects Res B Dev Reprod Toxicol.* 2006;77: 268–79.

6. Shane-McWhorter L, Fermo J. Nausea and vomiting. In: Berardi RA, Kroon LA, McDermott JH, et al., eds. *Handbook of Nonprescription Drugs: An Interactive Approach to Self-Care.* 15th ed. Washington, DC: American Pharmacists Association; 2006: 381–401.

7. American College of Obstetricians and Gynecology. Nausea and vomiting of pregnancy. ACOG Practice Bulletin No. 52. *Obstet Gynecol.* 2004;103:803–14.

8. Badell ML, Ramin SM, Smith JA. Treatment options for nausea and vomiting during pregnancy. *Pharmacotherapy.* 2006;26:1273–87.

9. Borrelli F, Capasso R, Aviello G, et al. Effectiveness and safety of ginger in the treatment of drug-induced nausea and vomiting. *Obstet Gynecol.* 2005;105:849–56.

10. Marcus DM, Snodgrass WR. Do no harm: avoidance of herbal medicines during pregnancy. *Obstet Gynecol.* 2005;105:1119–22.

11. Marcus DM, Snodgrass WR. Effectiveness and safety of ginger in the treatment of pregnancy-induced nausea and vomiting. *Obstet Gynecol* 2005;106:3;640.

12. Wigle P, Kim K, King A, et al. OTC medications for GI disorders in pregnancy. *US Pharm.* 2006;31:1.

13. Scolaro K. Disorders related to cold and allergy. In: Berardi RA, Kroon LA, McDermott JH, et al., eds. *Handbook of Nonprescription Drugs: An Interactive Approach to Self-Care.* 15th ed. Washington, DC: American Pharmacists Association; 2006:201–28.

14. Black RA, Hill DA. Over-the-counter medications in pregnancy. *Am Fam Physician.* 2003;67:2517–24.

15. Hansen WF, Peacock AE, Yankowitz J. Safe prescribing practices in pregnancy and lactation. *J Midwifery Womens Health.* 2002;47: 409–21.

16. Koehn R, Ormond K, Pergament E. Over the counter cold medications in pregnancy. *Fetal Expos.* 1998;7:1–5.

17. Wigle PR, Mcneal SM, Tibbs K. Pregnancy and OTC cough, cold and analgesic preparations. *US Pharm.* 2006 31:33–47.

18. Blaiss M. Management of rhinitis and asthma in pregnancy. *Ann Allergy Asthma Immunol.* 2003;90(suppl 3):16–22.

19. Pharmacologic treatment of cough: evidence-based guidelines. *Pharm Lett Prescr Lett.* 2006;22:221006.

20. Gastrointestinal drug use in pregnancy. *Pharm Lett Prescr Lett.* 2006;22:221210.

21. Roy PK, Barakat J, Shojamanesh H, et al. Gastrointestinal disease and pregnancy. eMedicine from WebMD. Available at: http://www.emedicine.com/med/topic3265.htm. Last accessed November 8, 2008.

22. Zweber A, Berardi RR. Heartburn and dyspepsia. In: Berardi RA, Kroon LA, McDermott JH, et al., eds. *Handbook of Nonprescription Drugs: An Interactive Approach to Self-Care.* 15th ed. Washington, DC: American Pharmacists Association; 2006:265–82.

23. Mahadevan U, Kane S. American Gastroenterological Association Institute medical position statement on the use of gastrointestinal medications in pregnancy. *Gastroenterology.* 2006;131:278–82.

24. American Gastroenterological Association Institute Technical Review on use of gastrointestinal medications in pregnancy. *Gastroenterology* 2006;131:28–311.

25. Williams DB, Schade RR. Gastroesophageal reflux disease. In: Dipiro JT, Talbert RL, Yee GC, et al., eds. *Pharmacotherapy: A Pathophysiologic Approach.* 6th ed. New York: McGraw-Hill; 2005:613–28.

26. Curry CE Jr, Butler DM. Constipation. In: Berardi RA, Kroon LA, McDermott JH, et al., eds. *Handbook of Nonprescription Drugs: An Interactive Approach to Self-Care.* 15th ed. Washington, DC: American Pharmacists Association; 2006:299–326.

27. Jewell DJ, Young G. Interventions for treating constipation in pregnancy. *Cochrane Database Syst Rev.* 2001;2:CD001142.

28. OTC medication use while breastfeeding. *Pharm Lett Prescr Lett.* 2007;23:220412.

29. Banta-Wright SA. Minimizing infant exposure to and risks from medications while breastfeeding. *J Perinat Neonatal Nurs.* 1997; 11:71–84.

30. American Academy of Pediatrics Committee on Drugs. Transfer of drugs and other chemicals into human milk. *Pediatrics.* 2001;108: 776–89.

31. Nice FJ, Snyder JL, Kotansky BC. Breastfeeding and over-the-counter medications. *J Hum Lact.* 2000;16:319–31.

32. Ito S. Drug therapy for breast-feeding women. *N Engl J Med.* 2000; 343:118–26.

59 Menstrual Disorders: Dysmenorrhea

Deanne L. Hall

Objectives

1. Assess for appropriateness of self-care in a patient presenting with dysmenorrhea.

2. Identify symptoms that require referral to a physician for evaluation.

3. Recommend appropriate nonprescription medication for treatment of dysmenorrhea.

4. Provide nonpharmacologic education about dysmenorrhea.

5. Explain appropriate therapeutic options for treatment of dysmenorrhea not controlled by nonprescription agents.

Scenario

You notice a young woman pacing the analgesic aisle of your community pharmacy for some time. As you approach her, you notice she is holding a box of Midol Complete Formula and a box of Midol Extended Relief. When you ask if you could be of assistance, she says that she does not need any help and takes a few steps away. You say, "I know there are many products and it can be confusing." The young woman does not acknowledge your comment. "Feel free to come to the pharmacy counter if you would like some assistance in selecting a product."

About 5 minutes later, the young woman approaches the pharmacy counter. She is in apparent discomfort. The patient says (speaking softly), "I have really bad cramps, which do you think would be better?" You respond, "Let's step over here where we can have some privacy. My name is Mary Jones and I am a pharmacist. May I ask you a few questions so that I may better assist you?"

Patient: "Sure. I'm Jan"

Pharmacist: "Hi, Jan. What kind of cramps are you having?"

Patient: "Menstrual. I am due to start my period tomorrow."

Pharmacist: "Have you had cramps like this before?"

Patient: "Yes. My mom took me to the doctor last year because they were so bad I missed 3 days of school 2 months in a row. The doctor started me on birth control pills, which helped."

Pharmacist: "What is the name of the oral contraceptive you are using and how do you take it?"

Patient: "I use Ortho 7/7/7 just like the package says."

Pharmacist: "You said that it has helped your cramping. Do you use any other medication, prescription or over-the-counter, to help with the pain?"

Patient: "No, not even Tylenol."

Pharmacist: "Do you have your medication filled here? I can pull up your profile."

Patient: "No, I get them filled at a pharmacy near home because I am still under my parent's health insurance, so it's covered."

Pharmacist: "Are you allergic to any medications?"

Patient: "No."

Pharmacist: "Are you being treated for any other medical conditions?"

Patient: "No, I really am healthy, just having a bad day."

Pharmacist: "I know not feeling well can affect everything you need to do that day. What other medications do you use, prescription or over-the-counter?"

Patient: "Nothing regularly. Sometimes naproxen if I get a headache, which is not often."

Pharmacist: "Is this the first time you have needed to take something in addition to the birth control pills to control your menstrual pain?"

Patient: "Yes, although it was pretty bad last month. But I just figured it was a fluke and dealt with it. But when I woke up this morning, it was just like last month. I did not even get out of bed to go to class. When my roommate came back at lunch, she recommended I get some Midol."

Pharmacist: "Where is your pain located?"

The patient rubs her lower abdomen with her hand and replies, "My lower stomach."

Pharmacist: "What other symptoms are you experiencing? For example, are you having pain in other areas of your body, headache, dizziness, nausea?"

Patient: "No, I feel fine otherwise. I am not even bloated or moody!"

Pharmacist: "Do you have bleeding or pain at times of the month not associated with your menses?"

Patient: "No."

Pharmacist: "Have you experienced any abdominal trauma or changes in bowel habits?"

Patient: "No."

Pharmacist: "Have you spoken to your doctor about this worsened pain?"

Patient: "No. She said if it was worse, I could use something nonprescription and to call if it did not work or I feel really, really bad."

Pharmacist: "So, I just want to make sure I understand how severe your pain is. On a scale of 1 to 10, with 1 being no pain and 10 being incapacitating pain, how would you rate your pain?"

Patient: "I would say about a 5. It is uncomfortable, but I do not feel it is bad enough that I need to see the doctor."

Pharmacist: "Well, it may be a good idea just to let your doctor know that you are in need of additional pain medication. When do you see your doctor again?"

Patient: "In 3 months, over break. I will let her know. She said that this may happen with moving away from home and being stressed with classes."

Pharmacist: "Just one last question to help choose the best product for you. I see that you are holding two combination products, do you have a price range in mind that you would like to spend?"

Patient: "Well, I only have $10 on me and I'm on a tight budget."

Questions and Activities

1. On the basis of the information obtained in the pharmacist's discussion with the patient, identify the drug- or disease-related problem, and state the current drug therapy for this problem. Also, state what risk factors are present for this patient to develop this problem and why this patient is or is not a candidate for self-care.

2. What are the goals of pharmacotherapy for this patient?

3. Identify the nonprescription treatment alternatives available for this drug-related problem.

4. Identify the intervention(s) to solve the problem(s) and anticipated outcome(s).

5. What drug(s), dosage form(s), schedule (s), and duration(s) of therapy are optimal for treatment of this patient's problem?

6. What intervention (e.g., patient recommendation, call to provider or family member, contact emergency medical services, etc.) is necessary for implementing this treatment?

7. What monitoring parameters available in the community pharmacy setting should be used to evaluate therapy in this patient, including efficacy and adverse effects?

8. What nondrug or lifestyle modifications might be useful in managing this patient's problem?

9. What are the pertinent topics to address during patient education?

10. Develop a follow-up plan for this patient; include time to follow up and method of contact.

Additional Activities

1. After your discussion with the patient about her product selection, she asks if you are aware of what other prescription medications are used to treat severe menstrual cramps. List the available prescription medications and their mechanism for improving menstrual cramping.

2. List the causes of amenorrhea and the treatment approaches to help restart menses.

3. Describe endometriosis and list the treatment options available to patients (include alternative approaches, surgical approaches, and medication approaches).

Information Sources

1. French L. Dysmenorrhea. *Am Fam Physician.* 2005;71:285–91.

2. Dawood MY. Primary dysmenorrhea: advances in pathogenesis and management. *Obstet Gynecol.* 2006;108:428–41.

3. Adams Hillard PJ. Dysmenorrhea. *Pediatr Rev.* 2006;27:64–71.

4. Shimp LA. Disorders related to menstruation. In: Berardi RR, Kroon LA, McDermott JH, et al., eds. *Handbook of Nonprescription Drugs: An Interactive Approach to Self-Care.* 15th ed. Washington, DC: American Pharmacists Association; 2006:155–176

5. Proctor M, Farquhar C. Diagnosis and management of dysmenorrhoea. *BMJ.* 2006;332:1134–8.

6. Marjoribanks J, Proctor ML, Farquar C. Nonsteroidal anti-inflammatory drugs for primary dysmenorrhoea. *Cochrane Database Syst Rev.* 2003;4:CD001751.

7. Proctor ML, Murphy PA. Herbal and dietary therapies for primary and secondary dysmenorrhoea. *Cochrane Database Syst Rev.* 2001;3: CD002124.

8. Barnard ND, Scialli AR, Hurlock D, Bertron P. Diet and sex hormone binding globulin, dysmenorrhea and premenstrual symptoms. *Obstet Gynecol.* 2000;95:245–50.

9. Campbell MA, McGrath PJ. Non-pharmacologic strategies used by adolescents for the management of premenstrual discomfort. *Clin J Pain.* 1999;15:313–20.

10. Akin M, Weingand KW, Hengehold DA, et al. Continuous, low-level, topical heat wrap in the treatment of dysmenorrhea. *Obstet Gynecol.* 2001;97:343–9.

11. Eccles NK. A randomized, double-blinded, placebo-controlled pilot study to investigate the effectiveness of a static magnet to relive dysmenorrheal. *J Altern Complement Med.* 2005;11:681–7.

12. Pouresmail Z, Ibrahimzadeh R. Effects of acupressure and ibuprofen on the severity of primary dysmenorrheal. *J Tradit Chin Med.* 2002; 22:205–10.

13. Chen HM, Chen CH. Effects of acupressure at the Sanyinjiao point on primary dysmenorrhoea. *J Adv Nurs.* 2004;48:380–7.

Section

13

Men's Health

60 Benign Prostatic Hyperplasia

Brandon T. Jennings and Amy L. Whitaker

Objectives

1. Recognize clinical manifestations of benign prostatic hyperplasia.

2. Evaluate various treatment options for benign prostatic hyperplasia.

3. Explain the role of saw palmetto in the management of benign prostatic hyperplasia.

4. Develop counseling points pertinent to community practice regarding benign prostatic hyperplasia.

Scenario

Michael Harris, a 56-year-old white male, presents to your pharmacy with a bottle of saw palmetto and asks, "Does this stuff really work?" You recognize Mr. Harris as a regular customer of your pharmacy, and before answering his question you check his most recent medications (Case Table 60–1).

You notice that Mr. Harris has adhered to his medication regimen and has been receiving refills at the properly scheduled intervals. You also notice that the patient started Proscar 2 months ago.

CASE Table 60–1	Prescription Medications for Patient Michael Harris Filled July 12		
Drug Name	**Directions**	**Quantity**	**Prescriber**
Hydrochlorothiazide 25 mg	1 tablet by mouth every day	30	Thomson
Lisinopril 10 mg	1 tablet by mouth every day	30	Thomson
Proscar 5 mg	1 tablet by mouth every day	30	Lee
Protonix 40 mg	1 tablet by mouth every day	30	Jacobs

Upon questioning the patient further, you learn that he has trouble urinating even though he feels that he needs to void. He is waking frequently during the night to urinate but is not always able to go. Mr. Harris does not currently complain of sexual or erectile dysfunction.

The patient has full prescription coverage through his employer with a $5 generic co-pay and a $25 brand co-pay.

Questions and Activities

1. On the basis of the patient's presentation and drug therapy, identify the drug-related problems for this case.

2. What are the goals of pharmacotherapy for this patient?

3. What is saw palmetto's mechanism of action?

4. What is your answer to the patient's question, "Does this stuff really work?" with regard to the saw palmetto?

5. Identify the treatment alternatives for the drug therapy problem.

6. What monitoring parameters available in the community pharmacy setting should be used to evaluate this patient, including efficacy and adverse effects?

7. Develop a medication action plan for the patient; include short- and long-term goals.

8. What are pertinent topics to address with regard to patient education?

9. Develop a follow-up plan for this patient.

Additional Activities

1. Investigate which medications can worsen urinary symptoms.

2. Describe the use of heat therapy for benign prostatic hyperplasia. What are the advantages and disadvantages?

3. Describe the adverse effects of the medications used for benign prostatic hyperplasia, and compare them with the adverse effects of alternative therapies.

Information Sources

1. Gerber GS. Saw palmetto for the treatment of men with lower urinary tract symptoms. *J Urol.* 2000;163:1408–12.

2. Goepel M, Hecker U, Krege S, et al. Saw palmetto extracts potently and noncompetitively inhibit human α_1-adrenoceptors in vitro. *Prostate.* 1999;38:208–15.

3. Bent S, Kane C, Shinohara K, et al. Saw palmetto for benign prostatic hyperplasia. *N Engl J Med.* 2006;354:557–66.

4. AUA Guideline on Management of Benign Prostatic Hyperplasia. Chapter 1: diagnosis and treatment recommendations. *J Urol.* 2003; 170:530–47.

5. Kaplan SA, McConnell JD, Roehrbron CG, et al. Combination therapy with doxazosin and finasteride for benign prostatic hyperplasia in patients with lower urinary tract symptoms and a baseline total prostate volume of 25 mL or greater. *J Urol.* 2006 January; 175:217–21.

6. Proscar [package insert]. Whitehouse Station, NJ: Merck & Co; April 2004.

7. Cardura [package insert]. New York: Pfizer; February 2006.

61 Erectile Dysfunction

Lynne M. Roman

Objectives

1. Evaluate and compare the treatment options for erectile dysfunction.

2. Describe the adverse effects and drug interactions associated with the treatment options for erectile dysfunction.

3. Evaluate the nondrug therapies that can be used to treat erectile dysfunction.

4. Identify the obstacles to counseling a patient on erectile dysfunction, and develop strategies for overcoming these obstacles.

Scenario

You are working at Sunshine Pharmacy and one of your regular customers, John Smith, comes in to drop off a new prescription. You know that Mr. Smith is a 5-year post–myocardial infarction (MI) patient, and that he has been very adherent with his medications since his MI. He is a 60-year-old white male, and you know that he also has high cholesterol. Mr. Smith drops off a prescription today (Case Figure 61–1).

Case Table 61–1 contains his prescription profile. After reviewing Mr. Smith's patient profile, you decide to ask him some questions before filling his prescription. Afterwards you find out that Mr. Jones has been feeling great since his MI 5 years ago, when they placed three stents in his heart. He has lost approximately 30 pounds, and he quit smoking right after his heart attack. He tells you that the last time he was at his doctor's office his blood pressure was 120/75, his total cholesterol was 180, and his "bad" cholesterol was 75. He tells you that his wife makes sure that he eats low-fat meals, and that he exercises at least 5 days a week by walking or riding his bike for about 1 to 2 hours. When you ask him about his use of nitroglycerin, he tells you that he has not needed to use it for over 2 years, but his wife makes him get a new bottle every once in a while because she heard somewhere that the "pills" go bad quickly. In addition, he tells you that over the last year or so he has been having problems with erectile dysfunction and he finally decided to see a urologist about it. He is hoping that the medication the doctor pre-

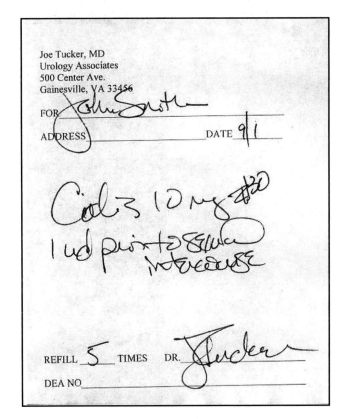

CASE Figure 61–1 Prescription for patient John Smith.

scribed helps him with his problem. Mr. Smith has Medco prescription coverage, and you explain to him that the plan will cover only 10 tablets per month.

Questions and Activities

1. On the basis of the patient's presentation and drug therapy, identify the drug- or disease-related problem, and state the current drug therapy for the problem.

2. What medication classes and diseases might contribute to erectile dysfunction (ED)?

3. What are the goals of pharmacotherapy for this patient?

4. Identify the treatment alternatives available for ED.

CASE Table 61-1 Prescription Medication Profile

John Smith
200 Gator Way Dr.
Gainesville, VA 20155

Phone: 571-224-3333   **DOB:** 01/25/46   **Insurer:** Medco

Allergies/Intolerances: ACE inhibitors (angioedema)

Rx No.	Drug Name	Directions	Date	R/F	Prescriber	Qty	RPh
678781	Lipitor 40 mg	1 tablet by mouth every day	8/15	4	Carter	30	LR
678782	Toprol XL 50 mg	1 tablet by mouth every day	8/15	4	Carter	30	LR
678783	Plavix 75 mg	1 tablet by mouth every day	8/15	4	Carter	30	LR
678786	Nitroglycerin 0.4 mg	1 tablet sublingually as needed	4/30	PRN	Carter	25	LR
679721	Z-Pack	Take as directed	2/21	0	Carter	6	LR

5. Identify the intervention(s) to solve the ED problem and the anticipated outcome(s).

6. What drug(s), dosage form(s), schedules(s), and duration of therapy are optimal for the treatment of the patient's ED?

7. What intervention (e.g., patient recommendation, call to provider or family member, contact emergency medical services, etc.) is necessary for implementing this treatment?

8. What monitoring parameters available in the community pharmacy setting should be used to evaluate therapy in this patient, including efficacy and adverse effects?

9. What nondrug therapies or lifestyle modifications might be useful in managing this patient's ED?

10. Develop a medication action plan for the patient; include short-term and long-term goals.

11. What are the pertinent topics to address during patient education?

12. Develop a follow-up plan for this patient; include time to follow up and method of contact.

Additional Activities

1. Research the type of devices available for ED.

2. Evaluate the dietary supplements or herbs that patients might use to help with ED.

3. Investigate what treatments are available for female sexual dysfunction.

Information Sources

1. National High Blood Pressure Education Program. *The Seventh Report of the Joint National Committee on Prevention, Detection, Evaluation, and Treatment of High Blood Pressure.* Bethesda, Md: National Heart, Lung, and Blood Institute, National Institutes of Health; 2003. NIH Publication No. 03-5233.

2. Grundy SM, Cleeman JI, Merz CN, et al. Implications of recent clinical trials for the National Cholesterol Education Program Adult Treatment Panel III Guidelines. *Circulation.* 2004;110:227–39.

3. Gibbons RJ, Abrams J, Chatterjee K, et al. ACC/AHA 2002 guideline update for the management of patients with chronic stable angina—summary article: A Report of the American College of Cardiology/American Heart Association Task Force on Practice Guidelines (Committee on the Management of Patients with Chronic Stable Angina). *Circulation.* 2003;107:149–58.

4. Kloner RA. Pharmacology and drug interaction effects of the phosphodiesterase 5 inhibitors: focus on alpha-blocker interactions. *Am J Cardiol.* 2005;96(12B):42M–6M.

5. Mayo Clinic Health Information. Erectile Dysfunction. Available at: http://www.mayoclinic.com/health/erectile-dysfunction/DS00162/DSECTION=7. Last accessed September 23, 2008.

6. Kloner RA, Mullin SH, Shook T, et al. Erectile dysfunction in the cardiac patient: how common and should we treat? *J Urol.* 2003;170:S46–S50.

7. National Kidney and Urologic Diseases Information Clearinghouse. *Erectile Dysfunction.* Bethesda, Md: National Institute of Diabetes and Digestive and Kidney Diseases, National Institutes of Health; 2005. NIH Publication No. 06-3923.

8. Brown DA. The management of erectile dysfunction and identification of barriers to treatment. *US Pharm.* 2006; 31:53–64.

9. Erectile Dysfunction Guideline Update Panel. *The Management of Erectile Dysfunction: An Update.* Baltimore, Md: American Urological Association Education and Research; 2005.

Geriatric Health

62 Managing Medication Use in the Geriatric Patient

Ron Gregory and Kimberly A. Cappuzzo

Objectives

1. Identify and prioritize medication-related problems in a complicated older patient.

2. Make recommendations for changes to drug therapy that address medication-related problems in a complicated older patient.

3. Describe techniques to improve adherence in an older patient, taking into account problems that are unique to older persons.

4. Communicate therapeutic recommendations to the patient and appropriate health care practitioner.

5. Formalize a plan to educate an older patient about dietary considerations.

6. Describe the laboratory values that would be helpful in guiding choices to improve drug therapy.

7. Summarize recommendations for the treatment of diabetes mellitus in an older patient compared with a younger patient.

8. Describe a plan for follow-up to assess patient progress and health outcomes.

Scenario

Mrs. Jayne Roberts is an 80–year-old black female who comes to a "brown bag" event held in your community pharmacy. She is accompanied by her son. The patient is alert and cooperative, but she uses a cane and has trouble walking without her son's assistance. Mrs. Roberts says that she lives with her son who assists her with her medications and other daily activities. However, no one is at home to help her during the day while her son is at work.

Mrs. Roberts' brown bag of medications is included in Case Table 62–1.

CASE Table 62–1   Patient's Brown Bag Medications

Medication	Strength	Directions
Metoprolol tablet	25 mg	Take 1/2 tablet by mouth every 12 hours
Amlodipine tablet	10 mg	Take 1 tablet by mouth every day
Aspirin tablet, EC	81 mg	Nonprescription medication
Ferrous sulfate tablet	325 mg	Nonprescription medication
Os-Cal+D tablet	500 mg/200 IU	Nonprescription medication
Sinemet CR tablet	50/200 mg	Take 1 tablet every 12 hours
Folic acid tablet	1 mg	Take 1 tablet by mouth every day
Felodipine ER tablet	10 mg	Take 1 tablet by mouth every day
Fosinopril tablet	40 mg	Take 1 tablet by mouth every day
Catapres TTS-2 patch	0.2 mg/24 hours	Apply 1 patch every 7 days
Candesartan tablet	8 mg	Take 1 tablet by mouth every day
Prednisone tablet	10 mg	Take 1 tablet by mouth every day
Insulin glargine	100 U/mL	Inject 15 units subcutaneously at bedtime each evening[a]
Regular insulin	100 U/mL	Inject 6 units subcutaneously if blood glucose is greater than 400 units at bedtime

[a] Doctor's instructions: If also giving regular insulin, reduce glargine dose to 12 units.

Her son tells you that his mother has been treated for diabetes for about 20 years. She also has been treated for high blood pressure, anemia, osteopenia, chronic renal insufficiency, and polymyalgia rheumatica (PMR). In addition, he tells you that his mother has a small retirement income, and the cost of her medications is sometimes a problem.

When asked why she is taking Sinemet, she replies that she is taking it for "leg pain."

When asked about how she is taking her aspirin, she replies that her doctor told her to take one tablet every day. She takes 1 tablet of Os-Cal+D three times a day, and she takes 1 tablet of ferrous sulfate three times a day.

When asked about the daily supplement of folic acid, Mrs. Roberts says that she once took methotrexate for her PMR and started taking the folic acid at the same time. However, she no longer takes the methotrexate because she started the prednisone.

Mrs. Roberts also has her glucose meter with her. The most recent glucose readings in the meter's memory are listed in Case Table 62–2.

Mrs. Roberts says that her doctor wants her to take glucose readings in the morning before breakfast and at bedtime, but she has difficulty doing finger sticks on her own, because she has had some numbness and tingling in her fingers for the past 2 or 3 years. Her son leaves early for work but is home to assist her in the evenings. Mrs. Roberts denies having any pain or numbness in her legs or feet.

When questioned, Mrs. Roberts denies feeling lightheaded or dizzy, having any changes in vision, or falling. However, her son adds that she was hospitalized a month earlier because of a fall caused by fainting. At the emergency department, her blood glucose was low (32 mg/dL). In addition, she was severely anemic and required a transfusion before being discharged.

When asked about her diet, Mrs. Roberts says that she rarely eats more than 2 meals a day. She knows that she should be on a diabetic diet, but she admits that she does not follow the diet well. Her son adds that his mother spends long hours in her chair watching television while he is at work. He leaves her healthy snacks on a table beside the chair. Mrs. Roberts likes to sip sweetened green tea throughout the day. Because of her kidney problems and blood work at the hospital, she was told she needs to be on a low-potassium diet, but she is unsure what that means.

During this appointment, Mrs. Roberts' blood pressure is 178/92 mm Hg, and her heart rate is 56 beats/min. Mrs. Roberts says that this blood pressure reading is "about average" for her.

Questions and Activities

1. How would you characterize Mrs. Roberts' control of her diabetes?

2. What improvements in her diet would you recommend?

3. Describe Mrs. Roberts' (suspected) nonadherence to blood glucose testing and insulin administration and what improvements may be needed.

4. What are the signs and symptoms of hypoglycemia, and how should users of insulin be prepared to act if these symptoms appear?

5. What are the recommended blood glucose and hemoglobin A1c values for patients 65 years and older? Are these goals different from those in younger patients and, if so, why?

6. Characterize Mrs. Roberts' hypertensive control. In light of this patient having both diabetes and chronic kidney disease, what are her blood pressure goals according to the Seventh Report of the Joint National Committee on Prevention, Detection, Evaluation, and Treatment of High Blood Pressure, and the American Diabetes Association guidelines?

7. What are the options for improving Mrs. Roberts' hypertensive therapy? What are the benefits and risks associated with the different classes of hypertensive medications available? Recommend an optimal plan for treating hypertension in this patient.

8. Mrs. Roberts has chronic renal insufficiency (CRI). In addition to kidney function tests, what other laboratory tests are important for patients with CRI?

9. Mrs. Roberts is being treated for polymyalgia rheumatica (PMR). What is the first-line therapy for PMR? What are the therapeutic goals?

10. What are "activities of daily living" (ADLs)? Why are ADLs pertinent to older patients and their pharmacotherapy plans of care?

CASE Table 62–2	Patient's Blood Glucose Readings	
Date	Glucose (mg/dL)	Time
8/7	464	Bedtime
8/8	360	Bedtime
8/9	207	Bedtime
8/11	291	Bedtime
8/12	157	Bedtime
8/13	351	9:00 am
8/14	439	11:00 am
8/15	509	Bedtime

11. What complications can result from long-term glucocorticosteroid therapy? How are these potential complications pertinent to Mrs. Roberts' other disease states?

12. List possible causes for Mrs. Roberts' anemia. What is the most likely cause? What are the important patient education points and monitoring measures for patients taking iron sulfate? What is the recommended daily dose of iron sulfate for patients older than 80 years compared with younger patients? Under what conditions would you recommend epoetin therapy for patients with CRI?

13. Mrs. Roberts received a diagnosis of osteopenia based on a standard X-ray. What tests would you recommend to confirm a diagnosis of osteoporosis? What are Mrs. Roberts' risk factors for osteoporosis? Is Mrs. Roberts a good candidate for bisphosphonate therapy and why? What are current guidelines for daily elemental calcium and vitamin D intake for women older than 70 years?

14. Mrs. Roberts was told that she has hyperkalemia. Which of her medications and disease states can contribute to this condition? Describe what foods and quantities of those foods would constitute a low-potassium diet.

15. Describe all medication-related problems you can find with Mrs. Roberts' therapeutic regimen (drug–drug interactions, duplicate medications, indication not being treated, etc.). Make recommendations for changes in therapy to optimize her regimen.

16. Plan a follow-up visit 60 days after the initial visit. What questions would you ask Mrs. Roberts, her son, or her physician to determine whether therapeutic changes and other recommendations were implemented?

Additional Activities

1. Would Mrs. Roberts benefit from alternate site testing of her blood glucose levels and why?

2. What factors or differences should be considered in testing blood glucose at different sites?

3. Describe which type of glucose meter you think is best for Mrs. Roberts and why.

4. In addition to monitoring of blood glucose and hemoglobin A1c, what other monitoring or testing should Mrs. Roberts receive, considering her diabetes?

5. What is the "Beers list?" How could the Beers list be used in assessing medication-related problems in older patients? What does the Beers list have to say about ferrous sulfate dosing in elderly persons?

6. Prepare a medication action plan to summarize your recommended changes in therapy.

Information Sources

1. American Diabetes Association. Tight diabetes control. Available at: http://www.diabetes.org. Last accessed September 8, 2008.

2. American Diabetes Association. Standards of medical care in diabetes–2006. *Diabetes Care.* 2006;29(suppl 1):S28–9.

3. Reuben DB, Herr KA, Pacala JT, et al. *Geriatrics at Your Fingertips.* 7th ed. New York: American Geriatrics Society; 2005:61–4.

4. Brown AF, Mangione C, Saliba D, et al. Guidelines for improving the care of the older person with diabetes mellitus. *J Am Geriatr Soc.* 2003;51(5 suppl):S265–80.

5. Chobanian AV, Bakris GL, Black HR, et al. The Seventh Report of the Joint National Committee on Prevention, Detection, Evaluation and Treatment of High Blood Pressure: the JNC 7 report. *JAMA.* 2003;289:2560–72.

6. Rossing K, Jensen BR, Christensen PK, et al. Dual blockade of the renin-angiotensin system in diabetic nephropathy: a double-blind crossover study. *Diabetes Care.* 2002;25:95–100.

7. Fick DM, Cooper JW, Wade WE, et al. Updating the Beers criteria for potentially inappropriate medication use in older adults: results of a U.S. consensus panel of experts. *Arch Intern Med.* 2003;163; 2716–24.

8. Semla TP, Beizer JL, Higbee MD. *Lexi-Comp's Geriatric Dosage Handbook.* 11th ed. Hudson, Ohio: Lexi-Comp; 2006:303–5, 1111–3.

9. Dirckx JH, Stedman TL, eds. *Stedman's Concise Medical Dictionary for the Health Professions.* 4th ed. Dayton, Ohio: Lippincott Williams & Wilkins; 2001:14.

10. Hunder GG. Polymyalgia rheumatica. Literature review. UpTo-Date [subscription database online]. Version 14.2. Available at: http://www.uptodate.com. Last accessed September 28, 2006.

11. Ineck B, Mason BJ, Thompson EG. Anemias. In: DiPiro JT, Talbert RL, Yee GC, et al., eds. *Pharmacotherapy: A Pathophysiologic Approach.* 6th ed. New York: McGraw-Hill; 2005:1805–31.

12. Rimon E, Kagansky N, Kagansky M, et al. Are we giving too much iron? Low-dose therapy is effective in octogenarians. *Am J Med.* 2005;118:1142–7.

13. Dietary Supplement Fact Sheet: Vitamin D. Bethesda, Md: National Institutes of Health, Office of Dietary Supplements. Available at: http://ods.od.nih.gov/factsheets/vitamind.asp. Last accessed September 8, 2008.

14. National Osteoporosis Foundation. Clinician's guide to prevention and treatment of osteoporosis, 2008. Available at: http://www.nof.org/professionals/Clinicians_Guide.htm. Last accessed September 15, 2008.

15. Bischoff-Ferrari HA, Dawson-Hughes B, Willett WC, et al. Effect of vitamin D on falls: a meta-analysis. *JAMA.* 2004;291:1999–2006.

16. Morgan SL, Baggott JE, Vaughn WH, et al. Supplementation with folic acid during methotrexate therapy for rheumatoid arthritis: a double-blind, placebo-controlled trial. *Ann Intern Med.* 1994;121; 833–41.

17. MICROMEDEX Healthcare Series: Interactions Table [subscription database online]. Available at: http://www.thompsonhc.com. Last accessed September 15, 2008.

18. Haynes RB, Yao X, Degani A, et al. Interventions for enhancing medication adherence [review]. The Cochrane Library [subscription database online]. New York: John Wiley & Sons; 2006:issue 3. Available at: http://www.thecochranelibrary.com. Last accessed September 15, 2008.

19. National Kidney Foundation. Potassium and Your CKD Diet. Available at: http://www.kidney.org/atoz/atozItem.cfm?id=103. Last accessed September 8, 2008.

63 Parkinson's Disease

Melody Ryan

Objectives

1. List the classic symptoms of Parkinson's disease.

2. Construct appropriate pharmacotherapy goals for a patient with Parkinson's disease.

3. Develop an appropriate pharmacy care plan for a patient with Parkinson's disease.

4. Identify adverse effects associated with Parkinson's disease pharmacotherapy.

Scenario

Randolph Lativa is a patient who has gotten his medications for years at your pharmacy. He has had Parkinson's disease for the past 2 years and recently had some gastrointestinal issues. Otherwise, he is generally healthy.

Today, he brings you a prescription from his neurologist (Case Figure 63–1). He tells you that his Parkinson's disease symptoms have been getting worse for the past month or so. He is particularly having problems with slow movements and initiating movements, but his tremor has also visibly worsened. You are able to access Mr. Lativa's prescription medication profile in the pharmacy computer (Case Table 63–1).

Questions and Activities

1. What are the four classic symptoms of Parkinson's disease? Which ones are problematic for Mr. Lativa?

2. What additional information would you like from Mr. Lativa?

3. On the basis of the patient's presentation and drug therapy, identify the drug- or disease-related problem(s).

4. Identify the treatment alternatives available for the drug therapy problem.

5. You realize that Dr. Slevin should be contacted. You are able to reach him by phone and explain the drug therapy problem. What action will you advise Dr. Slevin to take?

6. Dr. Slevin agrees with your assessment and recommendation, but he does not feel comfortable making any changes to medications written by another prescriber. He asks you to contact Dr. Mattson and then get back in touch with him. Unfortunately, it is now Friday afternoon and Dr. Mattson's office is closed for the weekend. You will not be able to reach anyone there until Monday. What action should you take at this time (e.g., patient recommendation, call to provider or family member, contact emergency medical services, etc.)?

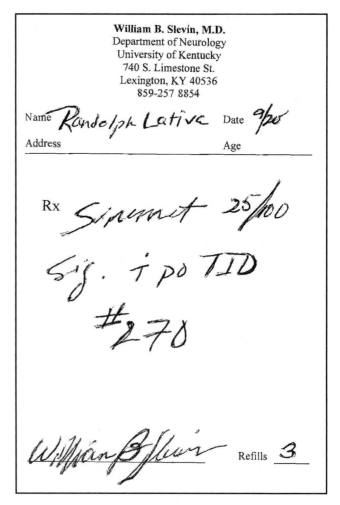

CASE Figure 63–1 Prescription for patient Randolph Lativa.

CASE Table 63–1   Prescription Medication Profile

Randolph Lativa
763 Maple Street
Lexington, Kentucky 40516

Phone: 859-256-5691   **DOB:** 07/10/44   **Insurer:** Blue Cross/Blue Shield of Kentucky

Allergies/Intolerances: Codeine (causes stomach upset)

Rx No.	Drug Name	Directions	Date	R/F	Prescriber	Qty	RPh
621753	Omeprazole 20 mg	1 capsule by mouth every morning	9/1	10	Mattson	30	MR
621752	Metoclopramide 10 mg	1 tablet by mouth 30 minutes before each meal and at bedtime	9/1	10	Mattson	120	MR
621200	Requip 2 mg	1 tablet by mouth three times a day	8/19	2	Slevin	270	LC
621753	Omeprazole 20 mg	1 capsule by mouth every morning	7/31	11	Mattson	30	TM
621752	Metoclopramide 10 mg	1 tablet by mouth 30 minutes before each meal and at bedtime	7/31	11	Mattson	120	TM
621200	Requip 2 mg	1 tablet by mouth three times a day	5/15	3	Slevin	270	MR
620622	Requip 2 mg	1 tablet by mouth three times a day	2/17	0	Slevin	270	TM
620622	Requip 2 mg	1 tablet by mouth three times a day	11/19	1	Slevin	270	TM
620622	Requip 2 mg	1 tablet by mouth three times a day	08/18	2	Slevin	270	LC

7. What monitoring parameters available in the community pharmacy setting could be used to evaluate therapy in this patient, including efficacy and adverse effects?

8. Develop a follow-up plan for this patient; include time to follow up and method of contact.

9. If all of your recommendations are accepted, what additional monitoring might be necessary for Mr. Lativa over the next few months?

10. What other medications might worsen symptoms of Parkinson's disease?

11. What short- and long-term adverse effects are associated with carbidopa/levodopa therapy?

12. How can long-term adverse effects be addressed pharmacologically?

Additional Activities

1. A long-time patient in your pharmacy who cares for her mother who has Parkinson's disease asks to speak to you to have a question answered. She says she heard that drugs for Parkinson's disease can cause gambling. She is concerned because this sounds so strange. She wants to know if it is true and if she should be concerned for her mother. How do you counsel her?

2. What is the relationship between Parkinson's disease and restless legs syndrome? Why are some drugs used for both conditions? Do patients being treated for restless legs syndrome have a higher risk of developing Parkinson's disease later in life?

Information Sources

1. Nelson MV, Berchou RC, LeWitt PA. Parkinson's disease. In: DiPiro JT, Talbert RL, Yee GC, et al., eds. *Pharmacotherapy: A Pathophysiologic Approach.* 6th ed. New York: McGraw-Hill; 2005:1075–104.

2. Jimenez-Jimenez FJ, Garcia-Ruis PJ, Molina JA. Drug induced movement disorders. *Drug Saf.* 1997;16: 180–204.

3. Olanow CW, Watts RL, Koller WC. An algorithm (decision tree) for the management of Parkinson's disease (2001): treatment guidelines. *Neurology.* 2001;56(11 suppl 5):S1–S88.

4. Requip [product information]. Research Triangle Park, NC: GlaxoSmithKline; 2006.

5. Mills W. Nervous system. In: Jones RM, Rospond RM, eds. *Patient Assessment in Pharmacy Practice.* Baltimore: Lippincott Williams & Wilkins; 2003:359–85.

6. Chen JJ, Swope DM. Movement disorders. In: Tisdale JE, Miller DA, eds. *Drug-Induced Diseases: Prevention, Detection, and Management.* Bethesda, Md: American Society of Health-System Pharmacists; 2005:137–67.

7. Ristic AJ, Vojvodic N, Jankovic S, et al. The frequency of reversible parkinsonism and cognitive decline associated with valproate treatment: a study of 364 patients with different types of epilepsy. *Epilepsia.* 2006;47:2183–5.

8. Pahwa R, Factor SA, Lyons KE, et al. Practice parameter: treatment of Parkinson disease with motor fluctuations and dyskinesia (an evidence-based review). Report of the Quality Standards Subcommittee of the American Academy of Neurology. *Neurology.* 2006; 66:983–95.

9. Chen JJ, Oberling C. A review of intermittent subcutaneous apomorphine injections for the rescue management of motor fluctuations associated with advanced Parkinson's disease. *Clin Ther.* 2005;27: 1710–24.

64 Alzheimer's Disease

Heather Allison Greene and Patricia W. Slattum

Objectives

1. List signs of cognitive decline that may manifest in the community pharmacy setting.

2. Describe current therapy for cognitive impairment in Alzheimer's disease.

3. Identify medications that may contribute to cognitive decline in patients with Alzheimer's disease.

4. Develop a care plan to assist patients with Alzheimer's disease to remain as independent as possible in managing their medications.

Scenario

The independent pharmacy you work for is located in an affluent part of town near a large retirement community. Most of the pharmacy customers you serve are older than 65 years. Your pharmacy is dedicated to helping seniors live healthier, more independent lives. To prepare yourself for the task, after graduation from pharmacy school, you received credentialing as a Certified Geriatric Pharmacist (CGP). In addition to dispensing prescriptions you have clinical responsibilities that include conducting weekly blood pressure (BP) screenings.

Molly Bricklayer, one of your loyal and regular customers, came in today to have her blood pressure checked. As you sat with her a few minutes, she was pleased to report that her son, the lawyer, took time out of his busy schedule just to have lunch with her today. On their way out they decided to stop by the pharmacy to pick up her prescription and a few odds and ends; she had been out of juice for a week. She seemed surprised to see the BP screening and stated that she did not know it was a service you offered, even though she has participated in BP screenings before at your pharmacy. She and her son are glad to pay for the clinical services your pharmacy offers because they understand the value in properly monitoring chronic medical conditions and the medications used to manage them.

Although you allowed Mrs. Bricklayer to rest for a few minutes, her BP was unexpectedly elevated at 188/104 mm Hg (left arm, regular cuff). You ask her to rest another 5 minutes before taking a second reading. While she waited, you asked if she felt rested and if she was under a lot of stress or in pain. She said was not under stress or in pain. You asked if she recently had any caffeinated beverages or took any medications for sinus, cold, or allergy symptoms. She had not. You took her BP a second time; it was still elevated at 182/104 mm Hg. It has been 5 weeks since she was last at your BP screening, and her readings have never been this high; in fact, her average is usually 134/78 mm Hg (left arm, regular cuff). You print out her prescription medication profile to see what kind of blood pressure medications she takes (Case Table 64–1).

After evaluating Ms. Bricklayer's prescription medication profile, you note that she is on several medications to lower her BP. You ask her a few questions to help determine a cause for her elevated BP readings. During your conversation you find out the following information.

She never fills prescriptions at any other pharmacy. She has been taking BP medicine since her husband died 8 years ago. Although she cannot explicitly say how she takes her medicine, she reports taking it every morning with a glass of juice, just as her doctor prescribed it. She does not recall her doctor making any changes to her directions over the past few months. She states that she feels fine and does not complain of having had any headaches, chest pain, dizziness, or vision changes. Her chief complaint is that, although she finds it easy to nod off while watching her afternoon stories, she finds it difficult to get to sleep at night unless she takes a Tylenol PM.

Questions and Activities

1. On the basis of the patient's presentation and her prescription medication profile, identify her medical conditions and the current drug therapy to solve the problems.

2. What are the goals of therapy for each of Mrs. Bricklayer's medical conditions?

3. Identify five drug-related or disease-related problems in this case. Include your rationale, and/or list potential contributing factors for each problem identified.

CASE Table 64–1 Prescription Medication Profile

Molly Bricklayer
4516 W. Main Street
Richmond, VA 23220

Phone: 804 555-1234   **DOB:** 12/10/30   **Insurer:** Advance PCS

Allergies/Intolerances: PCN

Rx No.	Drug Name	Directions	Date	R/F	Prescriber	Qty	RPh
621414	Atenolol 100 mg	1 tablet by mouth twice daily	6/7	2	Harris	60	HAG
622125	Diovan hydrochlorothiazide 160/25 mg	1 tablet by mouth every morning	6/4	3	Harris	30	HAG
621762	Aricept 10 mg	1 tablet by mouth every day	5/18	3	Joyner	30	PWS
626283	Namenda 5 mg	1 tablet by mouth twice daily	5/18	1	Joyner	60	PWS
622126	Detrol LA 4 mg	1 tablet by mouth every day	5/6	2	Joyner	30	PWS
621414	Atenolol 100 mg	1 tablet by mouth twice daily	4/25	3	Harris	60	HAG
621831	Ditropan XL 5 mg	1 tablet by mouth every day	4/25	1	Harris	30	HAG
622125	Diovan hydrochlorothiazide 160/25 mg	1 tablet by mouth every day	4/20	4	Harris	30	PWS
621762	Aricept 10 mg	1 tablet by mouth every day	4/11	4	Joyner	30	HAG
622126	Detrol LA 4 mg	1 tablet by mouth every day	4/8	3	Joyner	30	PWS
621414	Atenolol 100 mg	1 tablet by mouth twice daily	3/12	4	Harris	60	HAG

4. Describe the interventions you propose to address each problem. List the outcomes you anticipate and with whom you need to communicate to perform each intervention.

5. You realize that you cannot solve all of these problems in the pharmacy today, but a call to Mrs. Bricklayer's physician is definitely in order. Which physician do you need to contact today? What would you like to discuss with him or her?

6. You are able to reach Mrs. Bricklayer's physician. She appreciates your call, but does not want to make any changes in her therapy until she can see the patient in the office. She is also concerned by Mrs. Bricklayer's BP and would like her to schedule a follow-up appointment as soon as possible. What is the most important point you would like Mrs. Bricklayer and her son to take home with them today?

7. How would you document today's interaction with Mrs. Bricklayer?

8. Develop a follow-up plan for Mrs. Bricklayer; include time to follow up and method of contact.

9. How might a patient's cognitive impairment manifest itself in the typical interactions in a community pharmacy?

10. What is the recommended starting dose of Aricept and Namenda, how are they titrated, and what is the optimal therapeutic dose for a person such as Mrs. Bricklayer in the moderate stage of Alzheimer's disease?

11. Which monitoring parameters could be used to evaluate dementia therapy in this patient in the community pharmacy setting, including efficacy and advers effects?

12. What nondrug therapies, lifestyle modifications, and support organizations in the community might be useful in the management of Mrs. Bricklayer's dementia?

13. What options are available to you as the pharmacist to help Mrs. Bricklayer adhere to her drug therapy?

Additional Activities

1. Visit the Alzheimer's Association Web site (www.alz.org), and identify resources for the pharmacist and ways to become involved in your community.

2. Develop a brief plan to identify or screen other patients in your practice who may be showing signs of cognitive decline.

3. Visit www.geriatricsatyourfingertips.org, register as a user (at no cost), and explore treatment options for common conditions that are often comorbid with dementia, including urinary or fecal incontinence, insomnia, agitation or aggression, and depression.

Information Sources

1. Chobanian AV, Bakris GL, Black HR, et al. Seventh report of the Joint National Committee on Prevention, Detection, Evaluation, and Treatment of High Blood Pressure. *Hypertension.* 2003;42: 1206–52.

2. Lyketsos CG, Colenda CC, Beck C, et al. Position Statement of the American Association of Geriatric Psychiatry regarding principles of care for patients with dementia resulting from Alzheimer's disease. *Am J Geriatr Psychiatry.* 2006;14:562–73.

3. Doody RS, Stevens JC, Beck C, et al. Practice parameter: management of dementia (an evidence-based review). Report of the Quality Standards Subcommittee of the American Academy of Neurology. *Neurology.* 2001;56:1154–66.

4. Kamel NS, Gummack JK. Insomnia in the elderly: cause, approach, and treatment. *Am J Med.* 2006;119: 463–9.

5. Ancoli-Israel S, Ayalon L. Diagnosis and treatment of sleep disorders in older adults. *Am J Geriatr Psychiatry.* 2006;14:95–103.

6. Ancoli-Israel S, Vitiello MV. Sleep in dementia. *Am J Geriatr Psychiatry.* 2006;14:91–4.

7. MacLaughlin EJ, Raehl CL, Treadway AK, et al. Assessing medication adherence in the elderly. Which tools to use in clinical practice? *Drugs Aging.* 2005; 22:231–55.

8. Chapman DP, Williams SM, Strine TW, et al. Dementia and its implications for public health. *Prev Chronic Dis.* 2006. Available at: http://www.cdc.gov/pcd/issues/2006/apr/05_0167.htm. Last accessed September 9, 2008.

9. Gill SS, Mamdani M, Naglie G, et al. A prescribing cascade involving cholinesterase inhibitors and anticholinergic drugs. *Arch Intern Med.* 2005;165:808–13.

10. Edwards KR, O'Connor JT. Risk of delirium with concomitant use of tolterodine and acetylcholinesterase inhibitors. *J Am Geriatr Soc.* 2002;50:1165–6.

11. Jewart RD, Green J, Lu C, et al. Cognitive, behavioral and physiological changes in Alzheimer's disease patients as a function of incontinence medications. *Am J Geriatr Psychiatry.* 2005;13:324–8.

12. Mulsant BH, Pollock BG, Kirshner M, et al. Serum anticholinergic activity in a community-based sample of older adults: relationship with cognitive performance. *Arch Gen Psychiatry.* 2003;60: 198–203.

13. Fick DM, Cooper JW, Wade WE, et al. Updating the Beers criteria for potentially inappropriate medication use in older adults: results of a US panel of experts. *Arch Intern Med.* 2003;163: 2716–24.

14. Rovner ES, Wyman J, Lackner T, Guay D. Urinary incontinence. In: DiPiro JT, Talbert RL, Yee GC, et al., eds. *Pharmacotherapy: A Pathophysiological Approach.* 6th ed. New York: McGraw-Hill; 2006:1553.

15. Mintzer J, Burns A. Anticholinergic side effects of drugs in elderly people. *J R Soc Med.* 2000;93:457–62.

16. Beier MT. Cholinesterase inhibitors and anticholinergic drugs: is the pharmacologic antagonism myth or reality? *J Am Med Dir Assoc.* 2005;Nov–Dec:413–4.

17. Kay GG, Abou-Donia MB, Messer WS, et al. Antimuscarinic drugs for overactive bladder and their potential effects on cognitive function in older patients. *J Am Geriatr Soc.* 2005;53: 2195–201.

18. Folstein MF, Folstein SE, McHugh PR. "Mini-mental state": a practical method for grading the cognitive state of patients for the clinician. *J Psychiatr Res.* 1975;12:189–98.

19. Beier MT. Harmless herbs? Think again: merits of a complete medication history. *J Am Med Dir Assoc.* 2006 September:446–7.

20. Donepezil. Geriatric Lexi-Drugs Online. Lexi-Comp [subscription required]. Available at: http://www.crlonline.com/crlsql/servlet/crlonline.Last accessed September 23, 2008.

21. Memantine. Geriatric Lexi-Drugs Online. Lexi-Comp [subscription required]. Available at: http://www.crlonline.com/crlsql/servlet/crlonline. Last accessed September 23, 2008.

22. Lleó A, Greenberg SM, Growdon JH. Current pharmacotherapy for Alzheimer's disease. *Annu Rev Med.* 2006;57:513–33.

23. Alzheimer's Association. Available at: http://www.alz.org. Last accessed September 9, 2008.

24. TabSafe Medical Systems Inc. Available at: http://www.tabsafe.com. Last accessed September 9, 2008.

25. e-pill Medication Reminders. Available at: http://www.epills.com. Last accessed September 9, 2008.

Neurologic Disorders

65 Headache

Carrie Foust Koenigsfeld and Darla Klug Eastman

Objectives

1. Compare and contrast the presentation of different types of headaches.

2. Demonstrate understanding of effective communication skills in gathering all the necessary information from a patient with a headache.

3. Develop patient-specific recommendations for pharmacologic and nonpharmacologic treatment of headaches.

4. Devise a plan for monitoring headache treatment.

Scenario

You are working at Anderson's Pharmacy, a privately owned community pharmacy, when Megan Clayton, a 24-year-old white woman, comes to the pharmacy to pick up her prescription for Seasonale (Quasense) and has a question about a nonprescription item. Ms. Clayton is holding a bottle of extra strength acetaminophen and asks if you could recommend anything stronger for her tension headaches. You begin by asking Ms. Clayton to tell you more about her tension headaches.

She tells you she recently has been having throbbing pain above her left temple. The pain starts without warning and usually lasts for several hours. The headache progressively gets worse, until she is forced to go to bed where it is quiet and dark. The headache typically resolves while she is sleeping, but in the morning her head still feels tender. She estimates that she has been getting these headaches about once weekly for the past couple of months.

She has been taking 2 extra strength acetaminophen tablets at the onset of the headache with little relief. Her bottle of acetaminophen is now gone and she wants to be prepared for her next headache. It has been almost a year since she has seen her physician. She recently made an appointment for 2 weeks from today. In the meantime she wants your recommendation for a nonprescription item to treat her headaches. You pull up her prescription medication profile on the computer and find the information available in Case Table 65–1.

Questions and Activities

1. What type of headache do you suspect Megan Clayton is experiencing and why?

CASE Table 65–1 Prescription Medication Profile

Megan Clayton
112 3rd Avenue
Owatonna, MN 55060

Phone: 555-334-3364 (cell)   **DOB:** 10/30/83   **Insurer:** Blue Cross/Blue Shield

Allergies/Intolerances: NKDA

Rx No.	Drug Name	Directions	Date	R/F	Prescriber	Qty	RPh
63002	Seasonale (Quasense)	1 tablet every day	12/22	1	Huber	84	TJ
63002	Seasonale (Quasense)	1 tablet every day	9/26	2	Huber	84	TJ
63003	Bactrim DS	1 tablet twice daily for 10 days	6/30	0	Huber	20	RF
63002	Seasonale (Quasense)	1 tablet every day	6/30	3	Huber	84	RF
56890	Ortho Tri-Cyclen Lo	1 tablet every day	4/1	0	Huber	84	AS
56890	Ortho Tri-Cyclen Lo	1 tablet every day	1/3	1	Huber	84	TJ

2. What further information would you like to gather from Megan Clayton? What questions might you want to ask her?

As the pharmacist you ask Ms. Clayton if she has noticed any patterns or any triggers that seem to bring on her headaches. Specifically, you ask if her headaches seem to correlate at all with her menstrual cycle. Ms. Clayton states she had noticed a correlation but that she has had fewer problems since she switched her birth control to Seasonale.

3. Why might Seasonale have lessened the incidence of her headaches?

After reviewing the patient's profile you pull out a three-question migraine headache screening tool that you recently read about and have been using with your patients who complain of headache. You ask Ms. Clayton the following questions from the three-item migraine screener.[1] You remember reading that if a patient answers yes to two of three questions, it is likely that the headaches are migraines.

During the past 3 months, did any of the following occur with your headache?

1. *You felt nauseated or sick to your stomach?*
2. *Light bothered you (a lot more than when you do not have headaches)?*
3. *Your headaches have limited your ability to work, study, or complete other tasks for at least 1 day?*

Ms. Clayton tells you that, although her stomach has not been bothered by her headaches, light does bother her, and she is severely limited in her activities for about a day with each headache.

4. On the basis of the patient's presentation and drug therapy, identify the drug- or disease-related problem(s), and state the current drug therapy for the problem.

5. What are the goals of pharmacotherapy for this patient?

6. Identify the treatment alternatives available for the drug therapy problems.

7. Identify the interventions to solve the problems and the anticipated outcomes.

8. What drugs, dosage forms, schedules, and durations of therapy are optimal for the treatment of the patient's headaches?

9. What intervention (e.g., patient recommendation, call to provider or family member, contact emergency medical services, etc.) is necessary for implementing this treatment?

10. What monitoring parameters available in the community pharmacy setting should be used to evaluate therapy in this patient, including efficacy and adverse effects?

11. What nondrug therapies or lifestyle modifications might be useful in managing this patient's headaches?

12. Two weeks later Megan Clayton returns to your pharmacy with a prescription for Amerge (naratriptan) 1 mg, 1 tablet as needed for headache, may repeat once after 4 hours. Develop a medication action plan for this patient; include short-term and long-range goals.

13. What are the pertinent topics to address during patient education?

14. Before you begin counseling Ms. Clayton about her new prescription, she asks if this is like the Imitrex samples she tried a couple of months ago. On further discussion you learn that the Imitrex samples helped Megan's headaches initially but then the headaches would return after 2 to 4 hours. What could you tell her about the differences between the Imitrex she had tried and the Amerge that she is picking up today?

15. Develop a follow-up plan for this patient; include time to follow up and method of contact.

16. While Megan Clayton is in the pharmacy picking up her prescription for Amerge, she mentions that she has done some research on headaches on the Internet and is curious about the use of Topamax (topiramate) for headaches. What could you tell her?

Additional Activities

1. Compare and contrast available nonprescription therapies indicated for migraine headaches. Which of these agents (if any) would you recommend for patients? What patient counseling would you want to provide when recommending a nonprescription therapy for migraine?

2. Compare and contrast available triptans in respect to formulation, pharmacology, efficacy, onset of action, and duration of action. List any significant clinical differences among these agents and for which patient population each agent might be ideal (e.g., Frova in patients with long-lasting migraine).

3. List agents commonly used to prevent migraine therapy. Which agents have the most supporting evidence of efficacy and tolerability? Which patients with migraine are candidates for prophylactic therapy?

4. Discuss common drug interactions seen with the triptans. Which of these interactions are clinically significant? Is it advisable for patients to take triptans

and selective serotonin reuptake inhibitors together? Why or why not? Review the following article for more information on this topic.

- US Food and Drug Administration. Information for healthcare professionals. Selective serotonin reuptake inhibitors (SSRIs); selective serotonin-norepinephrine reuptake inhibitors (SNRIs); 5-hydroxytryptaminereceptor agonists (Triptans). Available at: www.fda.gov/cder/drug/InfoSheets/HCP/triptansHCP.pdf. Last accessed September 16, 2008.

5. Review the following references about the role of the ambulatory care or community pharmacist in patients with migraines. Discuss the potential role of the community pharmacist in optimizing outcomes in patients with headache.

- Wenzel RG, Schommer JC, Marks TG. Morbidity and medication preferences of individuals with headache presenting to a community pharmacy. *Headache*. 2004; 44:90–4.

- Wenzel RG, Lipton RB, Diamond ML, Cady R. Migraine therapy: a survey of pharmacists' knowledge, attitudes, and practice patterns. *Headache*. 2005;45: 47–52.

- Weitzel KW, Presley DN, Showalter ML, et al. Pharmacist-managed headache clinic. *Am J Health Syst Pharm*. 2004;61:2548–50.

Information Sources

1. Headache Classification Subcommittee of the International Headache Society. The international classification of headache disorders, 2nd ed. *Cephalalgia*. 2004;24:24–43.
2. Clinch CR. Evaluation of acute headaches in adults. *Am Fam Physician*. 2001;63:685–92.
3. King DS, Herndon KC. Headache disorders. In: DiPiro JT, Talbert RL, Yee GC, et al., eds. *Pharmacotherapy: A Pathophysiologic Approach*. 6th ed. New York: McGraw-Hill; 2005:1105–21.
4. Cady RK, Borchert LD, Spalding W, et al. Simple and efficient recognition of migraine with 3-question headache screen. *Headache*. 2004;44:323–7.
5. Sheftell FD, Cady RK, Borchert LD, et al. Optimizing the diagnosis and treatment of migraine. *J Am Acad Nurse Pract*. 2005;17: 309–17.
6. Lipton RB, Bigal ME, Amatniek JC, et al. Tools for diagnosing migraine and measuring its severity. *Headache*. 2004;44:387–98.
7. Tozer BS, Boatwright EA, David PS, et al. Prevention of migraine in women throughout the lifespan. *Mayo Clin Proc*. 2006;81:1086–92.
8. Seasonale [product information]. Pomona, NY: Duramed Pharmaceuticals; 2003.
9. Seasonique [product information]. Pomona, NY: Duramed Pharmaceuticals; 2006.
10. Landy S, Smith T. Treatment of primary headache: acute migraine treatment. In: *Standards of Care for Headache Diagnosis and Treatment*. Chicago: National Headache Foundation; 2004:27–39. Available at: http://www.guideline.gov/summary/summary.aspx?doc_id=6579. Last accessed September 16, 2008.
11. Pryse-Phillips WEM, Dodick DW, Edmead JG, et al. Guidelines for the diagnosis and management of migraine in clinical practice. *Can Med Assoc J*. 1997; 156:1273–87.
12. Silberstein SD, McCrory DC. Ergotamine and dihydroergotamine: history, pharmacology, and efficacy. *Headache*. 2003;43:144–66.
13. Tepper SJ, Dahlöf CGH, Dowson A, et al. Prevalence and diagnosis of migraine in patients consulting their physician with a complaint of headache: data from the landmark study. *Headache*. 2004; 44:856–64.
14. Lacy CF, Armstrong LL, Goldman MP, et al. *Drug Information Handbook Pocket*. Hudson, Ohio: Lexi-Comp; 2004:27–9.
15. Silberstein SD. Chronic daily headache. *J Am Osteopath Assoc*. 2005;105:23–9.
16. About MIDAS. AstraZeneca migraine disability information center. Available at: http://www.midas-migraine.net. Last accessed September 16, 2008.
17. Novartis Consumer Health, Inc. Headache Diary. Available at: http://www.excedrin.com/headache_center/diary.shtml. Last accessed September 16, 2008.
18. Boardman HF, Thomas E, Millson DS, et al. Psychological, sleep, lifestyle, and comorbid associations with headache. *Headache*. 2005; 45:657–69.
19. Halpern MT, Lipton RB, Cady RK, et al. Costs and outcomes of early versus delayed migraine treatment with sumatriptan. *Headache*. 2002;42:984–99.
20. Amerge [product information]. Research Triangle Park, NC: GlaxoSmithKline; 2006.
21. Berger BA. *Communication Skills for Pharmacists: Building Relationships Improving Patient Care*. Washington, DC: Jobson Publishing; 2003:43–4.
22. Tfelt-Hansen P. A review of evidence-based medicine and meta-analytic review in migraine. *Cephalalgia*. 2006;26:1265–74.
23. Topamax [prescribing information]. Titusville, NJ: Ortho-McNeil Neurologics; 2005.
24. Brandes JL, Saper JR, Diamond M, et al. Topiramate for migraine prevention: a randomized controlled trial. *JAMA*. 2004;291:965–73.
25. Diamond S. *Diagnosing and Managing Headaches*. 1st ed. Caddo, Okla: Professional Communications; 1994: 60–2.
26. National Headache Foundation. Low tyramine diet for migraine. Available at: http://www.headaches.org/consumer/topicsheets/consumertopics.html. Last accessed September 16, 2008.
27. Kando JC, Wells BG, Hayes PE. Depressive disorders. In: DiPiro JT, Talbert RL, Yee GC, et al., eds. *Pharmacotherapy: A Pathophysiologic Approach*. 6th ed. New York: McGraw-Hill; 2005:1235–55.

66 Epilepsy and Women of Childbearing Age

Angela M. Dyer and J. Tyler Stevens

Objectives

1. Identify potential complications of antiepileptic drugs in women of childbearing age.

2. Recognize the difficulties associated with epilepsy and the complications.

3. Assess patient information in a community setting to identify the drug- or disease-related problems.

4. Develop a plan to provide optimal patient care with pharmacologic and nonpharmacologic options.

5. Demonstrate competency in interpreting illegible prescriptions.

Scenario

Suzie Smith is a 28-year-old white woman who is a regular patient at Big T's Drug Emporium. Ms. Smith has a 12-year history of complex partial seizures that are a result of trauma associated with a motor vehicle accident. She has been seizure free for the past 6 years. Last year she married and began taking Ortho Tri-Cyclen. She presents to Big T's today with three prescriptions (Case Figures 66–1 through 66–3). Her past prescription medication profile is available in Case Table 66–1 and includes Ortho Tri-Cyclen, Allegra, and Depakote.

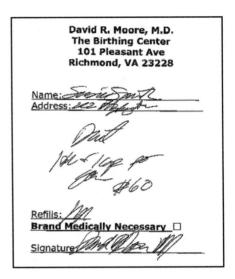

CASE Figure 66–2 Prescription #2 for patient Suzie Smith.

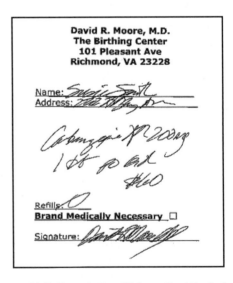

CASE Figure 66–3 Prescription #3 for patient Suzie Smith.

Questions and Activities

1. On the basis of the patient's drug therapy, identify the drug- or disease-related problem, and state the current drug therapy for the problem.

2. What are the goals of pharmacotherapy for this patient?

CASE Figure 66–1 Prescription #1 for patient Suzie Smith.

CASE Table 66–1   Prescription Medication Profile

Suzie Smith
222 Hitzhugh Ave.
Richmond, VA 23225

Phone: 804-555-1234   **DOB:** 01/01/80   **Insurer:** American Health

Allergies/Intolerances: NKDA

Rx No.	Drug Name	Directions	Date	R/F	Prescriber	Qty	RPh
210412	Depakote ER 500 mg	2 tablets by mouth every day	9/2	7	West	60	DW
210412	Depakote ER 500 mg	2 tablet by mouth every day	8/3	8	West	60	RD
210412	Depakote ER 500 mg	2 tablets by mouth every day	7/1	9	West	60	RD
226021	Ortho Tri-Cyclen	1 tablet by mouth every day	7/1	11	Moore	84	DW
210412	Depakote ER 500 mg	2 tablet by mouth every day	6/2	10	West	60	DW
226022	Allegra 180 mg	1 tablet by mouth every day	6/2	12	Moore	30	DW
226021	Ortho Tri-Cyclen	1 tablet by mouth every day	4/1	12	Moore	84	DW

3. Identify the drug-related or disease-related problem(s), the intervention(s) to solve the problem(s), and the anticipated outcome(s).

4. Identify the treatment alternatives available for the drug therapy problem.

5. After speaking with Ms. Smith, you were informed that she will be taking only these three new medications. What drug(s), dosage form(s), schedule(s), and duration(s) of therapy are optimal for the treatment of this patient's problem?

6. Why is an additional amount of folic acid needed for Ms. Smith?

7. What intervention (e.g., patient recommendation, call to provider or family member, contact emergency medical services, etc) is necessary for implementing this treatment?

8. What monitoring parameters available in the community pharmacy setting should be used to evaluate therapy in this patient, including efficacy and adverse effects?

9. What nondrug therapies or lifestyle modifications might be useful in the management of this patient's problem?

10. Develop a medication action plan for the patient; include short-term and long-range goals.

11. What are the pertinent topics to address during patient education?

12. Develop a follow-up plan for this patient; include time to follow up and method of contact.

13. About a year later, Ms. Smith returns to the pharmacy. Her pregnancy went well. She is on her way home from the hospital after her labor and delivery, and stops at the pharmacy to have some prescriptions filled. No additional changes were made in her antiepileptic drug (AED) regimen. What could be an issue for Ms. Smith with this drug regimen at this time?

14. If it is determined that a treatment change is needed, what treatment alternative(s) would be available to her at this time?

15. What monitoring parameters could be observed for adverse drug reactions in the breast-fed infant?

16. What effects do hormonal changes have on seizure status (especially during pregnancy and menstruation)?

17. Discuss the drug interaction between oral contraceptives and AEDs. What would you recommend to a patient receiving both of these medications?

18. In what situations would vitamin K supplementation be needed during the last month of pregnancy in a patient taking antiepileptic medications?

19. What are some similarities and differences between newer AEDs and older AEDs that may be used in the treatment of epilepsy?

20. What effect can AEDs have on osteoporosis?

21. Name some commonly used nonprescription and herbal remedies that would lower seizure threshold.

22. In community pharmacy practice, what are some implications or considerations about brand or generic substitutions of AEDs in patients with seizure disorders?

23. What effect might the prescription handwriting have had on this patient's therapy? Do you feel comfortable dispensing these prescriptions as written without clarification from the physician?

Information Sources

1. Gidal BE, Garnett WR. Epilepsy. In: Dipiro JT, Talbert RL, Yee GC, et al., eds. *Pharmacotherapy: A Pathophysiologic Approach.* 6th ed. 2005. New York: McGraw-Hill; 2005:1023–48.

2. American Academy of Neurology. AAN Guideline Summary for Patients and Their Families: Efficacy and Tolerability of the New Antiepileptic Drugs for Treatment of New Onset Epilepsy. Available at: http://www.aan.com/globals/axon/assets/2592.pdf. Last accessed September 17, 2008.

3. Clinical Pharmacology [subscription required]. Available at: http://clinicalpharmacology.com/Forms/Monograph/monograph.aspx?cpnum=340&sec=monpregPregnancy/Breast-feeding Category for Valproic Acid, Lamotrigine, and Carbamazepine. Last accessed September 25, 2008.

4. Yersy, MS. Antiepileptic Drug Use and Pregnancy. *CNS News Special Edition.* December 2001.

5. Pack, Alison M. Morrell, Marth J. Treatment of women with epilepsy. *Semin Neurol.* 2002;22:289–98.

6. Epilepsy Foundation. Available at: http://www.epilepsyfoundation.org. Last accessed September 17. 2008.

7. Practice parameter: management issues for women with epilepsy (summary statement). Report of the Quality Standards Subcommittee of the American Academy of Neurology. *Epilepsia.* 1998;39:1226–31.

8. American Academy of Pediatrics Committee on Fetus and Newborn. Controversies concerning vitamin K and the newborn. *Pediatrics* 2003;112:191–2.

9. Farley JF, Cline RR, Hansen RA. Resorptive drug use among community-dwelling women in Minnesota. *Am J Health Syst Pharm.* 2004;61:1577–85.

10. Tyagi A, Delanty N. Herbal remedies, dietary supplements, and seizures. *Epilepsia.* 2003;44:228–35.

11. Crawford P, Feely M, Guberman A, Kramer G. Are there potential problems with generic substitution of antiepileptic drugs? A review of issues. *Seizure.* 2006;15:165–76.

Psychiatric Disorders

67 Managing Attention Deficit Hyperactivity Disorder

Pamela C. Heaton and Kelly Swensgard

Objectives

1. Understand the differential diagnosis of attention deficit hyperactivity disorder, and list the diagnostic criteria as well as tools used in the diagnosis of attention deficit hyperactivity disorder.

2. List the pharmacologic treatment goals for attention deficit hyperactivity disorder.

3. Evaluate patient presentation, and recommend a therapeutic plan that includes drug(s), dosage form(s), schedule(s), and duration of therapy.

4. Understand and recommend appropriate adjunct therapy for the treatment of attention deficit hyperactivity disorder.

5. Redesign a patient care plan from follow-up information, and include response to therapy, side effects, cost of medication, and patient preference until the goals of therapy are achieved.

Scenario

A parent comes to your pharmacy with concerns about her child's behavioral issues and poor progress in school. She has questions about whether she should be concerned because her husband feels that their son's behavior is normal for his age. After she discusses this issue with her son's pediatrician as you recommended, she returns on several occasions for your advice on treatment options for attention deficit hyperactivity disorder (ADHD).

"I'm here to pick up my son's Singulair refill, and I would like to ask the pharmacist a couple questions about the behavior issues I am having with my 10-year-old son."

After introducing yourself as the pharmacist and directing her to the private counseling area, she introduces herself as Mrs. Harris, Matthew Harris's mother. She then explains that her son, who is 10 years old and currently in fourth grade, is seeing his pediatrician later today for his yearly physical. She explains, "Matthew's teacher and I are both concerned about his restless and disruptive behavior at school and at home." She states that he has too much energy and often gets into physical disagreements with his 4-year-old sister. She also states that he is having difficulty keeping up with his teacher's expectations. He regularly does not finish his homework because he is easily distracted by just about anything in his room.

Matthew's mother further elaborates on his past difficulties with school, stating that Matthew entered kindergarten at age 5. His overall performance throughout kindergarten was considered average, with reading and writing as his worst areas. After some discussion with his teacher, Matthew's parents chose to advance him to first grade the following year. Throughout first grade it was more apparent to Matthew's teacher that he was struggling with the basics. Matthew repeated first grade the following year and went on to complete the second and third grades on schedule. He typically earns low C's or D's with occasional B's. His worst subjects continue to be reading and writing; however, he usually performs slightly better in math and science and excels in physical education.

She mentions that one of her biggest concerns is that her husband is not so sure that there is a real problem. He feels that this is just "typical boy" behavior and thinks that his son's behavior is similar to his own when he was 10. He does not think that the issue needs to be addressed at Matthew's doctor appointment later today. He feels that things will work out if they just wait and see.

The following information was provided by Matthew's mother after your prompting:

- Past medical history is significant for typical childhood illnesses and asthma (currently well controlled); vision screening was normal (1.5 years ago through school third grade with right to sight program); and auditory screening was normal (4 years ago during prekindergarten physical).

- Family history: Mother has clinical depression (unipolar), father has questionable ADHD, and the sister has seasonal allergies.

- Social history: Mother denies that Matthew uses tobacco, alcohol, and illicit drugs.

- Matthew's weight is 65 pounds, and he is 4 feet 3 inches tall.
- Medications: See Case Table 67–1.

Questions and Activities

1. On the basis of the mother's description of Matthew's behavior, determine a likely diagnosis for his problem. Include the differential diagnoses and any medical tests that should be performed to confirm the diagnosis. Discuss potential diagnostic tools and criteria to help Matthew's father accept the diagnosis.

The next day, the mother returns and explains that her son's condition was diagnosed as attention deficit hyperactivity disorder (ADHD) combined type yesterday at his doctor's appointment. She says that the doctor gave her a prescription for methylphenidate (Ritalin) 10 mg by mouth at breakfast for her son, and she wants to know if this seems like a good choice.

2. Is the prescribed medication, methylphenidate (Ritalin), an appropriate first-line choice for Matthew's diagnosed attention deficit hyperactivity disorder (ADHD)? Why or why not? What are the goals of pharmacotherapy for Matthew?

3. Matthew's mother is also concerned about side effects of this medication. What can you tell her about what to expect while Matthew is taking this medication? What other counseling points should be included today?

4. Matthew's mother is grateful for all the information you have given her, but she is still unsure if she wants her son to take a medication on a regular basis. She asks about alternative therapies that can be used either instead of or in addition to medication. Identify alternative treatments available for ADHD, and include nonpharmacologic therapy or natural or dietary supplements.

Matthew's mother comes back to the pharmacy about 6 weeks after filling his initial prescription. She says his teacher sent a note home stating that overall Matthew's ability to focus and his impulsivity are much improved; however, he is still having difficulty focusing in class toward the end of the day.

5. Matthew's mother asks you for advice on how to address the issue of her son having difficulty focusing in class toward the end of the day. What therapeutic changes could be made to alleviate this problem?

6. Matthew's mother inquires about the effectiveness of dietary changes in treating ADHD. She states that her mother-in-law told her there may be dietary changes that can improve Matthew's behavior or potentially reduce the amount of medication he is on. She asks you if you could recommend dietary changes for Matthew.

Six months have elapsed since Matthew began treatment. He is now seeing a psychiatrist for his ADHD. Three weeks ago he was switched to Metadate CD 20 mg by mouth once daily. While you are talking to Matthew, he says he has difficulty swallowing his medication. His mother confirms Matthew's concerns and adds that he typically refuses the medication at least 3 days a week. He actually wants to stop his current medication.

7. Matthew's mother would like to switch from the recently prescribed Metadate CD to an alternative form of extended release methylphenidate because of her son's difficulty in swallowing the tablet. She wants to know if there is another formulation you can substitute for her to try without having to call the doctor. You look on your shelves and see you have Metadate ER and methylphenidate extended release. Can you substitute either of these for Metadate CD? What would you recommend for this problem?

8. Matthew's mother returns the next day with a prescription for Daytrana 10 mg applied once daily. Is

---

CASE Table 67–1   Prescription Medication Profile

Matthew Harris
7044 Bay View Street
Annapolis, MD 21401

Phone: 410-355-5555   **DOB:** 11/5/98   **Insurer:** BlueCross BlueShield

Allergies/Intolerances: NKDA

Rx No.	Drug Name	Directions	Date	R/F	Prescriber	Qty	RPh
623455	Singulair 10 mg	1 tablet by mouth every day	10/4	2	Kassar	30	JY
623457	ProAir HFA	Inhale 2 puffs four times daily as needed	9/2	1	Kassar	9	KT
623455	Singulair 10 mg	1 tablet by mouth every day	8/17	3	Kassar	30	JY
623457	ProAir HFA	Inhale 2 puffs four times daily as needed	7/31	2	Kassar	9	JY

this an appropriate dose for Matthew? How would you counsel them about using the patch?

A year later, Matthew's mother is in the pharmacy to get his prescriptions filled. Matthew is now taking Adderall XR 10 mg every morning and methylphenidate 5 mg at noon because the Daytrana did not seem to work for him. He feels that his current regimen controls his symptoms. However, his mother complains that Matthew now has difficulty falling asleep. She says her nephew takes clonidine at bedtime to calm down. Matthew's mother wants to know if clonidine would help her son with his difficulty falling asleep. On further questioning it is discovered that the school is not consistently giving Matthew his methylphenidate at lunchtime. On those days, when he comes home from school, he is so hyper that his mom gives him half of a methylphenidate 5 mg tablet.

9. Discuss any necessary patient education concerning the school's failure to administer the noon dose of methylphenidate every day and the mother's administering the missed dose when Matthew comes home. Indicate whether clonidine should be added to Matthew's therapy to help him with his difficulty falling asleep.

10. Also, at this visit to the pharmacy, Matthew's mother has two prescriptions for the Adderall XR. The first prescription has today's date on it, June 12. The second prescription is dated July 12 and has a note on it from the doctor that says "Do not fill until July 12 or later." After July 12, would it be acceptable to fill this second prescription?

11. Matthew's mother comes into the pharmacy and complains about having to pay $30 co-pay each month for his medications. She says her insurance company now prefers her to either use mail order or at least get a 3-month supply of each prescription for $45 co-pay. She knows she cannot get a 3-month supply of a controlled medication with her insurance, and she wants you to recommend another type of medication that can be dispensed in a 3-month supply. Discuss any options available and their pros and cons. Would you recommend that she try to make this switch for Matthew or stick with the current regimen?

12. Matthew's father realizes that he has symptoms that are similar to his son's symptoms. After seeing the improvement in his son, his father comes to the pharmacy and asks you about treating adult ADHD. Discuss adult treatment of ADHD. How does treatment differ for adults?

Additional Activities

1. Research Vyvanse (lisdexamfetamine), a relatively new long-acting stimulant option available for treatment of ADHD. How is it different from other existing long-acting stimulants? What advantages, if any, does it offer for patients?

2. A physician asks a pharmacist about placing an adult on a high dose of stimulant. What should the pharmacist do? How would the pharmacist contact the drug company to obtain more information about dosing.

3. Check with your state's board of pharmacy to determine what are the current laws in your state about multiple prescriptions postdated for schedule II controlled substances? How would you handle this situation in practice?

4. Assign two or more learners to teams to present and debate the pros and cons of drug therapy for ADHD in children. Parents are often concerned about the safety and efficacy of these agents, and this exercise can help learners understand opposing viewpoints and answer caregiver questions.

Information Sources

1. Clinical practice guideline: diagnosis and evaluation of the child with attention-deficit/hyperactivity disorder. American Academy of Pediatrics. *Pediatrics.* 2000;105:1158–70.

2. Clinical practice guideline: treatment of the school-aged child with attention-deficit/hyperactivity disorder. *Pediatrics.* 2001;108:1033–44.

3. Poulton A, Cowell CT. Slowing of growth in height and weight on stimulants: a characteristic pattern. *J Paediatr Child Health.* 2003;39:180–5.

4. Sund AM, Zeiner P. Does extended medication with amphetamine or methylphenidate reduce growth in hyperactive children? *Nord J Psychiatry.* 2002;56:53–7.

5. Palumbo D, Spencer T, Lynch J, et al. Emergence of tics in children with ADHD: impact of once-daily OROS methylphenidate therapy. *J Child Adolesc Psychopharmacol.* 2004;14:185–94.

6. Law SF, Schachar RJ. Do typical clinical doses of methylphenidate cause tics in children treated for attention-deficit hyperactivity disorder? *J Am Acad Child Adolesc Psychiatry.* 1999;38:944–51.

7. Lipkin PH, Goldstein IJ, Adesman AR. Tics and dyskinesias associated with stimulant treatment in attention-deficit hyperactivity disorder. *Arch Pediatr Adolesc Med.* 1994;148:859–61.

8. American Academy of Pediatrics. Available at: www.aap.org. Last accessed on June 5, 2005.

9. Mannuzza S, Klein RG, Moulton JL 3rd. Does stimulant treatment place children at risk for adult substance abuse? A controlled, prospective follow-up study. *J Child Adolesc Psychopharmacol.* 2003;13:273–82.

10. A 14-month randomized clinical trial of treatment strategies for attention-deficit/hyperactivity disorder. The MTA Cooperative Group. Multimodal Treatment Study of Children with ADHD. *Arch Gen Psychiatry.* 1999;56:1073–86.

11. Natural Database. Available at: www.naturaldatabase.com. Last accessed on March 27, 2007.

12. Ritalin LA [product information]. East Hanover, N.J.: Novartis Pharmaceutical Corporation; 2002.

13. Concerta [product information]. Fort Washington, Pa.: McNeil Consumer Healthcare; 2000.

14. Rojas NL, Chan E. Old and new controversies in the alternative treatment of attention-deficit hyperactivity disorder. *Ment Retard Dev Disabil Res Rev.* 2005;11:116–30.

15. Marcason W. Can dietary intervention play a part in the treatment of attention deficit and hyperactivity disorder? *J Am Diet Assoc.* 2005;105:1161–2.

16. Generic substitution for commonly prescribed drugs. *Pharm Lett Prescrib Lett.* 2006;22:220901.

17. Daytrana [product information]. Wayne, Pa.: Shire US Inc; 2006.

18. Olfson M, Gameroff MJ, Marcus SC, Jensen PS. National trends in the treatment of attention deficit hyperactivity disorder. *Am J Psychiatry.* 2003;160:1071–7.

19. Kappagoda C, Schell DN, Hanson RM, Hutchins P. Clonidine overdose in childhood: implications of increased prescribing. *J Paediatr Child Health.* 1998;34:508–12.

20. Cantwell DP, Swanson J, Connor DF. Case study: adverse response to clonidine. *J Am Acad Child Adolesc Psychiatry.* 1997;36:539–44.

21. Wilens TE, Spencer TJ, Swanson JM, Connor DF, Cantwell D. Combining methylphenidate and clonidine: a clinically sound medication option. *J Am Acad Child Adolesc Psychiatry.* 1999;38:614–22.

22. Hazell PL, Stuart JE. A randomized controlled trial of clonidine added to psychostimulant medication for hyperactive and aggressive children. *J Am Acad Child Adolesc Psychiatry.* 2003;42:886–94.

23. Carlson CL, Tamm L, Gaub M. Gender differences in children with ADHD, ODD, and co-occurring ADHD/ODD identified in a school population. *J Am Acad Child Adolesc Psychiatry.* 1997;36:1706–14.

24. Wilens TE, Spencer TJ, Biederman J. A review of the pharmacotherapy of adults with attention-deficit/hyperactivity disorder. *J Atten Disord.* 2002;5:189–202.

25. Stevenson CS, Whitmont S, Bornholt L, et al. A cognitive remediation programme for adults with Attention Deficit Hyperactivity Disorder. *Aust N Z J Psychiatry.* 2002;36:610–6.

26. Safren SA, Otto MW, Sprich S, et al. Cognitive-behavioral therapy for ADHD in medication-treated adults with continued symptoms. *Behav Res Ther.* 2005;43:831–42.

68 Insomnia

Erin L. St. Onge

Objectives

1. List the advantages and disadvantages for current treatments for insomnia.

2. Determine what information the pharmacist needs to obtain from the patient to formulate a drug therapy plan.

3. Explain to a patient the differences among pharmacologic therapies used to treat insomnia.

4. Assist a patient in understanding the medication guide required to be dispensed with hypnotics, and include what information is required and what the patient needs to do with such information.

Scenario

Linda Barnes is a 49-year-old white woman who is a frequent customer of your pharmacy. She comes in today to pick up her refill for lisinopril. In addition to her refill, Mrs. Barnes wants to purchase a bottle of melatonin. She asks if you have a few minutes to answer some questions she has about the use of melatonin.

After speaking with Mrs. Barnes for a few minutes, you learn that she is having trouble falling asleep at night, but she is able to stay asleep once she does fall asleep. She says that this has been going on for about 2 weeks, and her work performance is suffering because of her daytime sleepiness. She is upset by this sudden change and says she has never had trouble falling or staying asleep before. When you ask her about recent stress in her life, she says that she has been under a lot of stress at home. Her husband's father has been ill and recently passed away. Her husband has been too upset to handle the funeral and estate planning, so she is trying to do everything and is having trouble winding down at night to go to sleep.

You step back into the pharmacy to review Mrs. Barnes prescription medication profile (Case Table 68–1) over the past couple months. On talking further with Mrs. Barnes, you determine that her past medical history includes hypertension, hyperlipidemia, perimenopause, and seasonal aller-gies. She says her father died in his seventies of a stroke (father had type 2 diabetes mellitus and hypertension at time of death). Her mother is still alive at 73 years of age and has no significant medical conditions. Mrs. Barnes drinks socially (1–2 drinks/week), but she does not smoke. She also mentions that she is currently taking echinacea for cold symptoms and ibuprofen for headaches. Mrs. Barnes has no known drug allergies.

Questions and Activities

1. List Mrs. Barnes' current potential drug-related problems.

2. What factors may be contributing to Mrs. Barnes complaint of insomnia today?

3. What additional information do you need from Mrs. Barnes to help determine the cause of her insomnia?

After further discussion with Mrs. Barnes, you find out that she did originally think that her insomnia was related to her allergy symptoms, because she was also having quite a few headaches. About 2 weeks ago, she started taking her Claritin-D on a scheduled basis twice a day instead of just occasionally as she was doing in the past.

Mrs. Barnes then mentions that she would like to talk more about the melatonin supplement she has picked out. She looked on the nonprescription aisle for sleep products and just ended up being confused by all the choices. She has heard that melatonin might be helpful, but she would like your advice.

4. What are the advantages, disadvantages, and place in therapy of the following available nonprescription treatments for insomnia?

- Antihistamines
- Valerian
- Melatonin

After talking a little about these agents, Mrs. Barnes is a little disappointed in her nonprescription options for insomnia. She says she picked the melatonin because a friend of hers has been taking Rozerem (ramelteon) for insomnia, and she had heard it was really just an expensive form of melatonin.

CASE Table 68–1 Prescription Medication Profile

Linda Barnes
1234 Main Street
Chicago, IL 60601

Phone: 321-555-5555   **DOB:** 11/12/59   **Insurer:** MERIT health plan

Allergies/Intolerances: NKDA

Rx No.	Drug Name	Directions	Date	R/F	Prescriber	Qty	RPh
637912	Lisinopril 10 mg	1 tablet every day	5/11	3	Smith, A	30	TS
632604	Claritin-D 12 hour	1 tablet twice daily	5/11	1	Taylor, B	60	TS
635276	Hydrochlorothiazide 25 mg	1 tablet every day	5/11	5	Smith, A	30	TS
638429	Premarin 0.625 mg	1 tablet every day	5/11	0	Jackson, R	30	TS
638430	Provera 5 mg	Take as directed	5/11	0	Jackson, R	10	TS
637913	Mevacor 20 mg	1 tablet every day	5/11	1	Smith, A	30	TS
637912	Lisinopril 10 mg	1 tablet every day	4/15	4	Smith, A	30	ML
632604	Claritin-D 12 hour	1 tablet twice daily	4/15	2	Taylor, B	60	ML
635276	Hydrochlorothiazide 25 mg	1 tablet every day	4/15	6	Smith, A	30	ML
638429	Premarin 0.625 mg	1 table every day	4/15	1	Jackson, R	30	ML
638430	Provera 5 mg	Take as directed	4/15	1	Jackson, R	10	ML
637913	Mevacor 20 mg	1 tablet every day	4/15	2	Smith, A	30	ML

5. What can you tell Mrs. Barnes about the difference between ramelteon and melatonin supplementation?

6. What nondrug, nonprescription, or prescription medication recommendations can you make today for Mrs. Barnes?

A few days later, Mrs. Barnes returns to the pharmacy with a prescription and a drug company coupon for a free 7-day supply of Ambien CR (zolpidem) 12.5 mg at bedtime. She asks you to fill the 7-day prescription on the drug company coupon and put the other prescription on hold. She will be back in a week to pick up the prescription if the medication works for her.

7. What are the advantages, disadvantages, and place in therapy of the following prescription medications available for Mrs. Barnes' insomnia?

- Benzodiazepines
- Zolpidem
- Zaleplon
- Eszopiclone
- Ramelteon
- Trazodone
- Chloral hydrate

8. Is Mrs. Barnes' prescription for Ambien CR appropriate for treatment of her insomnia? Explain why or why not.

9. List three insomnia treatments that should be avoided in this patient, and explain why.

10. What monitoring parameters available in the community pharmacy setting can be used to evaluate Mrs. Barnes' new medication regimen, including efficacy and adverse effects?

11. What counseling does Mrs. Barnes need today when she picks up her Ambien CR prescription?

While you are going over her medication, you point out the Ambien CR medication guide. Mrs. Barnes sees this and becomes concerned. She wants to know if it is safe to take these medicines with all these new warnings.

12. How would you counsel Mrs. Barnes on the safety of sleep medications?

13. Why do insomnia medications require a medication guide? What information is included in this medication guide and why?

One week later, Mrs. Barnes returns to the pharmacy. She said that the Ambien CR has worked well, and she is pleased to be getting a good night's sleep for the first time in a while. She has not had any problems with it at all. She would like to get her full Ambien CR prescription filled. When she is paying for the prescription, she is shocked that her co-pay is $50 for a 1-month supply. She says that she just cannot afford this.

14. What other options does Mrs. Barnes have?

15. Mrs. Barnes appreciates your recommendation but is concerned about taking a generic. What is the difference between Ambien CR and available generic insomnia medications? Specifically, how do Ambien CR and Ambien differ? Is this difference likely to be clinically significant for Mrs. Barnes?

16. When you contact Mrs. Barnes' physician to explain the issue and request a change, he says that he prefers to use Ambien CR because it is "safer" for long term use than some other sleep medications. Is this true? How do you respond to this?

Additional Activities

1. You are working in a pharmacy when you get a new prescription for Ambien 10 mg, take 1 to 2 tablets nightly at bedtime, #60, 3 refills. You call the doctor to verify the dose, and he states that he uses this dose all the time and of course that is what he wants. How do you respond to him? What resources would you use to verify this dose? What action would you take? How would you document this action?

2. Three months later, the same patient comes into your pharmacy with a prescription from another doctor for Provigil to be taken during the day. How do you respond? Which physician would you contact? What action would you take? How would you document this action?

3. Go to the herbal and supplement aisle in the pharmacy, and identify any products that make the claim of promoting sleep or a good night's rest. Examine ingredients in these products and determine whether they are appropriate for patients complaining of insomnia.

4. Treatment of insomnia in the elderly revolves around different age-related causes, factors, and treatment options. List three differences in treating insomnia in the elderly compared with non–elderly patients. Identify appropriate patient counseling and ideal pharmacologic agents for treating sleep disorders in elderly patients.

5. Identify and research common medical conditions associated with insomnia such as sleep apnea, restless legs syndrome, depression and anxiety, and others. How do treatment strategies differ in these patients with insomnia?

Information Sources

1. Dopheide JA, Stimmel GL. Sleep disorders. In: Koda-Kimble MA, Young LY, Kradjan WA, et al., eds. *Applied Therapeutics: The Clinical Use of Drugs.* 8th ed. Philadelphia: Lippincott Williams and Wilkins; 2005:77-1–22.

2. Jackson CW, Curtis JL. Sleep disorders. In: DiPiro JT, Talbert RL, Yee GC, et al., eds. *Pharmacotherapy: A Pathophysiologic Approach.* 6th ed. New York: McGraw-Hill; 2005:1321–32.

3. Morin AK, Jarvis CI, Lynch AM. Therapeutic options for sleep-maintenance and sleep-onset insomnia. *Pharmacotherapy.* 2007; 27:89–110.

4. Taylor JR, Vazquez CM, Campbell KM. Pharmacologic management of chronic insomnia. *South Med J.* 2006;99:1373–7.

5. Benca RM. Diagnosis and treatment of chronic insomnia: a review. *Psychiatr Serv.* 2005;56:332–43.

6. Melatonin Drug Monograph. Gold Standard, Inc. Clinical Pharmacology [subscription required]. Available at: http://www.clinical pharmacology.com. Last accessed October 22, 2008.

7. Valerian Drug Monograph. Gold Standard, Inc. Clinical Pharmacology [subscription required]. Available at: http://www.clinical pharmacology.com. Last accessed October 22, 2008.

8. Hadley S, Petry JJ. Valerian. *Am Fam Physician.* 2003;67:1755–8.

9. Nguyen NN, Yu SS, Song JC. Ramelteon: a novel melatonin receptor agonist for the treatment of insomnia. *Formulary.* 2005; 40:146–55.

10. Holm KJ, Goa KL. Zolpidem: an update of its pharmacology, therapeutic efficacy, and tolerability in the treatment of insomnia. *Drugs.* 2000;59:865–89.

11. Weitzel KW, Wickman JM, Augustin SG, et al. Zaleplon: a pyrazolopyrimidine sedative-hypnotic agent for the treatment of insomnia. *Clin Ther.* 2000;22:1254–67.

12. Eszopiclone Drug Monograph. Gold Standard, Inc. Clinical Pharmacology [subscription required]. Available at: http://www.clinical pharmacology.com. Last accessed October 22, 2008.

13. Ambien CR Drug Monograph. Gold Standard, Inc. Clinical Pharmacology [subscription required]. Available at: http://www.clinical pharmacology.com. Last accessed October 22, 2008.

14. FDA requests label change for all sleep disorder drug products. *Pharm Lett Prescrib Lett.* 2007;23:230405.

69 Generalized Anxiety Disorder

Rebecca L. Stovall, Nancy Brahm, and Kimberly M. Crosby

Objectives

1. Compare and contrast the treatment options available for generalized anxiety disorder.

2. Identify potential problems associated with the elderly and selective serotonin reuptake inhibitors.

3. Explain the role of benzodiazepines for the treatment of generalized anxiety disorder.

4. Evaluate prescriptions for correct dosing, correct indication, and overall appropriateness before dispensing.

5. Formulate an appropriate treatment plan and follow-up for a patient experiencing generalized anxiety disorder.

Scenario

You are a staff pharmacist for a rural community pharmacy. One of your routine customers, Arlene Miller, comes in today with two new prescriptions (Case Figures 69–1 and 69–2). She states these prescriptions are for her "nerves," and they are both new medications. She does not know anything about the medications and would like you to explain them to her. Mrs. Miller is a 65-year-old, 59 kg, white woman living by herself since her husband died a few years ago. She refills her medication like clockwork on the 15th of every month, the day that she gets her social security benefits. You are able to move to the counseling area and ask her for a clearer understanding of what problems she is having with her nerves. She tells you feelings of stress and worry have gradually increased since the death of her husband. She now finds that she worries about common problems even before they could happen. When you ask her if she has enough energy to get through the day, she replies not really. She is tired almost all the time, cannot concentrate to make her grocery list, and has even been "snappish" with her grandchildren.

You were able to obtain additional information from the patient and from her prescription medication profile (Case Table 69–1). Her past medical history includes hypertension, gastroesophageal reflux disease, restless legs syndrome, coronary artery disease, anxiety, and allergic rhinitis. She uses the following OTC products: aspirin 325 mg, 1 tablet by mouth once daily; Centrum Silver, 1 tablet by mouth once daily; diphenhydramine 25 mg, 1 tablet by mouth as needed for allergies; and acetaminophen 325 mg, 1 tablet by mouth as needed for pain.

Questions and Activities

1. Describe typical symptoms associated with generalized anxiety disorder (GAD).

2. What are the goals of pharmacotherapy for this patient?

David McNeal, DO
4502 E. 41st St.
Tulsa, OK 47135

Patient: Arlene Miller___ DOB: 3/11/41
Address:_____ Date: 09/25

diazepam 2mg
one tablet po bid prn anxiety
#60

Refill 0 Time
DEA NO: AD1212122

Signature:

CASE Figure 69–1 Prescription #1 for patient Arlene Miller.

David McNeal, DO
4502 E. 41st St.
Tulsa, OK 47135

Patient: Arlene Miller___ DOB: 3/11/41
Address:_____ Date: 09/25

paroxetine 40mg
one tablet po qday ud
#30

Refill 1 Time
DEA NO: AD1212122

Signature:

CASE Figure 69–2 Prescription #2 for patient Arlene Miller.

CASE Table 69–1   Prescription Medication Profile

Arlene Miller
2000 East Sooner Road
Glenpool, OK 74033

Phone: 918-322-5555   **DOB:** 3/11/41   **Insurer:** Humana Medicare Part D (prescription) and Medicare and BCBS (medical)

Allergies/Intolerances: Streptomycin

Rx No.	Drug Name	Directions	Date	Refill	Prescriber	Qty	RPh
602125	Amlodipine 5 mg	1 tablet by mouth every morning	9/15	1	McNeal	30	RS
602124	Benazepril 40 mg	1 tablet by mouth every morning	9/15	1	McNeal	30	RS
602123	Ropinirole 2 mg	1 tablet by mouth at bedtime	9/15	1	Clark	30	RS
602122	Esomeprazole 40 mg	1 capsule by mouth every day	9/15	1	McNeal	30	RS
602121	Clopidogrel 75 mg	1 tablet by mouth every day	9/15	1	McNeal	30	RS
602125	Amlodipine 5 mg	1 tablet by mouth every morning	8/15	2	McNeal	30	RS
602124	Benazepril 40 mg	1 tablet by mouth every morning	8/15	2	McNeal	30	RS
602123	Ropinirole 2 mg	1 tablet by mouth at bedtime	8/15	2	Clark	30	RS
602122	Esomeprazole 40 mg	1 capsule by mouth every day	8/15	2	McNeal	30	RS
602121	Clopidogrel 75 mg	1 tablet by mouth every day	8/15	2	McNeal	30	RS

3. What nonpharmacologic therapies or lifestyle modifications might be useful in managing this patient's problem?

4. Compare and contrast available antidepressants indicated for the treatment of GAD.

5. Describe the role of benzodiazepines in the treatment of anxiety.

6. Identify the drug-related or disease-related problem(s), the intervention(s) to solve the problem(s), and the anticipated outcome(s) for this patient.

7. Develop a medication action plan for the patient; include short-term and long-range goals.

8. You are able to contact Dr. McNeal today, and he agrees to implement your recommendation about Mrs. Miller's SSRI. What are the pertinent topics to address during patient education once her prescriptions are filled?

9. What monitoring parameters available in the community pharmacy setting should be used to evaluate therapy in this patient, including efficacy and adverse effects?

10. Develop a follow-up plan for this patient; include time to follow up and method of contact.

Dr. McNeal has increased Mrs. Miller's diazepam dose over the past few weeks from the original prescription to diazepam 5 mg, *1 tablet three times daily. She says this dose is working for her now, but she does not want to continue to take diazepam indefinitely. She is a little concerned about getting off the medication because she has heard that it can be difficult.*

11. How would you counsel Mrs. Miller on her concerns about discontinuing the medication? What would an appropriate titration schedule of her benzodiazepine be from this dose when she is ready to discontinue her diazepam?

Mrs. Miller comes into your pharmacy to refill her paroxetine approximately 1 month later. She is complaining about taking the new medication and does not think it is really helping her. Her friend told her about an all-natural medication that might work. She asks, "Can I take kava?"

12. How would you counsel Mrs. Miller about taking kava? What counseling points about her current drug therapy would you reinforce?

13. Describe the role of kava in the treatment of anxiety.

Mrs. Miller returns to your pharmacy 6 months later complaining of dizziness, increased anxiety, headaches, and nausea and vomiting for 3 days. After further investigation, you determine she stopped taking her paroxetine because of financial reasons. It is late on a Friday evening, and she cannot contact her physician until Monday morning.

14. Counsel her on the complications of abrupt withdrawal of SSRIs.

15. Recommend an appropriate plan of action.

16. Identify appropriate options for a patient who has failed one SSRI. Include directions for switching to another medication.

Additional Activities

1. Research different available formulations and dosage forms of SSRIs (e.g., generic paroxetine compared with Paxil CR or Pexeva, generic fluoxetine compared with Prozac Weekly or Sarafem, etc.). Are there any advantages to newer dosage forms or formulations? When would you counsel patients to use these?

2. Would you counsel a child or adolescent taking an SSRI for anxiety or depression any differently than you would an adult? Why or why not?

3. Compare and contrast available benzodiazepines with regard to pharmacokinetic properties and efficacy in anxiety treatment. What factors (e.g., efficacy, onset, half-life) influence choosing which benzodiazepine to use as a first-line option in the treatment of anxiety?

4. Compare and contrast presentation and treatment of GAD and panic disorder. How do these conditions differ?

Information Sources

1. American Psychiatric Association. *Diagnostic and Statistical Manual of Mental Disorders: Text Revision*. 4th ed. Washington, DC: American Psychiatric Association; 2000.

2. Lyriad RB. An overview of generalized anxiety disorder: disease state-appropriate therapy. *Clin Ther*. 2000;22(suppl A):13–24.

3. Kirkwood CR, Melton ST. Anxiety disorders I: generalized anxiety, panic and social anxiety disorders. In: DiPiro JT, Talbert RL, Yee GC, et al., eds. *Pharmacotherapy: A Pathophysiologic Approach*. 6th ed. New York: McGraw-Hill; 2005:1285–306.

4. Augustin SG. Anxiety disorders. In: Koda-Kimble MA, Young LY, Kradjan WA, Guglielmo BJ, eds. *Applied Therapeutics: The Clinical Use of Drugs*. 8th ed. Baltimore, Md: Lippincott Williams & Wilkins; 2005:76:1–29.

5. McIntosh A, Cohen A, Turnbull N, et al. Clinical Guidelines for the Management of Anxiety. Management of Anxiety (panic disorder, with or without agoraphobia, and generalized anxiety disorder) in Adults in Primary, Secondary, and Community Care. London: National Institute for Clinical Excellence (NICE); 2004.

6. Fricchione G. Generalized anxiety disorder. *N Engl J Med*. 2004; 351:675–82.

7. Broman-Fulks JJ, Berman ME, Rabain, et al. Effects of aerobic exercise on anxiety sensitivity. *Behav Res Ther*. 2004;42:125–36.

8. Micromedex Healthcare Series [subscription required]. Greenwood Village, Colo: Thomson Micromedex. Available at: http://www.micromedex.com. Last accessed October 21, 2008.

9. Ditto KE. SSRI discontinuation syndrome. Awareness as an approach to prevention. *Postgrad Med*. 2003;114:79–84.

10. McCleod DR, Hoehn-Saric R, Porges SW, et al. Therapeutic effects of imipramine are counteracted by its metabolite, desipramine, in patients with generalized anxiety disorder. *J Clin Psychopharmacol*. 2000;20:615–21.

11. Sala M, Coppa F, Cappucciati C, et al. Antidepressants: their effects on cardiac channels, QT prolongation and torsade de pointes. *Curr Opin Investig Drugs*. 2006;7:256–63.

12. Fick DM, Cooper JW, Beers MH, et al. Updating the Beers Criteria for potentially inappropriate medication use in older adults: results of a US consensus panel of experts. *Arch Intern Med*. 2003;163:2716–24.

13. Baldwin DS, Anderson IM, Nutt DJ, et al. Evidence-based guidelines for the pharmacological treatment of anxiety disorders: recommendations from the British Association for Psychopharmacology. *J Psychopharmacol*. 2005;19:567–96.

14. Paxil [product information]. Research Triangle Park, NC: GlaxoSmithKline; June 2008.

15. Gosselin P, Ladouceur R, Morin CM, et al. Benzodiazepine discontinuation among adults with GAD: a randomized trial of cognitive-behavioral therapy. *J Consult Clin Psychol*. 2006;74:908–19.

16. Singh YN, Singh NN. Therapeutic potential of kava in the treatment of anxiety disorders. *CNS Drugs*. 2002;16:731–43.

17. Hume AL, Strong KM. Botanical medicines In: Berardi RR, Kroon LA, Newton DD, et al., eds. *Handbook of Nonprescription Drugs: An Interactive Approach to Self-care*. 15th ed. Washington, DC: American Pharmacists Association; 2006:1231–75.

70 Depression

Stacey Lauderdale

Objectives

1. Identify the signs and symptoms of a major depressive episode, and describe pharmacotherapeutic options for the treatment of depression.

2. Analyze the cause of an adverse drug reaction, and determine the appropriate intervention to resolve the reaction.

3. Develop a pharmaceutical care plan for a patient with major depression complicated by nonadherence and an adverse reaction.

4. Identify pertinent patient education to discuss with the patient.

Scenario

You are employed as a community pharmacist at Prescriptions for Life, a local independent pharmacy. Your technician approaches you and states that Connie McMaster, a regular patient, wants to consult with you about a medication she has been taking for a couple of weeks. After greeting Mrs. McMaster, you move her to the consultation area for privacy. During the consultation, you find out the following information.

Mrs. McMaster lost her sister to cancer approximately 4 months ago. She states her bereavement over her sister's death started to interfere with her activities of daily living. She described that she started to feel sad and empty almost every day, was fatigued to the point that she was sleeping or in bed 15 to 16 hours a day, stopped going out to dinner and the movies with her husband, and experienced a general loss of appetite with subsequent weight loss. Her doctor prescribed Lexapro after she sought treatment. Mrs. McMaster says she has been taking Lexapro for about 3 weeks without significant improvement in her symptoms. She admits she does not take the medication as regularly as she should, but her insurance does not cover Lexapro, and she cannot afford to spend almost $80 each month on one medication. In addition, she has been experiencing side effects. She says for the past day her heart has felt like it is racing, and she has experienced increased sweating and a tremor. She tells you she contacted her doctor, and he reassured her that these are common side effects of

Lexapro. However, Mrs. McMaster tells you she did not start experiencing the side effects until late yesterday evening, and she has been making an effort to take her Lexapro on a daily basis for the past week.

After further questioning, Mrs. McMaster explains she experienced a migraine yesterday and, in an effort to abort the headache, she took Relpax. She tells you her physician provided her with samples of Relpax to try before he wrote her a prescription. She took the Relpax without incident last week. Yesterday, she took the Relpax in combination with a pain medication her dentist prescribed. She says she has not felt "right" since taking the pain medication. Her pulse today is 120 beats/min. Case Table 70–1 is a printout of Mrs. McMaster's prescription medication profile.

Questions and Activities

1. On the basis of the patient's presentation and drug therapy, identify the drug- or disease-related problem, and state the current drug therapy for the problem.

2. What are the goals of pharmacotherapy for this patient?

3. Identify the treatment alternatives available for the drug therapy problem.

4. Identify the intervention(s) to solve the problem(s) and the anticipated outcome(s).

5. What drug(s), dosage form(s), schedule(s), and duration(s) of therapy are optimal for the treatment of the patient's problem(s)?

6. What intervention (e.g., patient recommendation, call to provider or family member, contact emergency medical services, etc.) is necessary for implementing these treatments?

7. What monitoring parameters available in the community pharmacy setting should be used to evaluate therapy in this patient, including efficacy and adverse effects?

8. What nondrug therapies or lifestyle modifications might be useful in managing this patient's problem?

CASE Table 70–1   Prescription Medication Profile

Connie McMaster
1341 Broadway Street
Birmingham, AL 35229

Phone: 205-919-3488   **DOB:** 09/25/1956   **Insurer:** Blue Cross Blue Shield of Alabama

Allergies/Intolerances: Sulfa

Rx No.	Drug Name	Directions	Date	R/F	Prescriber	Qty	RPh	Co-Pay
613924	Clindamycin 150 mg	1 capsule by mouth four times daily	9/25	0	Edgar	40	PM	$10
613923	Tramadol 50 mg	1 tablet by mouth every 4–6 hours as needed	9/25	1	Edgar	30	PM	$10
612455	Lexapro 10 mg	1 tablet by mouth every day	9/7	12	Ferrar	30	DL	$75.76
610800	Premarin 0.625 mg	1 tablet by mouth every day	7/12	2	Murphy	90	DL	$75
610646	Simvastatin 20 mg	1 tablet by mouth every day	7/03	2	Henderson	90	PM	$30
610645	Lisinopril 20 mg	1 tablet by mouth every day	7/03	2	Henderson	90	PM	$30
610800	Premarin 0.625 mg	1 tablet by mouth every day	4/13	3	Murphy	90	PM	$75
610646	Simvastatin 20 mg	1 tablet by mouth every day	4/02	3	Henderson	90	DL	$30
610645	Lisinopril 20 mg	1 tablet by mouth every day	4/02	3	Henderson	90	DL	$30
610800	Premarin 0.625 mg	1 tablet by mouth every day	1/10	4	Murphy	90	DL	$75
610646	Simvastatin 20 mg	1 tablet by mouth every day	1/05	4	Henderson	90	PM	$30
610645	Lisinopril 20 mg	1 tablet by mouth every day	1/05	4	Henderson	90	PM	$30

9. Develop a medication action plan for the patient; include short-term and long-range goals.

10. What are the pertinent topics to address during patient education?

11. Develop a follow-up plan for this patient; include time to follow up and method of contact.

12. Did the pharmacist have a duty to warn Mrs. McMaster about the potential drug–drug interaction when tramadol was dispensed? Why or why not?

13. After you educate Mrs. McMaster on potential side effects of SSRIs, she wants to know if it would be safer for her to receive St. John's wort for depression because it is a nonprescription product. How would you counsel Mrs. McMaster about the safety and efficacy of natural products for depression treatment compared with prescription products?

14. After hearing your response to her question about St. John's wort, Mrs. McMaster wants to know if any herbal products are safe and effective for the treatment of depression.

15. Mrs. McMaster asks you about the medication guide on suicide that was dispensed with her prescription of Lexapro. She wants to know if the medication guide is relevant to her, and, if not, why she received the medication guide.

16. Mrs. McMaster calls you several months later and reports she went out of town and left her medication at home. Consequently, she missed several doses of her prescribed antidepressant and is now experiencing nausea, insomnia, and dizziness. She is afraid this might mean she is "addicted" to the antidepressant. How would you counsel Mrs. McMaster?

17. During cough and cold season, Mrs. McMaster asks for your advice. She has a nonproductive cough, and her physician recommended purchasing a cough suppressant such as Robitussin DM. However, the label of Robitussin warns "Do not use if you are taking a prescription MAOI (certain drugs for depression, psychiatric, or emotion conditions, or Parkinson's Disease)." Mrs. McMaster wants to know what she should take for her cough because she is taking escitalopram for depression.

18. Mrs. McMaster returns to the pharmacy and tells you her physician is discontinuing her antidepressant. She remembers that you specifically told her not to abruptly stop the medication during her initial consultation. She mentioned this to her physician, and he told her to consult with the pharmacist about how to taper the dose. How should you counsel Mrs. McMaster to taper the dose?

Additional Activities

1. How should depression be treated in pregnancy? Are there any antidepressants that are relatively safe and recommended for use in pregnancy?

2. Which antidepressants are associated with sexual dysfunction? Which are not? List strategies to manage antidepressant-induced sexual dysfunction.

3. A physician calls your pharmacy and needs to switch a patient from Zoloft 100 mg daily to Wellbutrin XL 150 mg daily. How would you counsel the physician to switch this patient? How would this counseling differ if the patient were switching instead to another SSRI? To venlafaxine?

4. Compare and contrast pharmacologic, pharmacokinetic, and clinical differences among SSRIs. What agent would you recommend as a first-line option in this class of medications and why?

5. Review the references below along with any other pertinent sources. Discuss possible roles of the community pharmacist in identification and treatment of patients with depression.

   - Knox ED, Dopheide JA, Wincor MZ, Han PK. Depression screening in a university campus pharmacy: a pilot project. *J Am Pharm Assoc.* 2006;46: 502–6.

   - Rickles NM, Svarstad BL, Statz-Paynter JL, et al. Pharmacist telemonitoring of antidepressant use: effects on pharmacist-patient collaboration. *J Am Pharm Assoc.* 2005;45:344–53.

   - Rickles NM, Svarstad BL, Statz-Paynter JL, et al. Improving patient feedback about and outcomes with antidepressant treatment: a study in eight community pharmacies. *J Am Pharm Assoc.* 2006; 46:25–32.

Information Sources

1. *Diagnostic and Statistical Manual of Mental Disorders.* 4th ed. Washington, DC: American Psychiatric Association; 1994:320–3.

2. US Food and Drug Administration. Information for Healthcare Professionals: Selective Serotonin Reuptake Inhibitors (SSRIs), Selective Serotonin-Norepinephrine Reuptake Inhibitors (SNRIs), 5-Hydroxytryptamine Receptor Agonists (Triptans). Available at: http://www.fda.gov/cder/drug/InfoSheets/HCP/triptansHCP.htm. Last accessed September 19, 2008.

3. *Facts & Comparisons.* St Louis: Wolters Kluwer; 2008.

4. Drugs for psychiatric disorders. *Treat Guidel Med Lett.* 2006;4:35–46.

5. Boyer EW, Shannon M. The serotonin syndrome. *N Engl J Med.* 2005;352:1112–20.

6. Clinical Pharmacology Online [subscription required]. Available at: http://www.clinicalpharmocology.com. Last accessed October 21, 2008.

7. Micromedex Healthcare Series [subscription required]. Available at: http://www.micromedex.com. Last accessed October 21, 2008.

8. Lexapro Web site. Available at: http://www.leapro.com/pdf/lexapro_pi.pdf. Last accessed September 19, 2008.

9. Mahlberg R, Kunz D, Sasse J, et al. Serotonin syndrome with tramadol and citalopram [letter]. *Am J Psychiatry.* 2004;161:1129.

10. Teter CJ, Kando JC, Wells BG, et al. Depressive disorders. In: DiPiro JT, Talbert RL, Yee GC, et al., eds. *Pharmacotherapy: A Pathophysiological Approach.* 6th ed. New York: McGraw-Hill; 2008:1235–55.

11. Mann JJ. The medical management of depression. *N Engl J Med.* 2005;353:1819–34.

12. Karasu TB, Gelenberg A, Merriam A, et al. Practice guideline for the treatment of patients with major depressive disorder. In: *American Psychiatric Association Practice Guidelines for the Treatment of Psychiatric Disorders. Compendium 2004.* 2nd ed. Arlington, Va: American Psychiatric Association; 2004:441–524.

13. Which SSRI? *Med Lett Drugs Ther.* 2003;45:93–5.

14. Wagstaff AJ, Goa KL. Once-weekly fluoxetine. *Drugs.* 2001;61: 2221–8.

15. DeVane CL. Pharmacokinetics, drug interactions, and tolerability of paroxetine and paroxetine CR. *Psychopharmacol Bull.* 2003; 37(suppl 1):29–41.

16. Leo RJ, Barkin RL. Antidepressant use in chronic pain management. Is there evidence of a role for duloxetine? *Prim Care Companion J Clin Psychiatry.* 2003;5:118–23.

17. Sussman N. SNRIs versus SSRIs: mechanisms of action in treating depression and painful physical symptoms. *Prim Care Companion J Clin Psychiatry.* 2003;5(suppl 7):19–26.

18. Fava M, Rush AJ, Thase ME, et al. 15 years of clinical experience with bupropion HCL: from bupropion to bupropion SR to bupropion XL. *Prim Care Companion J Clin Psychiatry.* 2005;7:106–13.

19. Stahl SM. Basic psychopharmacology of antidepressants, part 1: antidepressants have seven distinct mechanisms of action. *J Clin Psychiatry.* 1998;59(suppl 4):5–14.

20. Schwetz BA. Warning on Serzone. *JAMA.* 2002;287:1103.

21. Perry PJ, Alexander B, Liskow BI, et al. *Psychotropic Drug Handbook.* 8th ed. Philadelphia: Lippincott Williams & Wilkins; 2006: 199–210.

22. *Professional's Handbook of Drug Therapy for Pain.* 1st ed. Springhouse, Pa: Springhouse; 2001:515–7.

23. King DS, Herndon KC. Headache disorders. In: DiPiro JT, Talbert RL, Yee GC, et al., eds. *Pharmacotherapy: A Pathophysiological Approach.* 6th ed. New York: McGraw-Hill; 2005:1105–21.

24. Bultman DC, Svarstad BL. Effects of pharmacist monitoring on patient satisfaction with antidepressant therapy. *J Am Pharm Assoc.* 2002;42:36–43.

25. Rickles NM, Svarstad BL, Statz-Paynter JL, et al. Pharmacist telemonitoring of antidepressant use: effects on pharmacist-patient collaboration. *J Am Pharm Assoc.* 2005;45:344–53.

26. Eisendrath SJ, Feldman MD. Psychotherapeutic and behavioral treatments. In: Goldman LS, Wise TN, Brody DS, eds. *Psychiatry for Primary Care Physicians.* 2nd ed. Chicago: American Medical Association Press; 2004:432–4.

27. American Pharmacists Association and National Association of Chain Drug Stores Foundation. Medication therapy management in community pharmacy practice: core elements of an MTM service (version 1.0). *J Am Pharm Assoc.* 2005;45:573–79.

28. Rovers JP. Patient care plan development. In: Rovers JP, Currie JD, Hagel HP, et al., eds. *A Practical Guide to Pharmaceutical Care.* 2nd ed. Washington, DC: American Pharmacists Association; 2003:69–81.

29. National Depressive and Manic-Depressive Association (NDMDA). *Beyond Diagnosis: A Landmark Survey of Patients, Partners and Health Professionals on Depression and Treatment.* New York: Schulman, Ronca & Bucuvalas; 2000.

30. Bull SA, Hu XH, Hunkeler EM, et al. Discontinuation of use and switching of antidepressants: influence of patient-physician communication. *JAMA.* 2002;288:1403–9.

31. Williams KG. Pharmacists' duty to warn of drug interactions. Dooley v. Everett. *Am J Hosp Pharm.* 1992;49:2787–9.

32. Brown, CH. Overview of drug interactions. Part 1. *US Pharm.* 2000;25:HS3, HS7, HS15–6, HS20, HS22, HS24, HS27–8, HS30.

33. Malone DC, Abarca J, Hansten PD, et al. Identification of serious drug-drug interactions: results of the partnership to prevent drug-drug interactions. *J Am Pharm Assoc.* 2004;44:142–51.

34. Fetrow CW, Avila JR. *Professional's Handbook of Complementary & Alternative Medicines.* 3rd ed. Philadelphia: Lippincott Williams & Wilkins; 2004:6–7.

35. Kelly BD. St. John's wort for depression: what's the evidence? *Hosp Med* 2001;62:274–6.

36. Brown RP and Gerberg PL. Herbs and nutrients in the treatment of depression, anxiety, insomnia, migraine and obesity. *J Psychiatr Pract* 2001;7:75–91.

37. Drug products with medication guides. *Pharm Lett Prescrib Lett.* 2006;22:220331.

38. US Food and Drug Administration. Medication guide: about using antidepressants in children and teenagers. Available at: http://www.fda.gov/cder/drug/antidepressants/MG_template.pdf. Last accessed September 19, 2008.

39. Young D. Antidepressant black-box warning should include young adults, panel urges. *Am J Health Syst Pharm.* 2007;64:125–6.

40. Shelton RC. The nature of the discontinuation syndrome associated with antidepressant drugs. *J Clin Psychiatry.* 2006;67(suppl 4):3–7.

41. Haddad PM. Antidepressant discontinuation syndromes. *Drug Saf.* 2001;24:183–97.

42. Fava M, Mulroy R, Alpert J, et al. Emergence of adverse events following discontinuation of treatment with extended-release venlafaxine. *Am J Psychiatry.* 1997;154:1760–2.

43. Rosenbaum JF, Fava M, Hoog SL, et al. Selective serotonin reuptake inhibitor discontinuation syndrome: a randomized clinical trial. *Biol Psychiatry.* 1998;44:77–87.

44. Michelson D, Fava M, Amsterdam J, et al. Interruption of selective serotonin reuptake inhibitor treatment. *Br J Psychiatry.* 2002;176:363–8.

45. Pratter MR. Cough and the common cold: ACCP evidence-based clinical practice guidelines. *Chest.* 2006;129(suppl 1):72S–4S.

46. Schatzberg AF, Blier P, Delgado PL, et al. Antidepressant discontinuation syndrome: consensus panel recommendation for clinical management and additional research. *J Clin Psychiatry.* 2006;67(suppl 4):27–30.

47. Shelton RC. Steps following attainment of remission: discontinuation of antidepressant therapy. *Prim Care Companion J Clin Psychiatry.* 2001;3:168–74.

71 Prescription Drug Abuse: Identifying Risk Factors and Warning Signs

Jennifer M. Strickland

Objectives

1. Identify potential warning signs of prescription drug abuse.

2. Identify risk factors that may increase the incidence and likelihood of prescription drug abuse.

3. Perform a patient assessment of the potential for prescription drug abuse.

4. Distinguish between appropriate medication use for valid symptoms and misuse or abuse of prescription drugs.

Scenario

This morning, the wife of Andrew Brim, a well-known customer, comes to the pharmacy and asks to speak to the pharmacist. She provides the pharmacist with a new prescription (Case Figure 71–1). She says that her husband has been receiving prescriptions for "pain medications" from this pharmacy frequently, but he has asked her to pick up prescriptions from other area pharmacies frequently as well. She says that he does have a history of low back pain, but she is concerned about his use of pain medications and feels he may be endangering his own safety. She has found him "unresponsive" multiple times after he takes his pain medication. She also reports that she often sees him take 4 to 6 tablets at a time instead of the 1 to 2 that are prescribed, and she has also seen him crush and snort at least one of the medications he has received in the past.

She reports that he recently was seen by a well-respected pain management physician in the area, Dr. Jones. He gave the patient prescriptions for non-narcotic medications, but Mr. Brim refused to have them filled. His wife tells you that she has tried to talk to her husband about his use of opioids, but he becomes agitated and upset. You are able to review Mr. Brim's prescription medication profile (Case Table 71–1) for more information.

On the basis of the conversation with Mr. Brim's wife and your review of his medication refill history, you ask her if she can request that her husband come in to talk with you and to pick up his prescription.

When Mr. Brim arrives, you ask him if you can speak to him briefly about his medication today and do a pain assessment. He appears anxious and hurried but agrees to speak to you briefly. During your interview, he does report "mild" pain in his low back and states "nothing works except the 'narcs'." He rates his pain as 7 on a scale of 0 to 10 and states that it feels like a "spasm." He reports that he is reluctant to use any other type of medication because he knows the "narcs work." In reviewing his social history, you discover that Mr. Brim has a history of alcohol abuse and a longstanding past history of drug abuse, including heroin and marijuana. He states that he "went through rehab a couple of times and he doesn't need that program anymore." He denies using any other pharmacy for medications and states he uses different physicians because "one physician won't give me the number of tablets I need."

Questions and Activities

1. On the basis of the patient's drug therapy and the interview, identify the medical problem.

2. What risk factors for prescription drug abuse and addiction can you identify in this case?

Patient Name: <u>Andrew Brim</u>   Date: <u>12/10</u>

Address: <u>1100 E 98th Street, Tampa, FL</u>

Allergies: <u>NKDA</u>

    Vicodin 5/500

    #60 tablets

    1-2 tabs po Q 6 hrs prn

refills: 1
Prescribing Physician:

CASE Figure 71–1 Prescription for patient Andrew Brim.

CASE Table 71–1 Prescription Medication Profile

Andrew Brim
5789 Flamingo Way
Lakeland, FL 33813

Phone: 863-555-0989   **DOB:** 3/5/1953   **Insurer:** United Healthcare

Allergies/Intolerances: NKDA

Rx No.	Drug Name	Date	Directions	R/F	Prescriber	QTY	RPh
462554	Hydrocodone/APAP 5/500	9/12	Take 1–2 tablets every 4 to 6 hours as needed for pain	1	Smith	60	JA
462778	Hydrocodone/APAP 7.5/750	9/18	Take 1 tablet three times daily as needed for pain	0	Payne	90	ST
462554	Hydrocodone/APAP 5/500	10/1	Take 1 to 2 tablets every 4 to 6 hours as needed for pain	0	Smith	60	JA
241133	Oxycodone/APAP 5/325	10/12	Take 1 tablet as directed as needed for pain	0	Rutten	45	MM
463225	Hydrocodone/APAP 10/325	10/28	Take 1 tablet three times daily as needed for pain	0	Payne	90	ST
646887	Ibuprofen 800 mg	11/1	Take 1 tablet three times daily with food	0	Payne	90	JA
251125	Morphine ER 30 mg	11/18	Take 1 tablet every day to every 12 hours for pain	0	Rutten	90	MM
453445	Hydrocodone/APAP 10/325	11/22	Take 1 tablet four times daily as needed for pain	0	Smith	120	LA
255789	Oxycodone/APAP 5/325	11/28	Take 1 tablet as directed as needed for pain	0	Deal	90	ST

3. Identify the drug-related or disease-related problem(s) and the intervention(s) that may be effective in treating the problem(s). Consider both nonpharmacologic and pharmacologic interventions.

4. What are the goals of treatment for this patient?

5. What changes would you suggest in his current drug therapy?

6. What nonopioid medications may be beneficial in treating Mr. Brim's low back pain? List drug(s), dosage form(s), schedule(s), and duration(s) of therapy.

7. What intervention (e.g., patient recommendation, call to provider or family member, contact emergency medical services, etc.) is necessary for implementing your treatment plan today?

8. What monitoring parameters available in the community pharmacy setting should be used to evaluate the interventions in this patient, including monitoring aberrant behaviors?

9. What are the pertinent topics to address during patient education? Other than the patient, whom else would you want to provide with education?

10. What are the pertinent topics to address during discussions with Mr. Brim's prescribing physician(s)?

11. Develop a follow-up plan for this patient; include time to follow up and method of contact.

Additional Activities

1. Talk with an experienced community pharmacist about prescription drug abuse issues in the community pharmacy setting. On the basis of professional experience, ask him or her to list drugs that are most frequently associated with abuse. Also, inquire about specific instances in which the pharmacist has been involved in his or her career and about practical tips learned over the years.

2. Contact your county or local prescription narcotics officer (usually in the local police or sheriff's department). Talk with the officer about his or her experience and about advice for community pharmacists in preventing prescription drug abuse.

3. Contact your state's board of pharmacy to determine when and whether it is appropriate to refuse to fill a prescription in your state because of concern about pre-

scription abuse or diversion. What factors influence this decision? What is the pharmacist's role and responsibility in determining the legitimacy of a prescription? Is it ever acceptable to refuse to fill a prescription and refuse to return that prescription to the patient?

Information Sources

1. Gourlay DL, Heit HA, Almahrezi A. Universal precautions in pain medicine: a rational approach to the treatment of chronic pain. *Pain Med*. 2005;6:107–12.

2. Isaacson JH, Hopper JA, Alford DP, et al. Prescription drug use and abuse. Risk factors, red flags, and prevention strategies. *Postgrad Med*. 2005;118:19–26.

3. Katz NP, Adams EH, Bennevan JC, et al. Foundations of opioid risk management. *Clin J Pain*. 2007;23:103–18.

4. Lafferty L, Hunter TS, Marsh WA. Knowledge, attitudes and practices of pharmacists concerning prescription drug abuse. *J Psychoactive Drugs*. 2006;38:229–32.

5. Michna E, Ross EL, Hynes WL, et al. Predicting aberrant drug behavior in patients treated for chronic pain: importance of abuse history. *J Pain Symptom Manage*. 2004;28:250–8.

6. Passik SD, Kirsh KL. Managing pain in patients with aberrant drug-taking behaviors. *J Support Oncol*. 2005;3:83–6.

7. Webster LR, Webster RM. Predicting aberrant behaviors in opioid-treated patients: preliminary validation of the Opioid Risk Tool. *Pain Med*. 2005;6:432–42.

8. Maizels M, McCarberg B. Antidepressants and antiepileptic drugs for chronic non-cancer pain. *Am Fam Physician*. 2005;71:483–90.

9. Martell BA, O'Connor PG, Kerns RD, et al. Systematic review: opioid treatment for chronic back pain: prevalence, efficacy, and association with addiction. *Ann Intern Med*. 2007;146:116–27.

10. Weaver M, Schnoll S. Abuse liability in opioid therapy for pain treatment in patients with an addiction history. *Clin J Pain*. 2002;18(4 suppl):S61–9.

11. Woolf CJ, Hashmi M. Use and abuse of opioid analgesics: potential methods to prevent and deter non-medical consumption of prescription opioids. *Curr Opin Investig Drugs*. 2004;5:61–6.

Objectives

1. Identify drug-related problems associated with antipsychotic use.

2. Discuss treatment interventions for antipsychotic adverse effects.

3. Compare and contrast available agents for the treatment of schizophrenia.

4. Develop a monitoring plan for a patient started on clozapine.

5. Evaluate potential misfills and drug interactions associated with antipsychotic use.

Please note the purpose of this case is not to diagnose schizophrenia but rather to identify issues surrounding the use of antipsychotics, common side effects, and monitoring parameters, as well as to help prevent medication errors and drug interactions. For the purpose of this case, the term *first-generation antipsychotic* refers to the older, conventional, typical antipsychotics (e.g., chlorpromazine, haloperidol, trifluoperazine), and the term *second-generation antipsychotic* refers to the atypical antipsychotics (e.g., risperidone, olanzapine).

Scenario

You work at the community pharmacy that fills the prescriptions for Sunrise Adult Home, which serves mental health patients in the area. Jason Beckenheimer's sister calls you today about her brother's new prescription Sinemet (carbidopa/levodopa), which he has been taking for about 1 week. He was recently prescribed the Sinemet after seeing a neurologist for new-onset tremor symptoms and a change in his gait (stooped and shuffling with no arm swing). She is concerned because he has a history of schizophrenia and, since starting the new medicine, his hallucinations (both auditory and visual) have become markedly worse. Before the new medicine she states his schizophrenia was fairly stable, he denied hearing any voices, and he was mildly paranoid. She also tells you she is concerned that he smokes 2 packs of cigarettes per day and drinks from 5 to 7 cans of Coke per day.

The patient's sister has power of attorney for his medical care, and you have this documented on file along with his HIPAA release, so you can discuss his medications with her. You pull up his prescription medication profile before discussing his history further with his sister (Case Table 72–1).

You first inquire about the break in his prescriptions between May and August, and again between August and October. You learn that he was originally hospitalized in July at the local acute psychiatric hospital, after refusing to take his medications because he felt "fat." It appears they changed him to ziprasidone at that time, but he remained not at baseline and was rehospitalized in October. Jason's sister informs you that many medication changes were made during that time, that he has lost some weight, and that his diabetes has actually improved; however, he displayed the tremor and other symptoms that sent him to the neurologist recently.

Questions and Activities

1. On the basis of the patient's drug therapy, identify the most recent drug-related problem(s) and the current drug therapy being used to solve the problem(s).

2. Review the patient's past medication history, and identify other current and past possible drug-related problem(s), the medications that are being used to treat these issues, and what interventions you suggest.

Once you have reviewed Jason's profile and talked to his sister, you begin to see what the problems might be. To address these problems, you first start by explaining to Jason's sister the difference between Parkinson's disease and parkinsonian symptoms associated with antipsychotic use.

3. What other extrapyramidal symptoms (EPS) and potential treatments for these symptoms are important for the patient's sister to know about?

4. What are the ideal goals of pharmacotherapy for this patient?

On further discussion with Jason's sister, she confirms that he has tried trifluoperazine, olanzapine, ziprasidone, and haloperidol in the past. She is interested in knowing what other alternatives there are in light of his recent problems. She explains that Jason either did not tolerate, or did not respond, to any of the agents he has tried so far.

CASE Table 72–1   Prescription Medication Profile

Jason Beckenheimer
Sunrise Adult Home
Norfolk, VA 23508

Phone: 757-655-5555   **DOB**: 11/23/66   **Insurer**: Sentara

Allergies/Intolerances: Haldol (reaction unknown)

Rx No.	Drug Name	Directions	Date	RF	Prescriber	Qty	RPh
698692	Sinemet 50/100	1 tablet three times daily	11/21	2	Johnson	90	AMB
498621	Clonazepam 0.5 mg	1 tablet nightly at bedtime	10/28	5	Ali	30	TLL
698620	Trihexyphenidyl 2 mg	1 tablet twice daily	10/28	6	Ali	60	TLL
698619	Trifluoperazine 2 mg	1 tablet twice daily	10/28	6	Ali	60	TLL
698512	Glipizide 5 mg	1 tablet twice daily	8/31	10	Maddex	60	TLL
697205	Geodon 80 mg	1 tablet twice daily with food	8/31	5	Patel	60	TLL
696895	Geodon 40 mg	1 tablet twice daily with food	8/14	3	Patel	60	JKT
698512	Glipizide 5 mg	1 tablet twice daily	5/29	11	Maddex	60	TLL
698504	Zyprexa 20 mg	2 tablets nightly at bedtime	5/29	2	Patel	60	TLL
698502	Zyrtec 10 mg	1 tablet at bedtime for allergies	5/29	2	Maddex	30	TLL
698500	Zyprexa 10 mg	1 tablet at bedtime	4/28	5	Patel	30	JKT
698512	Glipizide 5 mg	1 tablet twice daily	4/25	12	Maddex	60	TLL
698511	Metformin 500 mg	1 tablet twice daily	4/25	12	Maddex	60	TLL
6985110	Pravachol 40 mg	1 tablet at bedtime	4/25	12	Maddex	30	TLL

5. In light of the patient's history and the EPS, what treatment alternatives to trifluoperazine are available to treat his schizophrenia? Compare the risks and benefits (or pros and cons) of each therapy alternative.

6. The patient's sister is also concerned about weight gain and its resulting effects on cardiovascular risk factors with any drug change. What manifestations of schizophrenia may contribute to the development of metabolic syndrome?

7. What is your recommendation for the patient's sister today to address his drug-related complaints?

His sister calls you back a week later and states that Jason has been taken off the Sinemet, trihexyphenidyl, and trifluoperazine; his psychiatrist wants to start him on clozapine. She expresses her concern with any medication changes in light of the problems Jason has recently had.

8. Is a switch to clozapine appropriate for the patient?

9. What laboratory monitoring is required to dispense clozapine initially and throughout treatment?

10. With regard to the sister's concerns about the patient's weight gain and cardiovascular risk, what metabolic monitoring parameters do you suggest she discuss with his physician?

11. What other side effects of clozapine would you counsel the patient's sister about? What specific receptor is associated with each of these effects?

12. Before dispensing the first prescription of clozapine, what process must the pharmacist complete?

13. Two months after the patient starts clozapine, his sister calls and says he is doing better, but he has been drooling. He has never done this before with a medication. What do you tell her?

About a month later, you are checking a refill of Jason's clozapine prescription. You notice that there seem to be more pills in the bottle than you would expect. You look at the original prescription and see that the technician entering the prescription has mistakenly read it as "clozapine 750 mg at bedtime" instead of "clozapine 150 mg at bedtime." You quickly correct this error and talk to your staff to clarify its cause.

14. What specific concerns would you have if the patient had received this higher dose (clozapine 750 mg at bedtime, instead of clozapine 150 mg at bedtime)?

15. Six weeks later, the patient's adult home calls you late Friday afternoon to request a 7-day supply of his clozapine at 200 mg per day. When refilling the prescription, you notice that the patient has not had his clozapine filled in 21 days. What is your concern about filling the prescription at this time?

The nurse also informs you that Jason has been in the hospital for 2 weeks for an acute depressive episode. Once you have clarified that, though, you realize you do not have any recent blood work on Jason. The nurse from the adult home says his blood work was drawn this morning but is not back from the laboratory yet. He is going to be out of clozapine tomorrow night, so he needs it filled today because the laboratory is not open over the weekend.

16. Is it acceptable to fill the patient's clozapine prescription without his blood work in this situation?

The nurse also tells you that while he was in the hospital, Jason was started on a serotonin reuptake inhibitor antidepressant in combination with his clozapine.

17. Which two antidepressants would you recommend avoiding and why?

18. What would be optimal choices for the treatment of the patient's depression?

19. Two weeks later, the Sunrise Adult Home faxes the patient's blood work on a Friday and requests a refill. You go to the shelf and realize you are out of the generic that you normally fill for the patient. What steps do you take from here? What concerns do you have if you have to order generic and cannot get it until Monday?

Jason's sister returns a few months later and says she is relieved that he is finally doing well on his new medication. Now that he is more stable, she would also like to address her concerns about his smoking and caffeine intake.

20. What nonpharmacologic interventions would you suggest for the patient? How would these affect his drug therapy?

21. On the basis of a review of the patient's prescription medication profile, what potential look-alike sound-alike medication errors could have been made?

One month later, the nurse at the adult home calls for a new prescription for Jason. She requests Levaquin 250 mg daily for urinary tract infection for 10 days with no refills.

22. What potential problem is there with Levaquin?

23. What alternative(s) could you suggest to avoid these problems?

Jason's sister returns about a week later. While you are talking with her about Jason, she says she would like to get more information about schizophrenia.

24. What Internet or other resources can you recommend for information about schizophrenia?

Information Sources

1. Weiden PF. EPS profiles: the atypical antipsychotics are not all the same. *J Psychiatr Pract.* 2007;13:13–24.

2. Sadock BJ, Sadock VA. *Kaplan & Sadock's Pocket Handbook of Clinical Psychiatry.* 4th ed. Philadelphia: Lippincott Williams & Wilkins; 2005:462–9.

3. Crismon ML, Buckley PF. Schizophrenia. In: DiPiro JT, Talbert RL, Yee GC, et al., eds. *Pharmacotherapy: A Pathophysiologic Approach.* 6th ed. New York: McGraw-Hill; 2005:1209–33.

4. Nasrallah HA, Smeltzer DJ. *Contemporary Diagnosis and Management of the Patient with Schizophrenia.* Newtown, Pa: Handbooks in Healthcare; 2002.

5. Micromedex Healthcare Series. Vol 132 [subscription required]. Greenwood Village, Colo: Thomson Micromedex; eEdition expires June 2007.

6. Zyprexa [product information]. Indianapolis, Ind: Eli Lilly and Company; 2006.

7. Consensus Development Conference on Antipsychotic Drugs and Obesity and Diabetes. *J Clin Psychiatry.* 2004;65:267–72.

8. Newcomer JW, Haupt DW. The metabolic effects of antipsychotic medications. *Can J Psychiatry.* 2006;51:480–91.

9. Miller AL, Hall CS, Crismon ML, Chiles JA. TIMA Procedural Manual: Schizophrenia Module. January 2003. Available at: http://www.dhs.state.mn.us/main/idcplg?IdcService=GET_FILE&RevisionSelectionMethod=LatestReleased&Rendition=Primary&allowInterrupt=1&noSaveAs=1&dDocName=dhs_id_029346 Last accessed October 25, 2008.

10. National Institutes of Mental Health. Available at: http://www.nimh.nih.gov. Last accessed October 25, 2008.

11. Invega [product information]. Titusville, NJ: Janssen LP; 2007.

12. Abilify [product information]. Princeton, NJ: Bristol-Myers Squibb; 2006.

13. Clozaril [product information]. East Hanover, NJ: Novartis Pharmaceuticals; 2005.

14. Lehman AF, Lieberman JA, Dixon LB, et al. Practice Guideline for the Treatment of Patients with Schizophrenia, 2nd edition. *Am J Psychiatry.* 2004;161(suppl 2):1–56.

15. Novartis Clozaril Administration Registry Enrollment (CARE). Available at: http://www.clozarilcare.com. Last accessed October 25, 2008.

16. Miller DD. Review and management of clozapine side effects. *J Clin Psychiatry.* 2000;61(suppl 8):14–7.

17. Henderson DC. Schizophrenia and comorbid metabolic disorders. *J Clin Psychiatry.* 2005;66(suppl 6):11–20.

18. Praharaj SK, Arora M, Gandotra S. Clozapine-induced sialorrhea: pathophysiology and management strategies. *Psychopharmacology* (Berl) 2006;185:265–73.

19. Freudenreich O, Beebe M, Goff DC. Clozapine-induced sialorrhea treated with sublingual ipratropium spray: a case series. *J Clin Psychopharmacol.* 2004;24:98–100.

20. Sharma A, Ramaswamy S, Dahl E, et al. Intraoral application of atropine sulfate ophthalmic solution for clozapine-induced sialorrhea. *Ann Pharmacother.* 2004;38:1538.

21. Novartis. Frequently asked questions for health care professionals. Available at: http://www.clozaril.com/hcp/treating/faqs.jsp. Last accessed October 25, 2008.

22. DeLeon J, Armstrong SC, Cozza KL. Med-psych drug-drug interactions update: the dosing of atypical antipsychotics. *Psychosomatics.* 2005;46:262–73.

23. Bess AL, Cunningham SR. Novartis Pharmaceuticals Corporation. Dear Health Care Provider letter. Available at: http://www.fda.gov/medwatch/safety/2006/Clozaril_chart_letter_final12-2005.pdf. Last accessed October 25, 2008.

24. ISMP's List of Confused Drug Names. Institute for Safe Medication Practices. Available at: http://www.ismp.org/Tools/confuseddrugnames.pdf. Last accessed October 25, 2008.

25. Stollberger C, Huber JO, Finsterer J. Antipsychotic drugs and QT prolongation. *Int Clin Psychopharmacol.* 2005;20:243–51.

26. Titier K, Girodet PO, Verdoux H, et al. Atypical antipsychotics from potassium channels to torsade de pointes and sudden death. *Drug Saf.* 2005;28:35–51.

Renal and Genitourinary Disorders

73 Urinary Incontinence

Lakesha M. Butler

Objectives

1. Recognize and identify symptoms associated with overactive bladder syndrome.

2. Distinguish between the different types of urinary incontinence; include appropriate treatment options.

3. Identify the drug/disease-related problems and interventions to solve the problems.

4. Differentiate between the types of absorbent products and when they should be recommended for patients.

5. Discuss preventive measures for urinary incontinence, including nonpharmacologic and pharmacologic.

6. Develop an appropriate treatment plan for management of urinary incontinence.

Scenario

Lucy Williams, a 72-year-old white female well-known to your community pharmacy, presents with a new prescription (Case Figure 73–1). You know Mrs. Williams well because of her extensive past medical history, which includes atrial fibrillation, chronic obstructive pulmonary disease, type 2 diabetes, hypertension, and hyperlipidemia. When she presents the new prescription (Case Figure 73–1), she reports that her doctor says she has an overactive bladder. "I have been having a lot of 'accidents' lately because I can't get to the bathroom quick enough to urinate. When I have to go, I have to go right then and there. I also can't get enough sleep at night because I get up to go to the bathroom three to four times a night. I hope this medicine works because I have stopped walking in my neighborhood for exercise, and I have not been to church in 2 weeks because I am scared I may have an accident. I really hope this medicine helps." Mrs. Williams also requests assistance with choosing an absorbent product for daily and nightly use.

Mrs. Williams' patient profile is shown in Case Table 73–1.

Questions and Activities

1. On the basis of the patient's subjective information and drug therapy provided, identify and discuss any potential medication-related problem(s) with current and/or new medication(s).

2. Identify the intervention(s) needed to solve the current medical problem(s) and the anticipated outcome(s).

3. What drug(s), strength, and dosage form are most appropriate for the initial treatment of the patient's medical problem?

4. What medication(s) or social issues, if any, could be causing or exacerbating the patient's current medical problem?

5. What nondrug therapies or lifestyle modifications may be useful in the management of this patient's condition?

6. What types of absorbent products are available? When should they be recommended for patients?

7. What factors are important to consider when selecting an absorbent product?

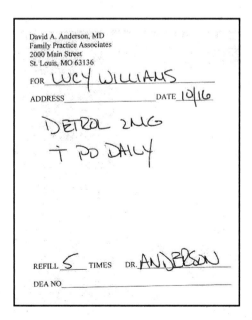

David A. Anderson, MD
Family Practice Associates
2000 Main Street
St. Louis, MO 63136

FOR LUCY WILLIAMS

ADDRESS_____ DATE 10/16

DETROL 2MG

+ PO DAILY

REFILL 5 TIMES DR. ANDERSON

DEA NO._____

CASE Figure 73–1 Prescription for patient Lucy Williams.

CASE Table 73–1   Prescription Medication Profile

Lucy Williams
123 Cobble Road
St. Louis, Missouri 63136

Phone: 314-555-2323   **DOB:** 2-17-1934   **Insurer:** Medicare Part B, D

Allergies/Intolerances: PCN, codeine

Nonprescription/Herbal Products: Calcium 500 mg 1 tablet by mouth two to three times daily; Centrum Silver multivitamin 1 tablet by mouth every day; Tylenol Arthritis as needed for pain

SH: Married, lives with husband; retired school teacher. Alcohol: 1 glass of red wine daily, beer occasionally. Tobacco: quit 8 years ago, used to smoke 1 ppd × 40 years

Rx No.	Drug Name	Directions	Date	R/F	Prescriber	QTY	RPh
614311	Metoprolol tartrate 50 mg	1 tablet by mouth twice daily	9/2	4	Anderson	60	NK
614310	Hydrochlorothiazide 25 mg	1 tablet by mouth every day	9/2	4	Anderson	30	NK
614309	Warfarin 2 mg	Take as directed	9/2	4	Bergman	45	NK
611987	Lisinopril 40 mg	1 tablet by mouth every day	9/2	4	Anderson	30	NK
611986	Simvastatin 40 mg	1 tablet by mouth at bedtime	9/2	4	Anderson	30	NK
611944	Spiriva inhaler	Inhale 1 puff daily	9/2	5	Johnson	1	NK
611943	Novolin	Inject 20 units in the morning and 10 units every evening	9/2	2	Anderson	10	NK
609876	Albuterol inhaler	Take as needed	7/3	5	Johnson	1	HT

8. Is there additional information you might need from this patient to make a recommendation for an absorbent product?

9. On the basis of this patient's signs and symptoms, what type of absorbent product would you recommend and why?

10. What complications may be expected from the use of absorbent products?

11. What should you recommend to prevent complications from the use of absorbent products and why?

12. What are the pertinent topics regarding the patient's new medication therapy to address during patient education?

13. What are the different types of urinary incontinence and recommended treatment options?

14. Discuss ways to assess the patient's adherence to medication therapy and the interventions you can make to increase adherence.

15. Develop a follow-up plan for this patient; include time to follow up and method of contact.

The patient returns to your pharmacy in 2 weeks to pick up refills on her other medications. You ask the patient how her new medication and absorbent product is working for her. She says that one of her bridge partners told her about an herbal tea that contains horsetail, which can help with her "leaking" problem. She would prefer to use the tea instead of taking the prescribed medication. She says, "I really don't want to take another pill if I don't have to."

16. Discuss alternative herbal treatments indicated for urinary incontinence with the patient. Make recommendations regarding use of the herb horsetail.

Additional Activities

1. Research the types of incontinence products available for males.

2. Compare and contrast the pharmacologic treatments available for females and males, including the mechanism of action, dosage, drug interactions, and adverse effects.

3. Develop a plan-o-gram for urinary incontinence products for the pharmacy.

Information Sources

1. Casaburi R, Mahler DA, Jones PW, et al. A long-term evaluation of once-daily inhaled tiotropium in chronic obstructive pulmonary disease. *Eur Respir J.* 2002;19:217–34.

2. Ansell J, Hirsh J, Poller L, et al. The pharmacology and management of the vitamin K antagonists: The Seventh ACCP Conference on Antithrombotic and Thrombolytic Therapy. *Chest.* 2004;126:204S–331S.

3. Hodgson SF, Watts NB. American Association of Clinical Endocrinologists Osteoporosis Guidelines. *Endocr Pract.* 2003;9(6):544–64.

4. National Institutes of Health, National Heart, Lung, and Blood Institute. National Asthma Education and Prevention Program. Expert panel report: guidelines for the diagnosis and management of asthma update on selected topics 2002. *J Allergy Clin* Immunol. 2002;110:S142–219.

5. Rovnew ES, Wyman J, Lackner T, et al. Urinary incontinence. In: Dipiro JT, Talbert RL, Yee GC, et al., eds. *Pharmacotherapy: A Pathophysiologic Approach.* 6th ed. New York: McGraw-Hill; 2005:1547–63.

6. Sullivan J, Abrams P. Pharmacological management of incontinence. *Eur Urol.* 1999;36(suppl 1):89–95.

7. Hampel C, Weinhold D, Benken N, et al. Definition of overactive bladder and epidemiology of urinary incontinence. *Urology.* 1997;50(suppl 6A):4–14.

8. O'Neil CK. Adult urinary incontinence and supplies. In: Berardi RR, Kroon LA, McDermott JH, eds. *Handbook of Nonprescription Drugs: An Interactive Approach to Self-Care.* 15th ed. Washington, DC: American Pharmacists Association; 2006:1077–91.

9. Brown JS, Nyberg LM, Kusek JW, et al. Proceedings of the National Institute of Diabetes, Digestive and Kidney Diseases International Symposium on Epidemiologic Issues in Urinary Incontinence in Women. *Am J Obstet Gynecol.* 2003;188:S77–S88.

10. Van Kerrebroeck P, Kreder K, Jonas U, et al.; Tolterodine Study Group. Tolterodine once-daily: superior efficacy and tolerability in the treatment of overactive bladder. *Urology.* 2001;57:414–21.

11. Anderson KE. The overactive bladder: pharmacologic basis of drug treatment. *Urology.* 1997;50(suppl 6A):74–84.

12. Dvorkin L, Song KY. Herbs for benign prostatic hyperplasia. *Ann Pharmacother.* 2002;36:1443–52.

Section

Dermatologic
Disorders

18

74 Acne

Andrea DiFalco and Jean-Venable "Kelly" R. Goode

Objectives

1. Identify the stages of acne severity and the treatments recommended for each stage.

2. Classify the prescription and nonprescription medications available for the treatment of acne vulgaris.

3. Describe the specific lifestyle modifications one can make for the management of acne vulgaris.

4. Develop a medication action plan for a patient given patient symptoms, and state short- and long-term goals of treatment.

5. Describe the pathogenesis of acne vulgaris.

6. Discuss the iPLEDGE program and the steps a pharmacist must take before dispensing oral isotretinoin.

Scenario

While working one Saturday morning at your pharmacy you notice Tina Jones, a young girl, browsing the skin care aisle. When you ask Ms. Jones if she would like help finding a particular product, you notice her skin. Her face looks very oily, and she has a breakout of whiteheads and blackheads across her forehead and chin. She also has red, raised inflammatory papules and pimples dispersed throughout her face. The total number of inflammatory and noninflammatory lesions appears to be about 25 to 30. She tells you that she is looking for a face wash or soap to help "clear up her face." She then shows you two prescriptions from her dermatologist, who told her to use the medications to wash her face twice a day (Case Figure 74–1).

Her medication profile is shown in Case Table 74–1.

CASE Figure 74–1 Prescriptions for patient Tina Jones.

CASE Table 74–1   Prescription Medication Profile

Tina Jones
100 Sunshine Drive
Richmond, VA 23222

Phone: 804-777-1111   **DOB:** 4/11/1990   **Insurer:** Anthem

Allergies/Intolerances: NKDA

Rx No.	Drug Name	Directions	Date	R/F	Prescriber	Qty	RPh
23456	Zithromax Z-Pak	Take as directed	11/4	0	Smith	6	AD

Questions and Activities

1. What other information would you like to know about the patient before recommending treatment?

2. Describe the pathogenesis of acne.

3. On the basis of the description and treatment, would the patient's' acne be classified as mild, moderate, moderate-to-severe, or severe? Explain the basis for your answer.

4. What are the criteria for exclusions for self-treatment of acne? Can the patient self-treat her acne?

5. What medications are prescribed for the patient and what are the directions for use? What medications will you dispense? Will you be dispensing brand or generic medication?

6. Is there a specific first-line treatment for this type of acne? Are the patient's treatment choices appropriate? Why or why not?

7. What are the patient's treatment goals?

8. What face wash product would you recommend to the patient?

9. What are some alternatives that could have been used to treat the patient's acne?

10. The prescribing physician did not indicate whether he wanted tretinoin gel or cream. Which would you recommend and why?

11. How would you counsel the patient on her prescribed medications and educate her on this condition? Give specific instructions and cautions.

12. What advice would you give the patient regarding lifestyle modifications to help treat her acne?

Ms. Jones presents to your pharmacy again in 8 weeks and her mother is with her. Her acne looks only slightly improved. She has just come from the dermatologist and has a new prescription: Ortho Tri-Cyclen. She would also like a refill on tretinoin and BenzaClin. The patient's mother comes to the pharmacy counter looking very concerned and says that she does not understand why her daughter was given birth control pills to treat her acne.

13. What would you tell the patient's mother regarding the use of oral contraceptives in the treatment of acne?

14. What would you counsel the patient about with regard to the oral contraceptives?

15. Develop a follow-up plan for this patient; include time to follow-up from the start of her acne therapy and method of contact.

16. What would be the next step if the patient's acne were still unresolved following an appropriate time course of treatment with the oral contraceptive?

17. If the patient's acne were to progress to a severe recalcitrant nodular form of acne, an alternative treatment would be isotretinoin (Accutane). What are the indications for use of oral isotretinoin? Discuss with the patient the iPledge system and the steps that would need to be taken to provide this medication.

Additional Activities

1. Research which medications might contribute to or cause acne.

2. Investigate how your treatment recommendations would change if Tina were a 40-year-old female with adult acne.

3. Develop a patient education handout for proper skin care.

4. Create a plan-o-gram in a community pharmacy for skin care products and acne treatment.

Information Sources

1. Foster KT Coffey CW. Acne. In: Berardi RR, Kroon LA, McDermott JH, et al., eds. *Handbook of Nonprescription Drugs: An Interactive Approach to Self-Care*. 15th ed. Washington, DC: American Pharmacists Association; 2006:803–16.

2. Institute for Clinical Systems Improvement (ICSI). Acne management. Bloomington, Minn: Institute for Clinical Systems Improvement (ICSI); May 2006:1–33.

3. Liao DC. Management of acne. *J Fam Pract*. 2003;52:43–51.

4. James WD. Acne. *N Engl J Med*. 2005;352:1463–72.

5. Cunliffe WJ, Meynadier J, Alirezai M, et al. Is combined oral and topical therapy better than oral therapy alone in patients with moderate to moderately severe acne vulgaris? A comparison of the efficacy and safety of lymecycline plus adapalene gel 0.1% versus lymecycline plus gel vehicle. *J Am Acad Dermatol*. 2003;49 (suppl):S218–26.

6. Layton AM. A review on the treatment of acne vulgaris. *Int J Clin Pract*. 2006;60(1):64–72.

7. OrthoNeutrogena, Ortho-McNeil Pharmaceuticals: USA. Retin-A [prescribing information]. Last revised February 2001. Available at: http://www.retinamicro.com/RetinA.pdf#zoom=200. Last accessed September 23, 2008.

8. sanofi-aventis. BenzaClin [prescribing information]. Last updated February 2006. Available at: http://www.benzaclin.com/hcp/Index.jsp. Last accessed September 23, 2008.

9. Ortho-McNeil Pharmaceuticals: USA. Ortho Tri-Cyclen [prescribing information]. Last revised March 2001. Available at: https://www.ortho-mcneilpharmaceutical.com/ortho-cneilpharmaceutical/shared/pi/Tri-Cyclen_Lo_PI.pdf. Last accessed October 26, 2008.

10. iPLEDGE: Committed to Pregnancy Prevention. 2005. Available at: https://www.ipledgeprogram.com/Default.aspx. Last accessed September 23, 2008.

75 Psoriasis

Richard N. Herrier

Objectives

1. Apply knowledge of treatment of psoriasis to a patient scenario.

2. Apply knowledge of drug interactions with commonly prescribed drugs used to treat psoriasis.

3. Apply knowledge of psoriasis and related diseases to a patient scenario.

Scenario

Davidia Crockett, a 52-year-old female, comes in to pick up her refills for enalapril and hydrochlorothiazide on October 2. She specifically requests to talk with a pharmacist. She shows you two approximately 2-cm plaques on the ulnar surface of each elbow. Covered with whitish silvery scales, the lesions are clearly due to psoriasis. According to her patient history, these lesions appeared over the last week. She was treated briefly for more severe psoriasis with "tar" and steroids 15 years ago, but the condition had not bothered her again until last week. Her primary care physician does not want to deal with it and referred her to a dermatologist. However, she cannot get an appointment for 7 weeks and wants your advice on what she can do in the meantime. When you ask her what other symptoms are associated with the lesions, she mentions that she has had aches and pains in her hands for about 2 weeks, and her manicurist noted some new depressions in her fingernails last week.

The patient's profile is shown in Case Table 75–1.

CASE Table 75–1	Prescription Medication Profile

Davidia Crockett
4212 W. Mercer Lane
Phoenix, AZ 85800

Phone: 623-868-3456 **DOB:** 11/2/53 **Insurer:** CIGNA

Allergies/Intolerances: NKDA

Diseases: Hypertension, recurrent UTI, asthma (childhood; current status unknown)

Rx No.	Drug Name	Instructions	Date	R/F	Prescriber	Qty	RPh
676002	Enalapril 20 mg	1 tablet every morning	10/2	2	Patton	30	RNH
676001	Hydrochlorothiazide 25 mg	1 tablet every morning	10/2	2	Patton	30	RNH
676003	Theodur 300 mg	1 tablet twice daily	9/27	4	Patton	60	JDA
654001	Septra	½ tablet at bedtime	9/15	4	Patton	15	KGB
676282	Septra	2 tablets twice daily	9/15	4	Patton	15	KGB
676002	Enalapril 20 mg	1 tablet every morning	9/2	3	Patton	30	RNH
676001	Hydrochlorothiazide 25 mg	1 tablet every morning	9/2	3	Patton	30	RNH
676003	Theodur 300 mg	1 tablet twice daily	9/1	5	Patton	60	JDA
654001	Septra	½ tablet at bedtime	8/18	5	Patton	15	KGB
676002	Enalapril 20 mg	1 tablet every morning	8/8	4	Patton	30	RNH
676001	Hydrochlorothiazide 25 mg	1 tablet every morning	8/8	4	Patton	30	RNH
676003	Theodur 300 mg	1 tablet twice daily	8/2	6	Patton	60	JDA
654001	Septra	½ tablet at bedtime	7/20	6	Patton	15	KGB
676282	Septra	2 tablets twice daily	7/20	5	Patton	40	KGB

Questions and Activities

1. On the basis of the patient's presentation and drug therapy, identify the potential drug- or disease-related problems.

2. What additional question(s) should you ask the patient to further clarify the nature of the problem?

3. What are the goals of care and pharmacotherapy for this patient?

The patient goes on to tell you that several knuckles on both hands are impacted, plus her back has been stiff in the mornings. She has been taking 400 mg of ibuprofen, and it helps the stiffness and discomfort in her hands and back. You notice that the involved joints are red and swollen; she points out the depressions in the nails.

When asked about her asthma, the patient says she developed it after a bad bout of the flu when she was 12 years old and has not had an attack since age 13. She has no history of hay fever, nasal allergies, or itching rashes on her face or arms. Upon observation she has no evidence of atopic dermatitis on arms or face and does not have allergic shiners, a nasal crease, or Dennie's lines. She does not awaken from sleep in the early morning coughing.

4. How does the additional information about the patient's current symptoms and childhood asthma impact your initial assessment? Explain the rationale behind your revised assessments.

5. What questions would you ask to identify potential problems between the current therapy and your proposed interventions or future treatment of her arthritis? Explain your rationale for each question.

The patient tells you that she has had recurrent urinary tract infections (UTIs). One prescription is for preventing UTI, and she takes the other medication when she gets dysuria, which happens five to six times a year. She tells you the theophylline is for her childhood asthma. Her physician has repeatedly told her she does not need this medication because she has not had an attack for almost 40 years. However, he checks her theophylline levels annually and says they are fine. She admits to being on theophylline out

of habit. She feels safer because she remembers how horrible her breathing problems were. Her blood pressure is under great control with home readings running close to 120/80 mm Hg.

6. For each additional problem revealed by the patient, identify the interventions to solve the problems and the anticipated outcomes; include drug, dosage, dosage form, and duration of therapy for the interventions.

7. For each problem, list other potential therapies, and their advantages and disadvantages.

8. How will you monitor for efficacy or adverse effects in the community pharmacy setting?

9. What pertinent topics need to be addressed during patient education?

Additional Activities

1. List risk factors for psoriasis; include prevalence rates based on gender, age, race, and lifestyle.

2. Develop a follow-up treatment plan for this patient; include a progress note that can be faxed to her physician.

3. Compare and contrast the topical prescription medications used for psoriasis; include the mechanism of action, efficacy rates, and side effects.

Information Sources

1. Manadan AM, Sequeira W, Block JA. Treatment of psoriatic arthritis. *Am J Ther.* 2006;13:72–9.

2. Methotrexate. Micromedex Healthcare Series [subscription required]. Greenwood Village, Colo: Thomson Micromedex; 2006. Available at: http://www.thomsonhc.com. Last accessed October 20, 2008.

3. Schoen MP, Boehncke WH. Psoriasis. *N Engl J Med.* 2005;352: 1899–912.

4. Smith CH, Barker JNWN. Psoriasis and its management. *BMJ.* 2006;333:380–4.

5. Lee NP, Arriola ER. Topical corticosteroids: back to basics. *West J Med.* 1999;171:351–3.

6. Albert X, Huertas I, Pereiro II, Sanfelix J, et al. Antibiotics for preventing recurrent urinary tract infections. *Cochrane Database Syst Rev.* 2004;3:CD001209.

76 Poison Ivy Dermatitis

Brice A. Labruzzo

Objectives

1. Identify patients for whom self-care of poison ivy is appropriate.

2. Develop an appropriate therapeutic regimen for poison ivy.

3. Identify effective prophylactic measures for poison ivy.

4. Provide thorough and appropriate patient education regarding a specific therapeutic regimen for poison ivy.

Scenario

Ray Tilson is a 46–year-old white male who approaches the counter at your northern California community pharmacy and asks to speak to a pharmacist. Mr. Tilson does not look familiar to you. He informs you that he gets all of his prescriptions filled at your pharmacy, but his wife always gets his prescriptions filled for him. You ask Mr. Tilson what you can do to help him today. He tells you that he has had a rash for a few days, which is becoming bothersome. He describes the rash as being itchy, streaky, and warm to the touch; he further describes the itchiness as being intense.

During your conversation with Mr. Tilson, you learn that he is married and has two children in high school. Full of pride, he tells you about his daughter, the basketball player, and his son, the musician.

Mr. Tilson reveals that he has been working as a fireman with the USDA Forest Service for years and was involved in fighting a forest fire last week. He informs you that, although he has diabetes and high blood pressure, he is in great physical condition and proudly mentions that he passed his work capacity test with flying colors. He also mentions that many of the forest trees in the area are covered with hairy vines that contain clusters of three red-tinted leaves. He thinks it may be poison ivy.

You ask Mr. Tilson to show you his rash. While examining his arms, you notice an erythematous, vesiculopapular rash accompanied by local edema. Mr. Tilson says the rash occurred with only intense itching at first, but over the past day or so the pain has become increasingly worse and he

has noticed blisters that have begun to ooze a clear liquid. The patient also says that the itching is worse at night, even keeping him from sleeping through the night. He tells you that his wife has complained about him being cranky the past few days, which he attributes to the lack of sleep. Mr. Tilson wants to know what the rash could be from and what he can do to help with the itching; he has been putting jewelweed extract on the rash for a few days and he has had no relief. The patient explains that a friend told him jewelweed was the most beneficial remedy. You confirm that it appears he has poison ivy and then ask him if he has a few minutes to answer more questions you would like to ask before making a recommendation.

You question Mr. Tilson regarding his diabetes and blood pressure. He informs you that he checks his blood glucose several times daily, that his fasting glucose usually ranges from 80 to 100 mg/dL, and that his postprandial glucose usually ranges from 110 to 130 mg/dL. The patient reports that at his last visit his hemoglobin A1c was 6.5%. He also tells you that he has an automatic blood pressure cuff at home. He checks his blood pressure several times per week and reports that his top number ranges from 120 to 130 mm Hg and his bottom number ranges from 75 to 85 mm Hg.

You ask Mr. Tilson about use of any herbal and/or non-prescription medications. He reports taking 3 ibuprofen (600 mg) as needed for headaches, which occur one or two times per month. He also tells you that he takes a baby aspirin daily because his doctor said it would be good for his heart.

Before suggesting treatment for Mr. Tilson, you research his current prescription use (Case Table 76–1).

Questions and Activities

1. Identify the patient's disease-related problem, and state the current drug therapy for the problem.

2. What information would you tell the patient regarding jewelweed extract as an effective treatment for poison ivy?

3. What are the goals of pharmacotherapy for this patient?

CASE Table 76–1 Prescription Medication Profile

Ray Tilson
18606 Hummingbird Ln.
Redding, CA 59875

Phone: 598-956-6782   **DOB:** 09/03/1965   **Insurer:** United Healthcare

Allergies/Intolerances: PCN

Rx No.	Drug Name	Directions	Date	R/F	Prescriber	Qty	RPh
668612	Glucovance 5 mg/500 mg	Take 1 tablet by mouth twice daily for diabetes	2/15	3	Zivney	60	DKH
662547	Lisinopril 10 mg	Take 1 tablet by mouth daily for blood pressure	02/15	3	Zivney	30	DKH
668612	Glucovance 5 mg/500 mg	Take 1 tablet by mouth twice daily for diabetes	3/13	2	Zivney	60	KNB
662547	Lisinopril 10 mg	Take 1 tablet by mouth daily for blood pressure	03/13	2	Zivney	30	KNB
668612	Glucovance 5 mg/500 mg	Take 1 tablet by mouth twice daily for diabetes	4/14	1	Zivney	60	DKH
662547	Lisinopril 10 mg	Take 1 tablet by mouth daily for blood pressure	04/14	1	Zivney	30	DKH
668612	Glucovance 5 mg/500 mg	Take 1 tablet by mouth twice daily for diabetes	5/12	0	Zivney	60	KNB
662547	Lisinopril 10 mg	Take 1 tablet by mouth daily for blood pressure	05/12	0	Zivney	30	KNB

4. Identify the treatment alternatives available for the drug therapy problem(s).

5. Is the patient a candidate for self-treatment of his poison ivy? Explain why or why not.

6. What intervention(s) can the pharmacist perform to solve the problem(s)? What is the anticipated outcome of these interventions?

7. What drug(s), dosage form(s), schedule(s), and duration(s) of therapy are optimal for the treatment of poison ivy?

8. What intervention (e.g., patient recommendation, call to provider or family member, contact emergency medical services, etc.) is necessary for implementing this treatment?

9. What monitoring parameters available in the community pharmacy setting should be used to evaluate this patient's therapy, including efficacy and adverse effects?

10. What FDA-approved pharmacologic agents may aid in the prevention of contact dermatitis from poison ivy exposure? Explain how you would counsel the patient on the use of these agents.

11. What lifestyle modifications might be beneficial in managing the patient's problem?

12. Develop a medication action plan for the patient; include short-term and long-range goals.

13. While you are counseling the patient about the recommended medications, he asks if he can apply diphenhydramine topically to the rash if the itching gets worse. What response would you give the patient?

14. Develop a follow-up plan for this patient; include time to follow up and method of contact.

During your follow-up, Mr. Tilson informs you that he has had some relief of itching with your recommended self-care treatment; however, since then, the rash has spread all over his body, including to his genitals. He has an appointment with his primary care provider this afternoon. He returns from his appointment with a prescription for the following:

Medrol dose pack #1 UAD. Mr. Tilson alerts you that this prescription should be covered by Worker's Compensation Insurance because it is related to the forest fires and hands you a piece of paper with contact information for a claim adjuster.

15. Does Worker's Compensation Insurance cover poison ivy treatment and medications?

16. What points do you want to make sure are addressed while counseling the patient?

Mr. Tilson once again returns to your pharmacy on the last day of treatment with the oral methylprednisolone. He reports the itching and rash improved during the first 3 days of treatment;

however, the rash and itching have recurred. He wants to know what he should do now.

17. Is this outcome consistent with your expectations? Why or why not?

18. What intervention can be made regarding this problem? What would you anticipate the outcome of the intervention to be?

Additional Activities

1. Research the location and appearances of the different types of poison ivy species.

2. Investigate an easy way to distinguish between poison ivy plants and nonallergenic look-alike plants.

3. Develop a patient education handout for prevention and treatment of poison ivy.

4. Investigate home remedies and/or alternative medications for the prevention and treatment of poison ivy.

Information Sources

1. Keefner KR. Contact dermatitis. In: Berardi RR, Kroon LA, McDermott JH, et al., eds. *Handbook of Nonprescription Drugs: An Interactive Approach to Self-Care*. 15th ed. Washington DC: American Pharmacists Association; 2006:745–64.

2. Long D, Ballentine NH, Marks JG Jr. Treatment of poison ivy/oak allergic contact dermatitis with an extract of jewelweed. *Am J Contact Dermat*. 1997;8:150–3.

3. Zink BJ, Otten EJ, Rosenthal M, et al. The effect of jewelweed in preventing poison ivy dermatitis. *J Wilderness Med*. 1991;2: 178–82.

4. Carpenter DO. *Professional Guide to Complementary and Alternative Therapies*. Springhouse, Pa; Springhouse Publishing: 2001.

5. Whaley-Connell A, Sowers JR. Hypertension management in type 2 diabetes mellitus: recommendations of the Joint National Committee VII. *Endocrinol Metab Clin North Am*. 2005;34:63–75.

6. Tanner TL. Rhus (toxicodendron) dermatitis. *Prim Care*. 2000;27: 493–502.

7. Brodell RT, Williams L. Taking the itch out of poison ivy. Are you prescribing the right medicine? *Postgrad Med*. 1999;106:69–70.

8. Kaidbey KH, Kligman AM. Assay of topical corticosteroids. Efficacy of suppression of experimental Rhus dermatitis in humans. *Arch Dermtaol*. 1976;112:808–13.

9. Bentoquatum. Lexi-Drugs Online [subscription required]. Available at: http://online.lexi.com. Last accessed August 28, 2008.

10. Methylprednisolone. Lexi-Drugs Online [subscription required]. Available at: http://online.lexi.com. Last accessed August 28, 2008.

11. Wildfire season: poison oak, ivy and sumac plants top cause of disability, sick time. *Los Angeles Firefighter*. 2005;43(5):9.

12. Kollef MH. Adult respiratory distress syndrome after smoke inhalation from burning poison ivy. *JAMA*. 1995;274:358–9.

13. Epstein WL. Occupational poison ivy and oak dermatitis. *Dermatol Clin*. 1994; 12:511–6.

Case

77 Sunburn

Richard N. Herrier

Objectives

1. Apply knowledge of sunscreen efficacy to identify potential sunscreen failures.

2. Apply knowledge of factors that may contribute to cause of sunburns.

3. Compare efficacy of various insect repellents.

4. Describe the contributions of ultraviolet A and B radiation to sunburn and other sun-damaging effects.

Scenario

Barnaby Jones, a 50-year-old male, comes in on October 2 to pick up his refills for enalapril and metformin. He specifically requests to talk with a pharmacist. He asks you, "What's good to treat this sunburn I got playing 18 holes of golf yesterday?" It is obvious that his face, neck, both arms, and both legs are mildly sunburned, but his left hand is spared. When questioned about sun protection measures,

he reveals that he lathered up just as he always does with a very-water-resistant sunscreen having a sun protection factor (SPF) of 50. He is surprised that he got burned.

He also says, "The bugs were out like crazy due to the recent rains and ate me alive." You notice several potential bite areas. When asked about them, he tells you that he used insect repellent, and that the bites are not painful and they do not itch. When asked for brand names of the insect repellent and sunscreen, he points out two popular products, one with 5% DEET, and a sunscreen that contains three compounds that have ultraviolet B (UVB) protection and 3% avobenzone for UVA protection.

The patient's profile is shown in Case Table 77–1.

Questions and Activities

1. On the basis of the patient's presentation and drug therapy, identify the potential drug- or disease-related problems.

CASE Table 77–1　Prescription Medication Profile

Barnaby Jones
1846 North Nowhere Lane
Surprise, AZ 85707

Phone: 623-546-6416　　　**DOB:** 11/2/55　　　**Insurer:** TRICARE

Diseases: HTN, T2DM

Allergies/Intolerances: Procaine penicillin injection (hives; 1961)

Rx No.	Drug Name	Directions	Date	R/F	Prescriber	Qty	RPh
176002	Enalapril 20 mg	1 tablet twice daily	10/2	6	Reepelsnap	60	RNH
176001	Glucophage 800 mg	1 tablet twice daily	10/2	6	Reeplesnap	60	RNH
182191	Glyburide 5 mg	1 tablet every morning	9/15	3	Reepelsnap	30	JNA
176002	Enalapril 20 mg	1 tablet twice daily	9/3	7	Reepelsnap	60	RNH
176001	Glucophage 800 mg	1 tablet twice daily	8/6	8	Reeplesnap	60	RNH
176002	Enalapril 20 mg	1 tablet twice daily	8/6	8	Reeplesnap	60	KGB
176001	Glucophage 800 mg	1 tablet twice daily	8/6	8	Reeplesnap	60	KGB
176002	Enalapril 20 mg	1 tablet twice daily	7/9	9	Reepelsnap	60	JNA
176001	Glucophage 800 mg	1 tablet twice daily	7/9	9	Reeplesnap	60	JNA
178655	Cephalexin 500 mg	1 capsule four times daily	7/6	0	Quincy	40	KGB

2. What additional question(s) should you ask the patient to further clarify the nature of the problem?

3. What are the goals of pharmacotherapy for this patient?

4. The patient applied both the insect repellent and the sunscreen just once, applying the sunscreen last. He was also wearing a baseball cap, and he wore a golf glove on his left hand because he is right-handed. How does this information impact your initial assessment? Explain the rationale behind your revised assessments.

5. What questions would you ask to identify potential problems between the patient's current therapy and your proposed interventions? Explain your rationale for each question.

Mr. Jones tells you that his blood pressure usually runs 110–120/65–75 and that he has been on enalapril for 10 years for his blood pressure. In addition, he was diagnosed 1 year ago with diabetes. His A1c was 9.2 two months ago Although he realizes that he will eventually have to use insulin, he would rather wait until he must use it.

6. For each of the patient's medical problems, identify the interventions to solve the problems and the anticipated outcomes; include drug, dosage, dosage form, and duration of therapy.

7. For each medical problem, list other potential therapies, and their advantages and disadvantages.

8. How will you monitor for efficacy or adverse effects in the community pharmacy setting?

9. What pertinent topics need to be addressed during patient education?

Additional Activities

1. Research the new sunscreen rules that have been proposed by FDA for sunscreen products. Explain the changes that have been suggested for these products.

2. Design a drug therapy regimen for both prevention and treatment of sunburn for a pediatric patient. Include the nonpharmacologic therapies for sunburn.

3. Research the different types of skin cancers that are related to sun exposure and how the ABCD's of melanomas can help to assess a patient.

Information Sources

1. Moore DE. Drug-induced cutaneous photosensitivity: incidence, mechanism, prevention and management. *Drug Saf.* 2002;25: 345–69.

2. Ferguson J. Photosensitivity due to drugs. *Photodermmatol Photoimmunol Photomed.* 2002;18:262–9.

3. DeLeo V. Sunscreen use in photodermatoses. *Dermatol Clin.* 2006; 24:27–33.

4. Ting WW, Vest CD, Sontheimer R. Practical and experimental consideration of sun protection in dermatology. *Int J Dermatol.* 2003;42:505–13.

5. Prevention of West Nile virus. *Pharm Lett.* 2005;21(6):1.

6. Fradin MS, Day JF. Comparative efficacy of insect repellents against insect bites. *N Engl J Med.* 2002;347:13–8.

78 Rash

Richard N. Herrier

Objectives

1. Apply knowledge of dermatologic conditions to a patient scenario.

2. Apply knowledge of use of corticosteroids in dermatologic conditions.

3. Apply knowledge of adjunctive treatment modalities in dermatologic conditions.

Scenario

Paul Rodriguez, a 16-year-old male, comes to the pharmacy to pick up his refills for Nasonex and Zyrtec. He specifically requests to talk with a pharmacist. He asks you, "What's good to treat this rash on my arms? It itches like crazy!" You observe that he has a pale pink area in both cubital fossae with evidence of excoriation (scratching). He also has several 3- to 4-cm patches on both upper arms that are considerably lighter than the surrounding skin. He thinks he may have been bitten by something. You also notice that he has rubbed his eyes three times since you began talking with him.

The patient's profile is shown in Case Table 78–1. (Today's date is October 2.)

Questions and Activities

1. On the basis of the patient's presentation and drug therapy, identify the potential drug- or disease-related problems.

2. What additional question(s) should you ask the patient to further clarify the nature of the problem?

3. What are the goals of pharmacotherapy for this patient?

Mr. Rodriquez tells you that the Nasonex controls his allergic rhinitis very well except for two 4-week periods, one in the summer and one in October. He uses the Zyrtec during that time period because it reduces sneezing and a runny nose, and takes care of his itchy eyes. His skin did itch for several days before he saw his skin change. You notice severe allergic shiners and a nasal crease.

4. How do the patient's description of his symptoms and your observations impact your initial assessment? Explain your rationale for your revised assessments.

5. For each problem identify the interventions to solve the problems and the anticipated outcomes; include drug, dosage, dosage form, and duration of therapy.

CASE Table 78–1 Prescription Medication Profile

Paul Rodriguez
241 Brook Road
Roanoke, VA 24018

Phone: 540-555-9876   **DOB:** 9/5/1992   **Insurer:** Anthem

Allergies/Intolerances: NKDA

Rx No.	Drug Name	Instructions	Date	R/F	Prescriber	Qty	RPh
662191	Nasonex	2 sprays each nostril in the morning	10/22	3	Bradley	1	abc
676002	Zyrtec 10 mg	1 tablet every morning	10/2	5	Bradley	30	rjb
662191	Nasonex	2 sprays each nostril in the morning	9/5	4	Bradley	1	rjb
662191	Nasonex	2 sprays each nostril in the morning	8/6	5	Bradley	1	rjb
662191	Nasonex	2 sprays each nostril in the morning	7/8	6	Bradley	1	abc
677655	Cephalexin 500 mg	1 tablet four times a day	7/6	0	Quincy	28	rjb
676002	Zyrtec 10 mg	1 tablet every morning	6/26	6	Bradley	30	abc

6. For each problem list other potential therapies, and their advantages and disadvantages.

7. How will you monitor for efficacy or adverse effects in the community pharmacy setting?

8. What pertinent topics need to be addressed during patient education?

Two weeks later Mr. Rodriquez returns to the pharmacy. His atopic dermatitis is almost gone, and he asks for something good for this cough that wakes him up at night. It has been waking his mom up 5 mornings a week. When you ask about the timing, he tells you it occurs between 3 and 5 am every morning.

9. In light of the patient's other health issues what is the most likely cause of his cough?

Additional Activities

1. Compare and contrast signs and symptoms of different types of rashes.

2. Investigate which medications are most likely to cause the following conditions:

   a. An allergic drug rash

   b. Pseudoallergy

   c. Photosensitivity

3. Research how to manage and treat diaper rash.

Information Sources

1. Williams HC. Atopic dermatitis. *N Engl J Med.* 2005;352:2314–24.

2. Boguniewicz M, Schmid-Grendelmeier P, Leung DYM. Atopic dermatitis. *J Allergy Clin Immunol.* 2006;118:40–3.

3. Akdis CA, Mubeccel A, Bieber T, et al. Diagnosis and treatment of atopic dermatitis in children and adults: European Academy of Allerology and Clinical Immunology/American Academy of Allergy, Asthma, and Immunology/PRACTALL consensus report. *J Allergy Clin Immunol.* 2006;118:152–69.

4. Lee NP, Arriola ER. Topical corticosteroids: back to basics. *West J Med.* 1999;171:351–353.

5. Chamlin SL, Kao J, Frieden IJ. Ceramide-dominant barrier repair lipids alleviate childhood atopic dermatitis: changes in barrier function provide a sensitive indicator of disease activity. *J Am Acad Dermatol.* 2002;47:198–208.

79 Warts

Emily Evans

Objectives

1. Compare available pharmacotherapy for warts (non-prescription and prescription), including efficacy, ease of use/convenience, duration of therapy, and cost.

2. Identify patients for whom self-care of warts is appropriate.

3. Develop an appropriate therapeutic regimen for warts that is based on clinical presentation and patient-specific factors.

4. Provide appropriate and thorough patient education for available pharmacotherapy for warts; include directions for use, adverse effects, cautions, and monitoring parameters.

Scenario

You are a pharmacist in a small, rural, independently owned community pharmacy. Ms. Loren Riley is a 63-year-old white female. She is well-known to you and the rest of the staff at the pharmacy as a patient who is somewhat "difficult," often complains about the price of her medications, and is always in a big hurry. She comes in one Monday morning and asks the cashier for some eucalyptus oil. You overhear her request and quickly walk out to find out what current problem she is having. She exasperatedly tells you that she has a wart on her foot, and that when she had a wart in her teens, her mother had put eucalyptus oil on it every day for a few weeks and it had cleared up beautifully.

You ask Ms. Riley to step into the private patient counseling room so that you can speak with her further. She is irritated and tells you that she just wants a little bottle of the oil, and she has a lunch date. You insist, however, and she agrees to talk with you briefly.

In the counseling room, Ms. Riley tells you that about 2 weeks ago she first noticed what felt like a "pebble" in her shoe during her 2-mile walk, and that the place on her foot has worsened somewhat since then. She describes it as "uncomfortable," rather than painful. It has, however, kept her from her normal walking routine but not from attending water aerobics at the local aquatics center twice weekly. When asked, she reluctantly takes off her shoe to show you

the bottom of her foot. You see an eraser-sized lesion on the ball of her foot. It is not noticeably raised and interrupts the normal whorls of the foot.

You agree with Ms. Riley that she has a plantar wart. "Well, I told you that," she replies. "That's why I asked for the eucalyptus. Do you have any or not?" You explain that you need to ask just a few more questions to determine if eucalyptus oil is a good choice for her. You learn that Ms. Riley was widowed about 5 years ago, and now lives with her daughter and son-in-law. She has never used any tobacco products and has a glass of wine when she goes to dinner with her "gentleman friend" about twice a month. She is a retired school librarian and lives off her husband's pension and Social Security benefits. She proudly tells you that she is very healthy, and that her "pressure" is under good control with only two prescription medications, but she cannot tell you the names of the medications. "And it's a good thing," she says, "as expensive as that one is!" (At this point, you ask your technician to give you a printout of the patient's prescription profile from the beginning of the year, and check Ms. Riley's blood pressure. It is 124/82.) She also says that she takes a baby aspirin every day, "just in case," and a couple of Tylenol Arthritis when she needs it (a couple of times a month). When questioned about herbal preparations, she tells you that she has been taking black cohosh for about a month, on the advice of her physician, to help with her hot flashes and mood swings, which she has been putting up with for years, but for which she refuses to take any "medicine" (i.e., prescription drugs). She has noticed a significant improvement and is planning on continuing to take it.

Your technician brings you Ms. Riley's prescription profile (Case Table 79–1).

Ms. Riley is now obviously ready to go. She asks what she should do if she should not use the eucalyptus oil for her wart. She just wants it to go away as quickly as possible.

Questions and Activities

1. On the basis of the patient's presentation and drug therapy, identify the drug- or disease related problem(s), and state the current drug therapy for the problem(s).

CASE Table 79–1 Prescription Medication Profile

Loren Riley
1265 Pace Street
Pensacola, FL 32501

Phone: 850-458-1111 **DOB:** 06/22/1943 **Insurer:** AARP (Medicare)

Allergies/Intolerances: NKDA

Rx No.	Drug Name	Directions	Date	R/F	Prescriber	Qty	RPh
6523635	Hydrochlorothiazide 25 mg	Take 1 tablet every morning for blood pressure	08/02	2	Denton	30	EW
6523634	Avapro 300 mg	Take 1 tablet every day for blood pressure	08/02	2	Denton	30	EW
6523635	Hydrochlorothiazide 25 mg	Take 1 tablet every morning for blood pressure	07/05	3	Denton	30	JD
6523634	Avapro 300 mg	Take 1 tablet every day for blood pressure	07/05	3	Denton	30	JD
6523635	Hydrochlorothiazide 25 mg	Take 1 tablet every morning for blood pressure	06/04	4	Denton	30	JD
6523634	Avapro 300 mg	Take 1 tablet every day for blood pressure	06/04	4	Denton	30	JD
6523635	Hydrochlorothiazide 25 mg	Take 1 tablet every morning for blood pressure	05/05	5	Denton	30	RE
6523634	Avapro 300 mg	Take 1 tablet every day for blood pressure	05/05	5	Denton	30	RE
6523633	Prempro 0.625/2.5	Take 1 tablet every day for hormones	05/05	5	Denton	30	RE
6502058	Hydrochlorothiazide 25 mg	Take 1 tablet every day	04/17	0	Littleton	30	RE
6502057	Avapro 150 mg	Take 1 tablet every day	04/17	0	Littleton	30	RE
6502058	Hydrochlorothiazide 25 mg	Take 1 tablet every day	03/15	1	Littleton	30	EW
6502057	Avapro 150 mg	Take 1 tablet every day	03/15	1	Littleton	30	EW
6516521	Levaquin 500 mg	Take 1 tablet every day until gone	03/01	0	Dandy	7	EW
6502058	Hydrochlorothiazide 25 mg	Take 1 tablet every day	02/17	2	Littleton	30	JD
L057	Avapro 150 mg	Take 1 tablet every day	02/17	2	Littleton	30	JD
6502058	Hydrochlorothiazide 25 mg	Take 1 tablet every day	01/17	3	Littleton	30	EW
6502057	Avapro 150 mg	Take 1 tablet every day	01/17	3	Littleton	30	EW

2. What are the goals of pharmacotherapy for this patient?

3. Identify the various treatment alternatives available for the drug therapy problem(s).

4. What will you tell the patient about the use of eucalyptus oil and her previous success in using it?

5. Is this patient a good candidate for self-care of her wart? Why or why not?

6. Identify the possible intervention(s) to solve the problem(s) and the anticipated outcome(s).

7. What drug(s), dosage form(s), schedule(s), and duration(s) of therapy are optimal for the treatment of this patient's problem? Justify why you consider this regimen "optimal."

8. What intervention (e.g., patient recommendation, call to provider or family member, contact emergency medical services, etc.) is necessary for implementing this treatment?

9. What monitoring parameters available in the community pharmacy setting should be used to evaluate therapy in this patient, including efficacy and adverse effects?

10. What nondrug therapies or lifestyle modifications might be useful in managing this patient's problem(s)?

11. Develop a medication action plan for the patient; include short-term and long-range goals.

12. What are the pertinent topics to address during patient education?

13. Develop a follow-up plan for this patient; include time to follow up and method of contact.

You see Ms. Riley again when she picks up her prescriptions a month later. You ask if she has time to talk with you about her previous problem. She is very quick to tell you that the "spot" on her foot has actually gotten slightly bigger and has become more painful to walk on. She continues, "So I found someone who would sell me the eucalyptus oil, like I asked for to begin with. We'll see how it works."

14. Given the failure of the recommended treatment and the patient's decision to use eucalyptus oil, what will you recommend to her now?

15. About 2 weeks later, the patient returns with two prescriptions (Case Figures 79–1 and 79–2). How will you counsel the patient on this prescription?

16. What is the rationale for this combination therapy?

Additional Activities

1. Compare and contrast the different types of warts; include prevention and treatment options.

2. Investigate how the treatment recommendations might change if the patient had presented with a common wart.

3. Research home remedies and/or alternative medications for the treatment and prevention of warts.

4. Create a plan-o-gram in a community pharmacy for products to treat warts.

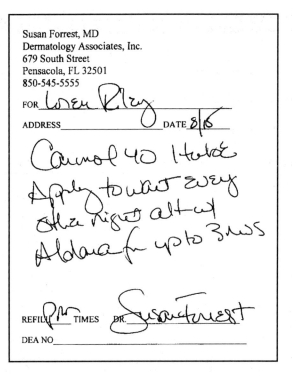

CASE Figure 79–2 Prescription #2 for patient Loren Riley.

Information Sources

1. US Department of Health and Human Services. National Institutes of Health, National Heart, Lung, and Blood Institute, National High Blood Pressure Education Program. *The Seventh Report of the Joint National Committee on the Detection, Evaluation, and Treatment of High Blood Pressure (JNC-VII)*. Bethesda, Md: US Department of Health and Human Services; 2004. NIH Publication No. 04-5230. Available at: http://www.nhlbi.nih.gov/guidelines/hypertension/jnc7full.pdf. Last accessed October 6, 2008.

2. Hansson L, Zanchetti A, Carruthers SG, et al. Effects of intensive blood-pressure lowering and low-dose aspirin in patients with hypertension: principal results of the Hypertension Optimal Treatment (HOT) randomised trial. *Lancet*. 1998;351:1755–62.

3. Jonsson B, Hansson L, Stalhammar N. Health economics in the Hypertension Optimal Treatment (HOT) study: costs and cost-effectiveness of intensive blood pressure lowering and low-dose aspirin in patients with hypertension. *J Int Med*. 20031;253:472–80.

4. Nedrow A, Miller J, Walker M, et al. Complementary and alternative therapies for the management of menopause-related symptoms: a systematic evidence review. *Arch Intern Med*. 2006;166:1453–65.

5. Mahady GB. Black cohosh (Actaea/Cimicifuga racemosa): review of the clinical data for safety and efficacy in menopausal symptoms. *Treat Endocrinol*. 2006;4:177–84.

6. Popovich NG, Newton GD. Warts. In: Berardi RR, Kroon LA, McDermott JH et al., eds. *Handbook of Nonprescription Drugs: An Interactive Approach to Self-Care*. 15th ed. Washington DC: American Pharmacists Association; 2006:907–16.

CASE Figure 79–1 Prescription #1 for patient Loren Riley.

7. Bacelieri R, Johnson SM. Cutaneous warts: an evidence-based approach to therapy. *Am Fam Physician*. 2005;72:647–53.

8. Habif TP. *Clinical Dermatology*. 4th ed. New York: Mosby; 2004: 368–408.

9. Gibbs S, Harvey I. Topical treatments for cutaneous warts. *Cochrane Database Syst Rev*. 2006;3:CD001781.

10. Fox P, Tung M. Human papillomavirus: burden of illness and treatment cost considerations. *Am J Clin Derm*. 2006;6:365–81.

11. Carpenter DO. *Professional Guide to Complementary and Alternative Therapies*. Springhouse, Pa: Springhouse; 2001:197–8.

12. Drugstore.com. Available at: http://www.drugstore.com. Last accessed October 6, 2008.

13. Imiquimod. Mosby's Drug Consult [subscription required]. Available at: http://home.mdconsult.com/das/drug/view/60861210-2/1/3328/top?sid=502564714&SEQNO=1. Last accessed October 6, 2008.

14. Skinner RB. Imiquimod. *Dermotol Clin*. 2003;21:291–300.

15. Focht DR, Spicer C, Fairchok MP. The efficacy of duct tape vs cryotherapy in the treatment of verruca vulgaris (the common wart). *Arch Pediatr Adolesc Med*. 2002;156:971–4.

80 Pediculosis

Adam C. Welch

Objectives

1. Distinguish common presentations of scalp and dermatologic conditions.

2. Identify appropriate pharmacologic and nonpharmacologic treatment approaches given a community-based scenario.

3. Determine appropriate physician referral given a self-care dermatologic condition.

4. Outline a procedure for follow-up with a self-care dermatologic condition.

Scenario

Lisa Blummer is 33-year-old white female who comes into your pharmacy with her oldest son Zach, who is 6 years old. You see Ms. Blummer often when she comes in for her migraine medication, and you remember her distinctly because she tends to ask many questions about her health. Although she usually comes to the pharmacy alone, this time her son is with her and he appears very miserable. Ms. Blummer was in the pharmacy 2 weeks ago for Zach's antibiotic. Today, he is pouting as he scratches the back of his head. His mother comes to you holding a bottle of Head and Shoulders. She asks if dandruff is usually itchy and if something can be added to the Head and Shoulders to help with the itch.

You pull up Zach's profile (Case Table 80–1). After examining Zach's profile, you decide to take a closer look at his head. You notice that as he scratches, there are no flakes falling on his shoulders. Upon closer examination you notice small grayish particles about the size of sesame seeds. His scalp does not appear significantly red despite his scratching, although you do notice small papules on his scalp. The particles on his scalp are primarily seen on the crown of his head and around his ears. Thinking that it is odd to not see any flakes on his shoulder, you ask Ms. Blummer when she started noticing these symptoms in her son. She replies that she noticed it about a week ago after he got back from a sleepover at his friend's house.

Questions and Activities

1. On the basis of the patient's presentation, identify the underlying problem.

CASE Table 80-1 Prescription Medication Profile

Zachary Blummer
123 Main St.
Wilkes-Barre, PA 18701

Phone: 570-555-5475   **DOB:** 06-12-2000   **Insurer:** Express Scripts rel:03

Allergies/Intolerances: None

Rx No.	Drug Name	Directions	Date	R/F	Prescriber	Qty	RPh
6475926	Amoxicillin/clavulanate potassium	Take 1 teaspoonful by mouth twice a day for 10 days	09-20	NR	Smith J	100	ACW
6471301	Sodium fluoride chewable tablets	Chew 1 tablet daily	09-01	11	Smith J	30	ACW
6435288	Sodium fluoride chewable tablets	Chew 1 tablet daily	08-01	NR	Smith J	30	LJR
6435288	Sodium fluoride chewable tablets	Chew 1 tablet daily	06-29	1	Smith J	30	ACW
6435288	Sodium fluoride chewable tablets	Chew 1 tablet daily	05-31	2	Smith J	30	LJR
6435288	Sodium fluoride chewable tablets	Chew 1 tablet daily	05-01	3	Smith J	30	LJR
6436694	Amoxicillin suspension	Take 1 teaspoonful by mouth three times a day	04-13	NR	Smith J	100	ACW
6435288	Sodium fluoride chewable tablets	Chew 1 tablet daily	04-02	4	Smith J	30	ACW

2. What are the goals of therapy to treat this problem?

3. Identify treatment options available for the underlying problem.

4. Is the patient a candidate for self-care? If so, choose the most appropriate pharmacologic agent.

5. What monitoring parameters regarding the problem should you explain to his mother?

6. What nonpharmacologic therapy would you also recommend to treat the underlying problem?

7. Develop a medication action plan for the underlying problem.

8. Identify some key counseling points that you would want to address with the mother about the underlying problem.

9. Outline a follow-up plan to monitor the patient's progress; include a specific method of communication.

10. Who else should the mother contact regarding her son's problem?

Additional Activities

1. Investigate the safety and efficacy of home remedies and/or alternative treatments for management of pediculosis capitis and pediculosis pubis.

2. Develop a patient education handout for the treatment of pediculosis capitis.

3. Investigate how the treatment would change if this patient were a 25-year-old female with pediculosis pubis.

Information Sources

1. Buff W, Fuhrman C. Insect bites and stings and pediculosis. In: Berardi RR, Kroon LA, McDermott JH, et al., eds. *Handbook of Nonprescription Drugs: An Interactive Approach to Self-Care.* 15th ed. Washington DC: American Pharmacists Association; 2006:781–801.

2. Centers for Disease Control and Prevention. Head lice treatment. May 16, 2008. Available at: http://www.cdc.gov/lice/head/treatment.html. Last accessed October 6, 2008.

3. Williams LK, Reichert A, MacKenzie WR, et al. Lice, nits, and school policy. *Pediatrics.* 2001;107:1011–5.

4. Mumcuoglu KY, Meinking TA, Burkhart CN, et al. Head louse infestations: the "no nit" policy and its consequences. *Int J Dermatol.* 2006;45:891–6.

5. Meinking TL, Entzel P, Villar ME, et al. Comparative efficacy of treatments for pediculosis capitis infestations: update 2000. *Arch Dermatol.* 2001;137:287–92.

Pain Management

81 Chronic Pain

Warren A. Narducci

Objectives

1. Assess the current drug therapy for appropriateness of the regimen for a patient with pain; include the use of adjuvant medications and nonprescription products.

2. Determine the appropriate means of pain assessment in a patient with complicated chronic pain with an acute injury.

3. Convert an oral pain medication regimen to alternative regimens using analgesic drug conversion tables.

4. Design a comprehensive drug therapy plan for a patient with chronic pain who also has an acute injury and other complicating diseases.

Scenario

Fern Gilbert is an 80-year-old white female with uncontrolled pain throughout her lower back and sides. Although Fern has experienced back pain for years, it has recently worsened as a result of two falls within the past 3 weeks. The latest incident occurred yesterday when she fell backward out of a bathtub and landed on her side. A computed tomography scan done 3 years ago showed a compound fracture and a bulging disk, and a magnetic resonance imaging scan indicated curvature of the spine. She had verteplasty done on January 10 of this year (a cement-like substance is injected into the vertebra to strengthen and stabilize it) and has had worse pain since then. Her pain is somewhat relieved when she is off her feet and is worse in the morning. Moreover, she reports pain radiating down her legs and numbness and tingling in the extremities.

A review of her pain therapies shows that she has tried Celebrex in the past but discontinued it because it did not work. Physical therapy was not successful for this patient. She had a trial of nonprescription ibuprofen and felt it worked well with her prescription pain medication. Neither constipation nor excessive sedation has occurred with her pain medications. Mrs. Gilbert is somewhat stoic and states that she can handle the pain without strong drugs and refuses to consider morphine or other narcotics. She has tried morphine once in the past, and it dramatically reduced her pain, but she had a "bad reaction" to it

almost right away. However, her pain is uncontrolled with the current therapy. She feels the pain is nearly a 10 at times throughout the day. Recently, the pharmacist contacted Dr. Jones with a recommendation to switch hydrocodone/APAP to oxycodone ER scheduled. The physician denied this request and instead wrote for gabapentin 300 mg by mouth every night and refilled her hydrocodone/APAP prescription. The patient states that the gabapentin helps her sleep, but it does not significantly reduce the pain.

The patient's past medical history includes gallbladder surgery in February of this year and both deep vein thrombosis (left leg) and pulmonary emboli since March 2006. She is also being treated for hypertension, frequent heartburn, osteoarthritis, and hypothyroidism. Ms. Gilbert is a nonsmoker, nondrinker, and only occasionally drinks caffeinated beverages. She says that she is allergic to morphine, with symptoms of moderate-to-severe itching. She has prescription coverage through her Medicare Part D plan. She comes to your pharmacy after an office visit to her physician with a new prescription (Case Figure 81–1). The patient's prescription medication profile is available in Case Table 81–1.

For _Fern Gilbert_ Date _5/7_
Address _12 James Ct. Essex_

℞

Methadone 10mg
30
Sig: one 3 times daily
for pain

Jones, C.

SUBSTITUTION PERMITTED   DISPENSE AS WRITTEN
REFILL **NR** TIMES   DEA No. _AF 1364273_

CASE Figure 81–1 Prescription for patient Fern Gilbert.

CASE Table 81–1   Prescription Medication Profile

Fern Gilbert
12 James Ct.
Essex, IA 51638

Phone: 712-255-9555   **DOB:** 12/5/28   **Insurer:** Medicare Part D

Allergies/Intolerances: Morphine (moderate-to-severe itching)

Rx No.	Drug Name	Directions	Date	R/F	Prescriber	Qty	RPh
449881	Hydrocodone/APAP 7.5 mg/500 mg	1 tablet by mouth every 6 to 8 hours as needed for pain	5/2	3	Jones	90	PC
649607	Gabapentin 300 mg	1 capsule by mouth every night	5/2	3	Jones	30	PC
647346	Miacalcin	1 spray in alternating nostrils once daily	4/12	5	Pedersen	1	PC
647350	Amlodipine 10 mg	1 tablet by mouth once daily	4/12	5	Pedersen	30	PC
647348	Levothyroxine 0.1 mg	1 tablet by mouth every day	4/12	5	Pedersen	30	PC
647347	Ranitidine 75 mg	1 tablet by mouth twice daily	4/12	5	Pedersen	60	PC
647349	Warfarin 4 mg	1 tablet by mouth every day	4/12	NR	Pedersen	30	PC
448969	Hydrocodone/APAP 7.5 mg/500 mg	1 tablet by mouth every 6–8 hours as needed for pain	4/12	1	Jones	60	PC
448969	Hydrocodone/APAP 7.5 mg/500 mg	1 tablet by mouth every 6–8 hours as needed for pain	3/23	1	Jones	60	PC
647346	Miacalcin	1 spray in alternating nostrils once daily	4/12	6	Pedersen	1	PC
647350	Amlodipine 10 mg	1 tablet by mouth once daily	4/12	6	Pedersen	30	PC
647348	Levothyroxine 0.1 mg	1 tablet by mouth once daily	3/14	6	Pedersen	30	PC
6473547	Ranitidine 75 mg	1 tablet by mouth twice daily	3/14	6	Pedersen	60	PC
646551	Warfarin 4 mg	1 tablet by mouth once daily	3/14	NR	Pedersen	30	PC
221662	Morphine ER 15 mg	1 tablet by mouth every 12 hours	2/28	NR	Jones	30	PC
447142	Hydrocodone/APAP 5 mg/500 mg	1 tablet by mouth every 6–8 hours as needed for pain	2/28	NR	Jones	90	PC

Questions and Activities

1. What medication therapy problems are evident in the patient's current drug regimen?

2. The patient expresses her concern about becoming addicted to "dope." Describe the psychosocial issues that influence the patient's acceptance of drug therapy for her acute and chronic pain condition. How would you counsel her to alleviate her addiction fears?

3. What other medical problems does this patient have that influence the choice of pain medications? Describe in detail how these comorbidities affect your choice of medications for her.

4. This patient states that her pain is often a 10. Describe the pain assessment scales routinely used to evaluate a patient's pain.

5. What are the preventable or treatable adverse effects associated with the use of narcotic analgesics? Describe the methods or therapies used to prevent or treat these adverse effects. What warnings would you give the patient when counseling her about these adverse effects?

6. On the basis of published analgesic equivalency tables, calculate the equivalent doses and frequency of administration of oral oxycodone ER, fentanyl transdermal, and methadone for this patient, according to the morphine dose that she took beginning on February 28.

7. The World Health Organization (WHO) recommends the use of an "analgesic ladder" for rational drug therapy for patients with pain. At which step should this patient be classified? What medication types should she be taking according to the WHO ladder?

8. What is an "analgesic ceiling?" Which of this patient's medications have an analgesic ceiling, and which do not?

9. List analgesic adjuvants that may improve this patient's pain therapy; include appropriate doses and routes of administration.

10. Classify the commonly used narcotic analgesics according to chemical structure. Why is this an important consideration in the treatment of patients with pain?

11. On the basis of this patient's medical and drug therapy history, formulate a comprehensive medication plan; include both short- and long-term goals and the medication regimens used to accomplish these goals.

12. What nondrug therapies could be recommended to this patient to improve the outcomes of her pain treatment?

13. What course of action should you take when you receive the methadone prescription written by Dr. Jones?

14. You contact Dr. Jones by telephone, and he agrees that a change is in order. He asks you whether you can update the prescription in the pharmacy according to his instructions or whether the patient needs a new prescription. How do you answer him (on the basis of laws applicable to community pharmacy practice in your state)?

15. When questioning the patient about nonprescription products, she tells you that she takes Tylenol Arthritis (3 times daily), "something for sleep," Aleve for headaches, and eye vitamins. Which of these should be discontinued, and why? Which nonprescription product(s) should the patient be advised to start taking?

16. The patient tells you that her gabapentin prescription is "worthless" and makes her so drowsy she cannot stay awake during the day. What alternative medication therapies should be considered?

17. Differentiate between true opioid allergy and routine adverse effects associated with morphine therapy. On the basis of the information you have, what is your assessment of the patient's allergy history?

18. If the patient has a true allergy to morphine, would she probably also be allergic to methadone? Why or why not?

19. The hydrocodone/acetaminophen product prescribed for this patient is unavailable from your wholesaler and from all other sources because of a manufacturing problem. Provide a solution for this drug shortage problem. Be sure to state whether your solution requires a new prescription from the prescriber.

20. Before the patient leaves the pharmacy today, she tells you that she has almost the whole morphine prescription at home from her February prescription because she could not take it. She wants to get rid of it, but does not know the best way to dispose of it. Does she just throw it in the trash? Can she bring it to the pharmacy for you to dispose of for her?

Additional Activities

1. Review the federal consumer guidelines for disposal of expired prescription drugs (www.whitehousedrug policy.gov/publications/pdf/prescrip_disposal.pdf). Review prescribing information with disposal instructions for Actiq, fentanyl patches, and OxyContin. Are these the same instructions a pharmacist would follow to dispose of these drugs? Why or why not?

2. Contact a community pharmacist in your area to discuss inventory issues with C-II drugs. Questions to ask might include the following: Do you use perpetual inventory for C-II agents? Do you order C-IIs electronically or with paper forms? If you do not have perpetual inventory, how do you determine order quantities? How often do you place a C-II order? Ask the pharmacist to describe instances in the past where he or she has discovered discrepancies between the on-hand supply and the C-II inventory records. How did you handle this issue?

3. Research and review trends in and causes of methadone toxicity and overdose. Why can methadone be more "dangerous" than other opioids? What patient counseling can you provide to prevent potential methadone toxicity or overdose?

Information Sources

1. Wilson PR, Caplan RA, et al. Practice guidelines for chronic pain management. A report by the American Society of Anesthesiologists Task Force on Pain Management, Chronic Pain Section. *Anesthesiology*. 1997;86:995–1004.

2. National Pharmaceutical Council, Joint Commission on Accreditation of Healthcare Organizations. Pain: Current Understanding of Assessment, Management, and Treatments. Available at: http://www.npcnow.org/resources/PDFs/painmonograph.pdf. Last accessed October 31, 2008.

3. American Pain Society. *Principles of Analgesic Use in the Treatment of Acute Pain and Cancer Pain*. 4th ed. Glenville, Ill: American Pain Society; 1999.

4. American Academy of Pain Medicine, American Pain Society. The use of opioids for the treatment of chronic pain. A consensus statement from the American Academy of Pain Medicine and the American Pain Society. *Clin J Pain*. 1997;13:6–8.

5. Jensen MP, Karoly P, Braver S. The measurement of clinical pain intensity: a comparison of six methods. *Pain*. 1986;27:117–26.

6. Levy MH. Pharmacologic treatment of cancer pain. *N Engl J Med*. 1996;335:1124–32.

7. World Health Organization. WHO's Pain Ladder. Available at: http://www.who.int/cancer/palliative/painladder/en. Last accessed October 31, 2008.

8. Dickinson BD, Altman RD, Nielsen NH, et al. Use of opioids to treat chronic, noncancer pain. *West J Med*. 2000;172:107–15.

9. Zenz M, Strumpf M, Tryba M. Long-term oral opioid therapy in patients with chronic nonmalignant pain. *J Pain Symptom Manage.* 1992;7:69–77.

10. Milligan K, Lanteri-Minet M, Borchert K, et al. Evaluation of long-term efficacy and safety of transdermal fentanyl in the treatment of chronic noncancer pain. *J Pain.* 2001;2:197–204.

11. Simpson RK Jr, Edmondson EA, Constant CF, et al. Transdermal fentanyl as treatment for chronic low back pain. *J Pain Symptom Manage.* 1997;14:218–24.

12. Glajchen M. Chronic pain: treatment barriers and strategies for clinical practice. *J Am Board Fam Pract.* 2001;14:211–8.

13. Marcus DA. Treatment of nonmalignant chronic pain. *Am Fam Physician.* 2000;61:1331–8, 1345–6.

14. AGS Panel on Persistent Pain in Older Persons. The management of persistent pain in older persons. *J Am Geriatr Soc.* 2002;50(6 suppl):S205–24.

15. Maizels M, McCarberg B. Antidepressants and antiepileptic drugs for chronic non-cancer pain. *Am Fam Physician.* 2005;71:483–90.

16. Analgesic options for patients with allergic-type opioid reactions. *Pharm Lett Prescr Lett.* 2006;22:220201.

17. Proper disposal of expired or unwanted drugs. *Pharm Lett Prescr Lett.* 2007;23:230401.

82 Neuropathic Pain

Bruce R. Canaday, Molly E. Graham, and Brice A. Labruzzo

Objectives

1. Identify the medication-related problem(s) associated with the case.

2. Formulate an optimal therapeutic treatment plan to resolve identified medication-related problem(s) and to provide appropriate follow-up.

3. Identify nondrug therapies or lifestyle modifications that might be useful in managing the patient's problem(s).

4. Develop a patient education and action plan to help optimize management.

Scenario

Mary Johnson is a 57-year-old African American woman who comes to the community pharmacy counter and requests the technician sell her some quinine. The technician refers the patient to you. On questioning, Mrs. Johnson reveals that she is experiencing pain in her legs. This pain is sometimes severe and makes it difficult for her to sleep. Her neighbor suggested that she was probably having leg cramps and that she should "see the druggist for some quinine." In further discussion she describes having "sugar," (consistent with a diagnosis of diabetes mellitus type 2), "high blood" (consistent with a diagnosis of hypertension), and "cholesterol" (consistent with a diagnosis of hyperlipidemia).

Mrs. Johnson is not new to your practice, so you have some additional historical information available to review. Case Table 82–1 is a printout of Mrs. Johnson's prescription medication profile.

On completing your profile review, you again speak to Mrs. Johnson. You determine that Mrs. Johnson is 5 feet 7 inches tall and her weight is 90 kg. She reports smoking on average

---

CASE Table 82–1   Prescription Medication Profile

Mary Johnson
4565 Rolling Oak Dr.
Wilmington, NC 25678

Phone: 910-555-1067   **DOB:** 8/21/49   **Insurer:** Blue Cross Health

Allergies/Intolerances: Shellfish, iodine, sulfa (rash to each)

Rx No.	Drug Name	Directions	Date	R/F	Prescriber	Qty	RPh
667895	Lisinopril 20 mg	1 tablet by mouth every day	8/25	4	Smith	30	MG
667436	Simvastatin 40 mg	1 tablet by mouth every night	8/25	4	Smith	30	MG
668342	Amlodipine 5 mg	1 tablet by mouth every day	8/25	5	Smith	30	BC
663411	Hydrochlorothiazide 25 mg	1 tablet by mouth every morning	8/25	4	Smith	30	MG
664586	Augmentin 875 mg	1 tablet by mouth every 12 hours	8/8	0	Lee	14	BC
664587	Clarinex 10 mg	1 tablet by mouth every day	8/8	1	Lee	30	BC
466214	Vicodin 5 mg/325 mg	1 tablet by mouth four times daily as needed for pain	7/29	1	Williams	120	BL
662895	Ibuprofen 800 mg	1–2 tablets four times daily as needed for pain	7/29	4	Mason	90	MG
667895	Lisinopril 20 mg	1 tablet by mouth every day	7/12	5	Smith	30	BC
667436	Simvastatin 40 mg	1 tablet by mouth every night	7/12	5	Smith	30	BL
663411	Hydrochlorothiazide 25 mg	1 tablet by mouth every night	7/12	5	Smith	30	BL

1 pack of cigarettes per day, and she denies drinking alcohol or using illicit drugs. Her typical physical activity regimen includes only walking to the mailbox and "fetching the newspaper" in the morning, but during the conversation she reveals that 1 week ago she began "mall walking" with a friend as suggested by her primary care physician. She is still employed in a nearby manufacturing facility and has Blue Cross health insurance. When asked about medications for her diabetes she says she takes 20 units of Novolin 70/30 in the morning and 10 units at night. Other past medical history appears to be noncontributory.

She describes the pain as "tingly, like your leg was asleep only a lot worse. It feels kind of like electricity in your legs; sometimes it's worse, sometimes a little better, but it's most always there in both of my legs." She rates the pain as peaking at 10 of 10 some nights and some nights being only about 2 of 10. The pain does not appear to be related to any activity. As she describes it, it is not focused in a joint or muscular area, but it is more diffuse and primarily more distal.

Questions and Activities

1. What test(s) may be performed in the community pharmacy that could help facilitate triaging this patient's pain complaint?

2. On the basis of the patient's presentation and drug therapy, identify the probable drug- or disease-related problem. What symptoms is she experiencing that are consistent with this problem?

3. What is the appropriate next step for the pharmacist to take at this point?

4. What topical and systemic treatment options are available for this problem? Include each agent, mechanism of action, target dose, and place in therapy.

On returning to the pharmacy 3 days later, the patient presents a new prescription as noted in Case Figure 82–1. The patient tells you she was able to see her physician a few days ago and was given samples to try for her pain. She appears a bit sluggish and seems to have trouble focusing during your conversation with her. She states the doctor said this medicine was "different" from other pain medications, but she still does not understand much about it. She is not really sure if it is helping much yet and expresses doubt about continuing to take it.

5. How would you counsel Mrs. Johnson on her concerns about the prescribed medication? Discuss using anticonvulsants for diabetic peripheral neuropathy, what results she should expect, adverse effects, and dose titration.

6. What information might you want to obtain to determine the cause of her altered mental status?

CASE Figure 82–1 Prescription for patient Mary Johnson.

7. What would you suspect as being the cause of her mental status change?

8. On the basis of a diagnosis of diabetic peripheral neuropathy, how is this type of pain different from other types of pain? What is the causative role of diabetes in neuropathic pain?

9. What are the goals of pharmacotherapy for this patient?

10. On contacting the prescriber, he requests that the patient be seen in his office the following day. The pharmacist relays this information to the patient. How would you advise the patient to continue taking the gabapentin before being seen by her physician to resolve the altered mental status?

The patient returns to the pharmacy the next afternoon with a new prescription. The physician has changed the gabapentin dose to 200 mg three times daily for 1 week, then 300 mg three times daily for 1 week, then increasing by 300 mg weekly to a maximum of 3600 mg or until the pain improves markedly. After 2 months of therapy, the patient returns to the pharmacy to pick up her gabapentin refill. You ask the patient if the gabapentin is helping relieve her pain. The patient tells you that, although the sedation has not been an issue, the pain has not improved. The patient informs you she is frustrated because her glucose readings have been "good" lately, but the pain has not gone away. The patient shows you her blood glucose log with all values within normal limits. She tells you a different friend of hers mentioned using "lipo acid," and she would like to know where to find this.

11. How would you answer the patient regarding her question about using alpha-lipoic acid for peripheral neuropathy?

12. Discuss other natural medicines available for the treatment of diabetic peripheral neuropathy.

After discussing the use of dietary supplements for her condition, you suggest that she make another appointment with her primary care provider to address the lack of pain relief with the gabapentin. The prescriber contacts you and asks you for an opinion as to what drug therapy change should be instituted and would like to know if you can offer any help in monitoring the patient.

13. What treatment alternatives available for managing this patient might you recommend as optimal and suggest to the prescriber at this point? What drug(s), dosage form(s), schedule(s), and duration(s) of therapy might you suggest? Note that there may be more than one correct answer.

While discussing the therapeutic options available, the physician decides to discontinue treatment with gabapentin and would like for the patient to begin duloxetine 60 mg daily.

14. How would you counsel Mrs. Johnson to discontinue her gabapentin? Can she just switch to the duloxetine?

15. How would you counsel the patient on the use of duloxetine? Discuss using an antidepressant for diabetic peripheral neuropathy, proper administration, and adverse effects.

16. After processing the prescription, you realize this medication is not covered on the patient's insurance. What do you do now?

You have your technician contact the patient's insurance company. You are told that several tricyclic antidepressants and gabapentin are covered. You have already discussed these therapeutic options with the prescriber, but you contact him to inform him of the bad news. Although he would prefer to use duloxetine because of its effectiveness and fewer side effects than other options, the prescriber decides to start the patient on desipramine so she will be able to afford the medication.

17. How would you counsel the patient on desipramine?

18. What monitoring parameters available in the community pharmacy setting should be used to evaluate therapy in this patient, including efficacy and adverse effects?

19. What nondrug therapies or lifestyle modifications might be useful in managing this patient's neuropathic pain?

20. Develop a medication action plan for the patient; include short-term and long-range goals.

21. What are the pertinent topics to address during patient education?

22. Develop a follow-up plan for this patient; include time to follow up and method of contact.

Information Sources

1. Stillman M. Clinical approach to patients with neuropathic pain. *Cleve Clin J. Med.* 2006;73:726–39.

2. American Diabetes Association. Standards of medical care in diabetes-2007. *Diabetes Care.* 2007; 30(suppl 1): S4–S41.

3. US Department of Health and Human Services, Bureau of Primary Care. Lower Extremity Amputation Program. Available at: http://www.hrsa.gov/leap. Last accessed October 20, 2008.

4. Screening Form for Diabetes Foot Disease. National Diabetes Education Program. Available at: http://ndep.nih.gov/resources/feet/screenfo.htm. Last accessed September 30, 2008.

5. Vinik A. Clinical review: use of antiepileptic drugs in the treatment of chronic painful diabetic neuropathy. *J Clin Endocrinol Metab.* 2005;90:4936–25.

6. Diabetic peripheral neuropathic pain consensus guidelines for treatment. *J Fam Pract.* 2006;(suppl):3–19.

7. Duby JJ, Campbell RK, Setter SM, et al. Diabetic neuropathy: an intensive review. *Am J Health Syst Pharm.* 2004;61:160–76.

8. Dworkin RH, Backonja M, Rowbotham MC, et al. Advances in neuropathic pain. *Arch Neurol.* 2003;60:1524–34.

9. Mendell JR, Sahenk Z. Painful sensory neuropathy. *N Engl J Med.* 2003;348:1243–55.

10. Argoff CE, Backonja MM, Belgrade MJ, et al. Consensus guidelines: treatment planning and options. *Mayo Clin Proc.* 2006;81 (4 suppl):S12–25.

11. Rowbotham MC, Twilling L, Davies PS, et al. Oral opioid therapy for chronic peripheral and central neuropathic pain. *N Engl J Med.* 2003;348:1223–32.

12. Adriaensen H, Plaghki L, Mathieu C, et al. Critical review of oral drug treatments for diabetic neuropathic pain – clinical outcomes based on efficacy and safety data from placebo-controlled and direct comparative studies. *Diabetes Metab Res Rev.* 2005;21:231–40.

13. Sindrup SH, Otto M, Finnerup NB, Jensen TS. Antidepressants in the treatment of neuropathic pain. *Basic Clin Pharmacol Toxicol.* 2005;96:399–409.

14. Bakonja M, Beydoun A, Edwards KR, et al. Gabapentin for symptomatic treatment of painful neuropathy in patients with diabetes mellitus: a randomized controlled trial. *JAMA.* 1998;280:1831–6.

15. Lyrica [product information]. New York: Pfizer Parke Davis; June 2007.

16. Shneker BF, McAuley JW. Pregabalin: a new neuromodulator with broad therapeutic indications. *Ann Pharmacother.* 2005;39: 2029–37.

17. Chong MS, Hester J. Diabetic painful neuropathy current and future treatment options. *Drugs.* 2007;67:569–85.

18. Kanich W, Brady WJ, Huff JS, et al. Altered mental status: evaluation and etiology in the ED. *Am J Emerg Med.* 2002;20:613–7.

19. Baumann TJ. Pain management. In: DiPiro JT, Talbert RL, Yee GC, et al., eds. *Pharmacotherapy: A Pathophysiological Approach.* 6th ed. New York: McGraw-Hill; 2005:1089–104.

20. Gundogdu BM. Diabetic peripheral neuropathy: an update on pathogenesis and management. *Curr Neurol Neurosci Rep.* 2006;6:1–4.

21. Ziegler D, Nowak H, Kempler P, et al. Treatment of symptomatic diabetic polyneuropathy with the antioxidant alpha-lipoic acid: a meta-analysis. *Diabet Med.* 2004;21:114–21.

22. Ziegler D, Ametov A, Barinov A, et al. Oral treatment with alpha-lipoic acid improves symptomatic diabetic polyneuropathy: the SYDNEY 2 trial. *Diabetes Care.* 2006;29:2365–70.

23. Alpha-lipoic acid monograph. *Natural Medicines Comprehensive Database.* Available at: http://www.naturalmedicines.com. Last accessed September 30, 2008.

24. American Diabetes Association. Nutrition recommendations and interventions for diabetes: a position statement of the American Diabetes Association. *Diabetes Care.* 2007;30(suppl 1):S48–S65.

25. Lipoic acid. Available at: http://www.drugstore.com/search/ search.asp?searchtype=1&trx=28198&trxp1=60&ipp=20&src htree=1&search=lipoic+acid. Last accessed September 30, 2008.

26. Lipoic acid. Available at: http://www.walgreens.com/search/ search_results.jsp?_dyncharset=ASCII&term=lipoic+acid. Last accessed September 30, 2008.

27. Halat KM, Dennehy CE. Botanicals and dietary supplements in diabetic peripheral neuropathy. *J Am Board Fam Pract.* 2003; 16:47–57.

28. Frampton JE, Foster RH. Pregabalin: in the treatment of postherpetic neuralgia. *Drugs.* 2005;65:111–8.

29. U.S. Food and Drug Administration. CDER New Molecular Entity (NME) Drug and New Biologic Approvals in Calendar Year 2004. Available at: http://www.fda.gov/cder/rdmt/ nmecy2004.htm. Last accessed September 30, 2008.

30. Galer BS, Jensen MP. Development and preliminary validation of a pain measure specific to neuropathic pain: the neuropathic pain scale. *Neurology.* 1997;48:332–8.

31. Krause SJ, Backonja MM. Development of a neuropathic pain questionnaire. *Clin J Pain.* 2003;19:306–14.

32. Swenson MR. Diabetic peripheral neuropathy. *Curr Ther Endocrinol Metab.* 1997;6:458–61.

33. Tanenberg RJ, Pfeifer MA. Neuropathy: the "forgotten: complication. *Diabetes Forecast.* 2000;53:56–60.

34. Russell D, Stading J. Diabetic peripheral neuropathy: minimizing and treating its pain. *US Pharm.* 2002;27:11. Available at: http://www.uspharmacist.com/index.asp?show=article&page=8_9 96.htm. Last accessed September 30, 2008.

35. American Pharmacists Association and National Association of Chain Drug Stores Foundation. Medication therapy management in community pharmacy practice: core elements of an MTM service (version 1.0). *J Am Pharm Assoc.* 2005;45: 573–79.

Persistent Pain in the Older Adult

Holly Divine and Amy Nicholas

Objectives

1. Identify signs and symptoms of persistent pain.

2. Identify any drug therapy problems with the patient's medication regimen.

3. Select appropriate therapy for chronic pain management in the older adult.

4. Assess safety and efficacy of medications for pain management.

5. Recognize appropriate and inappropriate medications for the management of pain in older adults.

Scenario

You are a recent pharmacy school graduate who has been working at Hometown Pharmacy for a few months. Mrs. Smith has been a regular patient at Hometown Pharmacy for many years. She has osteoporosis and has had multiple episodes of vertebral compression fractures with severe back pain. The pharmacy is next door to the senior adult apartment complex where she lives. Despite her medical condition, she is able to walk to the pharmacy several times each month to get her prescriptions and some necessary household and OTC items. You have been told she lives alone, is on a fixed income, and takes care of herself and her small apartment on her own.

She comes to the pharmacy counter where you are working today with a new prescription (Case Figure 83–1). She also places her OTC items on the counter to be "rung up" with the prescription when it is ready. The items she places on the counter are acetaminophen 500 mg, calcium carbonate 500 mg, naproxen sodium 220 mg, glucosamine 500 mg/chondroitin 400 mg, and a package of Depend briefs for bowel and bladder protection.

You are able to review a copy of her prescription medication profile in the pharmacy computer (Case Table 83–1).

After evaluating Mrs. Smith's prescriptions and reviewing her OTC products, you ask her if you can talk to her for a few minutes about her medications. She agrees, and you take her to a small counseling area next to the pharmacy to review her medications with her. During your interview, the following additional information is revealed:

- Other than her pain, diagnoses include isolated systolic hypertension, osteoporosis, and vertebral fracture history (due to osteoporosis).

- She is taking her furosemide at 9 am and 9 pm.

- She awakes several times during the night to urinate and, because of her limited walking ability, is sometimes unable to make it to the toilet in time.

- She has purchased the acetaminophen 500 mg for several years and takes 2 tablets four times daily.

- She had been having increased pain lately throughout the day and night, whereas she was having it just during the night before about the past 6 months.

Mary Jones, MD
Hometown Family Medicine
100 Main Street
Dawson, KY

FOR _Millie Smith_

ADDRESS_____ DATE_____

Darvocet N-100

T 4-6 x/day
PRN BP
#180

REFILL _5_ TIMES

DR. _Mary Jo___

CASE Figure 83–1 Prescription for patient Millie Smith.

CASE Table 83–1   Prescription Medication Profile

Millie Smith
123 Main Street, Apt. A
Dawson, KY 12345

Phone: 444-555-6666   **DOB:** 2/22/27   **Insurer:** Medicare

Allergies/Intolerances: NKDA

Rx No.	Drug Name	Directions	Date	R/F	Prescriber	Qty	RPh
601543	Alendronate 70 mg	Take as directed weekly	10/1	1	Jones	4	HSD
601541	Lisinopril 20 mg	1 tablet every day	10/1	0	Jones	30	HSD
601540	Furosemide 20 mg	1 tablet twice daily	10/1	1	Jones	60	HSD
601549	Ibuprofen 600 mg	1 tablet three times daily as needed for pain	9/30	1	Jones	90	ASN
601549	Ibuprofen 600 mg	1 tablet three times daily as needed for pain	9/8	2	Jones	90	ASN
601540	Furosemide 20 mg	1 tablet twice daily	9/1	2	Jones	60	HSD
601543	Alendronate 70 mg	Take as directed weekly	9/1	2	Jones	4	HSD
601541	Lisinopril 20 mg	1 tablet every day	9/1	1	Jones	30	HSD
601549	Ibuprofen 600 mg	1 tablet three times daily as needed for pain	8/15	3	Jones	90	HSD
601540	Furosemide 20 mg	1 tablet twice daily	8/5	3	Jones	60	ASN
601541	Lisinopril 20 mg	1 tablet every day	8/5	2	Jones	30	ASN
601543	Alendronate 70 mg	Take as directed weekly	8/5	3	Jones	4	ASN

She talked with some of her friends over lunch in the past month, and each of them had recommended some OTC items that worked for them (glucosamine and naproxen sodium) so she thought she would "try them out." She has been using her friend's glucosamine/chondroitin for approximately 1 month and takes 1 tablet in the morning.

After asking about her frequent refills on ibuprofen, she confirms that she has been taking more ibuprofen than prescribed because of the increased pain. When questioned further, she indicates she will sometimes take 4 tablets instead of 3, and she uses consistently three times daily instead of as needed.

She denies any recent trauma that would attribute to worsening pain control (i.e., no falls or new events). She thinks that since the weather has been so nice this fall that she has been more active than usual. Her doctor prescribed a new medication today that was "more powerful" than the ones she was currently taking.

You ask her on a scale of 0 to 10, with 10 being the most pain she has ever experienced and 0 being no pain at all, what her current pain status is. Her response is 8.

Questions and Activities

1. On the basis of the patient's presentation and drug therapy, identify the medical problem and the current drug therapy to solve the problem.

2. What are the goals of pharmacotherapy for each of the patient's medications?

3. Identify the drug therapy problem(s) with this patient's medication regimen.

4. Identify the treatment alternatives available for the drug therapy problem(s).

5. What intervention (e.g., patient recommendation, call to provider or family member, contact emergency medication services, etc.) is necessary for implementing this treatment?

6. What monitoring parameters available in the community pharmacy setting should be used to evaluate therapy in this patient, including efficacy and adverse effects?

7. What nondrug therapies or lifestyle modifications might be useful in managing this patient's problem?

8. Develop a medication action plan for the patient; include short-term and long-range goals.

9. What are the pertinent topics to address during patient education?

10. During patient counseling, Mrs. Smith asks if she can still take the OTC products her friends recommended. What would you tell her and why?

11. Develop a follow-up plan for this patient; include time to follow up and method of contact.

Information Sources

1. Cipolle RJ, Strand LM, Morley PC. *Pharmaceutical Care Practice: The Clinician's Guide.* 2nd ed. New York: McGraw-Hill; 2004:171–200.

2. Fine PG. Pharmacological management of persistent pain in older patients. *Clin J Pain.* 2004;20:220–6.

3. Fick DM, Cooper JW, Wade WE, et al. Updating the Beers' criteria for potentially inappropriate medication use in older adults. *Arch Intern Med.* 2003;163:2716–24.

4. AGS Panel on Persistent Pain in Older Persons. The management of persistent pain in older persons. *J Am Geriatr Soc.* 2002; 50(suppl):S205–24.

5. Tylenol [product information]. Available at: http://www.tylenol. com. Last accessed October 31, 2008.

6. Watkins PB, Kaplowitz N, Slattery JT, et al. Aminotransferase elevations in healthy adults receiving 4 grams of acetaminophen daily. JAMA. 2006;296:87–93.

7. American Liver Foundation press release July 18, 2006. Available at: http://www.liverfoundation.org/about/news/33. Last accessed October 31, 2008.

8. National Pharmaceutical Council. *Pain: Current Understanding of Assessment, Management, and Treatments.* Reston, Va: National Pharmaceutical Council; 2001. Available at: http://www.npcnow. org/resources/PDFs/painmonograph.pdf. Last accessed October 31, 2008.

9. American Pharmacist Association. *A Pharmacist's Guide to the Clinical Assessment and Management of Pain.* Washington, DC: American Pharmacist Association; 2004.

10. Partners Against Pain. Purdue Pharma L.P. 2005. Available at: http://www.partnersagainstpain.com. Last accessed October 31, 2008.

11. Nadler SF. Nonpharmacologic management of pain. *J Am Osteopath Assoc.* 2004;104(suppl):S6–S12.

12. Glucosamine and chondroitin: recent osteoarthritis research. *Pharm Lett.* 2006 January:22.

13. Tanveer E, Anastassiades TP. Glucosamine and chondroitin for treating symptoms of osteoarthritis: evidence is widely touted but incomplete. JAMA. 2000;283:1483–4.

14. National Institutes of Health. NIH Study on Glucosamine/Chondroitin Sulfate for Knee Osteoarthritis. Available at: http://www. nih.gov/news/pr/sept99/nccam-15a.htm. Last accessed October 31, 2008.

15. National Center for Complementary and Alternative Medicine Clearinghouse. Available at: http://nccam.nih.gov. Last accessed October 31, 2008.

Abbreviations Used without Expansion in Text and Pharmacy Records and Forms

AARP	American Association of Retired Persons		Ht	height
ACE	angiotensin-converting enzyme		ICD-9	International Statistical Classification of Diseases-9th Revision
ACEI	angiotensin-converting enzyme inhibitor		IR	immediate release
AIDS	acquired immunodeficiency disease		LDL	low-density lipoprotein
AL	Alabama		LDL-C	low-density lipoprotein
ALT	alanine transferase		LFT	liver function test
A1c	glycosylated hemoglobin		MAO	monoamine oxidase
APAP	acetaminophen		MAOI	monoamine oxidase inhibitor
ASAP	as soon as possible		MD	physician
AST	aspartate transferase		MedHx	medical history
AUD	take as directed		NCEP	National Cholesterol Education Program
BCBS	Blue Cross Blue Shield		NKDA	no known drug allergy
BC/BS	Blue Cross Blue Shield		NSAID	nonsteroidal anti-inflammatory drug
BMI	body mass index		OBRA '90	Omnibus Budget Reconciliation Act of 1990
BP	blood pressure		OTC	over-the-counter
bpm	beats per minute		PCN	penicillin
BUN	blood urea nitrogen		PCS	patient care system
CAD	coronary artery disease		PDA	personal digital assistant
CC	chief complaint		PERRLA	pupils equal, round, reactive to light and accommodation
CDC	Centers for Disease Control and Prevention		PMH	past medical history
CHD	coronary heart disease		ppd	pack per day
CK	creatine phosphokinase		PRN	as needed
CMS	Centers for Medicare & Medicaid Services		Qty	quantity
CPT	Current Procedural Terminology		R/F	refill
CR	controlled release		ROS	review of systems
CYP	cytochrome P450		RPh	registered pharmacist
DOB	date of birth		SHx	social history
DUR	drug utilization review		SR	sustained release
DX	diagnosis		S/S	signs and symptoms
EC	enteric coated		SSRI	selective serotonin reuptake inhibitor
ER	extended release		T	temperature
EtOH	alcohol		Td	tetanus-diphtheria
FDA	Food and Drug Administration		T2DM	type 2 diabetes mellitus
FHx	family history		TC	total cholesterol
FPG	fasting plasma glucose		TG	triglyceride
GERD	gastroesophageal disorder		TIA	transient ischemic attack
HDL	high-density lipoprotein		TLC	therapeutic lifestyle changes
HEENT	head, eyes, ears, nose, and throat		TSH	thyroid stimulating hormone
HFA	hydrofluoroalkane-134a		UTI	urinary tract infection
HIPAA	Health Insurance Portability and Accountability Act		VLDL	very-low-density lipoprotein
HIV	human immunodeficiency virus		Wt	weight
HMG-CoA	3-hydroxy-3-methylglutaryl coenzyme A		XL	extended release
HMO	health maintenance organization		XR	extended release
HPI	history of personal illness		y.o.	years old
HR	heart rate			